CURRICULUM OF
THE BASIC PRINCIPLES OF MARXISM-LENINISM

PART 2

HISTORICAL MATERIALISM

For University and College Students
Not Specializing in Marxism-Leninism and Ho Chi Minh Thought

VANGUARD EDITION
LIMITED TO THE FIRST ONE THOUSAND PRINTINGS

Translated, Annotated, and Cover Illustrated by Luna Nguyen

Introduction by Gerald Horne and Anthony Ballas

Edited, Annotated, and Illustrated by Emerican Johnson

Contributing Editor: David Peat

Banyan House
PUBLISHING

LICENSE

This work is licensed under a
Creative Commons Attribution-NonCommercial-ShareAlike 4.0 International License.

You are free to:

Share — copy and redistribute the material in any medium or format

Adapt — remix, transform, and build upon the material

The licensor cannot revoke these freedoms as long as you follow the license terms.

Under the following terms:

Attribution — You must give appropriate credit, provide a link to the license, and indicate if changes were made. You may do so in any reasonable manner, but not in any way that suggests the licensor endorses you or your use.

NonCommercial — You may not use the material for commercial purposes.

ShareAlike — If you remix, transform, or build upon the material, you must distribute your contributions under the same license as the original.

No additional restrictions — You may not apply legal terms or technological measures that legally restrict others from doing anything the license permits.

The full text of this license is available at:
https://creativecommons.org/licenses/by-nc-sa/4.0/

"Communism is the riddle of history solved, and it knows itself to be this solution."

— *Karl Marx*

SUPPORT FOR THIS WORK

Translating, annotating, and typesetting this book has taken three years, which would not have been possible without our crowdfunding supporters. These donations enabled us to make the digital version of this entire text available for free online.

We would therefore like to recognize all of our supporters:

William M.	Juan P.	Callum L.	Kacy Y.
Derek R.	Simon S.	James W.	Tuan D. N.
Ibrahin H.	Jordi N.	Carl M.	Kaleb L.
Duncan B.	Benjamin S.	Jacob N.	Trent T.
Daryl L.	Michael M.	Jeremy C.	Victor J.
Evan W.	Ryan F.	Renato D.	Thomas S.
Dante C.	Mitchell S.	John V.	Robert C.
Kengo K.	Shun F.	Benjamin G.	Carlos S. P.
Tyler S.	Arian P.	Joel P.	Diana T.
Mario H.	Spencer S.	Seth W.	Pulu A.
Robert D.	Lux N.	Joseph B.	Cameron S.
O. B.	Mark B.	Matthew B.	Jaivir G.
Ezra D. L.	Justin J.	Yasser M.	Robert H.
Mickey M.	Tim B.	Lucy F.	Joseph B.
Diangelo J.	Gassoh G.	Michael T.	Benjamin S.
Jason P.	Josh T.	Justin H.	Djordje M.
Stephen R.	Jake K.	Elliot O.	Robert K.
Nicolas S.	Trevor H.	Marc P.	Georgio M.
Joshua J.	Christian E.	Grahame S.	Gullern M. F.
Adrian R.	Michael T.	John V. Z.	Cora L.
Diego L.	Marshall L.	Kyle M.	Rowan G.
Felipe F.	Del S.	Simon T.	Steven N.
Alfonso G.	Trevor S.	Michael C.	Jacob P.
Joshua B.	David T.	Daniel L.	Dante C.
Michael F.	Jaye D.	Landon N.	The Slopstache

We have already begun work on Part 3 of this curriculum: *Political Economy*. If you would like to support this effort and be credited, consider donating at:

BanyanHouse.org/donate

DEDICATION

This book is dedicated to all of the backers of the crowdfunding campaign that raised the funds to allow me to translate this text. As with the first part of this series, we once again vastly underestimated how long it would take to complete this work, and once again our donors were incredibly patient and supportive throughout the process. Your enthusiasm is so deeply appreciated and we simply could not have taken the time to finish this project without you all.

Thank you, again, to my partner and comrade Emerican Johnson, who constantly elevated the work's clarity and philosophical sturdiness with the constant demand to "prove it!" – letting no claim go unsourced. His ability to write clear and easy to follow annotations to go along with the text make this series what it is, and his illustrations make the book much more accessible to readers who might be unfamiliar with the subject matter.

I offer my sincerest gratitude to Anthony Ballas and Dr. Gerald Horne for taking the time to read our very messy rough draft and, in addition to providing their feedback and eminent perspectives, wrote a profoundly important introduction which stands on its own as a great contribution to the historiography of socialist revolution. I know that both of you have many responsibilities in the important work that you do, both professionally and as activists, and so I am humbled that you have taken the time to help us with this project.

I would also like to thank contributing editor David Peat for once again offering a meticulous and learned helping hand. We could not have produced such a professional product without your attention to detail and all the wonderful little touches you've added to the final draft.

Finally, I want to thank again the Vietnamese intellectuals and experts who undertook the rigorous and imposing task of producing the original work from which this series is being translated. The breadth and depth of their understanding of Marx, Engels, and Lenin is simply astounding. Thanks to their efforts millions of Vietnamese students have been able to learn the principles of Historical Materialism and we hope that now, with this First English Edition, workers and students around the world can benefit from their contribution. My hope remains that my translation might do their work justice.

Luna Nguyen
July, 2025

PREFACE

The text of this book constitutes part two of a four-part curriculum on Marxism-Leninism developed and published by the Ministry of Education and Training of Vietnam. This curriculum is intended to give every Vietnamese student a firm grounding in the political philosophy of Marxism-Leninism.

The entire curriculum consists of:

Part 1: The Worldview and Philosophical Methodology of Marxism-Leninism

Part 2: Historical Materialism (this text)

Part 3: Political Economy

Part 4: Scientific Socialism

In Vietnam, each part of the curriculum encompasses one full semester of mandatory study for all college students. Each part builds upon the previous, meaning that readers of this book are expected to be familiar with the principles of Dialectical Materialism and Materialist Dialectics which were covered in Part 1.

It should be noted that this curriculum is not the first encounter which Vietnamese students will have had with these ideas, because Vietnamese students also study Dialectical Materialism, Historical Materialism, Political Economy, and Scientific Socialism from primary school all the way through high school.

As such, the text of this book—in and of itself—would probably seem overwhelmingly condensed to most foreign readers who are new to studying Historical Materialism. Therefore, we have decided to extensively annotate and illustrate this text with the information which would have been previously obtained in a basic Vietnamese high school education and/or provided by college lecturers in the classroom.

It is our desire that these annotations will be helpful for students who hope to learn these principles for application in political activity, but we should also make it clear to academic researchers and the like that our annotations and illustrations are not present in the original Vietnamese work.

We hope that this book will be useful in at least three ways:

- As a comprehensive introductory textbook on Historical Materialism and for self-study, group study, classroom use, cadre training, etc.
- As a quick and easy to reference handbook for reviewing the basic concepts of Historical Materialism for students of theory who are already familiar with the concepts.
- As a companion book for further reading of theory and political texts rooted in Historical Materialist philosophy.

Also, please note: because this book is intended to be used as a quick reference and handbook for further study, there are many instances where we duplicate references, quotations, and other such information. We hope that this repetition may be double as an aid for study by reinforcing important concepts and quotations.

This book—Part 2 of the curriculum, which focuses on the application of Dialectical Materialist philosophy and methodology to the study of human history and human society—serves as the foundation of Historical Materialist theory and practice in the Vietnamese educational system.

The contents of this book are derived primarily from the written works of three important historical figures:

Karl Marx and **Friedrich Engels** — who initially developed the framework of Historical Materialism through the application of their dialectical materialist philosophy to the study of humanity;

and **Vladimir Illyich Lenin** — who further developed and defended the principles of historical materialism, expanded the analysis of imperialism, demonstrated how to apply Historical Materialist analysis to local material conditions specific to Russia at the turn of the 20th century, and made many other important contributions to what would come to be called Historical Materialism.

Obviously, there are countless other writers, revolutionaries, philosophers, and scientists who have contributed to Historical Materialist philosophy and analysis. This book focuses primarily on Marx, Engels, and Lenin, because these figures laid the foundations and formulated the basic principles of the philosophy and methodology of Historical Materialism in their immortal writings.

At the end of the book we have provided three resources for your continued theoretical development:

- An afterword, in which we offer advice for the application of Historical Materialism and further study.
- A glossary of terms which doubles as an index.
- Appendices with summaries of important concepts and principles as well as texts which show how Historical Materialism is utilized by experts to analyze human society.

At the time of publication we are already in the process of translating and annotating Part 3 of this curriculum, which focuses on Political Economy, with the hopes of eventually releasing the full curriculum. Once Part 3 is complete, it will also be made available at BanyanHouse.org - where we also invite questions, constructive feedback, and suggestions.

INTERNATIONALISM IN PRACTICE:
HO CHI MINH AND BLACK LIBERATION

An Introduction to the Text by
Gerald Horne and Anthony Ballas

"It is well known that the black race is the most oppressed and most exploited of the human family. It is well known that the spread of capitalism and the discovery of the New World had as an immediate result the rebirth of slavery which was, for centuries, a scourge for the Negroes and a bitter disgrace for mankind. What everyone does not perhaps know is that after sixty-five years of so-called emancipation, American Negroes still endure atrocious moral and material sufferings, of which the most cruel and horrible is the custom of lynching."[1]

—Ho Chi Minh, "Lynching" (1924)

Ho Chi Minh and The Black World

Although often unacknowledged, Ho Chi Minh's numerous written contributions on the history of global Black subjugation under the boot of European colonial and imperial expansion compose an impressive, early 20th century record of internationalism in practice. Before founding the Indochinese Communist Party (ICP) in 1930, many of these early writings, such as "The Revolt of Dahomey,"[2] "Uprising at Dahomey,"[3] "Lynching" (cited above), and "Ku Klux Klan"[4] were penned just prior to his arrival in Moscow where it's widely believed he began studies at the University of the Toilers of the East (KUTV) in 1923.[5] Although the historical record is imperfect, Ho's attendance at KUTV would make rational sense given the school's reputation for training some of the 20th century's most celebrated internationalists as various as Harry Haywood who attended in 1925, Maude White Katz in 1927, and anti-colonial leaders such as Jomo Kenyatta in 1933, among others.[6] In Moscow, Ho was "considered the specialist on colonial affairs," and worked for five years as the Comintern's European representative.[7] As an agent of the Comintern, Ho also delivered a "Report On The National And Colonial Questions" at the Fifth World Congress in 1924, following on the heels of the Fourth World Congress, where Jamaican poet and novelist Claude McKay delivered his "Report on the Negro Question,"[8] and drafted "Resolutions" alongside Surinamese-born Otto Huiswoud[9] in 1922. Ho passionately asserted in July 1924 that it was the "task of the communist newspapers to introduce the colonial question to our militants to awaken the working masses in the colonies, [and] win them over to the cause of Communism." Not without a bit of rhetorical flair to punctuate his trenchant remarks, Ho follows his ardent plea with a question, "but what have our newspapers done?" to which he replies, "nothing at all."[10] In retrospect, we might consider Ho's report as a sort of vanishing mediator, bridging McKay and Huiswoud's 1922 "Resolutions" and the Comintern's adoption of the Black Belt Thesis at the revolutionary Sixth World Congress in 1928.

While Ho's remarks not only indicate a serious blind spot in the reportage on the colonial question, they also exemplify a certain confidence and self-criticism in equal measure on his own part: "If we compare the number of columns devoted to the colonial question in the bourgeois newspapers such as The Times, Figaro, Evre," he explains, "or in those of different opinions such as Le Populaire, or Liberty, with those devoted to the same question in L'Humanité, the central organ of our Party, [then] we are bound to

Nguyen Ai Quoc (1890 - 1969), who would later become known as Ho Chi Minh, attending the French Communist congress as the Indochinese delegate in 1921.

say that this comparison will not be favourable to us."[11] It is clear from these words that although Ho must have been aware that he was more prolific than most in his reporting on the colonial question in the pages of L'Humanité, for instance, he also demonstrates an acute reflexivity in his awareness that still more was to be done to encourage the proliferation of this question evermore to international audiences.

Even prior to his studies in Moscow, Ho began to develop his analysis of French colonialism. As early as 1919, Ho penned a letter to the U.S. Secretary of State Robert Lansing appealing for support against French colonialism in Vietnam in the hope that it might grace the desk of President Woodrow Wilson.[12] Undaunted by the lack of reciprocation, Ho continued pressing his materialist analysis of the colonial question through such writings as "Jim Crow" and "About Siki," the latter an account of the racist double standards of the news coverage of Senegalese boxer Louis Mbarick Fall, who defeated the white boxer, George Carpentier, in a 1922 upset to become light heavyweight world champion.[13] In a moment which not only exemplifies Ho's rhetorical acumen, but as well sheds light on his politics in the early 1920s, Ho describes how Carpentier, "after being knocked out by a Black... calmly went to visit Russia, the land of Reds. We congratulate Siki on his victory. We also congratulate Carpentier on his open-mindedness."[14]

Ho's Harlem Sojourn and Atlantic Travels

As one of Ho's biographers, William Duiker, puts it, although his "visit to America remains one of the most mysterious and puzzling periods in his entire life," it is through his "own account and in recollections to acquaintances" that we know with confidence that Ho "spent a period of time in New York City," particularly in the fertile political soils of Harlem. We also know, for instance, that, despite "earning... the princely salary of forty dollars a month" as a laborer "and as a domestic servant to a wealthy family, [Ho] found time to attend meetings of black activists" with the Universal Negro Improvement Association (UNIA).[15]

Ho lived and worked in Boston and Harlem, and may even have traveled on the same train route that would eventually shuttle Malcolm X therebetween decades later while he worked as a "sandwich man on the 'Yankee Clipper,'" a railroad connecting Boston and New York. Ho also may have worked as a baker at Parker House Hotel, where a young Malcolm was later employed as a busboy while living in Boston.[16] While some parallels remain vague or coincidental, others remain, at best, superficial. For instance, we ought not let the contingent fact of history that Ho and Malcolm X (along with Yuri Kochiyama and Lorraine Hansberry) share the same birthday (March 19) cloud the fact that, although they never met in person, both Malcolm and Ho were exposed to Garveyism at a young age. Malcolm's parents, he tells us in his autobiography, were dedicated Garveyites. His mother, Louise Little, as Erik S. McDuffie explains, "insisted that her children read newspapers such as the Negro World, the official periodical of the UNIA,"[17] while his father, Earl Little, who Malcolm describes as "a dedicated organizer" and "disciple" of Garvey, would often bring young Malcolm with him to UNIA gatherings.[18]

Robert F. Williams, who "swapped Harlem stories" with Ho in the mid-1960s, describes how a "saintly... and very jolly" Ho "recounted his visits to Harlem in the 1920s as a merchant seaman" where he "heard Marcus Garvey speak" as a young man.[19] Williams, who was part of a "peace delegation that visited Hanoi," later reiterated Ho's account of how he "had been strongly moved by the plight of black peoples around the world and had contributed generously to the movement." Indeed, Ho was "so inspired," as Timothy Tyson writes, "that he 'emptied his pockets' into the [UNIA] collection plate."[20] When Williams asked him if he had been a Communist during these early years, Ho is reported to have answered in the affirmative.[21]

It is likely that "Lynching," "Ku-Klux-Klan," and various of his writings on the plight of Black people in the United States during this period were inspired by Ho's sojourn in Harlem; as active participant in an emergent and militant internationalism, and as a skilled and meticulous researcher, Ho carefully documented the brutal violence executed upon Black women and men at the hands of white supremacist terror U.S.-style.[22]

Through historically and statistically-backed research, Ho also chronicled the tragic fates of Black soldiers who were victims of racist attacks, and even lynched after returning from the First Imperialist War—a subject taken up by James Wheldon Johnson and W.E.B. Du Bois in the same era, and which Toni Morrison would dramatize in her novel *Jazz* some decades later.[23] It is worthy of mention that Ho offered such a pointed critique of the mysticism of the KKK, providing a well-nigh psychological analysis of their "strange garb, bizarre rituals," and the way "its mysteries attracted the curiosity of whites in the southern states and became very popular."[24]

As a merchant sailor and ship cook on the *Amiral de Latouche-Tréville* under the alias Văn Ba, Ho traveled widely, including to former slave port cities in the Atlantic such as Rio de Janeiro and Dakar. About the latter, Ho would later recount the story of his time as a worker on the French vessel when he witnessed the cruelty of white, French sailors jeering and laughing at four Black sailors who tragically fell victim to drowning; a formative experience that made it into the pages of Ho's early autobiography, and also would have surely influenced his early writings on the plight of colonized Africans.[25] Similar to the great seafarers of the 19th and 20th centuries, Ho's travels on the high seas were formative of his political development. In this way, one may find certain parallels in Ho's biography to that of Denmark Vesey, John S. Jacobs, or, a bit later on, Benito Sylvain, Garvey, and Ferdinand Smith, co-founder of the National Maritime Union.[26] Like many of the great Caribbean internationalists and revolutionaries, Ho traveled, worked, conversed, and bore witness to the mistreatment of the non-white world at the hands of Euroamerican supremacy while sailing in open waters and docking on ports across the globe, leaving behind a written record of the development of his political consciousness inspired by these early experiences.[27]

Like all great internationalists, Ho "was quite adept at foreign languages," and even mastered several, becoming a proficient speaker and writer of "English, French, Chinese, and Russian" in addition to Vietnamese, his native tongue.[28] We can turn to the written record in the 1920s alone to detail the fact that, as Duiker points out, "his voluminous writings (including pamphlets, articles, reports, and letters) were written in a variety of languages."[29] Even a cursory glance at some of his early writings in *La Paria*, *L'Humanité*, *Inprecor*, as well as his *La race noir*, which was also translated into Russian, attests to this fact.[30] It is no wonder that the great internationalist Paul Robeson, himself a polyglot fluent in dozens of languages, extolled Ho Chi Minh, granting him the honorable title as "the Toussaint l'Ouverture of Indo-China" in 1954.[31]

In a reciprocal display of internationalist recognition, Ho wrote eloquently in *La Race Noir* in 1925 on the "uprising on the Island of Saint-Domingue," concluding that examples such as "Toussaint Louverture [leading] the black slaves to victory over armies unleashed by Napoleon and the British" as well as "the countless uprisings by slaves in the South of the United States… are enough to refute the argument put forth by our adversary that freedom is not important to Blacks, that they regard slavery as a better life for themselves." "To the contrary," he continues, "no one loves liberty as much as the oppressed do in the colonies."[32] It should not go unmentioned that Ho's words on the Haitian Revolution came over a decade prior to the publication of C.L.R. James's landmark text, *The Black Jacobins*, at a time when the import of the events of 1791-1804 remained little publicized, and even less acknowledged, in the anglophone world beyond the Black diaspora. It is no wonder as well that Ho regarded Henri Grégoire, the ardent 18th century abolitionist and leading member of the *Société des Amis des Noirs*, as "the apostle of the liberty of peoples."[33]

Ho's Anti-Colonial Theory

Ho's critical account of German colonialism ought to be read not only as a scathing rebuke of the German intelligentsia extant in his own time, but as well all succeeding generations who have failed and, indeed, continue to fail, with regard to acknowledging Germany's genocide of the Hererro and the Nama (1901-1906)—the first genocide of the 20th century. Long neglected by Western thinkers, including by some of the most vaunted critics of German fascism such as Theodor Adorno, Max Horkheimer, and Jurgen Habermas[34] among others, Ho addresses how the Herero and Nama tribes "in the former German colonies in Africa were completely exterminated," linking the latter as part of "the same system of pillage, extermination and destruction [which] prevails in the African regions under Italian, Spanish, British or Portuguese rule," as well as "in the Belgian Congo," where "the population in 1891 was 25 million, but... had fallen to eight and a half million by 1911."[35] It is notable that Ho writes about the genocide as early as 1925 which would subsequently take the German government over a century to acknowledge even nominally.[36]

To further emphasize this point, Ho's analysis was penned only a few years before Sigmund Freud would write his much celebrated *Civilization and its Discontents*, wherein he diagnoses aggressivity as a fundamental drive in human nature, exploding as the unconscious result of the repressive features of civilization. Although Freud was living in Leipzig during the Herero and Nama genocide, it was only after the First Imperial War that he even endeavored an attempt at understanding what drove humanity to mass atrocity—a fact which reveals the blindspot of German colonial thinking more generally, and perhaps more particularly Freud's own drive to effectively gainsay German barbarism on the African continent by providing a theoretical cover—concealing the history of European colonialism altogether behind a purported theory of universal aggression.[37]

While Freud was busy lambasting a strawman version of Communism in *Civilization and its Discontents*, abstracting aggressivity while also diluting intoxication as a mere form of fantasy and escapism, Ho was applying materialist analysis to history in order to diagnose the way slavery had become sublimated through the colonial process in the form of "corvées, porterage, forced labor, alcohol and syphilis" which, as he put it pithily in 1924, "complete the work of civilization."[38] Or, as stated in his poignant the final line of "Lynching," "among the collection of the crimes of American 'civiization,' lynching has a place of honour."[39] In works such as the "Monstrosity of Civilization" and "Civilization that Kills," Ho provides razor sharp historical analyses of the colonial situation faced by the people of the darker nations on par with Du Bois's own from the same era—an analysis which continues to evade an inordinate amount of Euroamerican intellectuals. Against the plaudits and popular sentiments of bourgeois apologists and paternalists too numerous to mention, Ho described in 1925 how the "cruel horrors have worsened a thousand fold" in the transition to colonialism in the late 19th and early 20th centuries.[40]

In 1925, Ho wrote "In the Slaughterhouse," a section of La race noir, in which he offers an analysis of Black soldiers fighting in colonial armies. Often recruited at the barrel of a gun, and subsequently dying on foreign battlefields and in Jim Crow hospitals, Ho argues that despite their ultimate sacrifices, these efforts "did not improve the laws of the Blacks in the United States," for instance.[41] In the 1940s, Ho, then leader of the Việt Minh, confronted Black soldiers on the battlefields of the Indo-China War with whom he would otherwise have been in an objective alliance with against the European powers. Though record keeping often conflated dead, missing, and deserted tirailleurs sénégalais soldiers (e.g. West and Central African soldiers conscripted into the French colonial army), of the 5,000 plus accounted for during the Indo-China years, a good number were likely deserters, as Sarah Zimmerman explains: "Exploiting the French military's inability to account for missing troops, some tirailleurs sénégalais crossed enemy lines to join up with the Vietminh." Zimmerman recounts one "celebrated tale… of a Guinean soldier, General Zaoro, who… deserted the tirailleurs sénégalais" and was so dedicated that it "led to his rapid promotion [to]… general among the ranks of the Vietminh." Another account even claims that "some deserters took advantage of the chaos of evacuation following the Fall of Điện Biên Phủ."[42]

Presaging events that would occur during the Vietnam War, the Việt Minh "segregated colonial soldiers from metropolitan French soldiers in POW camps," much "like the French." However, "instead of using this tactic to respect racial hierarchy like the French, the Việt Minh bifurcated troops to better serve the dissemination of their anti-colonial propaganda," tailoring "their propaganda for the tirailleurs sénégalais by focusing on their shared colonial identity as mistreated subjects of the French" and "fan[ning] the flames of military disobedience among POWs and active tirailleurs sénégalais."[43]

In this way, the Indo-China War "was the first large-scale anticolonial war where evidence suggests that tirailleurs sénégalais questioned their role in French colonialism," deserting and "abandon[ing] the French army for political reasons."[44] Thus, while Ho was actively fighting against French colonialism, a budding internationalist and anti-colonial consciousness[45] was brewing underfoot, cultivated and even spurred on by the Việt Minh's deft propaganda efforts, not only calling back to Ho's time as a journalist endeavoring to spread the colonial question to the masses, but also presaging similar phenomena during the Vietnam War when African American soldiers deserted the front, with many absconding to the famed "Soul Alley" in Saigon in order to escape the flagrant racism experienced in their own regiments. As Roger Goodwin observes, "a 1970 Army Counterintelligence investigation revealed that a large group of African Americans, most of whom had gone AWOL or deserted, were living in Saigon with Cambodians in the area surrounding Truong Minh Ky Street," and, "allegedly," even "had 'a mutual understanding of one another as 'oppressed minorities.'"[46]

Reflecting in 1925, and with typically rhetorical flair, Ho asks "did we not witness Hindu soldiers who refused to attack China?" suggesting that this ought to serve as "a grave warning for all imperialists who are thinking of sending native soldiers against the Soviet Republic, against the only loyal and resolute defender of all oppressed and exploited countries."[47] It is clear that the United States did not heed Ho's sage observation, given the way it would go on to, *inter alia*, stoke the flames for war between the Soviet Union and religious zealots in Afghanistan in the 1980s, the recoil of which was felt on 11 September 2001.

Black America and Ho Chi Minh

When Robert F. Williams met with Ho in the mid-1960s, he is said to have participated in producing some anti-war propaganda directed at Black soldiers. "Williams's experiences in Vietnam," his meeting with Ho Chi Minh not least, "left him with a passionate new depth of commitment to stopping the Vietnam War, a political priority that he shared with the increasingly radical young insurgents of the freedom movement in the United States." This new anti-war passion culminated in Williams sending "a batch of telegrams to freedom movement leaders including James Forman of SNCC and James Farmer of CORE" on 27 April 1965, in which he states: "Racial terrorists exterminating colored humanity of Vietnam. Decency and conscience requires all freedom fighters to join the battle for peace." On the very same day, Martin Luther King Jr. also "received another of Williams's patented political taunts," which read as follows: "'As nonviolent advocate and winner of the Nobel Peace Prize,' he told the minister, 'decent people of the world await your resolute condemnation of racist America's savage slaughter of the colored humanity of Vietnam.'"[48]

As President of the Monroe, North Carolina chapter of the NAACP, Williams's anti-war efforts cut against the grain in the years following the compromise of 1954 when the NAACP turned its back on internationalism, particularly under Executive Secretary Roy Wilkins. Wilkins viciously attacked Martin Luther King Jr. for his pro-peace stance on Vietnam: "'When an American Negro Soldier kills a Viet Cong, he is not killing a colored brother. Why should we consider the Viet Cong our colored brothers,' he asked querulously, since purportedly 'they don't feel the Negro is his brother.'"[49]

In 1968, the Black Panther Party sent a delegation to Montreal, including Bobby Seale and David Hilliard, to attend the Hemispheric Conference to End the War in Vietnam.[50] The BPP recognized the NLF as the government of South Vietnam, while the NLF recognized in turn the BPP as the vanguard of liberation in the United States: "Though we have different colors of skin," Ho writes in 1964, "the yellow Vietnamese and Black Americans are battling a common enemy—the cruelty of American imperialism."[51] Likewise, "when representatives of the Black Panther Party... met[52] the representatives of the National Liberation Front (NLF) of Vietnam in Montreal, Canada, the Vietnamese said, 'He Black Panther, we Yellow Panther!'[53] and the Panthers replied, 'Yeah, you're Yellow Panthers, we're Black Panthers. All power to the people!'[54] It would not be a stretch to suggest that Ho and the NLF were as much symbols for the BPP during the 1960s as the BPP were symbols for Ho and the NLF in the same era.[55] When, for instance, Ho describes the Vietnamese as "Yellow American Slaves," he is surely linking their common cause for liberation, which is why he also described the Vietnamese and Black Americans as fighting the first and second fronts against U.S. imperialism: "The Vietnamese People strongly support our Black brothers in America, for we believe their struggle is just and they shall overcome."[56]

A year after Ho's death in September 1969, Eldridge Cleaver penned an address in *The Black Panther* entitled "To My Black Brothers in Vietnam," encouraging Black soldiers to either go AWOL or "sabotage supplies and equipment and turn them over to the Vietnamese,"[57] a call which, again, harks back to the deserting tirailleurs sénégalais during the Indo-China years.[58] It should come as no surprise that Ho's death was also commemorated in the 13 Septmeber 1969 issue of *The Black Panther* in which his early essay "Lynching" was reprinted.[59] *The Black Panther* would also print Ho's New Year's Message on the cover of the 3 March 1969 issue,[60] while Korean leader Kim Il-Sung graced the front page alongside Ho Chi Minh in *The Black Panther* on 3 October 1970.[61]

Ho and Malcolm

In 1964, Ho commented in the pages of *Nhân Dân* how the "ink... barely had been dry" on the Civil Rights Act when racial terror by "American fascists" was unleashed from Mississippi to Harlem.[62] Ho then links this crusade of racial terror to the violence that the U.S. empire was executing contemporaneously upon the "'yellow American' slaves" of South Vietnam.

In his commentary, Ho also makes an allusion to "one black leader who warned, quite

THE BLACK PANTHER, SATURDAY OCTOBER 4, 1969 PAGE 14

TO MY GI BROTHERS

I want to say something to you, my G.I. brothers. I want to tell you something, something that you already know. Because we all came from the same place, that place being this fascist society, this capitalist society, this imperialistic society. Do you remember, brothers, when you were on the block and you would say, "I don't want to go." And you would then say, "But I got to go." I remember, just like it was only yesterday. I had to drop out of school, and I got me a job and said to myself, now I can make me some money and I can get all the things I wanted to get for myself. Do you know out of all the working I did, I still didn't have a goddamn thing. And I was still unsatisfied. All the while I was working I said to myself, I am a man, because I got me a job and I'm taking care of myself.

Now, brothers, dig this: Whenever they wanted me to do something, they would say, "Hey, boy, come here, " or "Hey, boy, do this or do that." So one day, when I was on my way home from work, I passed this recruiting station, and I saw in the window a sign that said, "JOIN THE ARMY AND BE A MAN". So after a lot of meditation, I decided to join the U.S. Marine Corps. For some goddamn reason, I believed that the U.S.M.C. made a man out of anybody. And I wanted to be a MAN more than anything in this whole goddamned world.

I put four years in that man's fascist U.S.M.C. I learned how to kill. They told me that the Koreans were communists and that they were coming over to our country to take over. But now dig this shit. I said to my top sergeant, "But, Seageant, that's the North and the South fighting, and they're coming over here?" He said, "Boy, can't you see we got to stop that shit right where it is. So you are going over there, so your mother and father and your sisters and brothers can be free; so they can have the right to do what they want; so they can say what they want to say; so they can go where they want to go. And when you come back home, you'll be a man. And you'll be able to get you a good job."

Now I want you to listen to this very closely, because I didn't know what he meant then; but I do now. He said, don't you want "us" to be the most powerful country in the world. Brothers, did I fall for that shit. I didn't know that he was talking about himself and not me, nor my brothers and sisters, nor my mother and father. He was talking about HIS racist, capitalistic, imperialistic, fascist society. So brothers, I stayed in there for four years. I put two and a half years in Korea. Then I came home. I had gotten wounded, so when I got back to the place I had fought for, to be free for me, I got my first taste of fascism. My leg was pretty well messed up, so I was walking with a cane. Also there were two more brothers with me, one blind and the other had lost one of his legs. We were on our way back to New York, and the train had to stop over in the U.S. capitol, Washington, D.C. We had two hours of waiting to do, so we decided to go get a malt. We went to the cafe and ordered a malt. Now dig this shit: Here we were standing there, one brother blind, and another on a cane, and the other with one leg, all of us were in uniform, with a chest full of ribbons and 2 1/2 pounds of battle stars. We ordered these malts and the bill came to 90 cents. So, Leroy gave the racist clerk $1.00. Do you know before she would pick it up, this racist, fascist pig wiped the money off and gave us our change on a napkin. Now this was one of the people whom I had been fighting for, so she could have a good job and be free.

Well, I finally got out. Then I tried to get a job. Brothers, let me tell you I couldn't find one. After my 26-26 ran out (that's $26.00 for 26 weeks), I was in the same shape I was in when I first left home. I was oppressed. I had been put in the biggest trick of my life. I had fought for freedom, for employment and equality. But in turn, I received racism, capitalism, and fascism. I didn't know that HE (the U.S. government) was the real enemy, and not the people I was fighting. For you see racism is his mother, capitalism is his father, imperialism is his sister, fascism is his goddamn brother. So you see HE is YOUR enemy, and not the Koreans or the Vietnamese. BE RUTHLESS TO YOUR ENEMY, AND KIND AND LOVING TO YOUR COMRADES. I'll close now, brothers, but I'll write you again soon.

ALL POWER TO THE PEOPLE
Ex-U.S. Marine
Present-Liberation Fighter
Brother Omar

"DUNG LAI" (HALT) GI

Yes, stop! Seize the time, and re-evaluate yourself and the conditions surrounding the situation you're in. Check it out and see how you're nothing but puppets and pawns for the greedy, bloodthirsty, lying American businessmen (Rockefeller, Hunt, Hughes, and some 800 big businessmen) who control the wealth, the big monies, all over the world.

Think about those thousands of Biafran people dying only because Standard Oil Co. (owned by Rockefeller) is trying to suck the 1000 barrels of oil per day which Biafra can produce. And think about how Nigeria is being used to move on those people.

Think about the Palestinean people who only want to live peacefully in their homeland, dying at the hands of the Israeli forces. The Israeli are supported by the United States so that it can steal the natural resources of that area. (That area can produce more oil than Biafra.)

Think about the Cuban people and their valuable sugar, and how they lost human lives fighting to protect their homeland. Whereas, the U.S. and their faithful bootlickers (Batista's regime) lost lives fighting to monopolize the sugar industries.

Think brothers and sisters and realize the fact that Vietnam is what was once called the "Rice Basket of the Far East" and that it produced more rice than any other country in its general millieu. Now Vietnam must buy rice from the United States. Also, that the K.K.K., along with the Birchites, both secured by 'their army', the Minutemen, have vested interest in Vietnamese products and various other imports from all over the world.

The Military-Industrial Complex is a network of big businessmen and key personnel in the U.S. Armed Forces (Pentagon) that starts and perpetuates wars in order to make money. Over 3 billion dollars every six months (6 billion dollars a year) is paid to Douglas Aircraft Co. Over 2 billion a year is paid for excess small arms ammo, and 20.0 million goes for musical instruments, and similar amounts of money go for various "goods" for the U.S. Military.

From the very beginning, the U.S. Military has had elaborate formal contract procedures with big businessmen. The Wright brothers made their first sale to the Signal Corps of the U.S. Army under a committment contract (#486) that called for payments of $85,000 per 'Flying Machine'.

Ever since World War I, there have been a number of so-called Advisory Corporations that the U.S. Government pays billions of dollars. System Development Corp. (S.D.C.) demands and receives millions to... 'develop I.B.M. Machines'?.. the Rand Corp. gets rich... 'aiding the Air Force'?... the Hudson Institute, formed in 1961, gets big money for 'Technological Advice'? All of the aforementioned have been founded by the most greedy, exploitative, tycoons ever known, who are warmongers, sucking the blood from all of the poor and oppressed people in the country.

So we see a whole conglomeration of jive capitalist juggernauts, organized and designed to exploit, that neglect the fact that millions of lives have been lost all across the world. In this country alone, Black people, in particular, and all poor and oppressed people in general, are still suffering and dying as a result of malnutrition, rat infested homes, disease, police brutality etc.

It's very important that you understand what's being said here, that you realize that the bubble of fantasy, money, and adventure you're caught up in is nothing more than an actual re-run of all those John Wayne, war loving movies that have conditioned your mind to believe that its your duty to kill innocent people in their own land. You are conditioned to act in the manner of American benchmen employed by motherf-----s who sit behind their desks wasting the peoples money, while you waste the peoples blood.

So, brothers and sisters you'd better mark time. Halt? Study the situation in its totality. Delve deep into the matter until you've educated yourself to that level of consciousness, to that degree of understanding, where you can plainly see that the government you're supporting is deteriorating, because it doesn't represent the people, and that you are sanctioning and stimulating the same tycoons that make money off you, the same jackanapes that cause little poor children to go unsheltered and hungry, the same mammy f----r that kidnapped Huey and Bobby and caused Papa (Eldridge) to go into exile. This government has dehumanized and brainwashed you to believe that this is a just system, that it's okay to oppress and exploit. So therefore, you become an enemy to yourself because you're representing another entity and not yourself. And until you purge yourself of all those evil elements that combine and make up the enemy within you, until you grasp the essesnce of the definition of capitalism, and get hip to the wrongness of the exploitation of man by man, only then can you truthfully say that 'no longer am I an enemy to myself, and I'm no longer a tool of this fascist government."

Then you'll realize more clearly all the repression and atrocious acts (the homes of our people being broken into, the inhabitants being forced to stand outside half naked and handcuffed etc.) being imposed and perpetrated upon the peace loving people that only want to live in harmony with each other. And when you see the same tactics that are used in Vietnam (helicopters with big fog lights and M-60 machine guns, nine man patrols, that patrol our community, gas shot into our homes) being used throughout the community, then it becomes explicitly clear that the ruling class of this country has no concern whatsoever, for the masses of people. So then, to anyone who is geared to the preservation of all just and honest people, it becomes a matter of concern, a matter of vital importance. A matter of who wins or who dies.

So, "Lai Dai G I", get on and get to stepping, stepping in the right direction, on a true azimuth that will surely guide you to the liberation and the self-determination of all poor and oppressed peoople of the world.

ALL POWER TO THE PEOPLE

A Note From Marine Corp History

"There isn't a trick in the racketeering bag that the military gang is blind to. It has its 'finger men' (to point out enemies), its 'muscle men' (to destroy enemies), its 'brain guys' (to plan war preparations), and a 'Big Boss' (supernationalistic capitalism).

It may seem odd for me, a military man to adopt such a comparison. Truthfulness compels me to do so. I spent 33 years and 4 months in active military service as a member of our country's most agile military force--the Marine Corps. I served in all commissioned ranks from a Second Lieutenant to Major-General. And during that period I spent most of my time being a high-class muscle man for Big Business, for Wall Street and for the bankers. In short, I was a racketeer, a gangster for capitalism.

I suspected I was just a part of a racket at the time. Now I am sure of it. Like all members of the military profession I never had an original throught until I left the service. My mental faculties remained in suspended animation while I obeyed the orders of the higher-ups. This is typical with everyone in the military service.

Thus I helped make Mexico and especially Tampico safe for American oil interests in 1914. I helped make Haiti and Cuba a decent place for the National City Bank boys to collect revenues in. I helped in the raping of half a dozen Central American republics for the benefit of Wall Street. The record of racketeering is long. I helped purify Nicaragua for the international banking house of Brown Brothers in 1909-12. I brought light to the Dominican Republic for American sugar interest in 1916. In China in 1927 I helped see to it that the Standard Oil went its way unmolested.

During those years, I had, as the boys in the back room would say, a swell racket. I was rewarded with honors, medals and promotion. Looking back on it, I feel that I might have given Al Capone a few hints. The best he could do was to operate his racket in three city districts. I operated on three continents."

--Manor Gen. Smedley D. Butler, U.S.M.C., Ret.
From Common Sense,

Bring the troops home now!

Join the march in San Francisco on Nov. 15

A page from The Black Panther newspaper addressing American soldiers serving in Vietnam.

accurately, that this was only a deceptive swindle that was propagated by America's ruling class."[63] Given that Malcolm X traveled the globe railing against the Civil Rights Act in highly publicized speaking engagements in Ghana, Nigeria, Egypt, Saudi Arabia, and England, it is possible, even probable, that Ho had Malcolm in mind when he wrote these lines[64] (Malcolm also referred to "three civil rights workers... murdered in cold blood" in Mississippi after the passage of the Civil Rights Act, for instance). Malcolm also would go on to give his landmark speech, "Not Just an American Problem, But a World Problem," in Rochester, New York on 16 February 1965, where, amid thunderous applause, he would make bold reference to "American planes, American bombs, escorted by American paratroopers, armed with machine guns" arriving in South Vietnam. Exposing certain hackneyed euphemisms often employed by agents of U.S. empire, Malcolm spoke of "Twenty thousand" soldiers, who we are made to believe were "not soldiers," but rather "escorts" and "just advisers"—a rhetoric all too familiar to anyone with even a passing knowledge of the way the U.S. war machine operates. "They're able to do all of this mass murder and get away with it," he continues, "by labeling it 'humanitarian,' an act of humanitarianism... or 'in the name of freedom,' 'in the name of liberty,'" and "all kinds of high-sounding slogans, but it's cold-blooded murder, mass murder."

It was likely no coincidence that FBI memos dated 18 and 21 February 1965—just days after Malcolm's rip-roaring speech in Rochester—make reference to how he "spoke at numerous meetings and functions, appeared on various radio and television shows," and "spoke at meetings sponsored by militant and subversive groups including the Socialist Workers Party," as well as "participated in debates, and held press conferences," in which "he urged Negroes to obtain guns for self protection and to register to vote; criticized the government, President Lyndon B. Johnson, and Negroes fighting in Vietnam."[65]

Though they never met in person or exchanged correspondence, Ho Chi Minh and Malcolm X shared more than a birthday in common. Forged in the furnaces of European colonialism and U.S. empire, from their youthful experiences as workers bouncing between Boston and Harlem, as well as the inspiration they drew from Garveyism and the UNIA, to their dedicated and principled commitments to internationalism, Ho and Malcolm were as much contemporaries to one another as they remain our contemporaries today.

* * *

Reflecting on Ho Chi Minh's time in Harlem, his meeting with Robert F. Williams, as well as the "Maoist inflections in both the National Liberation Front (of Vietnam) and Black Panther politics," Vijay Prashad encourages us "to appreciate the vitality of the idea of Third World solidarity," and asserts that the "radical visions that emerged in the twentieth century enabled the sense of enchanted comradeship of the 1960s and 1970s," and are "a legacy worth revisiting in this new century."[66] With the publication of this curriculum in English, we can be assured that these radical visions of Third World solidarity remain intact and in focus in our present era. We ought to be reminded not only of this shared history in the global struggle of oppressed nations against Western imperialism, but also of the cultivation of analytical and practical forms so desperately needed to galvanize, orient, and, in some cases, *re*orient and retrain our theoretical and organizational sights on forms of collective action toward the continuing development of international socialism. This volume thus fills the vacuum left open by the intersection of rampant anti-intellectualism, rabid anti-Communism, and, ultimately, rapacious capital; a veritable unholy trinity which looms vulturelike over the political and social landscape of much of Anglophone world—particularly in the United States.

As an aid in the development of materialist, global analysis trained on international solidarity, these volumes challenge the dominant philosophical and political modes fashionable on much of the Western left today with its monopoly on eclecticism, through which it often serves as an unwitting participant in the retreat from class analysis and thus as an unknowing handmaiden of historical amnesia. It is with hope that these volumes might aid in the development of political consciousness and perhaps even offer insight into the much-needed analysis of ultraleftism and other infantile disorders which remain prevalent in our present era. As well, we remain hopeful that these volumes might assist in the further development of an analysis of class collaboration historically and in our own time, as well as the stubborn attachment of some of our friends on the left to virulent white supremacy, aiding and abetting the global rise of right wing extremism, which in turn, we're afraid to say, lubricates the path for the emergence of a unique form of neo-fascism.

Gerald Horne
Victoria, British Columbia

Anthony Ballas
Durham, North Carolina

July, 2025

Endnotes
1. Ho Chi Minh (as Nguyen Ai Quoc), "The Martyrdom of the Negro: American Lynch-Justice," *Inprecor*, Vol. 4. No. 70, 2 October 1924, p. 772. Reprinted under the title "Lynching" in Fall, Bernard B (ed.), *Ho Chi Minh on Revolution: Selected Writings, 1920-66*, New American Library, 1967, p. 51-55; and Ho Chi Minh, *Selected Works, Vol. 1*. Foreign Languages Press, 2021; see also Silva, Luis (editor) and Nguyen, Dai Trang. *The Black Race by Ho Chi Minhi and Selected Works on Systemic Racism*, New Vietnam Publishing, 2021.
2. *L'Humanité*, 18 March 1923.
3. *La Vie Ouvrière*, 30 March, 1923.
4. "Le Ku-Klux-Klan," *La Correspondance Internationale*, vol. IV, no. 74, 4 November, 1924, pp. 628-629.
5. These writings have recently been reprinted in Luis Silva's edited volume entitled *The Black Race by Ho Chi Minh and Selected Works on Systemic Racism*, New Vietnam Publishing, 2021.

6   Haywood, Harry, *Black Bolshevik*, Liberator Press, 1978, pp. 154-165; Brocheux, Pierre, *Ho Chi Minh: A Biography*, Cambridge University Press, 2007, pp. 25-26; Horne, Gerald, *Mau Mau In Harlem?: The U.S. and the Liberation of Kenya*, Palgrave, 2009, p. 98; McDuffie, Erik S., *Sojourning for Freedom: Black Women, American Communism, and the Making of Black Left Feminism*, Duke University Press, 2011, p. 54; Higashida, Cheryl, *Black Internationalist Feminism: Women Writers of the Black Left, 1945-1995*, University of Illinois Press, 2001: "While enrolled at Moscow's Communist University of the Toilers of the East (KUTV) along with Ho Chi Minh, Deng Xiaoping, and Jomo Kenyatta, Maude White attended the 6th World Congress of the Comintern as it debated and passed the 1928 resolution on Black self-determination" (p. 36); and Lux, Talia, "The History of the Soviet Union's KUTV," *Peace, Land, & Bread*, 20 June, 2021.
7   Brocheux, *Ho Chi Minh*, pp. 25; 47.
8   *Inprecor*, Vol. 3, No. 2, 5 January 1923, pp. 16-17.
9   *Resolutions & Theses of the Fourth Congress of the Communist International, held in Moscow, Nov. 7 to Dec. 3, 1922*. As Harry Haywood recounts, Huiswoud "visited Lenin and became the first Black man to meet the great Bolshevik," and later also "became the first Black to serve as a candidate member of the Executive Committee of the Communist International." Haywood, *Black Bolshevik*, p. 147.
10 Ho Chi Minh (as Nguyen Ai Quoc), "Talk during the 22nd Session of the Fifth Congress of the Communist International, 1 July 1924," *La Correspondance Internationale*, Vol. 4, No. 53, pp. 558-559; Ho Chi Minh (as Nguyen Ai Quoc), "Report On The National And Colonial Questions At The Fifth Congress Of The Communist International," Selected Works of Ho Chi Minh Vol. 1, Foreign Languages Press, 2021, p. 181.
11 Ibid.
12 Letter from Nguyen Ai Quoc [Ho Chi Minh] to Secretary of State Robert Lansing (with enclosure); 6/18/1919; 851G.00; General Records, 1918 - 1931; Records of the American Commission to Negotiate Peace, Record Group 256; National Archives at College Park.
The letter, typed in French, references the Annamites, the group for which Minh would later be credited as the leader when he was arrested in Hong Kong under the alias Nguyen Ai Quoc, an accusation that he denied under questioning in 1931. See Gunn, Geoffrey C. "Media Coverage of the Arrest and Trial, in *Ho Chi Minh in Hong Kong*, 172–87. Cambridge University Press, 2021, p. 181. Refer also to Robert F. Williams's Testimony where he recounts how Ho described his "illusions about the United States" and "that he really expected the United States to help them liberate the country, because he thought the United States was opposed to colonialism" (p. 95).
13 This was the era in which the hunt for the so-called "Great White Hope" was still in the background, haunting the sweet science. See also Horne, Gerald, *The Bittersweet Science: Racism, Racketeering, and the Political Economy of Boxing*, International Publishers, 2020.
14 Ho Chi Minh (as Nguyen Ai Quoc), "About Siki," Le Paria, No. 9, 1 December, 1922. *Le Paria* was the first newspaper founded by Minh in 1922.
15 Duiker, William J. *Ho Chi Minh: A Life.* Hyperion, 2001, p. 50
16 Malcolm X, *The Autobiography of Malcolm X as Told By Alex Haley*, Ballantine Books, 1973, pp. 69-70. See also, Vincent, Ted. "The Garveyite Parents of Malcolm X," The Black Scholar, Vol. 20, No. 2 (1989): 10–13.
17 Blain, Keisha N., "On Louise Little, the Mother of Malcolm X: An Interview with Erik S. McDuffie," *Black Perspectives*, 19 February 2017.
18 Ibid., pp. 1 & 6..
19 Tyson, Timothy B., *Radio Free Dixie: Robert F. Williams and the Roots of Black Power Statement Of Responsibility*, Chapel Hill: University of North Carolina Press, 1999, p. 295; See also United States. Congress. Senate. Committee on the Judiciary. Subcommittee to Investigate the Administration of the Internal Security Act and Other Internal Security Laws, and Robert F. (Robert Franklin) Williams. Testimony of Robert F. Williams: Hearings, Ninety-first Congress, Second Session. Washington: U.S. Govt. Print. Off., 1971, in which Williams continues his description of Ho as follows: "if a person didn't know his record he wouldn't think that he was even a revolutionary" (p. 95.); See also Dellinger, David, "Conversations with Ho,"

Liberation, October 1969. pp. 2-6: "Earlier, when I had asked Ho about the time he lived in the United States shortly after World War I, he talked warmly about the people in Brooklyn for whom he had worked as a houseboy. Instead of condemning them as exploiters and class enemies, he said that they were fine people. 'I didn't have to work very hard,' he said. 'I used to have a lot of free time to study and to take trips to other sections of the city.' He spoke of taking the subway to Harlem and being shocked by the conditions of the black people. 'When you get back to the United States,' he said, 'you can say that when I worked as a domestic servant in Brooklyn I earned $40 a month and now that I am President of Vietnam I get paid $44 a month'" (p. 4); See also See also Quinn-Judge, *Ho Chi Minh: The Missing Years 1919-1941*, University of California Press, 2002: "A remark made to the US peace activist David Dellinger in 1969 reinforces the notion that his stay in America came after 1916. Ho Chi Minh told Dellinger that when he was in America, he heard Marcus Garvey speak in Harlem. Garvey, the leader of the 'return to Africa movement', did not arrive in the United States from his native Jamaica until 1916. In 1917 and 1918 he spoke frequently in Harlem on issues of racism, which had flared up in the US following the 1915 reappearance of the Ku Klux Klan. Ho Chi Minh published an article about the Ku Klux Klan in 1924 which described the practice of lynching in the American South—his information could have been drawn from Garvey's speeches or the US press of the time" (p. 21); See also Quinn-Judge p. 261n36.

20 Duiker, William J. *Ho Chi Minh: A Life*. Hyperion, 2001, p. 50; Tyson, *Radio Free Dixie*, 295. See also Duiker p. 588n8 where the author cites "an oral interview of Robert F. Williams by Archimedes F. Patti, contained in the Patti archives at the University of Central Florida in Orlando."

21 Robert F. WIlliams, Testimony, p. 95.

22 There are many such parallels and intersections to be drawn between Ho Chi Minh's early years and the long arc of Black liberation and internationalism in the 20th century that often remain unacknowledged. Ho was witness to the charnel house of French colonialism and especially to the cruelty of the latter on the coast of Dakar as a merchant sailor (see note 25 below), as well as his youthful experiences of "Harlem and the poverty of Negroes he saw there." "Ho Dead, War Policy Unchanged," *The Independent*, Vol. 32, No. 176, 4 September 1969, pp. A1 & A6.

23 Anticipating the global outcry garnered through Billie Holiday's "Strange Fruit," written by Jewish Communist, Abel Meeropol, Ho was not only hyper-aware of this most grotesque fixture of American life, but actively engaged and even ahead of the curve in terms of spreading the news and fomenting international outcry for the plight of Black Americans. It is noteworthy that Ho was covering such events for an international readership in the decade preceding the notorious persecution of the Scottsboro Boys and Angelo Herndon, both of which were to foment mass international movements in the 1930s. See Horne, Gerald, *Black Liberation/Red Scare: Ben Davis and the Communist Party*, University of Delaware Press, 1994; Horne, Gerald, *Powell V. Alabama: The Scottsboro Boys and American Justice*, Franklin Watts, 1997. See also Horne, Gerald, *Jazz and Justice: Racism and the Political Economy of the Music*, Monthly Review Press, 2019.

24 Silva, *The Black Race*, 2021, p. 17.

25 See Duiker, *Ho Chi Minh: A Biography*, pp. 50 & 588n7. See also Ho Chi Minh (as Trần Dân Tiên), *Những mẩu chuyện về đời hoạt động của Hồ Chủ tịch*, Shanghai: Ba Ywe, 1949, and, abridged English translation, *Glimpses of the Life of Ho Chi Minh*, Hanoi: Foreign Languages Press, 1958: "Bọn Pháp cười sặc sụa trong khi đồng bào ta chết đuối vì chúng nó. Đối với bọn thực dân, tính mạng của người thuộc địa, da vàng hay da đen cũng không đáng một xu" ["The French laughed heartily while our compatriots drowned because of them. To the colonialists, the lives of the colonized, whether yellow or black, were not worth a penny"]. For more on the aquatic connection to Black diasporic cultures, see also Dawson, Kevin, *Undercurrents of Power: Aquatic Culture in the African Diaspora*, University of Pennsylvania Press, 2021. Refer also to note 22 above.

26 See Horne, Gerald, *Red Seas: Ferdinand Smith and radical black sailors in the United States and Jamaica*, New York University Press, 2005.

27 As Marv Truhe writes: "During the Revolutionary War, more than five thousand free Black men fought for the colonists, despite General Washington's initial opposition. After the war, however, virtually all Black men were excluded from the military. During the Civil War and after the Emancipation Proclama- tion, the Union began widespread enlistment of Black men. They proved to be excellent soldiers but were discriminated against in pay, pensions, and equipment. Of particular interest is that Black men also served honorably in the Union Navy, making up fully one-fourth of its fleet. That ratio was double the Black population of the country at the time. By the close of the Civil War, more than thirty-eight thousand Black men had given their lives fighting for the Union cause. See Truhe, Marv, *Against All Tides: The Untold Story of the USS Kitty Hawk Race Riot*, Lawrence Hill Books, 2022, p. 6. See also Jacobs, John Swanson & (ed.) Jonathan D. S. Schroeder, *The United States Governed by Six Hundred Thousand Despots: A True Story of Slavery; A Rediscovered Narrative, with a Full Biography*, Chicago University Press, 2024.
28 Duiker, pp. 34 & 4. *Nhân Dân*, the newspaper of the Communist Party of Vietnam, continues to publish parallel editions multiple in Vietnamese, Russian, Chinese, French, Spanish, and English.
29 Ibid., p. 4.
30 Ho's polyglottal prowess was apparently a known attribute quite early on, as Geoffrey C. Gunn describes: "The first report on the arrest of Nguyen Ai Quoc entering the Hong Kong media appears to be a piece published in the Hong Kong Telegraph (June 22, 1931). Identified as the leader of "Annamite" revolutionaries in Hong Kong, his arrest was represented as a major coup for the French authorities, who had been tracking him for many years with agents fanned out across China. However, in a passage which caught the attention of Laprade, the French consul in Hong Kong, Ho Chi Minh was also depicted as, "A most accomplished man, speaking half a dozen European languages" See Gunn, Geoffrey C. "Media Coverage of the Arrest and Trial." Chapter. In *Ho Chi Minh in Hong Kong*, 172–87. Cambridge: Cambridge University Press, 2021, p. 174.
31 Robeson, Paul. "Ho Chi Minh is the Toussaint l'Ouverture of Indo-China (March 1954)," In *Freedomways Reader: Prophets in Their Own Country*, ed. Esther Cooper Jackson and Constance Pohl, Basic Books, 2000, pp. 147–149. Horne, Gerald, *Paul Robeson: The Artist as Revolutionary*, Pluto Press, 2016.
32 Luis, *The Black Race*, pp. 81-82. Ho also comments on escaped slaves in Portuguese controlled Brazil, who fled from the "plantations at Pernambuco" in the 17th century, comparing their "association of free settlements" at Palmares with "the ancient Spartan Republic" (Ibid., p. 81).
33 "Ho Chi Minh to Société des Amis de l'abbé Grégoire," July 6, 1946, reprinted in Gérard Lyon-Caen, "Grégoire et les droits des peuples," *Europe* 34, nos. 128–29 (1956): 84–85. In the latter, Ho Chi Minh cites Grégoire's "Déclaration du Droit des Gens" at length. See also Goldstein-Sepinwall, Alyssa, *The Abbé Grégoire and the French Revolution: The Making of Modern Universalism*, University of California Press, 2005. Goldstein-Sepinwall describes Grégoire as "an icon of anti-racism, a hero to people from Ho Chi Minh to French Jews," recalling how "he received further attention… as movements for decolonization spread through Asia and Africa. The Vietnamese Communist leader Ho Chi Minh called him 'the apostle of the liberty of peoples' in 1946; the celebrated Martiniquan poet and statesman Aimé Césaire praised him in 1950 as 'the first scientific refuter of racism' and 'the first anticolonial militant,' whilst baptizing a Place de l'abbé Grégoire in Fort-de-France" (Ibid., p. 224).
34 Habermas has been criticized, justifiably, as recently as 2024 for his inability or, more likely, his unwillingness to come to grips with the reality and legacy of German colonial pillage in Africa, as well as Germany's continuing colonial brokering in its obstinate allegiance with Israel and genocidal onslaught in Historic Palestine. As Hamid Dabashi writes, "Palestine is today an extension of the colonial atrocities" perpetrated by Germany and other colonial powers on the non-European world. "Habermas" he continues, "appears ignorant that his endorsement of the slaughter of Palestinians is completely consistent with what his ancestors did in Namibia during the Herero and Namaqua genocide. Like the proverbial ostrich, Ger-

man philosophers have stuck their heads inside their European delusions, thinking the world does not see them for what they are." Dabashi, Hamid, "Thanks to Gaza, European philosophy has been exposed as ethically bankrupt," 18 January 2024.

35 Ho Chi Minh, "Report On The National And Colonial Questions At The Fifth Congress Of The Communist International," Selected Works of Ho Chi Minh Vol. 1, Foreign Languages Press, 2021. See also, Fall, Bernard B., *Ho Chi Minh on Revolution: Selected Writings, 1920-66*. New American Library, 1967, pp. 71-72.

36 Onishi, Norimitsu & Melissa Eddy, "A Forgotten Genocide: What Germany Did in Namibia, and What It's Saying Now," 28 May 2021.

37 Had critical accounts like Ho's or Aimé Césaires's been available to the inordinately influential Freud, then perhaps the European intelligentsia would've better understood violence as mass atrocity perpetrated *on Europeans by Europeans* as what Césaire would later diagnose as the "imperial boomerang" coming back like whiplash against the European populus—the result of formerly exported colonial methods of torture and depravity turned inward. See Césaire, *Aimé, Discourse on Colonialism*, Monthly Review Press, 2000; Fanon, Frantz, "Colonial War and Mental Disorders," in *The Wretched of the Earth*, Grove, 1968, pp. 181-233; and Khanna, Ranjana, *Dark Continents: Psychoanalysis and Colonialism*, Duke University Press, 2003.

38 Silva, *The Black Race*, p. 6.

39 Ibid., p. 15.

40 Ibid., p. 37.

41 Ibid., p. 75.

42 Zimmerman, Sarah, *Living Beyond Boundaries: West African Servicemen in French Colonial Conflicts, 1908–1962*, Dissertation, University of California Berkeley, 2011, p. 109: "Veterans had mixed feelings about desertion in Indochina. Some viewed desertion as an act of cowardliness and others read it as a sign of bravery. The second opinion was particularly prominent among Guinean veterans. None of this projects' informants admitted to desertion, but the circulating rumors were fascinating. One veteran explained how tirailleurs sénégalais could join forces with the Vietminh. Under the cover of darkness, a soldier slipped out of a French military post and when he neared a Vietminh encampment, the absconding soldier waved a white handkerchief to indicate his peaceful intentions. He would then negotiate his integration into the Vietminh. West African veterans hypothesized that there were very few tirailleurs sénégalais who deserted, but those who did were aware that the Vietminh did not execute their POWs. Thus, deserting tirailleurs sénégalais knew that they could weather the war in Indochina with the Vietminh" (Ibid.).

43 Ibid., p. 108. Zimmerman continues: "In one attempt to inspire soldiers to defect to the Vietminh, they sent messages to tirailleurs sénégalais that there were anti-colonial riots in Dakar in 1951. The Vietminh promised that if soldiers deserted, they would finance their repatriation to West Africa."

44 Ibid., p. 3.

45 It should not go unremarked that the CIA orchestrated a coup to overthrow Kwame Nkrumah in 1966 whilst he was en route to China and Hanoi on a diplomatic peace mission to meet with Ho Chi Minh and find a peaceful end to the War in Vietnam—a meeting that the United States encouraged Nkrumah to attend, and even promised to cease bombing North Vietnam to ensure his safe passage. Upon his departure, coup leaders told some 600 Ghanaian troops that Nkrumah's intention for traveling to Hanoi was in order to make preparations to deploy troops to Vietnam, leading to the coup.

46 Goodwin, Gerald F., *Race in the Crucible of War: African American Servicemen and the War in Vietnam*, University of Massachusetts Press, 2023, p. 161. The Viet Cong also distributed leaflets highlighting racism in Alabama as part of these efforts, which ought to be read in tandem with the events of the "Kitty Hawk incident" in 1972, which famously saw a physical fight break out between white and Black soldiers as the result of racial tensions on the aircraft carrier stationed off North Vietnam. See Truhe, Marv, *Against All Tides: The Untold Story of the USS Kitty Hawk Race Riot*, Lawrence Hill Books, 2022.

47 Silva, *The Black Race*, p. 79. See also Ho's obituary for V.I. Lenin: "'Lenin is dead!' This news

struck the people like a bolt from the blue. It spread to every corner of the fertile plains of Africa and the green fields of Asia. It is true that the black or yellow people do not yet know clearly who Lenin is or where Russia is. The imperialists have deliberately kept them in ignorance. Ignorance is one of the chief mainstays of capitalism. But all of them, from the Vietnamese peasants to the hunters in the Dahomey forests, have secretly learnt that in a faraway corner of the earth there is a nation that has succeeded in overthrowing its exploiters and is managing its own country with no need for masters and Governors General. They have also heard that that country is Russia, that there are courageous people there, and that the most courageous of them all was Lenin. This alone was enough to fill them with deep admiration and warm feelings for that country and its leader…But this was not all. They also learned that that great leader, after having liberated his own people, wanted to liberate other peoples too. He called upon the white peoples to help the yellow and black peoples to free themselves from the foreign aggressors' yoke, from all foreign aggressors, Governors General Residents, etc. And to reach that goal, he mapped out a definite programme." See: Ho Chi Minh, "Lenin and the Colonized Peoples," *Pravda*, 27 January, 1924; Reprinted in Ho Chi Minh, *Selected Works, Vol. 1. Foreign Languages Press*, 2021, pp. 158-159.

48 Tyson, Timothy B., *Radio Free Dixie*, p. 295.
49 Horne, Gerald, *Armed Struggle?: Panthers and Communists, Black Nationalists and Liberals in Southern California, Through the Sixties and Seventies*, International Publishers, 2024, p. 217.
50 See Committee on Internal Security Report, The Black Panther Party, Its Origin and Development as Reflected in Its Official Weekly Newspaper, the Black Panther: Black Community News Service; Staff Study, Ninety-first Congress, Second Session. United States: U.S. Government Printing Office, 1970, specifically pp. 11, 69, 102.
51 Silva, *The Black Race*, p. 92.
52 Prisoner exchanges were proposed involving Bobby Seale and Huey Newton in exchange for POWs in North Vietnam, which was unsurprisingly rejected by the Nixon administration. Although they were "confiscated by customs agents in New York," "the North Vietnamese did send 379 letters from prisoners of war home to their families in the United States through the Black Panther Party." See Bloom, Joshua & Waldo E. Martin, Jr., *Black against Empire: The History and Politics of the Black Panther Party*, University of California Press, p. 318 and Cleaver, Kathleen Neal, "Back to Africa: The Evolution of the International Section of the Black Panther Party (1969–1972)," in *The Black Panther Party [Reconsidered]*, ed. Charles E. Jones, Black Classic Press, 1998, p. 234.
53 "M. Hoang Minh Giam, North Vietnamese Minister of Culture, Hemispheric Conference to End the War in Vietnam, November 19, 1968," quoted in Lewis, Raymond, "Montreal: Bobby Seale—Panthers Take Control," *The Black Panther*, Vol. 2, No. 18, 21 December 1968, p. 5; and Bloom & Martin, Jr., *Black against Empire*, pp. 267 & 310; and Hillard, David & Lewis Cole, *This Side of Glory: the Autobiography of David Hilliard and the Story of the Black Panther Party*, Little, Brown, 1993, p. 247; as well as Prashad, Vijay, "Bruce Lee and the Anti-imperialism of Kung Fu: A Polycultural Adventure," *positions: east asia cultures critique* Vol. 11, No. 1, 2003, p. 64.
54 Prashad, Vijay, "Bruce Lee and the Anti-imperialism of Kung Fu: A Polycultural Adventure," *positions: east asia cultures critique* Vol. 11, No. 1, 2003, pp. 64-65.
55 That the coinage "Viet Watts" appeared in popular parlance "and was perhaps "more than a slogan" in Southern California during the Watts uprising and the Vietnam War demonstrates this throughline. See Horne, Gerald, *Fire This Time: The Watts Uprising and the 1960s*, University Press of Virginia, 1995, pp. 45-63; 102 & 107. Likewise, *People's World* reported on how "the commitment to kill Vietnamese made it impossible to save lives in Watts," linking the way the attack on Vietnam "obstructs a serious war on poverty" in Southern California (Ibid., 273).
56 Silva, *The Black Race*, p. 88 & 95.
57 Cleaver, Eldridge, "To My Black Brothers in Vietnam," *The Black Panther*, Vol. 4, No. 16, 21 March 1970, pp. 4 & 20; Also cited in Horne, *Armed Struggle?*, p. 359.
58 A year later in 1970, while in Hanoi as part of a BPP delegation, Eldridge Cleaver would

broadcast similar appeals via the radio, calling for Black soldiers to either "refuse to fight, desert, or sabotage the war from within." Quoted in Cleaver, "Back to Africa," p. 234. A citation also appears on p. 254 in the latter in reference to a "Statement by Eldridge Cleaver to GIs in South Vietnam," in *The Black Panther*, 26 September, 1970, p. 14.

59 "Lynching," *The Black Panther*, Vol. 3, No. 21, 13 September 1969, p. 16.

60 *The Black Panther*, Vol. 2, No. 24, 3 March 1969.

61 *The Black Panther*, Vol. 5, No. 14, 3 October 1970; See also Ho Chi Minh, 22 May 1976, "Advice to Oneself," "On the Road," "Build the Country," and "Fine Weather," excerpted from "Ho Chi Minh's Prison Diary," reprinted in *The Black Panther* to honor Ho Chi Minh's birthday, *Freedom Archives*; See also Horne, *Armed Struggle?*, p. 381.

62 Silva, *The Black Race*, 91-92. See also "In Support of the Struggle of Americans," *Nhân Dân*, No. 3772, 28 July 1964.

63 Ibid., p. 91.

64 In another late writing in the pages of *Nhân Dân* in August 1966—just a year after the assasination of Malcolm—Ho quotes "a Black leader" as saying "in America, a dog has more rights than a Negro… American history is a history vault of Negroes being treated like cattle—the worst and most brutal history vault!" (Ibid.). It is possible that Ho may have had Malcolm in mind here as well, though there is no way to be certain. For example, from Malcolm X's Speech at the Founding Rally of the Organization of Afro-American Unity 28 June 1964: ""Convinced that, in order to translate this determination into a dynamic force in the cause of human progress conditions of peace and security must be established and maintained;" – And by "conditions of peace and security," [we mean] we have to eliminate the barking of the police dogs, we have to eliminate the police clubs, we have to eliminate the water hoses, we have to eliminate all of these things that have become so characteristic of the American so-called dream. These have to be eliminated. Then we will be living in a condition of peace and security. We can never have peace and security as long as one black man in this country is being bitten by a police dog. No one in the country has peace and security." And, finally, at a Washington, D.C. rally, 10 May 1963: "If anybody sets a dog on a black man, the black man should kill that dog—whether he is a four-legged dog or a two-legged dog."

65 FBI File 100-399321: Section 19. June 1964 - June 1980. MS Federal Surveillance of African Americans, 1920-1984: FBI File on Malcolm X. Federal Bureau of Investigation Library. Archives Unbound.

66 Prashad, Vijay, *Everybody was Kung Fu Fighting: Afro-Asian Connections and the Myth of Cultural Purity*, Beacon Press, 2001, p. 141.

EDITOR'S NOTE

Working on this book was one of the most exciting and enlightening experiences of my life. While developing Part 1 of this curriculum, I learned that Dialectical Materialism is crucial for understanding our universe. Historical Materialism focuses that understanding by applying Dialectical Materialist analysis to to our own existence.

One of the great achievements of Karl Marx was his accurate description of the ways in which objective material processes determine the course of human society as well as the ways in which a revolutionary economic class plays a subjective role in historical development. This discovery transformed the study of history into a scientific field and a revolutionary phenomenon. By grasping, utilizing, and building upon the discoveries of Marx and Engels, Ho Chi Minh and other revolutionary figures throughout modern history have been able to achieve incredible things.

I hope that workers worldwide will eventually learn this applied philosophy and use its lessons to hasten the liberation of humanity from class society. I hope that this work can contribute to the education of the masses by making the tremendous work of Vietnamese intellectuals available to the English-speaking world.

I am forever grateful to the Vietnamese professors and intellectuals who produced the original work, and to my wife and dearest comrade, who translated their words, for teaching me how to see the world from a comprehensive and historical perspective.

Emerican Johnson
July, 2025

CONTRIBUTING EDITOR'S NOTE

A few miles up the road from where this note was written lies Karl Marx's final resting place in Highgate Cemetery, London. At the funeral on March 17, 1883, his closest comrade, friend, and intellectual partner Friedrich Engels summed up the major contribution of Marx's theoretical work thus:

> Just as Darwin discovered the law of development of organic nature,
>
> so Marx discovered the law of development of human history.

Of course, Engels went on to list just a few of the many other world-historic theoretical breakthroughs that Karl Marx made during his life, but it is no accident that Engels foregrounded Historical Materialism as a key to understanding the Marxist method of analysis and praxis. This text, then, which seeks to be a foundational understanding of the meaning and use of the Historical Materialist method, could not be more essential, and more timely. In a world of dizzying ruptures, realignments, and radicalisation, the tool of Historical Materialism is essential to guiding our responses and our actions. Such grounding has led revolutionary movements to victory in many places, and of course most pertinently in Vietnam itself, this year celebrating 50 years since the Vietnamese people successfully liberated themselves, reunified their country, and began the process of socialist construction, which continues to this day and has always been undergirded by a historical materialist and dialectical materialist perspective.

Luna Nguyen and Emerican Johnson's outstanding work bringing the Curriculum of the Basic Principles of Marxism-Leninism to an Anglophone audience is to be applauded. For readers, it is a rare and generative opportunity to access 'actually existing socialist' education materials, alongside the insightful commentary of Luna and EJ. One initial shock from this text for Western audiences, used to the blinkered perspectives of our own academic institutions, is to see the respect and seriousness these topics are afforded by Vietnam's education system, with this robust curricula on the subject of historical materialism being necessary for all students in higher education, and specifically "for university students not specializing in Marxism-Leninism"(!). Of course, beyond this initial lesson there is so much more to learn from this text, and alongside Part 1 on Dialectical Materialism (and future forthcoming volumes), the Curriculum is a treasure trove and toolkit for those serving liberation movements globally.

In Engels' oration at Marx's funeral, he went on to stress "For Marx was before all else a revolutionist. His real mission in life was to contribute, in one way or another, to the overthrow of capitalist society and of the state institutions." And as such with any Marxist text we must consider this. In this work, the possibilities for practical application from study are enormous, and activists and organizers worldwide can implement the forms of analysis, the historical lessons, and the revolutionary optimism into their praxis. Who better to learn effective organising from than those who successively liberated themselves from French, Japanese, and American colonial invaders? Che Guevara, in his message to the Tricontinental, argued that those seeking the liberation of the peoples of the world should "create two, three, many Vietnams" and it is in that spirit that we should utilize these books.

David Peat
July, 2025

NOTES ON TRANSLATION

Vietnamese is a very different language from English, which has presented many challenges in translating this book. Whenever possible, I have tried to let the "spirit" of the language guide me, without altering the structure, tone, and formatting of the book.

One thing you will likely notice right away: this book is highly condensed! This is because most Vietnamese students are already familiar with these concepts. We have added annotations to try to make the book more digestible for those of you who are new to Marxism-Leninism, and these annotations are explained on the next page.

I have worked hard to try to make the language in this book consistent with the language used in popular translations of works from Marx, Lenin, etc., that would be familiar to English-language students of Marxism-Leninism. That said, a multitude of translators have been translating these texts into English for well over a century, such that different word choices have been used to relate the same concepts, and even Marx, Engels, and Lenin used different terms to describe the same concepts in many instances (not to mention the fact that Marx and Engels wrote primarily in German, whereas Lenin wrote primarily in Russian).

With all this in mind, I have made it my first priority to keep the language of this translation internally consistent to avoid confusion and, again, to match the spirit of the original text as much as possible. As a result, you may find differences between the translation choices made in this text and other translations, but it is my hope that the underlying meaning of each translation is properly conveyed.

Another note on "Large Language Models" and machine-translation, which was not nearly so wide spread when I began translating this curriculum:

Translation is an incredibly subtle and challenging undertaking. It requires a very human insight to properly convey emotional and intellectual content from not just one language, but also from one culture, to another. I have tried my hand at using machine translation for political and philosophical concepts and I conclude that machine translation is very much a double-edged sword. In some ways, they do open up communications for the workers of the world, but they can also be dangerously inaccurate in moments when accuracy is needed the most. We did not use any large language models or machine translation for this text and we hope that the reader will take care in using automated translation.

In your future studies I urge you to understand the severe misunderstandings which can emerge from systems that lack a human's ability to think critically and understand what is being said. I don't discourage anyone from using such tools, but I only hope that we will not rely on them overmuch in our attempts to commune with our fellow human beings as we create history together.

July, 2025

Luna Nguyen

GUIDE TO TEXT AND ANNOTATIONS

This book was written as a textbook for Vietnamese students who are not specializing in Marxism-Leninism, and so it is meant to be a simple and condensed survey of the most fundamental principles of Historical Materialism to be used in a classroom environment with the guide of an experienced lecturer. A typical Vietnamese college student will already have been exposed to many of the concepts presented herein throughout twelve years of primary and secondary education. As such, in translating and preparing this book for a foreign audience who are likely to be reading it without the benefit of a lecturer's in-person instruction, we realized that we would need to add a significant amount of annotations to the text.

These annotations will take the following forms:

Short annotations which we insert into the text itself [will be included in square brackets like these].

> Longer annotations which add further context and background information will be included in boxes like this.

We have also added diagrams to our annotations, as well as a detailed glossary/index and appendices, which are located in the back of the book.

Words that have a dotted underline like this are words that can be found in the glossary/index. Note that such words may have a very different use in the context of Dialectical and Historical Materialist philosophy, so it may be useful to check the definition in the glossary even if you are already familiar with the underlined word.

We will frequently reference Part 1 (*The Worldview and Philosophical Methodology of Marxism-Leninism*) and other parts of this curriculum. The text for Part 1 is currently available in a previously published volume. The ebook can be found for free at BanyanHouse.org. Other parts of the curriculum will be published in the future. Whenever another part of the curriculum is referenced, it will be featured in bold italics, like this: ***Part 1, Part 2, Part 3***, etc.

We hope these will resources will also be of use in studying other texts which are rooted in Marxist-Leninist philosophy.

ORIGINAL VIETNAMESE PUBLISHER'S NOTE

In 2004, under the direction of the Central Government, the Ministry of Education and Training, in collaboration with Sự Thật [Vietnamese for "The Truth," the name of a National Political Publishing House], published a [political science and philosophy] curriculum for universities and colleges in Vietnam. This curriculum includes 5 subjects: Marxist-Leninist Philosophy, Marxist-Leninist Political Economy, Scientific Socialism, Vietnamese Communist Party History, and Ho Chi Minh Thought. This curriculum has been an important contribution towards educating our students - the young intellectuals of the country - in political reasoning, so that the next generation will be able to successfully conduct national innovation.

With the new practice of education and training, in order to thoroughly grasp the reform of the Party's ideological work and theory, and to advocate for reform in both teaching and learning at universities and colleges in general, on September 18th, 2008, the Minister of Education and Training, in collaboration with Sự Thật, have issued a new program and published a textbook of political theory subjects for university and college students who are not specialized in Marxism - Leninism with Associate Professor and Doctor of Philosophy Nguyen Viet Thong as chief editor. There are three subjects:

Curriculum of the Basic Principles of Marxism-Leninism

Curriculum of Ho Chi Minh Thought

Curriculum of the Revolutionary Path of the Communist Party of Vietnam.

Curriculum of the Basic Principles of Marxism-Leninism was compiled by a collective of scientists and experienced lecturers from a number of universities, with Pham Van Sinh, Ph.D and Pham Quang Phan, Ph.D as co-editors. This curriculum has been designed to meet the practical educational requirements of students.

We hope this book will be of use to you.

April, 2016

NATIONAL POLITICAL PUBLISHING HOUSE - SỰ THẬT

ORIGINAL VIETNAMESE PREFACE

To implement the resolutions of the Communist Party of Vietnam, especially the 5th Central Resolution on ideological work, theory, and press, on September 18th, 2008, The Ministry of Education and Training has issued Decision Number 52/2008/QD-BGDDT, issuing the subject program: The Basic Principles of Marxism-Leninism for Students Non-Specialised in Marxism-Leninism and Ho Chi Minh Thought. In collaboration with Truth - the National Political Publishing House - we published the Curriculum of the basic principles of Marxism-Leninism for Students Non-Specialised in Marxism-Leninism and Ho Chi Minh Thought.

The authors of this text have drawn from the contents of the Central Council's previous programs (Marxist-Leninist Philosophy, Marxist-Leninist Political Economy, and Scientific Socialism) and compiled them into national textbooks for Marxist-Leninist science subjects and Ho Chi Minh Thought, as well as other curriculums for the Ministry of Education and Training. The authors have received comments from many collectives, such as the Ho Chi Minh National Academy of Politics and Administration, the Central Propaganda Department, as well as individual scientists and lecturers at universities and colleges throughout the country. Notably:

Associate Professor To Huy Rua, Ph.D, Professor Phung Huu Phu, Ph.D, Professor Nguyen Duc Binh, Professor Le Huu Nghia, Ph.D, Professor Le Huu Tang, Ph.D, Professor Vo Dai Luoc, Ph.D, Professor Tran Phuc Thang, Ph.D, Professor Hoang Chi Bao, Ph.D, Professor Tran Ngoc Hien, Ph.D, Professor Ho Van Thong, Associate Professor Duong Van Thinh, Ph.D, Associate Professor Nguyen Van Oanh, Ph.D, Associate Professor Nguyen Van Hao, Ph.D, Associate Professor Nguyen Duc Bach, PhD. Pham Van Chin, Phung Thanh Thuy, M.A., and Nghiem Thi Chau Giang, M.A.

After a period of implementation, the contents of the textbooks have been supplemented and corrected on the basis of receiving appropriate suggestions from universities, colleges, the contingent of lecturers of political theory, and scientists. However, due to objective and subjective limitations, there are still contents that need to be added and modified, and we would love to receive more comments to make the next edition of the curriculum more complete.

MINISTRY OF EDUCATION AND TRAINING

Table of Contents

Introduction to the Basic Principles of Marxism-Leninism
Part 2: Historical Materialism

Introduction 1

Chapter 1: The Role of Material Production

I. Material Production and Its Roles
   1. Material Production and the Mode of Production 10
   2. The Role of Material Production and the Role of the Mode of Production in the Origin and Development of Human Society 18

II. The Law of Suitability Between the Relations of Production and the Development of the Productive Forces
   1. Definitions of Productive Forces and Relations of Production 42
   2. Dialectical Relationship Between Productive Forces and Relations of Production 47

Chapter 2: Dialectics of the Base and Superstructure

I. Definitions of the Base and the Superstructure
   1. Definition of the Base 73
   2. Definition of the Superstructure 82

II. Dialectical Relationship Between the Base and the Superstructure
   1. The Base Determines the Superstructure 90
   2. The Superstructure's Impact on the Base 97

Chapter 3: Social Being Determines Social Consciousness; and the Relative Independence of Social Consciousness

I. Social Being Determines Social Consciousness
   1. Definitions of Social Being and Social Consciousness 106
   2. The Decisive Role of Social Being in Determining Social Consciousness 124

II. The Relative Independence of Social Consciousness 131

Chapter 4: Social-Economic Formation Theory

I. Category of Social-Economic Formation 159

II. The Natural-Historical Process of the Development of Social-Economic Formations 164

III. Scientific Value of the Theory of Social-Economic Formations 175

Chapter 5: The Role of Class Struggle and Social Revolution

I. Class and the Role of Class Struggle in the Development of Class Society

1. Definition of Class 181
2. Origin of Class 191
3. The Role of Class Struggle in the Motion and Development
   of Class Society 200

II. Social Revolutions and Their Role in the Development of Class Society

1. Definition of Social Revolution and Its Causes 207
2. The Role of Social Revolution in the Development of Class Society 209

Chapter 6: Historical Materialist Viewpoints About Humans and the History-Creating Role of the Masses

I. Humans and Human Nature

1. Definition of Humans 212
2. Human Nature 217

II. Definition of the Masses and the History-Creating Role of the Masses

1. Definition of the Masses 230
2. The History-Creating Role of the Masses and of Individuals 232

Afterword 238

Appendices

- Appendix A: Dialectical Materialism Fundamentals 240
- Appendix B: Laws of Historical Materialism 241
- Appendix C: Principles of Social Formation Theory and
  Rules of Historical Materialist Methodology 242
- Appendix D: Structure of Human Society 243
- Appendix E: Subjectivity and Objectivity 244
- Appendix F: Historical Development of Vietnam 252
- Appendix G: Productive Forces and Relations of Production in Vietnam 254
- Appendix H: Bypassing the Capitalist Mode of Production 269
- Appendix I: Transitional Period Towards Socialism in Vietnam 273
- Appendix J: What Are Socialist Values and Socialist Manners? 276
- Appendix K: History of Class Society 277

Glossary and Index 284

Total Victory of Vietnam
The Nation, United, Advances Towards Socialism

INTRODUCTION TO THE BASIC PRINCIPLES OF MARXISM-LENINISM

PART II

HISTORICAL MATERIALISM

Historical Materialism is a system of Dialectical Materialist viewpoints of human society as well as the result of applying the methodologies of Dialectical Materialism and Materialist Dialectics to the study of social life and human history.

> **Annotation 1**
>
> Following is a list of key words and concepts that will be used throughout the remainder of this text. It is important to note that within the Dialectical Materialist and Historical Materialist methodologies, many words are used differently or have different definitions from how they are used in mainstream bourgeois-dominated fields of philosophy, economics, history, etc.
>
> As such, we suggest reviewing the definitions of vocabulary words supplied in this text even if you are already familiar with them. For easy reference, there is a glossary and index at the end of the book, starting on page 284. Words that are underlined like this can be found in the glossary.
>
> **Dialectical Materialism**
>
> Dialectical Materialism is a universal philosophical and methodological system which forms the theoretical core of a scientific worldview which was first developed by Karl Marx and Friedrich Engels with the express goal of achieving communism.
>
> Dialectical Materialism is the subject of Chapter 1 of *Part 1* of this series: *Curriculum of the Basic Principles of Marxism-Leninism: the Worldview and Philosophical Methodology of Marxism-Leninism*, which will be referenced throughout this volume. Print and electronic copies of this book are available at BanyanHouse.org.
>
> As a universal philosophical and methodological system, Dialectical Materialism can be used to analyze and engage with all things, phenomena, and ideas.
>
> **Materialist Dialectics**
>
> Materialist Dialectics is a scientific system of philosophy concerned with motion, development, and common relationships, and with the most common rules concerning the motion and development of nature, society, and human thought. Materialist Dialectics is the subject of Chapter 2 of *Part 1* of this series and will also be referenced throughout this volume, along with Chapter 1, as mentioned above. The framework of Materialist Dialectics can be used to analyze the change, motion, and development of all things, phenomena, and ideas.

Annotation 1 (continued)
Viewpoints

A *viewpoint* (also known as a *point of view* or a *perspective*) is, in the Dialectical Materialist framework, the starting point of analysis which determines the direction of thinking from which phenomena and problems are considered [see *Part 1*, p. 12].

History

History, as used in Historical Materialism, typically refers to *human history.* Vietnam's *History Textbook for 10th Grade Students* gives the following definition of history:

> History includes everything that happened in the past. Human history is the entirety of human activities from the origin of humanity to the present day. Human history includes the history of human interaction with nature as well as the history of humans interacting with each other. There is a distinction between historical fact and historical perception.

Historical fact refers to objective facts which simply describe what has occurred in the past, including the material conditions of the past. Historical perception refers to opinions and perceptions of history which rely on interpretations that are influenced by political, cultural, or other biases or philosophical framings. The Vietnamese history textbook referenced above provides the following examples:

> **Historical Fact:** In early August 1945, the United States dropped two atomic bombs on the Japanese cities of Hiroshima and Nagasaki.
>
> **Historical Perception:**
>
> *Perception 1:* The United States dropped atomic bombs on Japan, causing World War II to end many months earlier, limiting the loss of life for the warring parties.
>
> *Perception 2:* America did not need to drop atomic bombs. It was a war crime, an atrocity against humanity.

Note that the perceptions above go beyond mere objective descriptions of occurrences in the past. Note also that historical perceptions can impact and influence human understandings of historical truth. For instance, some humans may be more likely to believe falsehoods and inaccurate narratives about historic truths because of attitudes and prejudices which arise from philosophical, religious, cultural, or other such biases. In an article titled "History, Truth, and Historiography," Professor Ha Van Tan, a Vietnamese historian and archeologist, offered this definition of history:

> History is objective. Historical truth is the truth that exists independently of our consciousness. But historical perception (consciousness/awareness) is subjective. And history is written by humans for different purposes.

Dialectical Materialist analysis demands that we seek a comprehensive and *historical* perspective in studying all subjects [see *Part 1*, p. 185]. It is a requirement to study human history and the historical development of human society in order to understand human society as it exists today. As such, the study of history and the study of contemporary human society are not considered distinct from one another but rather are seen as one pursuit. *Historical Materialism* is what we call this pursuit of understanding human society and its historical development through the lens of Dialectical Materialist philosophy and Materialist Dialectical methodology.

Introduction

Annotation 1 (continued)

In *The German Ideology*, Marx and Engels offer the following definition of history:

> History is nothing but the succession of the separate generations, each of which exploits the materials, the capital funds, the productive forces handed down to it by all preceding generations, and thus, on the one hand, continues the traditional activity in completely changed circumstances and, on the other, modifies the old circumstances with a completely changed activity. This can be speculatively distorted so that later history is made the goal of earlier history, e.g. the goal ascribed to the discovery of America is to further the eruption of the French Revolution. Thereby history receives its own special aims and becomes "a person rating with other persons" (to wit: "Self-Consciousness, Criticism, the Unique," etc.), while what is designated with the words "destiny," "goal," "germ," or "idea" of earlier history is nothing more than an abstraction formed from later history, from the active influence which earlier history exercises on later history.

Historical Materialism

When the Dialectical Materialist system is applied to the analysis of human society, various viewpoints are derived. These viewpoints serve as starting points for further theoretical and practical development in the realm of human society.

In the Dialectical Materialist philosophical and methodological framework, all things, ideas, and phenomena are considered to be in a constant state of change and development. This includes human society. As such, human society can be studied and understood through the framework of Materialist Dialectics, which is a system of understanding change and motion through the lens of Dialectical Materialism.

Historical Materialism therefore constitutes a system of viewpoints which are derived from the application of the Dialectical Materialist framework to the analysis of the development of human society. Taken as a system in its own right, Historical Materialism becomes a framework for further theoretical understanding of and practical engagement with human society. Historical Materialism allows us comprehend the change and development of human society in a manner which is consistent with the objective laws of Dialectical Materialism. Historical Materialism, like Dialectical Materialism, is approached from the viewpoint of the working class. It explicitly serves the revolutionary function of allowing the working class to comprehend itself and its own historical mission.

In "The Three Sources and Three Component Parts of Marxism," Lenin expounded on the importance of the discovery of Historical Materialist analysis by Karl Marx:

> Marx deepened and developed philosophical materialism to the full and extended the cognition of nature to include the cognition of human society. His Historical Materialism was a great achievement in scientific thinking. The chaos and arbitrariness that had previously reigned in views on history and politics were replaced by a strikingly integral and harmonious scientific theory, which shows how, in consequence of the growth of productive forces, out of one system of social life another and higher system develops—how capitalism, for instance, grows out of feudalism.

In *Karl Marx*, Lenin further expanded on the importance of the development of Historical Materialism:

> **Annotation 1 (continued)**
>
> The discovery of the materialist conception of history, or more correctly, the consistent continuation and extension of materialism into the domain of social phenomena, removed the two chief shortcomings in earlier historical theories. In the first place, the latter at best examined only the ideological motives in the historical activities of human beings, without investigating the origins of those motives, or ascertaining the objective laws governing the development of the system of social relations, or seeing the roots of these relations in the degree of development reached by material production; in the second place, the earlier theories did not embrace the activities of the masses of the population, whereas Historical Materialism made it possible for the first time to study with scientific accuracy the social conditions of the life of the masses, and the changes in those conditions. At best, pre-Marxist "sociology" and historiography brought forth an accumulation of raw facts, collected at random, and a description of individual aspects of the historical process. By examining the totality of opposing tendencies, by reducing them to precisely definable conditions of life and production of the various classes of individual aspects of the historical process. By examining the choice of a particular "dominant" idea or in its interpretation, and by revealing that, without exception, all ideas and all the various tendencies stem from the condition of the material forces of production, Marxism indicated the way to an all-embracing and comprehensive study of the process of the rise, development, and decline of socio-economic systems. People make their own history but what determines the motives of people, of the mass of people—i.e., what is the sum total of all these clashes in the mass of human societies? What are the objective conditions of production of material life that form the basis of all man's historical activity? What is the law of development of these conditions? To all these Marx drew attention and indicated the way to a scientific study of history as a single process which, with all its immense variety and contradictoriness, is governed by definite laws.
>
> In short, Historical Materialism is the system of ideas and practices which arises from the application of Dialectical Materialism and Materialist Dialectics to the specific subject of the development of human society.

By putting Dialectical Materialism and Materialist Dialectics into practice, Historical Materialism perfects and develops both Dialectical Materialism and Materialist Dialectics. In this manner, Historical Materialism perfects and develops the worldview and philosophical methodology of Marxism-Leninism.

> **Annotation 2**
>
> Dialectical Materialist philosophy and methodology asserts that the truth of human ideas can only be discovered through practice. The correctness of a theory is determined through experimentation, observation, and experience in objective reality. Practice includes any intentional conscious activity which improves the understanding of human beings about the world. Theory and practice have a dialectical relationship, and each is necessary to develop the other. Through practice, we discover and imagine new theories. Through theory, we imagine better ways of performing practice.

Annotation 2 (continued)

In this sense, theory and practice (the application of theory in the real world) mutually develop one other in a constant and dynamic feedback loop. This relationship between theory and practice is the subject of much of *Part 1* of this curriculum, and is discussed in particular on page 216. As Lenin wrote in *Materialism and Empirio-Criticism*: "The standpoint of life, of practice, should be first and fundamental in the theory of knowledge."

The laws of Historical Materialism are objective to humanity and subjective to the universal laws of Dialectical Materialism and Materialist Dialectics.[1] This constitutes a dialectical relationship between Historical Materialism and Dialectical Materialism: Historical Materialism developed from Dialectical Materialism just as the formulation of Historical Materialism has developed the Dialectical Materialist *worldview*.

A worldview is the whole of a human individual's or human group's opinions and conceptions about the world, about humanity itself, about life, and about the position of human beings in the world [see *Part 1*, p. 1]. As mentioned in the previous Annotation, the viewpoint of Dialectical Materialism is that of the working class. That is to say, Dialectical Materialism begins its analysis from the viewpoint of workers in the present circumstances of capitalism and is essentially concerned with the liberation of workers from capitalism and class society.

Class society is a formation of society which developed thousands of years ago. Class society separates human beings into groups based on their relations to the means of production. It is an inherently exploitative form of society in which one or more *ruling classes* dominate and exploit lower oppressed classes who are forced to work for the benefit of the ruling class. Understanding class society is vitally important if we are to understand the objective conditions of the working class and the subjective role of the working class in fulfilling its historical mission of ending class society. This understanding must include the origins of class society, the development of class society, the current form of class society (capitalism), and methods for bringing about an end to class society through social revolution.

Applying Dialectical Materialism and Materialist Dialectics to further our understanding of human society through Historical Materialism has led to many developments in the worldview and methodology of Marxism-Leninism, and in turn, the development of Dialectical Materialism and Materialist Dialectics leads to the further development of Historical Materialism. This is a relationship of dialectical unity and mutual development. Indeed, Friedrich Engels explained that it was through the study and observation of history that the objective laws of Dialectical Materialism were discovered by Marx and himself. Engels wrote in *Dialectics of Nature* that:

> It is, therefore, from the history of nature and human society that the laws of dialectics are abstracted. For they are nothing but the most general laws of these two aspects of historical development, as well as of thought itself.

Lenin summarized the importance of the contributions of Marx and Engels in developing Historical Materialism in the analysis of class society in *The Class Struggle*:

---

[1] This is further explained in Appendix E on p. 244.

Annotation 2 (continued)

It is common knowledge that, in any given society, the striving of some of its members conflict with the strivings of others, that social life is full of contradictions, and that history reveals a struggle between nations and societies, as well as within nations and societies, and, besides, an alternation of periods of revolution and reaction, peace and war, stagnation and rapid progress or decline. Marxism has provided the guidance, i.e., the theory of the class struggle, for the discovery of the laws governing this seeming maze and chaos. It is only a study of the sum of the strivings of all the members of a given society or group of societies that can lead to a scientific definition of the result of those strivings. Now the conflicting strivings stem from the difference in the position and mode of life of the *classes* into which each society is divided.

"The history of all hitherto existing society is the history of class struggles," Marx wrote in *The Communist Manifesto*... "Freeman and slave, patrician and plebeian, lord and serf, guild-master and journeyman, in a word, oppressor and oppressed, stood in constant opposition to one another, carried on an uninterrupted, now hidden, now open fight, a fight that each time ended, either in a revolutionary reconstruction of society at large, or in the common ruin of the contending classes... The modern bourgeois society that has sprouted from the ruins of feudal society has not done away with class antagonisms. It has but established new classes, new conditions of oppression, new forms of struggle in place of the old ones. Our epoch, the epoch of the bourgeoisie, possesses, however, this distinctive feature: it has simplified the class antagonisms. Society as a whole is more and more splitting up into two great hostile camps, into two great classes directly facing each other: Bourgeoisie and Proletariat."

...The following passage from Marx's *The Communist Manifesto* will show us what Marx demanded of social science as regards an objective analysis of the position of each class in modern society, with reference to an analysis of each class's conditions of development:

"Of all the classes that stand face to face with the bourgeoisie today, the proletariat alone is a really revolutionary class. The other classes decay and finally disappear in the face of Modern Industry; the proletariat is its special and essential product. The lower middle class, the small manufacturer, the shopkeeper, the artisan, the peasant, all these fight against the bourgeoisie, to save from extinction their existence as fractions of the middle class. They are therefore not revolutionary, but conservative. Nay more, they are reactionary, for they try to roll back the wheel of history. If by chance they are revolutionary, they are so only in view of their impending transfer into the proletariat; they thus defend not their present, but their future interests; they desert their own standpoint to place themselves at that of the proletariat."

In a number of historical works, Marx gave brilliant and profound examples of materialist historiography, of an analysis of the position of *each* individual class, and sometimes of various groups or strata within a class, showing plainly why and how "every class struggle is a political struggle."

> **Annotation 2 (continued)**
>
> The above-quoted passage is an illustration of what a complex network of social relations and *transitional* stages from one class to another, from the past to the future, was analyzed by Marx so as to determine the outcomes of historical development.
>
> The complexity of human society demands that we seek a comprehensive and historical perspective in analysis of human society (see *Part 1*, p. 116-118).

Historical Materialism is one of the greatest discoveries of Marxism because "the discovery of the materialist conception of history, or more correctly, the consistent continuation and extension of materialism into the domain of social phenomena, removed the two chief shortcomings in earlier historical theories."[2]

> **Annotation 3**
>
> The two chief shortcomings of earlier historical theories (which predated Historical Materialism) are described by Lenin in his work *Karl Marx*:
>
> 1. Earlier theories of history "examined only the ideological motives... of human beings, without investigating the origins of those motives, or ascertaining the objective laws governing the development of the system of social relations, or seeing the roots of these relations in the degree of development reached by material production." In other words, earlier conceptions of human history over-emphasized the ideological positions of humans and ignored the material basis of these positions in the objective world. This constituted an idealist conception of history.
>
> 2. The earlier theories "did not embrace the activities of the masses of the population." Rather, they focused on the activities and lives of the ruling classes, which composed only a small minority of the human population of historical societies. This offered only a small glimpse of the whole of human history, and a biased glimpse at that, as it over-emphasized the activities of the ruling minority while largely ignoring the activities and objective conditions and ideological development of the working masses.
>
> Historical Materialism was a major breakthrough because it offered a materialist conception of history which concretely explored the objective material conditions and motivations of ideological development of human society, and Historical Materialism also, in the words of Lenin, "made it possible for the first time to study with scientific accuracy the social conditions of the life of the masses, and the changes in those conditions." This fundamentally transformed the study of human history by putting it on a scientific, materialist basis which examined the entire scope of all classes within human society.

At the same time, "Marxism indicated the way to an all-embracing and comprehensive study of the process of the rise, development, and decline of social-economic systems"[3] from a materialist point of view.

---

2 *Karl Marx*, V. I. Lenin, 1914.
3 Ibid.

Annotation 4

The above quotation is taken from the following passage from *Karl Marx*, by Lenin:

> At best, pre-Marxist 'sociology' and historiography brought forth an accumulation of raw facts, collected at random, and a description of individual aspects of the historical process. By examining the totality of opposing tendencies, by reducing them to precisely definable conditions of life and production of the various classes of individual aspects of the historical process (and) by examining the choice of a particular 'dominant' idea or in its interpretation, and by revealing that, without exception, all ideas and all the various tendencies stem from the condition of the material forces of production, Marxism indicated the way to an all-embracing and comprehensive study of the process of the rise, development, and decline of social-economic systems.

Lenin's critique of pre-Marxist history is that it was not scientific in the Dialectical Materialist sense of the word. In Dialectical Materialism, scientific is an adjective which describes methodologies, approaches, and practices of gaining knowledge and insight which are methodological and/or systematic (see *Part 1*, p. 38). Lenin points out that before Marx, historians focused on gathering and assembling facts and focused too heavily on the "dominant" ideological concepts of the ruling classes while ignoring the material processes which led to these ideas (and ignored the ideas of the working classes entirely).

Lenin points out that the Marxist conception of Historical Materialism rightly attributes the origin of all social ideas to material forces of production. This relationship between material forces of production and social ideology will be explained in more detail throughout the rest of this book, but the main point is that all ideas are determined by objective/material processes (though those ideas can impact the material world through the conscious activities of human beings). This concept is foundational to the Dialectical Materialist understanding of reality, and is explained in more detail in *Part 1*, p. 88.

Lenin continues:

> People make their own history, but what determines the motives of people, of the mass of people—i.e., what is the sum total of all these clashes in the mass of human societies? What are the objective conditions of production of material life that form the basis of all man's historical activity? What is the law of development of these conditions? To all these Marx drew attention and indicated the way to a scientific study of history as a single process which, with all its immense variety and contradictoriness, is governed by definite laws.

Here, Lenin explains that history is governed by definite laws which are rooted in material processes which can be understood and explained through the study of Historical Materialism. This fact is of particular importance to communists who wish to bring about revolution, because understanding these concrete objective laws of history enable us to more successfully intervene in the processes of history through our subjective activities, and to bring about revolution more quickly and more effectively.

Finally, Lenin points out that Historical Materialism is of vital importance to humanity because it allows us to make sense of the seemingly chaotic and random events of the past by properly identify class struggle as an objective determiner of history:

Annotation 4 (continued)

Marxism has provided the guidance —i.e., the theory of the class struggle— for the discovery of the laws governing this seeming maze and chaos. It is only a study of the sum of the strivings of all the members of a given society or group of societies that can lead to a scientific definition of the result of those strivings. Now the conflicting strivings stem from the difference in the position and mode of life of the classes into which each society is divided.

CHAPTER 1

THE ROLE OF MATERIAL PRODUCTION AND THE LAW THAT RELATIONS OF PRODUCTION MUST SUIT THE DEVELOPMENT OF THE PRODUCTIVE FORCES

I. MATERIAL PRODUCTION AND ITS ROLES

1. Material production and the mode of production

Production is a special type of human activity within human society, which can take three forms: material production, mental production, and human reproduction[4].

> **Annotation 5**
>
> Production is a process in which humans interact with one another, with nature, with tools, and with other factors in order to develop that which is needed to survive. There are three broad categories of production in human society:
>
> **Material Production**
>
> Material Production is a practical activity with the aim of transforming objects of the natural world in order to suit the needs of existing humans and the development of human society. Material production takes place through human conscious activity which we call *labor* in conjunction with other factors such as nature, tools, production processes, and so on.
>
> **Mental Production**
>
> Mental Production is the production of ideological systems such as philosophy, religion, art, and so on. Historical Materialism considers mental production to be secondary to material production: material production *determines* mental production while mental production can *impact* back on material production. Historical Materialism holds that mental production is always dominated by the ruling class within any class society. As Marx and Engels wrote in *The German Ideology*:
>
>> The class which has the means of material production at its disposal, has control at the same time over the means of mental production, so that thereby, generally speaking, the ideas of those who lack the means of mental production are subject to it. The ruling ideas are nothing more than the ideal expression of the dominant material relationships, the dominant material relationships grasped as ideas; hence of the relationships which make the one class the ruling one, therefore, the ideas of its dominance.
>
> The primacy of material production over mental production is an extension of the Dialectical Materialist concept that matter determines consciousness, which is discussed in detail in *Part 1*, p. 88. This is the basis of the Law of the Economic Base Determining the Superstructure, which will be discussed on p. 90. Humans who engage in mental production are called intellectuals. Intellectuals and mental production are discussed more in Annotation 102, p. 185).
>
> **Human Reproduction**
>
> According to the Vietnamese textbook *The Philosophy of Marxism-Leninism*:

---

4 Not to be confused with "human production," which is material production carried out by humans.

Annotation 5 (continued)

Human reproduction is, at the individual and family scale, the act of giving birth and raising children to maintain mankind; At the social scale, it is population growth and human development as socio-bio entities.

Just as material and mental production develop over time, human reproduction also develops over time. For instance, as human society has developed, infant mortality rates have decreased and various other factors have allowed the human population to grow more rapidly over time.

Notes on the Dialectical Unity of Humanity and Nature

In Dialectical Materialism, nature has a specific meaning, referring to the external world which humans inhabit. Nature includes all of the material things and phenomena which surround us and which we interact with and utilize in our daily existence. Humans exist in dialectical unity with nature: humans are derived from nature and have a dialectical relationship with nature, meaning that as we change and develop nature, nature simultaneously changes and develops us. Marx explained in his *Economic and Philosophical Manuscripts* that:

> Man is directly a natural being. . . Nature is man's inorganic body – nature, that is, insofar as it is not itself human body. Man lives on nature – means that nature is his body, with which he must remain in continuous interchange if he is not to die. That man's physical and spiritual life is linked to nature means simply that nature is linked to itself, for man is a part of nature.

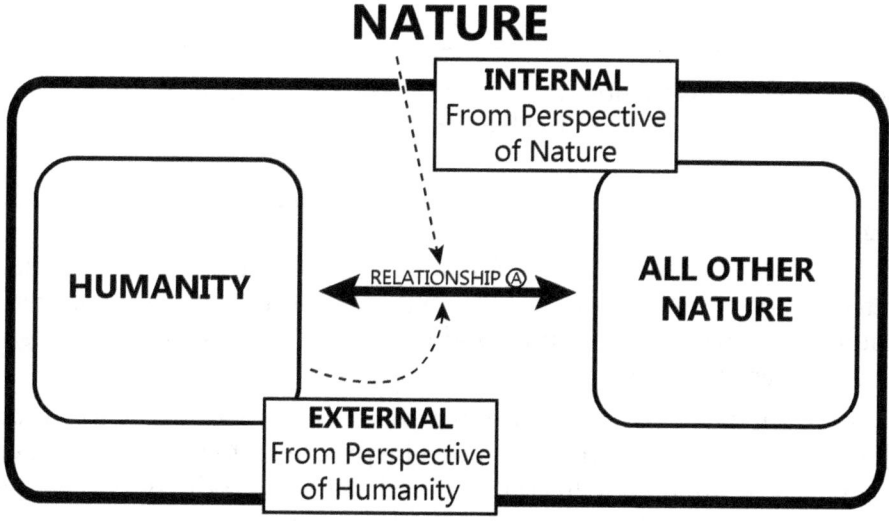

The relationship between humanity and all other nature (Relationship A) is external from the perspective of humanity, but an internal relationship within the full system of nature.

In Dialectical Materialist philosophy, we define things by internal and external relationships. Humanity, as a "particular natural being," is defined in large part by the relationship between humanity and the natural world within which humanity exists. Simultaneously, nature is defined in part by the internal relationship between humanity and all other elements of nature.

> **Annotation 5 (continued)**
>
> Engels refuted the idea that humanity is metaphysically separate from nature and dismissed the notion that humanity could therefore "conquer nature" as false consciousness,[5] as he wrote in *The Part Played by Labor in the Transition from Ape to Man*:
>
>> Let us not, however, flatter ourselves overmuch on account of our human conquest over nature. For each such conquest takes its revenge on us. Each of them, it is true, has in the first place the consequences on which we counted, but in the second and third places it has quite different, unforeseen effects which only too often cancel out the first. The people who, in Mesopotamia, Greece, Asia Minor, and elsewhere, destroyed the forests to obtain cultivable land, never dreamed that they were laying the basis for the present devastated condition of these countries, by removing along with the forests the collecting centers and reservoirs of moisture. When, on the southern slopes of the mountains, the Italians of the Alps used up the pine forests so carefully cherished on the northern slopes, they had no inkling that by doing so they were cutting at the roots of the dairy industry in their region; they had still less inkling that they were thereby depriving their mountain springs of water for the greater part of the year, with the effect that these would be able to pour still more furious flood torrents on the plains during the rainy seasons... Thus at every step we are reminded that we by no means rule over nature like a conqueror over a foreign people, like someone standing outside nature – but that we, with flesh, blood, and brain, belong to nature, and exist in its midst, and that all our mastery of it consists in the fact that we have the advantage over all other beings of being able to know and correctly apply its laws.

These three forms of production are closely linked with one another through interaction. Material production serves as the basis for the existence and development of society.

> **Annotation 6**
>
> Material Production, Mental Production, and Human Reproduction are all dialectically related to one another. As discussed in the previous annotation, material production determines mental production, and the dominant class within a class society therefore dominates mental production.
>
> Human Reproduction must take place in order for all other human production activities to take place, because new humans must be produced to take the place of humans who die or otherwise are unable to contribute to material production processes. However, at the social/macro scale, material production must develop in order to sustain growing human populations who will consume more resources. This constitutes a dialectical relationship since human reproduction and material production mutually develop one another and neither process can take place without the other.
>
> Material Production is considered the basis for the existence and development of *society* because it is through material production that human society first developed and it is through material production that society can sustain itself. Individual humans can

---

5 "False Consciousness" has a particular meaning in Dialectical Materialist philosophy. It refers to consciousness that does not align with reality. This is further explained on p. 94.

> **Annotation 6 (continued)**
> be produced through human reproduction, but a *society* of human beings can only be sustained through material production processes which provide the needs for humans to live. Indeed, society is defined as a collection of human beings which exists to carry out material production processes so as to provide the material needs for their own continued existence.

According to Engels, "the essential difference between human and animal society consists in the fact that animals at most *collect* while men *produce*."[6]

> **Annotation 7**
> Marx discussed this difference between human beings and animals in "Estranged Labor," writing:
>> It is true that animals also produce. They build nests and dwelling, like the bee, the beaver, the ant, etc. But they produce only their own immediate needs or those of their young; they produce only when immediate physical need compels them to do so, while man produces even when he is free from physical need and truly produces only in freedom from such need; they produce only themselves, while man reproduces the whole of nature; their products belong immediately to their physical bodies, while man freely confronts his own product. Animals produce only according to the standards and needs of the species to which they belong, while man is capable of producing according to the standards of every species and of applying to each object its inherent standard; hence, man also produces in accordance with the laws of beauty.
>
> In his letter to Pyotr Lavrov, Engels explained that "this sole but cardinal difference alone [that animals *collect* while humans *produce*] makes it impossible simply to transfer laws of animal societies to human societies."
>
> To understand why this is important in the context of developing a scientific understanding of human history, one must first understand the concept of *Social Darwinism* which was being pushed forward by bourgeois sociologists at that time.
>
> Social Darwinism is the pseudoscientific belief that animals share a common set of social laws, and that human society follows these same laws. According to Social Darwinism, the most fundamental social law of both animal and human society is *competition*. Engels accepted the theory of evolution formulated by Charles Darwin (1809-1882), but he believed that it was a major error to contend that human society was rooted in the concept of "survival of the fittest" and that competition was the most essential characteristic of human society. This concept of competition as the defining characteristic of humanity was often compounded with similar ideas from bourgeois philosophers such as Thomas Hobbes and Thomas Robert Malthus.
>
> Hobbes (1588–1679) was an English philosopher who was heavily influenced by his experiences in the English Civil War. Having witnessed a great deal of suffering and strife during this period, Hobbes conceptualized human society as a "war of all against all," and believed that human beings were inherently violent and prone to constant conflict with one another.

---

6   Letter from Friedrich Engels to Pyotr Lavrov in London, 1875 (original emphasis).

> **Annotation 7 (continued)**
>
>
>
> *Thomas Malthus*   *Charles Darwin*
>
> Malthus (1766-1834) was another English philosopher who believed that human societies overused resources for population growth and that this invariably led to catastrophe. Malthus had the pessimistic view that over time all societies tend to collapse into disarray as overpopulation led to overconsumption of resources and that this made human society essentially unstable and prone to crisis, war, famine, and so on. Engels pointed out that Social Darwinists muddled the pseudoscience of Hobbes and Malthus into the ideas of Charles Darwin in an unscientific manner. This adulterated conception of Darwinism was then overlaid onto human society, which Engels described a rhetorical "trick" with no foundation in objective reality. As Engels explains:
>
>> The whole [social] Darwinists teaching of the struggle for existence is simply a transference from society to living nature of Hobbes's doctrine of *bellum omnium contra omnes* ["the war of all against all"] and of the bourgeois-economic doctrine of competition together with Malthus's theory of population. When this conjurer's trick has been performed... the same theories are transferred back again from organic nature into history and it is now claimed that their validity as eternal laws of human society has been proved. The puerility [childish silliness] of this procedure is so obvious that not a word need be said about it. But if I wanted to go into the matter more thoroughly I should do so by depicting them in the first place as bad economists and only in the second place as bad naturalists and philosophers.
>
> Engels objected to both the merging of Darwin's theories with bourgeois pseudoscientific theories of human nature as well as the notion that human society must strictly follow the laws of the animal kingdom when there are essential differences between animal society and human society, particularly in the realm of material production activities. Such false consciousness about human nature remains a throughline of reactionary ideological defenses of capitalism to this day, and thus it is vital for workers to learn the true nature of humanity as a prerequisite for gaining class consciousness.

Thus, material production is one of the essential activities of humans. As a type of practical activity with the aim of transforming objects of the natural world according to the needs of existing humans and the development of society, material production is an objective, social, historical, and creative activity. Every material production process is carried out with certain purposes and in certain manners.

Annotation 8

The *purpose* of material production processes ultimately derive from the material needs of the life processes of human beings such as: food, water, shelter, sexual reproduction, etc. The *manner* can vary considerably depending upon objective factors such as the material base of society as well as subjective factors (see: Appendix E, p. 244).

Examples of Purpose and Manner of Material Production:

Factory farming and foraging are two different material production processes. Factory farming involves large-scale, industrial, mechanized development of animals and vegetables for human consumption. Foraging, on the other hand, involves small groups of human beings searching through natural environments for food. The material production process of factory farming is very different in *manner* from foraging for wild fruits and vegetables, though both production processes serve the same *purpose* of providing food for human beings. Factory farming is similar in *manner* to factory textile production. Both material production processes involve the use of large-scare industry and mechanization, however they serve different purposes (food production and clothing production, respectively).

Characteristics of Material Production

Material production is:

- **Objective**, because it consists of activities which take place externally from the perspective of any individual human subject and humanity as a whole. Many human beings must work together and utilize various tools, as well as resources from nature, to engage in material production.

- **Social**, because it requires multiple human beings working together as a society to take place.

- **Historical**, because it develops over time through many stages of development.

- **Creative**, because human beings use conscious labor activities to engage in and develop material production processes over time, leading to ever more advanced processes, tools, and techniques, and ever more efficient output of material needs.

The manner of production can be referred to as the *mode of production*. In Historical Materialism, the term *mode of production* refers specifically to the manner in which humans carry out the production processes of society within certain historical periods.

Annotation 9

A mode is a way or manner in which something exists. Historical Materialism uses the term "mode of production" to refer to the overall, predominant manner of production being utilized by a human group in a particular time-period. For example, the *capitalist mode of production* is typified by private ownership of the means of production by capitalists. Other modes of production may exist under capitalism, such as small-scale craft production or worker-owned cooperatives, but the overwhelmingly predominant mode of production under capitalism involves private ownership of the means of production.

Historical Materialism

Every society develops through specific historical periods, and each period is defined [in Historical Materialism] by its mode of production. The mode of production of each historical period has specific characteristics. For example: the mode of production of a foraging society has the characteristic of less technological mechanization and industrialization, while the mode of production of capitalist society has the characteristic of more technological mechanization and industrialization.

> **Annotation 10**
>
> Historical Materialism is, in essence, a methodology for examining a society's development (i.e., changes over time), particularly as it pertains to the mode of production. To expand on the examples in the text above, foraging societies tend to not use much mechanization and industrialization in material production processes, whereas capitalist societies predominantly utilize mechanization and industrialization. Foraging societies also tend to have a lower population density as compared to capitalist societies, and foraging societies tend to have collective ownership of the means of production (i.e., the tools and resources needed for material production processes).
>
> We would like to make it clear that terms used throughout this book such as "higher/lower level" or "more/less developed" should not be construed with moral or cultural judgment within the framework of Materialist Dialectics; "higher"/"more developed" should not be interpreted as "superior," nor should "lower"/"less developed" be interpreted as derogatory. This language simply reflects an increase in productive output and labor productivity as the productive forces develop over time. This morally neutral viewpoint of development is described in more detail in **Part 1**, p. 119.

Each mode of production has two basic aspects: technical and economic. These two aspects are closely linked together:

The *technical aspect* of a mode of production indicates the technology used in production processes to transform objects to suit the needs of humanity.

The *economic aspect* of the mode of production indicates the economic organization of production processes.

> **Annotation 11**
>
> Technical aspects of a mode of production include all sorts of technologies, including machines, communications equipment, chemistry, and so on. Economic aspects include economic organization factors. According to an article put out by Vietnam's Ministry of Trade and Industry[7], there is no single definition of "economy" which can be universally agreed on, but the most accurate and general definition as it pertains to Historical Materialism is:
>
>> The sum total of the dialectical relationships within a human society which are directly related to production, trading, distribution, and consumption of commodities and services in order to meet the demands of that society, given a limitation of available resources. In other words, economics is the attempt by human beings (both as individuals and as a society), faced with a limitation of resources, to answer these three fundamental questions:

---

7 "Analysis of the Tourism Sector – Today's General Service Economic Sector," by Mai Anh Vu, MA, and Le Thi Thanh Loan, MA, *Online Trade and Industry Magazine*.

Annotation 11 (continued)
- What to produce?
- How to produce?
- Produce for whom?

With this definition of "economy" in mind, we can conclude that "economic organization of production processes" refers to the relationships between humans (both as individual human beings and collectively as human society) and our material production processes.

So, while the *technical aspect* deals with technological advancement and development of production, the *economic aspect* deals more with social aspects, including relationships between human beings as they pertain to production processes as well as related economic aspects such as: ownership of the means of production, distribution of products, social organization of production processes, and so on.

MODE OF PRODUCTION

TECHNICAL ASPECT
Technological Aspects and Development of Mode of Production

⟷ Each is Defined by This Dialectical Relationship ⟷

ECONOMIC ASPECT
Social Aspects and Relations of Mode of Production

The mode of production is defined by the relationship between its technical and economic aspects. This relationship is also what defines both aspects of the mode of production.

Examples of technical aspects of production include: tools, machines, chemical compounds, computer software, means of transportation, etc.

Examples of economic aspects of production include: business organizations, team production procedures, government regulation of production, labor unions, etc..

In feudal societies, the technical aspect of production is defined by manual, small-scale tools and technologies, while the economic aspect is defined by local, self-contained markets. In contrast, in capitalist societies, the technical aspect of production is defined by large-scale industry while the economic aspect is defined by ever-expanding and overlapping markets.

2. The role of material production and the role of mode of production in the origin and development of human society

According to the materialist conception of history, material production is:

1. A decisive factor in the survival and development of humanity and society.
2. A fundamental activity that causes and develops human social relationships.
3. The basis of the formation, transformation, and development of human society.

Annotation 12

Materialism is the perspective that matter is the *primary existence* which precedes and determines consciousness. Here, materialism refers to *Dialectical Materialism*, which is currently the highest known form of materialist philosophy. Dialectical Materialism holds that matter determines consciousness, while consciousness can impact back on matter. This is explained in more detail in *Part 1*, p. 88.

The Dialectical Materialist conception of history referenced above is Historical Materialism. According to Historical Materialism, material production is:

1. A Decisive Factor in the Survival and Development of Humanity and Society

The primary existence of human beings is *material existence*. All human thought processes ranging from the ideas and brain activities of individuals to the cultural manifestations and practices of human society rely on and stem from material processes of survival. As such, material production processes—rendered through human labor [see Annotation 14, p. 25]—determine all other aspects of human life. One significant proof of this concept is that human beings simply could not survive without material production processes; and as such, all other human activities depend on material production processes to begin with. This is related to the fact that labor has a dialectical relationship with human consciousness and that human consciousness arose from and in conjunction with human labor [see *Part 1*, p. 74].

2. A Fundamental Activity That Causes and Develops Human Social Relationships

Human production activities lead to powerful and varied human relationships. As social animals, humans are not able to survive on their own as individuals for extended periods of time. Instead, humans must work together to provide the necessities of human life. This leads to strong bonds in every stage of human development, as human beings must work with and rely on other human beings to survive and develop human society over time.

3. The Basis of the Formation, Transformation, and Development of Human Society

Development in material production processes lead directly to changes in human society, especially as it pertains to *relations of production* [see p. 42] which serve as the material basis of human society in every time period. This is one of the fundamental laws of Historical Materialism and the most essential driving force of human history. This law—the Law of Suitability Between the Relations of Production and the Development of Productive Forces—is discussed specifically on p. 51.

In developing this materialist conception of history, Marx broke away from previous idealist conceptions of history.

> **Annotation 13**
>
> *Idealism* is the erroneous perspective that human consciousness precedes and determines the material world. Before the development of Historical Materialism by Marx and Engels, previous conceptions of history suffered from notions of idealism. Marx explained the materialist conception of human history in the preface to his *Contribution to the Critique of Political Economy*:
>
>> In the social production of their life, men enter into definite relations that are indispensable and independent of their will, relations of production which correspond to a definite stage of development of their material productive forces.
>
> "Social production of life," here, simply refers to social activities which yield all that is necessary to sustain human life (food, shelter, etc.). These social activities lead to social relationships. At any given stage of development, these social activities and relationships constitute an overall *mode of production* which *defines* that stage of development for that society.
>
>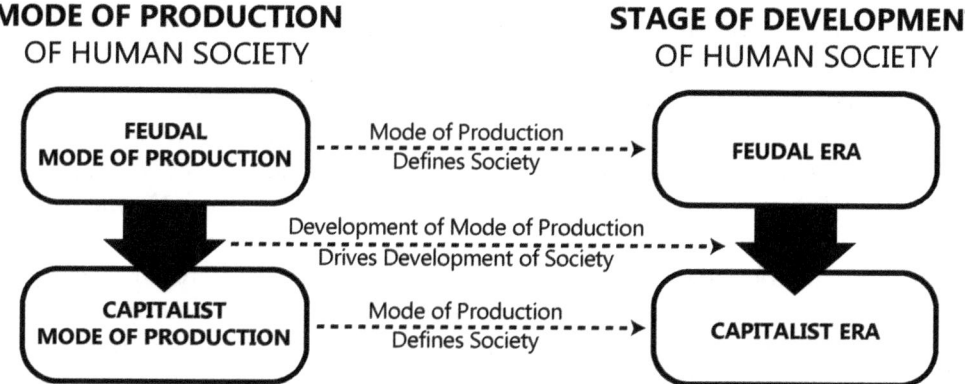
>
> *Every era of human society is defined by its mode of production. Development of the mode of production drives the development of human society from one stage of development to the next.*
>
> As an example, during the feudal era, human beings had certain relationships with one another which revolved around the production of the necessities of life. First and foremost, peasants were responsible for growing food through agricultural production. However, peasants during this time did not own the means of production (i.e., the land on which food was grown). Rather, the land was owned by feudal lords. This relationship between peasants and feudal lords (as well as relations with and between other classes, such as the clergy, crafts guilds, etc.) defined the era of feudalism.
>
> Marx continues:
>
>> The sum total of these relations of production constitutes the economic structure of society, the real foundation, on which rises a legal and political superstructure and to which correspond definite forms of social consciousness.
>>
>> The mode of production of material life conditions the social, political and intellectual life process in general. It is not the consciousness of men that determines their being, but, on the contrary, their social being that determines their consciousness.

Annotation 13 (continued)

Here, Marx defines the material basis for human history. The mode of production and relations of production constitute an objective material basis for human society. "Social being" refers to the material aspects of human society (chiefly defined by the current mode of production), and Marx indicates that this social being is what determines social consciousness of human beings. This relationship between social being and consciousness is discussed more on p. 106.

This contention that material existence—i.e., social being, consisting of the mode of production and relations of production—was an important departure from previous ways of viewing human society and human history. Prior to Marx's conception of Historical Materialism, it was believed that human ideas shaped history and pushed human society forward through stages of development. By defining a materialist basis for history and exploring history through the lens of Dialectical Materialism and Materialist Dialectics, Marx was able to create a scientific methodology for studying history which revolutionized our ability to understand and intervene in the processes of development of human society.

Marx continues:

> At a certain stage of their development, the material productive forces of society come in conflict with the existing relations of production, or—what is but a legal expression for the same thing—with the property relations within which they have been at work hitherto. From forms of development of the productive forces these relations turn into their fetters. Then begins an epoch of social revolution. With the change of the economic foundation the entire immense superstructure is more or less rapidly transformed. In considering such transformations a distinction should always be made between the material transformation of the economic conditions of production, which can be determined with the precision of natural science, and the legal, political, religious, aesthetic or philosophic—in short, ideological forms in which men become conscious of this conflict and fight it out.

This is Marx's formulation of *class struggle*, which is a fundamental concept in Historical Materialism and the primary way in which communists can engage with historical processes of change in human society. Class struggle is discussed more on p. 200.

Finally, Marx explains why idealist notions of history are invalid. Marx considered the ideological output of a society to be a poor basis for discovering historical truth because:

> Just as our opinion of an individual is not based on what he thinks of himself, so we cannot judge of such a period of transformation by its own consciousness; on the contrary, this consciousness must be explained rather from the contradictions of material life, from the existing conflict between the social productive forces and the relations of production.

In *The Communist Manifesto*, Marx and Engels address the ruling class directly, rebuking the bourgeoisie for aiming to deceive workers into believing that capitalism is a "natural" state of affairs. In reality, the ideas and laws of capitalist class society emerge from the objective conditions of the economic base of society, and whenever the base changes, the ruling ideas will also change:

> **Annotation 13 (continued)**
>
> Your very ideas are but the outgrowth of the conditions of your bourgeois production and bourgeois property, just as your jurisprudence is but the will of your class made into a law for all, a will whose essential character and direction are determined by the economical conditions of existence of your class.
>
> The selfish misconception that induces you to transform into eternal laws of nature and of reason, the social forms springing from your present mode of production and form of property – historical relations that rise and disappear in the progress of production – this misconception you share with every ruling class that has preceded you. What you see clearly in the case of ancient property, what you admit in the case of feudal property, you are of course forbidden to admit in the case of your own bourgeois form of property.
>
> Throughout the history of class society, each ruling class has produced a ruling ideology to reinforce its own dominant position in society. In *Anti-Dühring*, Engels explains that morality (like every ideology) is class-based:
>
>> Men, consciously or unconsciously, derive their ethical ideas in the last resort from the practical relations on which their class position is based — from the economic relations in which they carry on production and exchange.
>
> In *The German Ideology*, Marx and Engels explain exactly how a ruling class determines the prevailing ideology of their own society; that the ideas of the ruling class "are the ruling ideas of the epoch." In other words, the *ideological* content of a class society reflects *material* class relationships.
>
>> The ruling ideas are nothing more than the ideal expression of the dominant material relationships, the dominant material relationships grasped as ideas; hence of the relationships which make the one class the ruling one, therefore, the ideas of its dominance.
>
> Furthermore, Marx and Engels argue that all conscious activity is determined by material existence. This is the Dialectical Materialist view of the relationship between matter and consciousness.[8] We must recognize the fact that matter determines consciousness when we examine history if we are to put the study of human history and human society on a scientific basis.
>
> Marx and Engels explain how the Dialectical Materialist viewpoint of matter and consciousness pertains to the study of human society in *The German Ideology*:
>
>> The production of ideas, of conceptions, of consciousness, is at first directly interwoven with the material activity and the material intercourse of men, the language of real life. Conceiving, thinking, the mental intercourse of men, appear at this stage as the direct efflux [outflow] of their material behavior. The same applies to mental production as expressed in the language of politics, laws, morality, religion, metaphysics, etc., of a people. Men are the producers of their conceptions, ideas, etc. – real, active men, as they are conditioned by a definite development of their productive forces and of the intercourse corresponding to these, up to its furthest forms. Consciousness can never be anything else than conscious existence, and the existence of men is their actual life-process.

---

8 *Part 1*, p. 88.

Annotation 13 (continued)

Since all ideology and intellectual products of a given society stem from material life-processes, it makes sense to take those material life-processes as the primary subjects of study when examining human history.

Marx and Engels explain that Historical Materialism "ascends from earth to heaven." By this, they mean that Historical Materialism begins with studying material processes and relations in order to understand human ideology, and not the other way around, as previous historians had done:

> That is to say, we do not set out from what men say, imagine, conceive, nor from men as narrated, thought of, imagined, conceived, in order to arrive at men in the flesh. We set out from real, active men, and on the basis of their real life-process we demonstrate the development of the ideological reflexes and echoes of this life-process.

While previous historians primarily examined the words and philosophies and religions and other ideological products of human society, Marx and Engels saw these as mere "phantoms" which only reflect the material basis of human society:

> The phantoms formed in the human brain are also, necessarily, sublimates of their material life-process, which is empirically verifiable and bound to material premises. Morality, religion, metaphysics, all the rest of ideology and their corresponding forms of consciousness, thus no longer retain the semblance of independence.

Marx and Engels argued that ideas themselves "have no history, no development; but men, developing their material production and their material intercourse, alter, along with this their real existence, their thinking and the products of their thinking." That is to say, material processes and relations give rise to ideas, and not the other way around. In short: "Life is not determined by consciousness, but consciousness by life."

Marx and Engels then directly contrast idealist methods of studying human history against Historical Materialism:

> In the first method of approach the starting-point is consciousness taken as the living individual; in the second method, which conforms to real life, it is the real living individuals themselves, and consciousness is considered solely as their consciousness.

This was a remarkable breakthrough in the study of history, as it allows us to view the development of human society throughout history on a scientific basis which is rooted in material reality. As Marx and Engels explain:

> This method of approach is not devoid of premises. It starts out from the real premises and does not abandon them for a moment. Its premises are men, not in any fantastic isolation and rigidity, but in their actual, empirically perceptible process of development under definite conditions. As soon as this active life-process is described, history ceases to be a collection of dead facts as it is with the empiricists (themselves still abstract), or an imagined activity of imagined subjects, as with the idealists.

It is important to note how Marx and Engels distinguish Historical Materialism from other conceptions of history. First, they distinguish Historical Materialism from "empiricist" conceptions of history.

Annotation 13 (continued)

Empiricism holds that we can *only* obtain knowledge through human sense perception. Marx and Engels rejected empiricism because it ignored objective relations and knowledge that went beyond sense data. This is discussed in more detail in Annotation 10, p. 10 of *Part 1*. Empiricist conceptions of history merely catalog "dead facts" such as names, dates, and other such trivia while ignoring both objective laws and factors (such as relationships between humans and the means of production) as well as subjective factors (such as the history-making role of the masses[9]).

After differentiating Historical Materialism from Empiricist conceptions of history, Marx and Engels describe idealist conceptions of history as "imagined activity of imagined subjects." This is because idealists give a central role to consciousness—i.e., ideology and intellectual products of human society—in examining human history. Since we know that the prevailing ideology of any given class society is the ideology of the ruling class, idealists put themselves in the position of primarily studying fanciful and dishonest musings of the ruling class and otherwise ignoring the material foundation of human society.

Historical Materialism rises above the problems of empiricist and idealist conceptions of history by grounding historical study in the material processes of *real life*, elevating the study of history to a scientific pursuit:

> Where speculation ends—in real life—there real, positive science begins: the representation of the practical activity, of the practical process of development of men. Empty talk about consciousness ceases, and real knowledge has to take its place. When reality is depicted, philosophy as an independent branch of knowledge loses its medium of existence. At the best its place can only be taken by a summing-up of the most general results, abstractions which arise from the observation of the historical development of men.[10]

It is critical to understand what Marx and Engels mean, here. By grounding the study of human history and human society in material life processes and material relationships, Historical Materialism displaces the very notion of "philosophy" as a subject which can be separated metaphysically from the material processes of history. This is because what idealists view as "philosophy" is really just a cataloguing and summarization of the various ideologies which have been put forward through the centuries – and almost always by ruling classes seeking to justify their own positions of power within their society.

Historical Materialism sees "philosophy" as dialectically linked to human history. One can never truly understand the ideological conceptions of a society without first understanding the material processes and relationships which serve as their foundation. And one must also recognize that any such ideology—whether philosophical, religious, moral, or political—stems from material life processes of human beings living real lives in the real world. Marx and Engels dismissed the study of any ideological construct (such as "philosophy") in and of itself, divorced from its material basis, stating in *The German Ideology* that: "viewed apart from real history, these abstractions have in themselves no value whatsoever."

---

9 See Chapter 2, Section 2, beginning on p. 230.
10 *The German Ideology* by Karl Marx and Friedrich Engels.

> **Annotation 13 (continued)**
>
> Historical Materialism holds that human history has a material basis, and that consciousness – including philosophy and all other ideology – stems from this material basis. Therefore, in order to study history, one must begin by studying the material life processes and relationships of human beings – of the life-process of "real, active men," while ideological content must be viewed as "echoes of this life-process."
>
> Lenin explained the importance of the discovery of Historical Materialism by Marx and Engels in "What the 'Friends of the People' Are and How They Fight the Social-Democrats:"
>
>> Hitherto, not knowing how to get down to the simplest primary relations such as those of production, the sociologists undertook the direct investigation and study of political and legal forms, stumbled on the fact that these forms emerge from certain of mankind's ideas in the period in question—and there they stopped; it appeared as if social relations are consciously established by men. But this conclusion, fully expressed in the idea of the *Contract social* (traces of which are very noticeable in all systems of utopian socialism), was in complete contradiction to all historical observations. It never has been the case, nor is it so now, that the members of society conceive the sum-total of the social relations in which they live as something definite, integral, pervaded by some principle; on the contrary, the mass of people adapt themselves to these relations unconsciously, and have so little conception of them as specific historical social relations that, for instance, an explanation of the exchange relations under which people have lived for centuries was found only in very recent times. Materialism removed this contradiction by carrying the analysis deeper, to the origin of man's social ideas themselves; and its conclusion that the course of ideas depends on the course of things is the only one compatible with scientific psychology. Further, and from yet another aspect, this hypothesis was the first to elevate sociology to the level of a science. Hitherto, sociologists had found it difficult to distinguish the important and the unimportant in the complex network of social phenomena (that is the root of subjectivism in sociology) and had been unable to discover any objective criterion for such a demarcation. Materialism provided an absolutely objective criterion by singling out "production relations" as the structure of society, and by making it possible to apply to these relations that general scientific criterion of recurrence whose applicability to sociology the subjectivists denied. So long as they confined themselves to ideological social relations (i.e., such as, before taking shape, pass through man's consciousness) they could not observe recurrence and regularity in the social phenomena of the various countries, and their science was at best only a description of these phenomena, a collection of raw material. The analysis of material social relations (i.e., of those that take shape without passing through man's consciousness: when exchanging products men enter into production relations without even realizing that there is a social relation of production here)—the analysis of material social relations at once made it possible to observe recurrence and regularity and to generalize the systems of the various countries in the single fundamental concept: social formation. It was this generalization alone that made it possible to proceed from the description of social phenomena (and their evaluation from the standpoint of an ideal) to their strictly scientific analysis, which isolates, let us say by way of

> **Annotation 13 (continued)**
>
> example, that which distinguishes one capitalist country from another and investigates that which is common to all of them.
>
> Finally, it should be noted that although material/objective relations and processes *determine* consciousness within human society, subjective factors of consciousness can also *impact* material development of society. The impact of such subjective factors is explained in more detail on p. 167; subjectivity and objectivity are fully explained in Appendix E, p. 244.

From Marx's concept of "real, active men" came the conclusion that:

> The first premise of all human existence and, therefore, of all history - the premise, namely, [is] that men must be in a position to live in order to be able to "make history." But life involves before everything else eating and drinking, habitation, clothing and many other things. The first historical act is thus the production of the means to satisfy these needs, the production of material life itself.[11]

Therefore, we can affirm that the process of becoming "human" and distinguishing ourselves from animals started as soon as humans began to produce the means of living.

> **Annotation 14**
>
> "The production of material life" is made possible through *labor*. Labor is any conscious activity performed by humans which changes or develops the world around us. Labor is, essentially, a dialectical process in which humans (as individuals and in groups) interact with the natural world, and and which results in some meaningful change and development in the world. These developments, being dialectical in nature, result in changes in both humans and the external world.
>
> In the dialectical relationship between matter and consciousness, matter determines consciousness but consciousness can also impact back upon the material world through labor activity (see *Part 1*, p. 88). Labor is, therefore, critically important in the development of human society and human history. Labor is how we as subjects are able to impact back on the objective processes of history. This makes labor a fundamentally important subject in the study of Historical Materialism.
>
> In *The Part Played by Labour in the Transition from Ape to Man*, Engels states that:
>
>> Labour is the source of all wealth, the political economists assert. And it really is the source – next to nature, which supplies it with the material that it converts into wealth... labor created man himself.
>
> The role which labor played in the development of consciousness is explained in more detail in *Social Sources of Consciousness* on p. 74 of *Part 1*.

In order to carry out the process of material production (that is, the process of transforming the natural world) humans must necessarily establish certain relationships with each other. We call these relationships the *relations of production*. And from these relations of production, other social relations arise, such as politics, morality, laws, and so on. These relations of production exist objectively and independently of human will.

---

11 *The German Ideology*, Karl Marx, 1845.

> **Annotation 15**
>
> Human beings are social animals; we rely on one another to survive within a collective which we call a society. Within any given society, human beings will have relationships with one another in order to produce everything needed to sustain human life. These relations of production vary in time and place but they are always defined by the ways in which human beings work together to sustain life. The relations of production are the material basis of all other social relations. As Marx explained in *A Contribution to the Critique of Political Economy*:
>
>> The totality of these relations of production constitutes the economic structure of society, the real foundation, on which arises a legal and political superstructure and to which correspond definite forms of social consciousness.
>
> Since all prevailing ideological and intellectual products of any given class society are produced by the ruling class to reinforce and justify their own power [see Annotation 68, p. 119], it can be understood that all other social relations and consciousness stem from these material-based relations of production. As Marx says:
>
>> It is not the consciousness of men that determines their existence, but their social existence that determines their consciousness.
>
> The relations of production within any class society are not entered into voluntarily, nor are they consciously designed nor willed into existence by human beings. Rather, they result from material processes and *class struggle*. Thus, relations of production exist objectively and independently of the subjective will of any humans. This is discussed more on p. 49.

According to Friedrich Engels:

> The production of the immediate material means of subsistence and consequently the degree of economic development attained by a given people or during a given epoch form the foundation upon which the state institutions, the legal conceptions, art, and even the ideas on religion [are developed].[12]

> **Annotation 16**
>
> Here, Engels is describing the base/superstructure of human society, which was discussed in *Part 1*, starting on p. 24. The base/superstructure is also explained in full in Chapter 2 of this book, starting on p. 73. To briefly summarize this concept:
>
>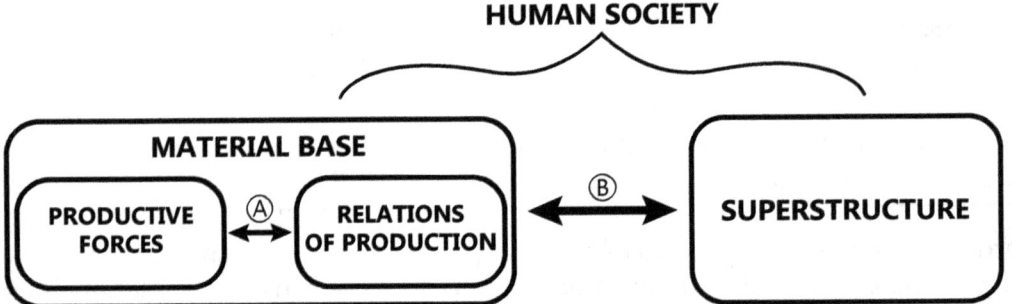
>
> *Human society is defined by the relationship between the base and the superstructure (B) which is, itself, defined by internal relations between productive forces and relations of production (A).*

---

12 Friedrich Engels' speech at the grave of Karl Marx, 1883.

Annotation 16 (continued)

The economic base (also known as the *material* base or just *base*) of society, as defined by Marx and Engels, refers to the material basis of society (as opposed to the conscious basis of society, i.e., the superstructure).

The material base of society is defined by internal and external relationships:

The internal relationships of the economic base consist of the relations between productive forces and the relations of production. Through these internal relations, the material base provides all of the material necessities of human life such as food, shelter, clothing, etc.

The external relationship which essentially defines the economic base of society is its relationship with the *superstructure*. The superstructure, conversely, is also defined by its external relationship with the base as well as internal relationships of its own.

Dr. Nguyen Ngoc Long defines superstructure in the Vietnamese textbook *Philosophy of Marxism-Leninism*:

> Superstructure is the totality of views about politics, rule of law, philosophy, ethics, religion, art, etc., along with corresponding social institutions such as the state, political parties, churches, social organizations, etc., that are formed on a certain economic base.

The internal relations of the superstructure of society include:

- **Forms of Social Consciousness:** Distinct collections of ideas, attitudes, and beliefs which are shared by a group of people in society (pertaining to such concepts as politics, rule of law, philosophy, ethics, religion, art, etc.)
- **Social Institutions:** An entity which has been established in order to promote, defend, and develop a corresponding form of social consciousness (such as the state, political parties, churches, social organizations, etc.)

Within the superstructure, each form of social consciousness has a corresponding social institution. This correspondence is a relationship of dialectical unity.

Within a class society, the superstructure consists of both dominant and non-dominant elements. The dominant elements are controlled by and serve the interests of the ruling class(es), while the non-dominant elements are controlled by remnant classes and oppressed classes. For example, in capitalist society the dominant social consciousness forms and social institutions are controlled by and serve the interests of the ruling capitalist class. Non-dominant elements might be controlled by the working class, which is currently the oppressed class in the current stage of development of human society. They may also be controlled by remnants of previous stages of development. For example, the system of monarchy and nobility in the modern day society of the United Kingdom is controlled by and serves the interest of remnants of the classes which dominated previously existing feudal relations of production.

Dr. Nguyen explains that the basic social function of the *dominant* superstructure is "to build, protect, and develop the economic base that gave rise to it, and to oppose any threats which might weaken or destroy the ruling economic regime. A class can only maintain economic dominance as long as it establishes and consolidates political and ideological dominance."

> **Annotation 16 (continued)**
>
> Non-dominant elements of superstructure exist to further the agenda of whichever class controls them by providing more power in society and more benefits from the means of production. For example, in our present society, the monarchy in the United Kingdom exists to provide benefits, power, and protection to the remnant feudal class, while a communist party might exist to provide benefits, power, and protection to the working class.
>
> **Nature of the Relationship Between Base and Superstructure**
>
> The economic base of society *determines* the superstructure, while the superstructure may impact back on the economic base. This follows the more general relationship between matter and consciousness in which the material determines consciousness while consciousness can impact back on the material through conscious human activity [see *Part 1*, p. 88].
>
> Dr. Nguyen explains in *Philosophy of Marxism-Leninism* that "in any given social regime, different elements of the superstructure will impact the base in different ways." In other words, not all social consciousness forms and institutions will impact the economic base at the same rate nor in the same direction of development.
>
> For example, in the modern USA, there are two political parties which are controlled by the ruling class: the Republican Party and the Democratic Party. Both of these parties exist to serve and protect the interests of the ruling capitalist class, however they often develop in different directions and at different rates of change and development.
>
> The economic base and superstructure are components of social being and social consciousness, respectively. Social being and social consciousness are explained in more detail in Annotation 60, p. 106.

In the process of material production, humans constantly transform nature, transform society, and at the same time transform themselves. Material production constantly develops. The development of material production determines the transformation and development of all aspects of society. Material production development determines social development.

> **Annotation 17**
>
> In Dialectical Materialism, *development* refers to the change and motion of things, phenomena, and ideas. Development is the subject of *Part 1*, Chapter 2: Materialist Dialectics (p. 98).
>
> It is important to recognize that dialectical development always results in changes occurring within all interacting subjects. This means that when human beings transform nature, human beings will also be transformed in countless ways. Likewise, as material production develops, the superstructure will also develop. It should also be noted that the material base of society *determines* the superstructure of society (see Annotation 50, p. 90). Such development follows the Law of Unification and Contradiction Between Opposites within the framework of Materialist Dialectics. This law is described in more detail in *Part 1* p. 175.

> **Annotation 17 (continued)**
>
>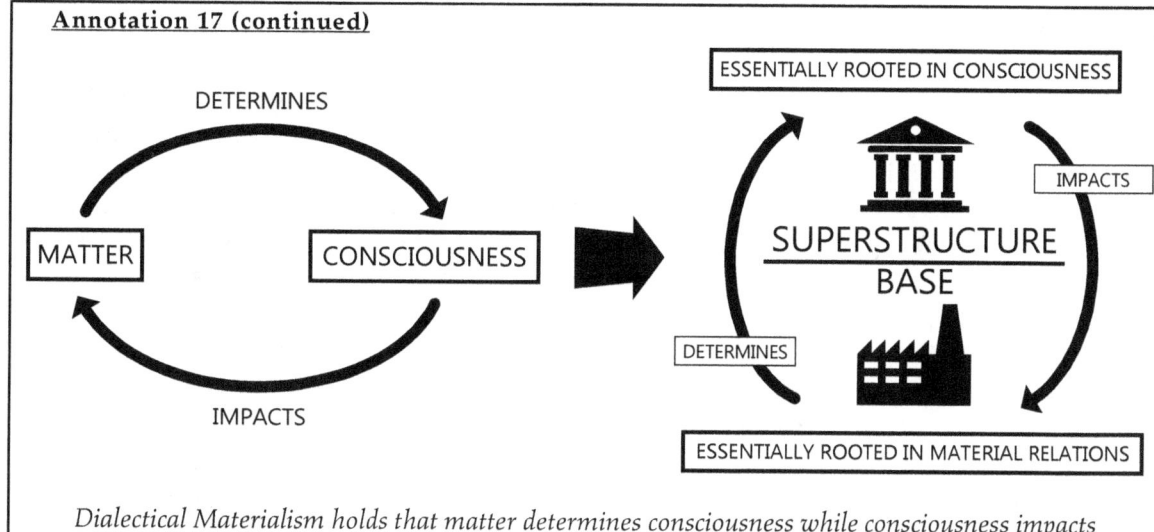
>
> *Dialectical Materialism holds that matter determines consciousness while consciousness impacts back upon matter. In accordance with this law, the economic base of human society determines superstructure while superstructure impacts back upon the economic base.*

Thus, the motion[13] and development of the entirety of a society, ultimately, is determined by the development of that society's material production processes. Therefore, in order to properly explain and solve the problems within a society, it is necessary to seek out the root causes of those problems within material production processes. This requires analysis of the development of that society's material production processes. Fundamentally, this means that the starting point of analysis of a society is determining the level of development of that society's *mode of production*.

> **Annotation 18**
>
> The mode of production constitutes the overall, predominant manner of production being utilized by humans in a particular time-period. Specifically, the mode of production is the predominant configuration of productive forces and relations of production at the current level of development. This will be further explained throughout the rest of this chapter.
>
> Under capitalism, the mode of production is typified by mechanized industrial production of goods and private ownership of the means of production by capitalists. The nature of the capitalist mode of production determines all other social problems which exist under capitalism, and all superstructural elements are rooted in the material foundation that is the mode of production.
>
> In *Manifesto of the Communist Party*, Marx and Engels described many ways in which the mode of production of capitalism led directly to severe social problems in their contemporary society. For example, the relentless demand which capitalists have for new markets led to the spread of imperialist oppression all around the world:
>
> > The need of a constantly expanding market for its products chases the bourgeoisie over the entire surface of the globe. It must nestle everywhere, settle everywhere, establish connexions everywhere.

---

13 In Dialectical Materialism, motion refers to change and development. See *Part 1*, p. 122.

Annotation 18 (continued)

In a letter to Sigfrid Meyer, Marx described how capitalism determined the form of racial antagonism between Irish and English workers. It is important to note that English oppression of the Irish did not *begin* with capitalism. However, once capitalism became the predominant mode of production, it directly determined the *form* of racial antagonism which existed between English and Irish workers and gave these antagonisms a proletarian character which was directly exacerbated by the ruling class (the bourgeoisie) to benefit their own class interests, as Marx describes:

> Every industrial and commercial center in England now possesses a working class divided into two hostile camps, English proletarians and Irish proletarians. The ordinary English worker hates the Irish worker as a competitor who lowers his standard of life. In relation to the Irish worker he regards himself as a member of the ruling nation and consequently he becomes a tool of the English aristocrats and capitalists against Ireland, thus strengthening their domination over himself. He cherishes religious, social, and national prejudices against the Irish worker. His attitude towards him is much the same as that of the "poor whites" to the black people in the former slave states of the U.S.A. The Irishman pays him back with interest in his own money. He sees in the English worker both the accomplice and the stupid tool of the English rulers in Ireland.
>
> This antagonism is artificially kept alive and intensified by the press, the pulpit, the comic papers, in short, by all the means at the disposal of the ruling classes. This antagonism is the secret of the impotence of the English working class, despite its organization. It is the secret by which the capitalist class maintains its power. And the latter is quite aware of this.

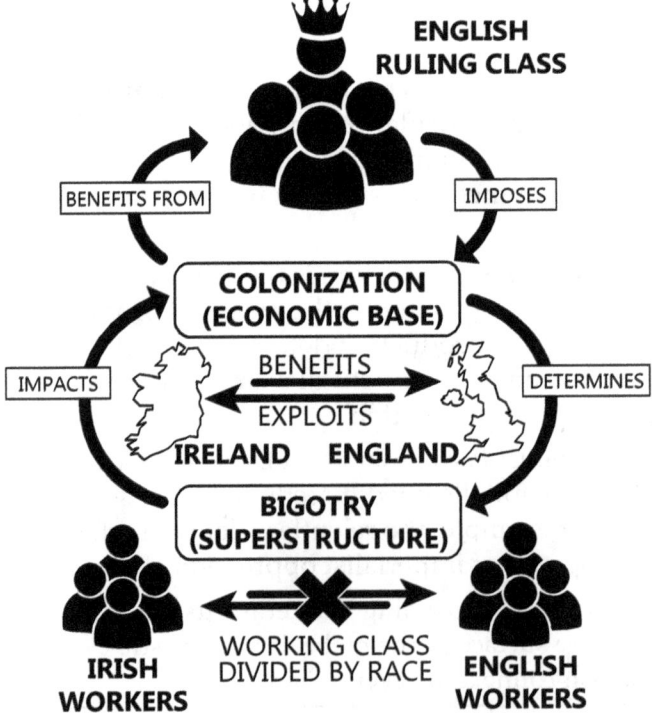

Superstructural bigotry against Irish workers reinforces the economic colonization of Ireland. This benefits the English ruling class to the detriment of both English and Irish workers.

Annotation 18 (continued)

We can thus conclude that capitalism did not *create* such social problems as sexism, racism, ableism, poverty, and so on. These are, in essence, manifestations of *false consciousness* and ideology-driven forms of bigotry and oppression as opposed to the material base class oppression through which workers are ruled over and exploited by the capitalist class. However, the capitalist mode of production does determine the *form* which all social problems and bigotries take within our current society. Most social problems and forms of oppression predate capitalism, but existed in different forms under previous modes of production than they do under the capitalist mode of production.

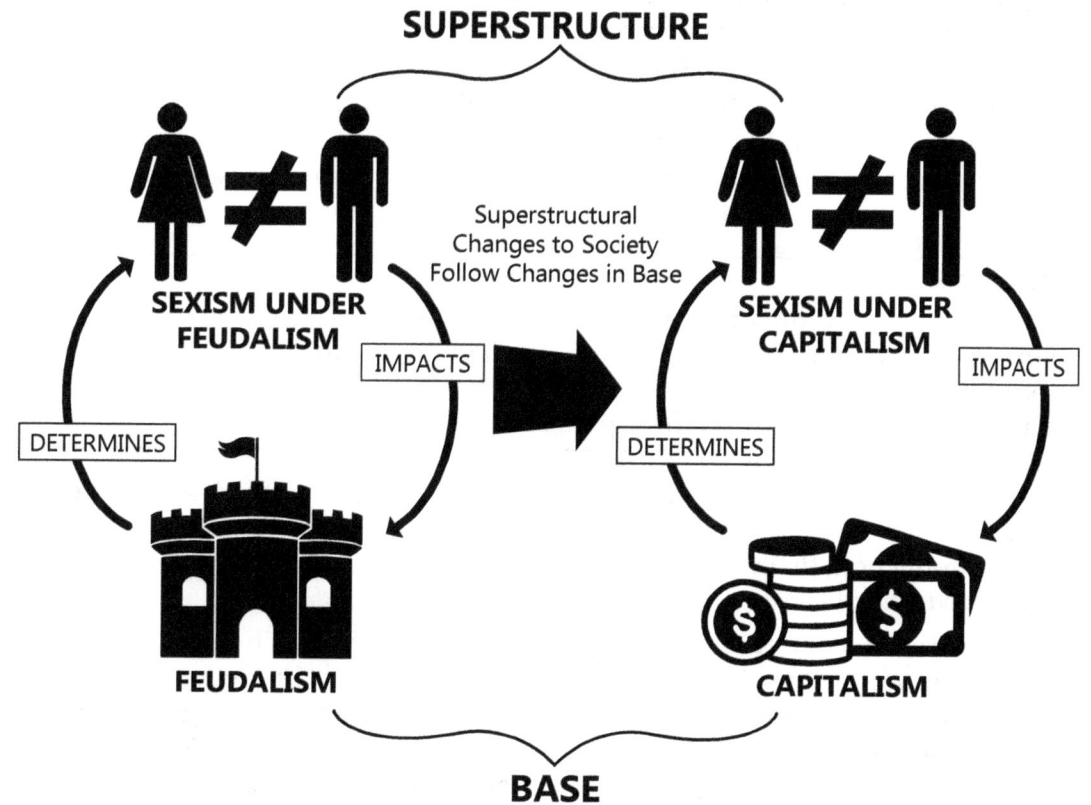

As the material base of society, the mode of production determines all other forms of oppression. Sexism, for example, existed differently under feudalism vs. how it exists today under capitalism. As the material base of society developed from feudalism to capitalism, sexism also developed.

In accordance with the principle that material determines consciousness and consciousness can impact back on the material through conscious activity, it follows that all of these various forms of oppression (which are rooted in ideology and stem from false consciousness) are able to impact back on the mode of production. In the above example of English-Irish racial antagonism, Marx makes it clear that the ruling class benefits as such racial antagonisms spread within the working class. Marx also points out that eroding such racial antagonisms (and ending the English colonization of Ireland) would weaken the position of the ruling class and strengthen the proletariat, which would bring about the end of capitalism all the sooner.

We can determine that capitalist society is at a higher stage of development than feudal society by examining the *mode of production* of each form of society.

> **Annotation 19**
>
> In Historical Materialism, a stage of development is considered to be at a "higher" or "lower" level based primarily on the development of productive forces. Under feudalism, the productive forces were at a much lower level of agrarian production. The essential means of production was the land which was used in the production of food. Tools and technology were relatively undeveloped. Compare this with the much higher level of development of the productive forces under capitalism, which utilize mechanization and other technologies for industrialized material production.

Capitalist society's mode of production utilizes industry with an increasingly complex market economy. Feudal society's mode of production was only able to use manual labor techniques and was limited to small, self-sufficient, self-contained economic organization. Therefore, capitalist society's mode of production can generate much higher labor productivity than the production mode of feudal society.

> **Annotation 20**
>
> Labor productivity simply refers to how much a single human being can produce in the workplace. A worker under capitalism is generally able to produce far more than a worker under feudalism because of the higher level of technology, industrialization, etc., which are employed within the capitalist mode of production.

Marx and Engels determined that economic eras do not differ from one another based on *what is* produced, but rather based on *how* production is carried out and *which tools* are used in production. [In other words, economic eras differ from one another based on the *mode of production*.]

This discovery – that the *mode of production* plays a decisive role in the development of production processes in society, and with the development of society in general – is the basis of Historical Materialism: understanding human history through the analysis of the history of development and replacement of the modes of production using Marxist-Leninist methodologies of Dialectical Materialism and Materialist Dialectics.

> **Annotation 21**
>
> In Dialectical Materialism, the words "development" and "replacement" have specific meanings.
>
> Development refers to changes over time which take place through dialectical relationships between all things, phenomena, and ideas. Development occurs through processes of contradiction: whenever one subject interacts with another subject, they are said to contradict, and both subjects are developed through this contradiction.
>
> Replacement refers to a specific form of negation. As two subjects contradict with one another, one subject will eventually negate the other subject – completely overcoming it. Replacement negation is a specific form of negation which occurs when one subject takes the place of another. Replacement is a dialectical process which always takes place gradually, since nothing can pop in and out of existence instantaneously.

> **Annotation 21 (continued)**
>
> Therefore, it is important to understand that the replacement of one mode of production by another is a gradual and dialectical process. Capitalism did not immediately and instantaneously replace the feudal mode of production. Instead, capitalism negated feudalism over many generations as the bourgeois class slowly but surely superseded the previous feudal ruling class through dialectical development processes. Marx and Engels describe this gradual development process in the *Manifesto of the Communist Party*:
>
>> Each step in the development of the bourgeoisie was accompanied by a corresponding political advance of that class. An oppressed class under the sway of the feudal nobility, an armed and self-governing association in the medieval commune: here independent urban republic (as in Italy and Germany); there taxable "third estate" of the monarchy (as in France); afterwards, in the period of manufacturing proper, serving either the semi-feudal or the absolute monarchy as a counterpoise against the nobility, and, in fact, cornerstone of the great monarchies in general, the bourgeoisie has at last, since the establishment of Modern Industry and of the world market, conquered for itself, in the modern representative State, exclusive political sway. The executive of the modern state is but a committee for managing the common affairs of the whole bourgeoisie.
>
> Similarly, communism will not instantaneously replace capitalism, but will negate capitalism gradually through the revolutionary advance of the working class.

The development and replacement of modes of production reflects the inevitable and objective trend of the development of human society from lower levels to increasingly higher levels: from the ancient production mode, to the feudal production mode, to the modern capitalist production mode, etc.

> **Annotation 22**
>
> Development of human society is both inevitable and objective. The Principle of Development[14] of Dialectical Materialism states that:
>
>> Development is a process that comes from within the thing-in-itself; the process of solving the contradictions within things and phenomena. Therefore, development is inevitable, objective, and occurs without dependence on human will.
>
> In accordance with this principle, it should be understood that all things, phenomena, and ideas are constantly and inevitably changing, and human society is no exception to these universal laws.
>
> Development of human society is considered *objective* because it cannot be subjectively controlled and directed by human will and consciousness. Rather, as is explained throughout the rest of this section, it is the material base of society which determines the development of human conscious activity: productive forces determine the material/economic base of human society, and this material base determines the superstructure which includes philosophy, political government, religion, art, and all other aspects of human society (see p. 90).

---

[14] The Principle of Development is described in detail in *Part 1*, p. 119.

> **Annotation 22 (continued)**
>
> The inevitable and objective development of human society reflects the forward tendency of development which is a characteristic of all development processes. This forward tendency is described in *Part 1*, Annotation 118, p. 122. Note that this is a tendency and there are exceptions. Occasionally, certain elements, regions, or aspects of human societies do tend to fall backward or degrade in some way or another. For example, industry may be degraded through the destruction of war or through economic difficulty. Also note that the terms "higher level" and "lower level" are value-neutral: to say that a society has a "higher level of development" does not imply that the society is "superior to" or "better than" a society with a "lower level of development."
>
> In Historical Materialism, to say that a society has moved to a "higher level of development" simply means that the mode of production has developed to a more complex form with a higher level of labor productivity and productive forces.

The sequential nature of the process of replacing and developing modes of production is also a general rule which governs the development process of human history.

> **Annotation 23**
>
> Sequential, here, means that development occurs in a specific sequence, from lower stages of development to higher stages of development. It is rare for such a sequential development process to reverse direction or to bypass a stage of development.
>
> This sequential nature of the process of human development is strongly related to the development of scientific knowledge of productive forces. As humans learn more about science, nature, and technology, there is a tendency for productive forces to develop in terms of efficiency and output.
>
> A simple example of this is the development of transportation methods by human beings. As humans progressed from transportation by foot, to transportation via beasts of burden, to transportation by steam engines, to modern systems of transportation which utilize efficient and powerful engines and high quality roads, rail systems, and airplanes, the productive forces also increased at every stage of development.
>
> Under normal circumstances, such scientific knowledge develops sequentially over time, but there are exceptions to this general tendency. For example, in some places and times, technological stages (and stages of development of production) may be bypassed through the introduction of high technology from abroad. As an example, Vietnamese industry and agriculture received many high technology production techniques and technologies from the Soviet Union during the revolutionary period of 1945 – 1975 which allowed the nation to bypass some steps of scientific development which rapidly increased productive forces.
>
> For the most part, looking at the big picture of humanity as a whole, it is generally necessary to go through the sequence of human development as new technologies are developed sequentially through the development of our scientific understanding of the world and of technology.
>
> The following excerpt is from the article "Karl Marx's View on Productive Forces and the Issue of Supplementing and Developing this View in the Current Period," from Vietnam's communist journal *Communist Review*:

Annotation 23 (continued)

Karl Marx believed that productive forces represent the practical capacity of humans in the process of transforming the natural world. When carrying out material production, humans use labor and tools to impact the natural world so that they can create material wealth which can serve their essential needs. Also in that process, humans come to understand the laws of nature, transforming the natural world from a wild, simple place into a "second world" with the participation of human hands and minds. Material production is always changing, so productive forces are a dynamic factor and a process that is constantly being innovated and developed.

Productive forces create material premises for the existence and development of human society. Productive forces are also the basic criterion to evaluate social progress in each specific historical period. That is why, in his work *The German Ideology*, Marx affirmed:

"History is nothing but the succession of the separate generations, each of which exploits the materials, the capital funds, the productive forces handed down to it by all preceding generations, and thus, on the one hand, continues the traditional activity in completely changed circumstances and, on the other hand, modifies the old circumstances with a completely changed activity."

Thus, from Karl Marx's point of view, it can be understood that the concept of productive forces refers to the combination of workers and means of production to create a certain material production power. According to Marx, in order to transform the natural world and create material wealth, workers need to have a synergy between physical and intellectual strength, as these are factors that create human working ability. As Marx wrote in *Capital*, Volume 1, Chapter 7:

"He opposes himself to Nature as one of her own forces, setting in motion arms and legs, head and hands, the natural forces of his body, in order to appropriate Nature's productions in a form adapted to his own wants."

However, if human activities were limited to human labor through the human body alone, then material production processes could not be developed to higher levels. Humans have thus developed other means of material production, such as "mak(ing) use of the mechanical, physical, and chemical properties of some substances in order to make other substances subservient to his aims."[15] These objects of material production, which Marx called "organs," give workers the ability to extend their hands and make the process of influencing the natural world more effective. If the means of production are a necessary condition for the material production process, then the workers are the main subjects in that process, playing a decisive role in the development of production. Thus, according to Karl Marx, if there were no humans who knew how to manufacture and use tools of labor to impact the natural world, there would be no process of material production.

In addition to discussing the two basic elements constituting the productive forces, Karl Marx also emphasized the important role of science in material production in general and in the development of productive forces in particular.

---

15 Karl Marx: *Capital* Volume 1, Chapter 7.

Annotation 23 (continued)

As Marx explained:

"The development of fixed capital [i.e., machinery of production] indicates to what degree general social knowledge has become a direct force of production, and to what degree, hence, the conditions of the process of social life itself have come under the control of the general intellect and been transformed in accordance with it. To what degree the powers of social production have been produced, not only in the form of knowledge, but also as immediate organs of social practice, of the real life process."[16]

According to the above thesis of Karl Marx, scientific knowledge has caused fixed capital such as factories and machines used in production to transform to a certain extent and become a direct productive force. In other words, scientific knowledge is applied and materialized into machines and into production tools, and used by workers in the production process, thus, scientific knowledge becomes a direct productive force. The conditions for scientific knowledge to become a direct productive force were affirmed by Karl Marx as follows:

"The development of machinery along this path occurs only when large industry has already reached a higher stage, and all the sciences have been pressed into the service of capital; and when, secondly, the available machinery itself already provides great capabilities. Invention then becomes a business, and the application of science to direct production itself becomes a prospect which determines and solicits it."[17]

Historical Materialism is essentially about looking for the root causes of historical change of human society. A material examination of human history shows this root cause to be change and development of the modes of production. The development of modes of production strongly depends on the level of development of the productive forces in each period of history, and this development is dependent upon the development of scientific knowledge that humans achieve through generations of theory and practice.[18]

Therefore, we can conclude that, as a general rule of Historical Materialism, the historical development of humanity is sequential, even if some societies with specific conditions may bypass some steps. This is the General Rule of Sequential Development of History.

It must also be noted that, within a society, different communities can exist at different levels of development, depending on certain objective and subjective conditions. There might be a mix of different production modes within a development period. Likewise, a community within a wider society might abandon or bypass the dominant mode of production and go straight to a higher mode of production.

That being said, the development of a conscious awareness of the objective laws of Historical Materialism has enabled some societies to consciously endeavor to bypass the stage of capitalism in attempts to go directly to a socialist mode of production.

---

16 Karl Marx: "Foundations of the Critique of Political Economy."
17 Ibid.
18 See Theory and Practice section of *Part 1*, p. 204.

> **Annotation 23 (continued)**
>
> **WORKERS** — PHYSICAL STRENGTH, INTELLECTUAL STRENGTH
>
> **MATERIAL PRODUCTION** — WORKERS DETERMINES / IMPACTS MACHINERY, TOOLS, ETC.
>
> *Human workers engage with the natural world to create wealth by applying intellectual and physical strength. This leads to the development of machinery and tools (what Marx calls the "organs of production") which enable humans to increase material production capabilities.*
>
> An example of a society bypassing a dominant mode of production and going straight to a higher mode of production is Vietnam during the revolutionary period. Before and during French colonial rule, Vietnam was essentially an agrarian feudal society. Despite the existence of some light industry and a nascent capitalist class, the vast majority of Vietnamese workers were peasants, slaves, and farmers. The ruling class of Vietnam before and during the Colonial period were not capitalists, but the emperor, feudal lords, and French colonialists who all constituted a landed class which was essentially feudalist in nature. During and after the revolutionary period of Vietnam, industrialization was rapidly implemented with great assistance from the Soviet Union and other foreign nations under the leadership of the Communist Party of Vietnam. The mechanization of Vietnamese industry and agriculture took place largely during the subsidizing period without a capitalist class. Vietnam was therefore able to transform itself into a modern industrial nation without having ever fully established a capitalist political economy.
>
> Agriculture in Vietnam reflects these efforts to bypass capitalist class society. Before and during the occupation of Vietnam, agriculture was feudalistic in nature. Feudal and colonial landowners employed hundreds of thousands of slaves and peasants who worked essentially within the framework of the traditional feudal mode of production. During the revolutionary period, the Communist Party of Vietnam implemented significant land reforms which transferred farmland directly to farmers and provided farmers with tools and training which allowed for mass mechanization.
>
> Today, Vietnamese agriculture—which employs approximately 70% of Vietnamese workers—is highly mechanized, and capitalist ownership of farmland is prohibited. In this way, Vietnamese farmers have managed to bypass the capitalistic agriculture by going straight to a mode of production which is mechanized, highly productive, and worker-owned. This is just one of the ways in which Vietnam has endeavored to transition to socialism while bypassing the capitalist mode of production. These efforts have resulted in many victories and failures in both theory and practice.[19]

---

19 Vietnam's efforts to bypass capitalism are discussed in more detail in Appendix H, p. 269.

The fact that multiple modes of production can exist within a society simultaneously is an expression of *unity in diversity* which leads to the richness of human history.

> **Annotation 24**
>
> Diversity in unity and unity in diversity is an aspect of the Principle of General Relationships of the Materialist Dialectical methodological and philosophical framework. These concepts are explained in detail in *Part 1*, Annotation 107, p. 110.
>
> Diversity in Unity means that there are an infinite number of diverse relationships between things, phenomena, and ideas, but that all these relationships share the same foundation in the material world.
>
> Unity in Diversity means that universal relationships which unite all things, phenomena, and ideas can manifest in infinitely diverse ways.
>
> Although human society develops sequentially, it does not develop mechanically or predictably. A given mode of production can manifest in a great diversity of forms in various human societies, and different modes of production can even exist simultaneously within one society.
>
> As an example, even though the United States of America is a highly capitalistic society, there are a small number of workers' cooperatives which are not owned by capitalists. There are also still examples of slave labor being employed in the United States of America: sometimes illicitly, such as with human trafficking, and sometimes legally, such as in American prisons.
>
> As a counterexample, we can look at socialist nations, both historically and in modern contexts (such as the Soviet Union, Vietnam, China, and Cuba) which have allowed capitalist-owned corporations to operate even though these nations are controlled by Communist Parties. This is discussed in the article "Approaching the Socialist-Oriented Market Economy and Human Issue from Goals and Driving Force of Development" in the Vietnamese communist journal *Communist Review*:
>
>> From a historical perspective, for a long time during the process of socialism building, both theoretically and practically, people have compared socialism and capitalism in an absolute and metaphysical way. They have also thought that what is in capitalism must be rejected by socialism and vice versa, including the market economy as the result in the development of human history. It should be clearly realized that the socialist society as a social-economic form cannot have everything available in a capitalist society, but it has prerequisites in many important aspects for the birth of a new social-economic form. One of these prerequisites is the well-developed market economy thanks to the extremely highly and strongly developed production forces. Lenin soon realized the mistake of haste in formulating and implementing the Wartime Communist Policy that he promptly corrected by proposing a New Economic Policy (NEP) for Russia to develop the production of multi-sector goods and start the market economy. He strongly asserted that "we cannot conceive of socialism other than socialism based on all the lessons drawn by the great civilization of capitalism."
>
> During transition periods between one mode of production and the next, there will be a mixture of modes of production within the developing society. In Europe and North America during the transition from feudalism to capitalism, there existed simul-

> **Annotation 24 (continued)**
>
> taneously for a time both capitalists and feudal lords. Even today around the world vestiges of feudal lords remain, such as entire nations ruled by monarchs. And even within the current capitalist era of human civilization, there exist a broad range of forms in which the capitalist mode of production manifests. For example, there is an obvious difference between a rich, developed capitalist country which has an economy dominated by local capitalists and an impoverished, imperialized country which is heavily dominated by foreign capitalists. All of this diversity exists within the current era of capitalism, demonstrating the concept of unity in diversity in capitalist society, just as unity in diversity was expressed in every preceding era of history.

However, no matter how rich and diverse the history of each human society might be, and even if a society goes through detours as it advances through a stage of development, in the end, history still follows the general direction of development: upward direction from lower-level to higher-level modes of production.

> **Annotation 25**
>
> As previously mentioned in Annotation 10 on p. 16, advancing from a "lower level" of production to a "higher level" of production merely refers to a general tendency and does not imply a tendency in a "better direction." As an example, many indigenous societies which were forced to "advance" into capitalist modes of production suffered tremendously or were even wiped out entirely in the process.
>
> It is also important to recognize that many "lower level" modes of production in indigenous societies were far more sustainable in terms of ecology and preferable to the indigenous populations in terms of satisfaction of life and wellbeing for the population at large. Certainly, the "development" of capitalism in what is today called the "United States of America" was certainly not seen as a beneficial development by indigenous peoples, as encapsulated in this quote from a speech by Satanta, chief of the Kiowa nation:
>
>> All the land south of the Arkansas River belongs to the Kiowas and Comanches and I don't want to give away any of it. I love the land and the buffalo, and will not part with any. I have heard that you intend to settle us on a reservation near the mountains. I don't want to settle there. I love to roam over the wide prairie, and when I do it I feel free and happy; but, when we settle down we grow pale and die. A long time ago, this land belonged to our fathers, but when I go up to the river, I see camps of soldiers on its banks. These soldiers cut down my timber, they kill my buffalo, and when I see that, my heart feels like bursting with sorrow.
>
> Similarly, French colonialism developed certain aspects of Vietnam by introducing railways, steam engines, and other such technology to the nation, but this was at great cost and caused untold suffering to the Vietnamese people who were enslaved and subjugated by the French. As socialists, we must seek ways to develop human society without causing such harm and subjugation. As Lenin explains in *What is to be Done*:
>
>> The building of railways seems to be a simple, natural, democratic, cultural and civilising enterprise; that is what it is in the opinion of the bourgeois professors who are paid to depict capitalist slavery in bright colours, and in the opinion of

> **Annotation 25 (continued)**
>
> petty-bourgeois philistines. But as a matter of fact the capitalist threads, which in thousands of different intercrossings bind these enterprises with private property in the means of production in general, have converted this railway construction into an instrument for oppressing a thousand million people (in the colonies and semicolonies), that is, more than half the population of the globe that inhabits the dependent countries, as well as the wage-slaves of capital in the "civilised" countries.
>
> In the Vietnamese journal *Communist Review*, Dr. Nguyen Trong Chuan discusses the ways in which Vietnam is attempting to develop productive forces in Vietnam in accordance with socialist principles:
>
>> Karl Marx once said that, in a capitalist market economy, each one sees others as the ones to exploit. Today, in the socialist-oriented market economy, we put people in the first place and regard them as the driving force and the development goal. Therefore, the Communist Party and State of Vietnam did not wait until the economy is highly developed for realizing social goals. At the very beginning, the Communist Party and the State of Vietnam advocated "economic growth together with social progress and justice in every step and throughout the process of development."
>>
>> The advocacy has been consistent throughout the Party Congresses and increasingly concretized in all aspects of the social life in order to facilitate human development in the best way. It is a correct, scientific, bold, creative, and humane choice. The inevitable choice is based on experience, selective inheritance of the strengths in the development of the market economy in the history. In addition, it shows socialism's human nature to affirm that building a socialist-oriented market economy with people as the driving force and development goal is a correct choice.
>
> Historical Materialism is considered a *science* not just because it analyzes history on a materialist basis, but also because it is intended to be applied by socialists working in the real world to bring about a transition away from capitalism and towards the stateless, classless society of communism.
>
> Communists like Marx, Engels, and Lenin did not study the material conditions of capitalism and previous eras of human history simply as an academic pursuit. They were committed communists who hoped to contribute to the end of capitalism through Scientific Socialism: a body of theory and knowledge (which must be constantly tested through practice) focused on the practical pursuit of changing the world to bring about socialism and, eventually, communism. Scientific Socialism demands that we study history to learn from the successes and failures of previous generations.
>
> Communists have at various times failed to understand the nature of human development which has led to failures, setbacks, and even collapse of entire movements. However, Scientific Socialism is unique within capitalist society in that this field seeks to understand how human development processes function—in large part through the science of Historical Materialism—in order to improve our political theory and practice over time, striving to constantly improve society and to ultimately free workers from the suffering which is inherent in class society.

Annotation 25 (continued)

"Move Forward to Build an Advanced Culture and Science"

As Friedrich Engels wrote in *Socialism: Utopian and Scientific*:

> To accomplish this act of universal emancipation is the historical mission of the modern proletariat. To thoroughly comprehend the historical conditions and thus the very nature of this act, to impart to the now oppressed proletarian class a full knowledge of the conditions and of the meaning of the momentous act it is called upon to accomplish, this is the task of the theoretical expression of the proletarian movement, Scientific Socialism.

II. THE LAW OF SUITABILITY BETWEEN THE RELATIONS OF PRODUCTION AND THE DEVELOPMENT OF THE PRODUCTIVE FORCES

1. Definitions of productive forces and relations of production

Any material production process must depend on factors of workers (such as workers' abilities, skills, knowledge, etc.) as well as on factors of the means of production (such as labor objects, tools, auxiliary means of production process, etc.). Together, these factors constitute the productive forces of the production process.

The productive forces are the synthesis of material and mental factors which together form a practical power to transform the natural world according to the needs of human survival and development.

> **Annotation 26**
>
> The productive forces of human society include human labor as well as all other factors which contribute to the means of production. This includes tools and processes designed by human beings as well as nature from which all material production processes draw. In *Critique of the Gotha Program*, Marx warns that labor alone does not constitute the entirety of the forces of production, writing:
>
>> Labor is not the source of all wealth. Nature is just as much the source of use values (and it is surely of such that material wealth consists!) as labor, which itself is only the manifestation of a force of nature, human labor power.
>
> Human beings *utilize* nature and, at the same time, are *of* nature. Human beings are not metaphysically distinct from nature; we are a part of the natural world and thus our activities are natural activities. What distinguishes human labor and human production processes from all other activities on Earth is that human production is *conscious* activity. This enables humans to intentionally develop our production activities over time through the sequential development of science, technology, and so on. Other animals may improve their life processes over time and may even use tools, but no other animal is known to have advanced through various stages of development of the mode of production through the conscious development of scientific knowledge in the same manner as human beings. This is discussed more in the next Annotation.

Therefore, the productive forces have the characteristic of creativity, and this creative characteristic develops through history.

> **Annotation 27**
>
> Creativity is the characteristic of human beings which allows human society and production processes to develop over time through conscious activity. Marx and Engels considered the creative ability of human beings to consciously produce and develop production over time to be the primary distinguishing characteristic which distinguishes us from other animals. As Marx wrote in "Estranged Labor:"
>
>> It is true that animals also produce. They build nests and dwellings, like the bee, the beaver, the ant, etc. But they produce only their own immediate needs or those of their young; they produce only when immediate physical need compels them to do so, while man produces even when he is free from physical need and truly produces only in freedom from such need; they produce only themselves,

> **Annotation 27 (continued)**
>
> while man reproduces the whole of nature; their products belong immediately to their physical bodies, while man freely confronts his own product. Animals produce only according to the standards and needs of the species to which they belong, while man is capable of producing according to the standards of every species and of applying to each object its inherent standard; hence, man also produces in accordance with the laws of beauty.
>
> In the same article, Marx wrote that:
>
>> The animal is immediately one with its life activity. It is not distinct from that activity; it is that activity. Man makes his life activity itself an object of his will and consciousness. He has conscious life activity. It is not a determination with which he directly merges. Conscious life activity directly distinguishes man from animal life activity.
>
> Because human beings are aware of our own production processes, we are able to creatively develop them over time through conscious activity. This creativity is rooted in a dialectical relationship between human consciousness and practical activities.

Therefore, the level of development of a society's productive forces reflects the level of development of a society's utilization of the natural world. The handicraft level of the productive forces reflects a lower level of utilization of the natural world compared to the productive forces that have a higher level of technology and industry.

> **Annotation 28**
>
> It should be noted that the development of a society's utilization of nature from lower to higher levels is not a value judgment of "good" or "bad." Marx and Engels recognized that wanton destruction of the natural environment to increase production is an example of human hubris, as Engels explained in "The Part Played by Labor in the Transition from Ape to Man" (see quoted passage in Annotation 5 on p. 12), and as Marx pointed out in *Capital*:
>
>> All progress in capitalistic agriculture is a progress in the art, not only of robbing the labourer, but of robbing the soil; all progress in increasing the fertility of the soil for a given time, is a progress towards ruining the lasting sources of that fertility. The more a country starts its development on the foundation of modern industry, like the United States, for example, the more rapid is this process of destruction. Capitalist production, therefore, develops technology, and the combining together of various processes into a social whole, only by sapping the original sources of all wealth—the soil and the labourer.
>
> Unfortunately, the capitalist mode of production is dictated entirely by a single factor: the profit motive of capitalists. This has led to widescale destruction of our natural environment in the name of capitalist profiteering. Given what we know now about climate change, the rapid extinction of thousands of species resulting from human production activities, and various other threats to our planetary environment, this only makes the necessity to move away from capitalism all the more urgent. As Scientific Socialists we must understand the ways in which improper utilization of nature can cause destruction and devastation and may even lead to our own downfall.

> **Annotation 28 (continued)**
>
> An aspect of the historical mission of the working class, therefore, is developing harmonious unity between humanity and nature. Class society has led to destructive exploitation of both the working class and of nature itself. In bringing about the stateless, classless society of communism, we must take into consideration the role which nature plays in the sustaining and development of human life. As Marx and Engels advised, we must strive to develop relations and forces of production which preserve nature and, by extension, preserve our own continued existence as a part of nature and as a species with a natural aspect.
>
> The natural aspect of humanity is discussed more in Chapter 6, starting on p. 212.

Among the factors that make up the productive forces (namely, worker factors and means of production factors), the worker factors play a decisive role. This is because, ultimately, the means of production are only products of human labor, and the value and actual effectiveness of the means of production depend on the efficiency and creativity of the workers. On the other hand, means of production factors (such as the technological level of tools) reflect most clearly the level of development of the productive forces as well as the level of human utilization of the natural world.

> **Annotation 29**
>
> Productive forces of human society consist broadly of two categories of factors:
>
> Worker Factors (related to the workers who carry out production processes in human society) and Means of Production Factors (related to the means by which workers carry out production. This includes nature and all of its resources as well as tools, machinery, and processes which humans have devised to produce our material needs).
>
>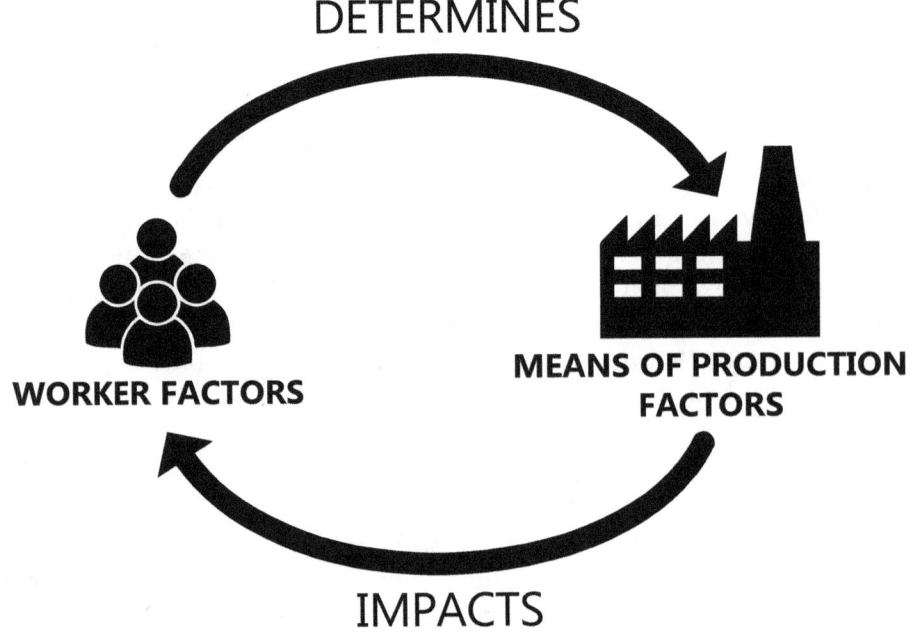
>
> *The productive forces are defined by a relationship between workers and means of production.*

> **Annotation 29 (continued)**
>
> In the capitalist mode of production it is the working class which develops the means of production over time. Without workers, the means of production would be useless and idle and production processes would be neither carried out nor developed to higher levels of efficiency and productive output. Thus, under capitalism, the productive forces are defined by a dialectical relationship which the workers have with the means of production. In this dialectical relationship, workers have the determining role while the means of production impact back on workers by making the labor of individual workers more efficient and productive, changing the circumstances of workers in many ways.

The *productive forces* are the fundamental and essential material content of the production process.

> **Annotation 30**
>
>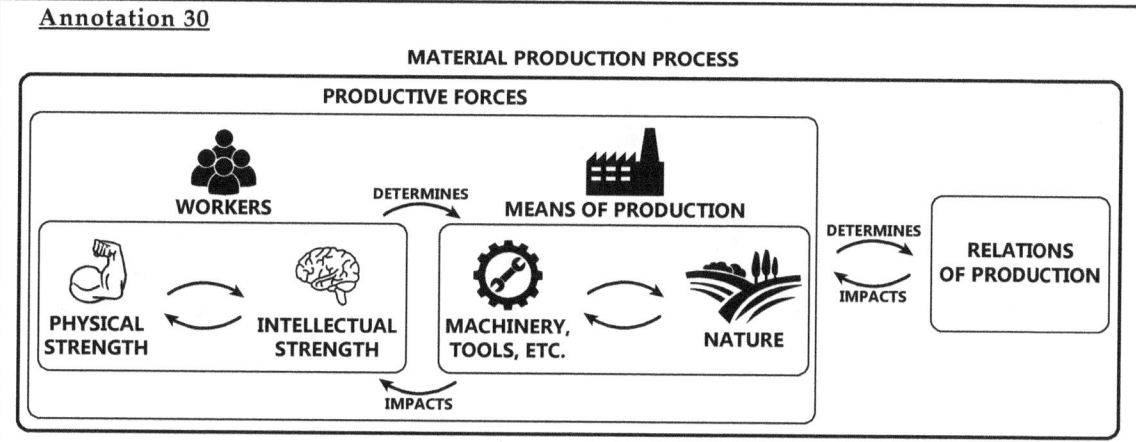
>
> *The productive forces are defined by internal relationships and, in turn, define the Material Production Process through its external relationship with the relations of production.*

The dialectical category pair of Essence and Phenomena is discussed in detail in **Part 1**, p. 156. To briefly summarize:

- **Essence** refers to the synthesis of all the internal aspects as well as the obvious and stable relations that define the existence, motion, and development of a thing, phenomenon, or idea.

- **Phenomena** refers to the external manifestations of those internal aspects and relations in specific conditions.

The dialectical category pair of Content and Form is discussed in detail in **Part 1**, p. 147. In summary:

- **Content** is the philosophical category which refers to the sum of all aspects, attributes, and processes that a thing, phenomenon, or idea is made from.

- **Form** refers to the mode of existence and development of things, phenomena, and ideas; in other words, form constitutes the relatively stable relationships which exist internally within a given thing, phenomenon, or idea.

46 ☭ Historical Materialism

Annotation 30 (continued)

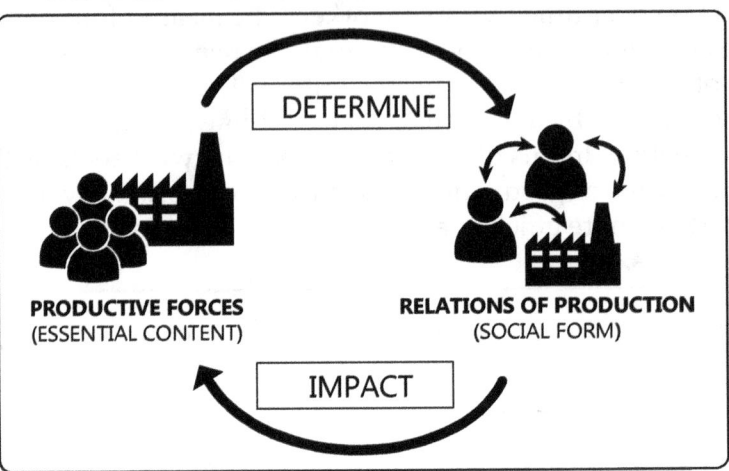

The material production process is defined by a dialectical relationship between the productive forces (which are the essential content) and the means of production (which are determined by the productive forces).

Content and Form have a dialectical relationship with one another in which content determines form and form can impact back on content. Thus, we can better understand that "the productive forces are the fundamental and essential material content of the production process." This statement contains the following truths:

1. The material production process has as *content* the productive forces; the productive forces manifest in human society in the *form* of relations of production.

2. In the dialectical relationship between the productive forces and the relations of production, the productive forces are the material content and are thus the determining factor.

3. As the determining factor, the productive forces constitute the essential content of the material production process.

4. The relations of production describe how the productive forces manifest in human society and are thus the social form of the production process.

No practical production process can take place without the presence of both factors of productive forces: labor [i.e., worker factors] and means of production. However, it must be understood that it is impossible for a production process to take place with productive forces alone. In addition to productive forces, it is also necessary to have relations of production for production processes to take place.

Relations of production are the relationships which exist between people in the production process. Relations of production include:

1. Ownership of the means of production.
2. Relations in the organizing and management of the production process.
3. Relations in the distribution of the results of that production process.

These relations exist in a unified relationship with each other. They also determine and impact each other on the decisive basis of the ownership of the means of production.

Annotation 31

RELATIONS OF PRODUCTION

[Diagram: RULING CLASS —EXPLOIT→ WORKING CLASS; RULING CLASS —OWN→ MEANS OF PRODUCTION; WORKING CLASS —OPERATE→ MEANS OF PRODUCTION; MEANS OF PRODUCTION —BENEFIT→ RULING CLASS]

The relations of production include relations between human beings which pertain to the ownership and operation of the means of production.

The relations of production are relationships in human society which pertain to the productive forces. Specifically, these include social relationships which humans have with each other and with the means of production.

---

2. Dialectical relationship between productive forces and relations of production

The relationship between productive forces and relations of production is a dialectical unity in which productive forces determine relations of production and relations of production impact the productive forces.

Productive forces and relations of production are two fundamental and essential aspects of the production process in which productive forces are the material content of the production process and relations of production are the social form of that process. No production process can take place without a certain social form [which we call the relations of production]. Conversely, no production process can take place without any material content [which we call the productive forces].

Thus, productive forces and relations of production mutually develop one another and, together, become unified.

Annotation 32

Whereas the productive forces include the *material* content of the material production process, the relations of production are the *social* form of the material production process. This includes all the relationships which humans have with each other to determine how material production processes are carried out in human society.

The productive forces and relations of production are not metaphysically distinct from each other. Rather, they exist together in dialectical unity, meaning that they are each defined by their relationship with one another and this relationship is what defines the material production process. The productive forces and relations of production define each other, in part, as follows:

> **Annotation 32 (continued)**
>
> - The relations of production include relations to the means of production (a component of the productive forces). In class society, these are the relationships which determine who owns and who operates the means of production.
> - The relations of production include relations of human labor (i.e., who operates the means of production).
> - The productive forces include human workers who labor together through social relations of production.
> - In a class society, the productive forces include the means of production which must be owned by some human beings and operated by others through social relations of production.

This is an essential and universal requirement that exists in all practical production processes within society. A specific level of development of the productive forces requires a suitable level of development of the relations of production in all three aspects:

1. Ownership of the means of production.
2. Organization and management of the production process.
3. Distribution of the results of the production process.

Only in this way can productive forces be maintained, used, and further developed.

> **Annotation 33**
>
> Suitability describes how appropriate or applicable a subject is for a specific application or role (see **Part 1**, Annotation 153, p. 154).
>
> In order for human production processes to be carried out efficiently, the productive forces and relations of production must be suitable with one another. This is the Law of Suitability Between the Relations of Production and the Productive Forces, or the Law of Suitability, which is a fundamental law of Historical Materialism. This law is further defined and explained in Annotation 33. This suitability between productive forces and relations of production can be broadly considered as it pertains to aspects of *ownership*, *organization*, and *distribution*.
>
> **Ownership:** The means of production must come under majority ownership of the capitalist class. Under feudalism, the means of production were owned by different classes. Land was owned by feudal lords, means of craft production were owned by craft guilds, etc. This system of ownership was unsuitable to emerging industrial production processes. However, as the bourgeois class emerged and came to own more and more of the means of production through the development of private capital, conditions became increasingly suitable for a industrial production process to dominate human society through the development of capitalism.
>
> **Organization:** Feudal society was organized very differently from capitalist society. Political power was primarily held by monarchs and feudal land owners, with significant amounts of power also being shared by clergy and (to a lesser extent) merchants and craft guilds. This was a much more complicated method of organizing human society which did not suit capitalist production processes. As capitalists came to own

> **Annotation 33 (continued)**
>
> the primary means of production in human society, they also shifted the organization of human society, so that capitalists came to dominate the organization of production more and more. Farms and factories reorganized so that capitalists dominated the overarching power structures and developed managers and enforcers (such as security guards, police, detective agencies, etc.) to maintain and manage production processes and control workers. As these organizational elements developed and improved, conditions became increasingly suitable for the capitalist mode of production to gain primacy over human civilization.
>
> **Distribution:** Under feudalism, land was owned by peasants and food was distributed through a relatively complex system in which peasants had access to a portion of farm yields and also had access to some common lands. Feudal lords took the majority of that which peasants produced, while religious institutions also took significant portions for the benefit of their own class. This was unsuitable to capitalist production processes. As capitalists came to own the means of production, they changed and simplified the ways in which material needs are distributed. The wage system was developed in which capitalists took surplus labor value from workers in the form of profits, and wages were distributed to workers so that they could pay for the basic materials needed for survival. The development of the wage system of capitalism made conditions increasingly suitable for capitalism to become the dominant mode of production in human society.
>
> Note that *ownership of the means of production* is the defining and dominant aspect which determines aspects of organization and distribution. Without taking ownership of the means of production, capitalists would not have been able to develop organization and distribution aspects of the human production process. This makes ownership the essential relationship in determining the relations of production; therefore, a revolutionary class *must* seize the means of production to enact social revolution.

The unified relationship between productive forces and relations of production is inevitable and objective: relations of production are determined by the actual development level of the productive forces in a certain historical period because relations of production are only the social-economic form of the production process, while the productive forces are the material and technical content of that process.

> **Annotation 34**
>
> Just as content determines form, it is also true that matter determines consciousness. This is the Dialectical Materialist conception of the relationship between matter and consciousness. This relationship is explained in detail in *Part 1*, p. 147.
>
> The productive forces include living human beings (workers), their material labor processes, and material elements of nature, as well as material elements such as factories, tools, etc. The productive forces therefore constitute the material basis of humanity's material production processes. Relations of production exist only as social-economic elements, and therefore must be determined by the material basis (i.e., the productive forces). That said, it is possible for the relations of production to impact back on the productive forces, as described in Annotation 34, p. 49.

> **Annotation 34 (continued)**
>
>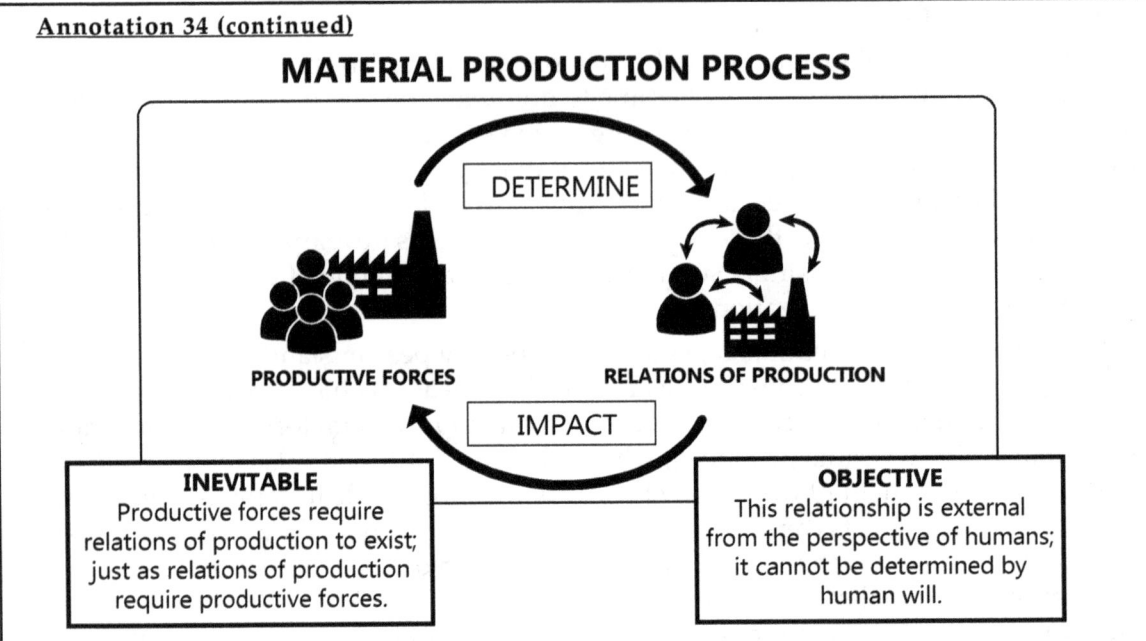
>
> *The relationship between the productive forces and the relations of production is considered to be inevitable and objective.*
>
> The unified relationship between productive forces and relations of production is said to be *inevitable* simply because one cannot exist without the other and both rely upon each other. Productive forces must exist as concrete relationships within human society, and human society must have productive forces to continue existing.
>
> The relationship between productive forces and relations of production is *objective* because it cannot be controlled through the subjective will of any human beings. In other words, no entity can willfully determine the material production process; material production processes arise from objective needs of humanity and are governed by objective laws of Dialectical Materialism and Historical Materialism.

However, relations of production, as the social-economic form of the production process, are always capable of impacting the motion and development of the productive forces. This impact can take place in a positive or negative direction, depending on how suitable or unsuitable the relations of production are with the development level of the productive forces. If these factors are suitable with one another, then it will have a positive effect on development, and vice versa, if they are not suitable, it will have a negative effect.

> **Annotation 35**
>
> While productive forces determine relations of production, it is also possible for relations of production to impact back on productive forces. Whether these impacts are "positive" or "negative" is subjective. From the perspective of the capitalist class, any impacts which strengthen capitalists would be considered "positive." Those same impacts would be considered "negative" from the perspective of the working class. Another way to look at the development of human production processes is in terms

> **Annotation 35 (continued)**
>
> of efficiency and output. Impacts might be seen as "positive" if they increase overall output (though this output may be seen as "negative" from other perspectives; for instance, the development of internal combustion engines was certainly "positive" in terms of total production output potential, but it has had very "negative" impacts in terms of effects on the natural environment of our planet).
>
> When it comes to the historical development of human society, "positive development" generally refers to increases in efficiency, output, and an increase in the capacity for human beings to produce material needs. As productive forces develop, they will eventually become so highly developed that they are no longer suitable with existing relations of production. For example, during the transition between feudalism and capitalism, productive forces advanced rapidly via industrialization and other technological developments. These developments in the productive forces were much more suitable to emerging capitalist relations of production than they were to feudal relations of production. Feudal lords and peasants simply were not able to keep up with the productive output of capitalists and the emerging proletariat. Peasants turned to wage work en masse and as conditions became increasingly unsuitable for feudalism, feudal relations of production were slowly but surely negated by capitalist relations of production. Thus, the development of the productive forces to such a high level that they were no longer compatible with feudal relations of production had given rise to capitalists as the new ruling class of human society.

The relationship between productive forces and relations of production is a unified relationship which includes the ability to generate contradictions.

The relations of production, being the social form of the production process, are relatively stable. This stability allows productive forces to develop over time, which by extension develops the production process.

The more suitable the productive forces and the relations of production are with one another, the higher the chance for the productive forces to develop. However, the development of productive forces will eventually become the root cause for the end of the relative stability of the relations of production.

Once the relations of production become unstable and no longer suitable with the productive forces, the development of productive forces (and, by extension, the productive process) will be disrupted.

The higher the stability and suitability of the relations of production to the productive forces, the more likely the productive forces are to develop, but it is precisely this development of the productive forces which leads to the possibility of disrupting the unity of relations of production that has so far served as the social-economic form for its development.

Once this occurs, social relations transition away from being the suitable and necessary basis for the development of the productive forces and become an impediment to that development. In other words, a contradiction forms between the productive forces and relations of production.

From this contradiction, an objective need to re-establish a unified relationship between the productive forces and relations of production arises.

Annotation 36

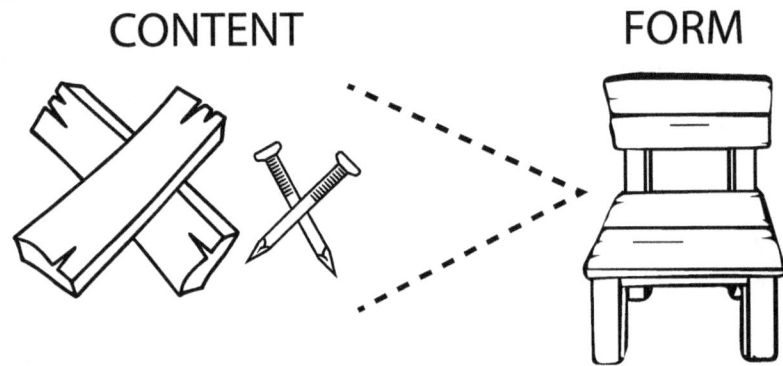

Form refers to a relatively stable set of relationships which exist over time. Content represents the internal composition of those relationships.

A form is a relatively stable set of relationships. Having a stable form allows a subject to develop over time through contradiction with other subjects. As the social form of the material production process, relations of production have an inherent degree of relative stability which means relations of production can develop over time. In general, the development of relations of production is driven by development of the productive forces. Throughout most of the duration of any given era of class society, the productive forces will steadily develop, and this will drive the development of relations of production. Eventually, however, the productive forces will develop beyond suitability with relations of production which leads to a crisis, and this crisis gives way to newly formed relations of production. As Marx explained in *Contribution to the Critique of Political Economy*[20], a society's productive forces will clash with the relations of production. When this happens, the old social structures, which once helped society develop, now hold it back. This conflict leads to a period of social revolution, and the resulting changes in the economic base eventually transform all of society.

Whenever new relations of production are established, there is a period of transition as the old relations of production are disrupted and negated. This is a period of instability for human productive processes as the old and new ruling classes battle for supremacy. Gradually, as the new relations of production become firmly established, productive forces begin to stabilize and resume steady development. Marx defines the development of productive forces in *Capital Volume I*:

> By increase in the productiveness of labor, we mean, generally, an alteration in the labor-process, of such a kind as to shorten the labor-time socially necessary for the production of a commodity, and to endow a given quantity of labor with the power of producing a greater quantity of use-value (or more goods).

In simple terms, "socially necessary labor-time" is the amount of labor and time needed to produce something within the material conditions of a certain human society. The amount of labor-time necessary to make something changes over time. The socially necessary labor-time needed to produce a hammer in an agrarian, pre-industrial society was quite different from that which is needed to produce a hammer in a modern society. This is because the standards and techniques of production have become far more advanced.

---

20 See relevant passage in Annotation 13, p. 20.

<u>**Annotation 36 (continued)**</u>

CYCLE OF DEVELOPMENT OF THE MODE OF PRODUCTION

① SUITABLE

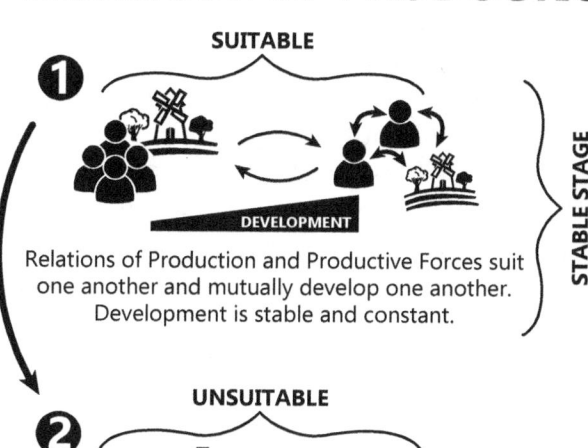

Relations of Production and Productive Forces suit one another and mutually develop one another. Development is stable and constant.

STABLE STAGE OF DEVELOPMENT

② UNSUITABLE

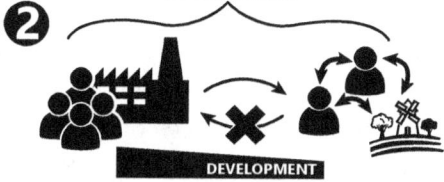

Productive Forces develop so much that they are no longer suitable with Relations of Production. Relations of Production now hinder development of Productive Forces.

③ UNSUITABLE → SUITABLE

Objective need for development leads to new Relations of Production that are suitable with Productive Forces.

UNSTABLE PERIOD OF TRANSITION

① SUITABLE

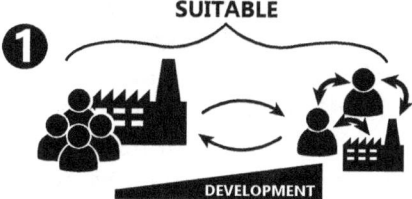

Cycle begins again. Relations of Production and Productive Forces are once again suitable with one another. Development is once again stable and constant.

STABLE STAGE OF DEVELOPMENT

The material production process has followed a pattern of development for as long as there has been class society. When productive forces are compatible with relations of production, development is stable and constant. Whenever productive forces grow to become unsuitable with relations of production, instability leads to an objective need for new relations of production.

Annotation 36 (continued)

Whenever productive forces develop so much that they become unsuitable with relations of production, this unsuitability will cause social disruption and, eventually, social revolution. This stems from what Marx identified as an "objective need" for the relations of production to be suitable with the development level of the productive forces. The productive forces will always eventually develop to such a point that new relations of production will *need* to arise which are more suitable. This, in turn, will allow the productive forces to be fully utilized by human society. Until this need is met, human society will struggle with stagnation and chaos which human society will objectively need to solve before stable progress of development can resume.

At the end of the feudal era, the ruling class of feudal lords restrained the productive forces. Early capitalists were much better suited to the newly emerging industrial processes which were developing. This made capitalists wealthy and powerful and much better suited to take control of the means of production. However, feudal lords tried to resist this change and maintain their grip on power over society. In the end, however, the feudal lords could only slow down the development of new relations of production. Ultimately, the capitalist class successfully waged social revolution which made capitalists the ruling class over a newly developed proletarian working class.

Even in the time of Karl Marx, the productive forces of human society had developed to such an extent that they were no longer compatible with capitalist relations of production. This is because the operation of productive forces is *socialized* while the ownership of the means of production is *private*. This creates an objective need for a social revolution that will lead to relations of production that are suitable to the socialized productive forces, i.e., socialist relations of production. The more the productive forces develop, the greater this objective need becomes, and the more pressing the need for social revolution by the working class.

Capitalists have worked for centuries to prevent the working class from successfully achieving social revolution, but the objective need persists for workers to rise up and develop relations of production that are more compatible with socialized operation of the means of production. This is the historical mission of the working class and the objective basis of Scientific Socialism as a methodology for carrying out this mission.

Transition periods occur at the threshold between one stage of development of relations of production and the next. These transition periods are times of high instability. Such instability was seen during the transition from feudalism to capitalism. As the bourgeoisie emerged and supplanted the feudal class, there was significant disruption in the lives of workers. Wars and social conflict combined with social upheaval leading to significant disruptions in the productive forces. These conditions persisted until the capitalist class was able to stabilize itself as the dominant economic class, at which point productive forces began to develop in terms of efficiency and suitability with the capitalist relations of production.

This stability, however, was short-lived, as mechanized industry enabled productive forces to develop and socialize at a rapid pace. For this reason, the productive forces very quickly became unsuitable with the relations of production under capitalism. As such, the history of the capitalist political economy has been fraught with instability. There have been many factors which have led to this inevitable instability. One such factor is the inherent contradiction stemming from the wage system of capitalism as it

> **Annotation 36 (continued)**
>
> pertains to the price of commodities. As productivity increases and the costs of commodities are driven lower, wages are also driven lower, leading to an inherent increase in instability over time. As Marx explains in *Capital*:
>
>> Hence there is immanent in capital an inclination and constant tendency, to heighten the productiveness of labor, in order to cheapen commodities, and by such cheapening to cheapen the laborer himself.
>
> This is only one of many internal contradictions of capitalism—caused by the unsuitability between the productive forces and relations of production—which lead to instability. Marx, Engels, and other socialists throughout the past two centuries have identified many other such contradictions and sources of instability which drive an objective need for social revolution and new relations of production. Understanding such contradictions and developments of the material production process within human society is what we call the science of Political Economy. As the productive forces continue to develop to higher and higher levels under capitalism it is inevitable that capitalist relations of production will become increasingly unstable and will eventually give rise to new relations of production. It is the duty of communists to apply Scientific Socialism as a political program in order to help bring about the end of capitalism and transition towards the stateless, classless society of communism as efficiently and smoothly as possible.

When analyzing the motion of the dialectical contradiction between the productive forces and the relations of production, Marx pointed out that:

> At a certain stage of development, the material productive forces of society come into conflict with the existing relations of production… with the property relations within the framework of which they have operated hitherto. From forms of development of the productive forces these relations turn into their fetters. Then begins an era of social revolution.

> **Annotation 37**
>
> The quote above comes from the preface to *A Contribution to the Critique of Political Economy*, in which Marx explains how the dialectical relationship between productive forces and the relations of production drive the development of human society. We shall now examine the full passage from which the above quotation is drawn:
>
>> In the social production of their existence, men inevitably enter into definite relations, which are independent of their will, namely relations of production appropriate to a given stage in the development of their material forces of production.
>
> Here, Marx is explaining that humans have an objective need to create social-economic forms – otherwise known as human societies – by working together to produce the material needs of life. The social relations which humans form to do this work are what we call relations of production. Marx describes these relations as "independent" of the "will" of human beings because humans do not have a choice when it comes to establishing these relationships. Rather, these relations are more or less forced upon human beings because they are a prerequisite for humans to survive. Just as the activities which humans undertake to procure food, clothing, and shelter are not taken as

> **Annotation 37 (continued)**

a "choice," entering into relations of production is equally necessary for humans to survive and for human society to continue existing. Furthermore, humans do not get to decide exactly what sorts of relations of production they will enter into. Instead, the relations of production arise from objective material conditions. Of these conditions, the most important factor is the current development level of the productive forces. Marx continues:

> The totality of these relations of production constitutes the economic structure of society, the real foundation, on which arises a legal and political superstructure and to which correspond definite forms of social consciousness.

Here, Marx explains that the relations of production, as the social form of the material production process which humans *must* participate in, serve as the material base for all other aspects of human society. Here, Marx is referring to the material/economic base and superstructure of human society.

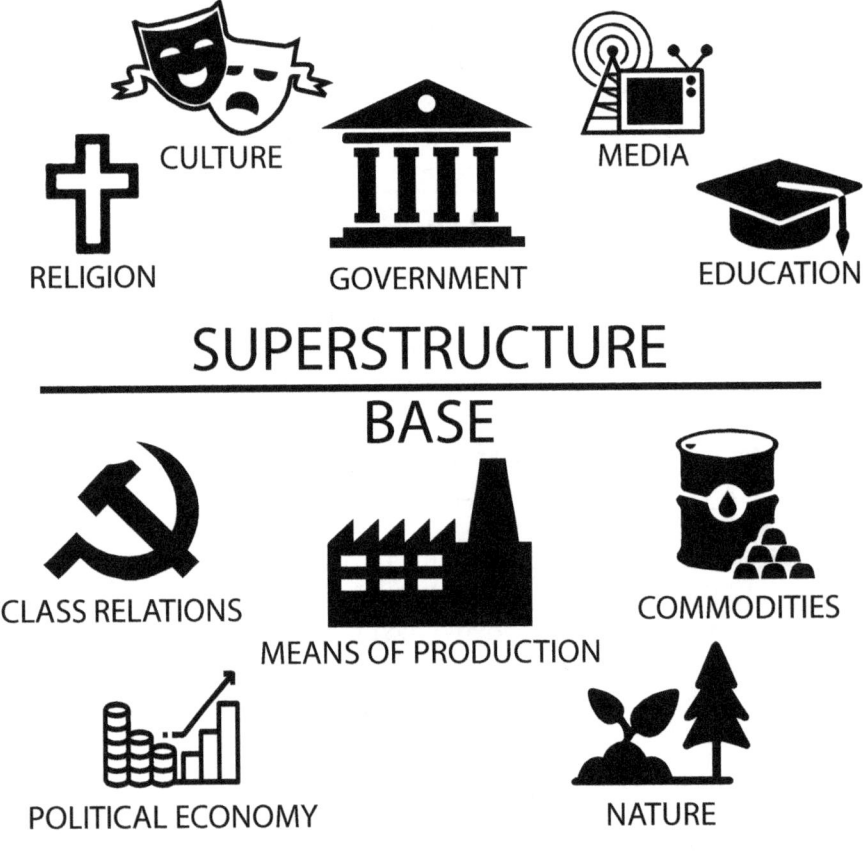

The base of society is the material aspect of a social-economic form. The superstructure is the aspect of social consciousness.

The base of society encompasses those aspects which are related to the material production process.

The superstructure of society includes social consciousness forms and institutions which reflect and protect the base.

.Annotation 37 (continued)

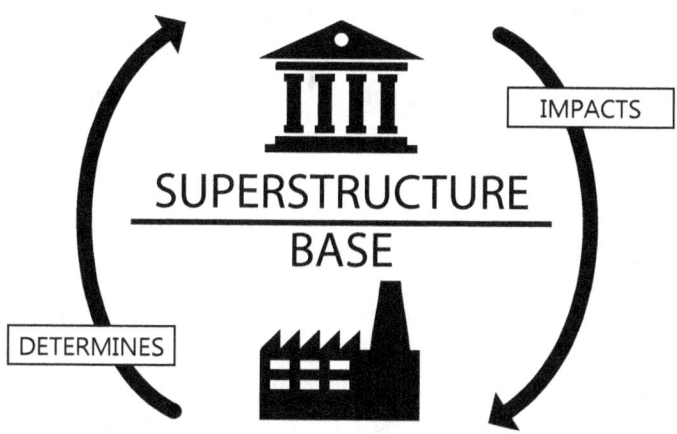

The base, as the material-based aspect of human society, determines the consciousness-based superstructure. The superstructure can also impact back upon the base.

All of the social consciousness forms and institutions which define the superstructure (including the legal system of human society, the state, religious institutions, art, etc.) are determined by the relations of production which serve as the material base of that society. The superstructure can never determine the material base of society but can only impact back upon the base. This reflects the Dialectical Materialist conception of the relationship between material and consciousness (see *Part 1*, p. 88).

As an example, we can look at the way religious institutions existed under feudalism vs. how they manifest under capitalism. Under feudalism, the relations of production determined how religious institutions existed. For example, churches owned lands and held serfs who worked those lands to provide for the material existence of the church in a manner which reflected and was suitable with the feudal relations of production. Another important source of revenue was donation and patronage from wealthy feudal lords. Feudal relations of production determined the very manner in which Christian churches existed in feudal Europe. The church could impact back on the base in various ways (such as collecting tithes from noble lords which impacted their material wealth, power, and status in society), but the church's very existence—the way in which it continued its existence in feudal society—was determined by feudal relations of production.

By contrast, today, religious institutions exist in very different conditions because the material base of capitalism is quite different from the material base of feudalism. Today, churches primarily continue their existence by collecting donations from workers (who earn wages) and from wealthy members of the bourgeoisie (who profit primarily from the labor of workers). This determines the manner in which religious institutions are able to exist under capitalism. Under capitalism, as under feudalism, churches—as superstructural institutions—can only impact back upon the economic base in various ways (such as influencing wealthy capitalists as well as workers).

Annotation 37 (continued)

Examining any superstructural element, institution, or phenomenon will demonstrate that this same relationship is true in all aspects of human society. The material base determines the way in which superstructural elements exist, while those superstructural elements can impact back upon the material base. As Marx continues:

> The mode of production of material life conditions the general process of social, political and intellectual life. It is not the consciousness of men that determines their existence, but their social existence that determines their consciousness.

This is crucial for understanding the relationships which define and propel human society forward. Human beings do not consciously decide their social existence, nor the objective laws which govern the world. Under feudalism, neither peasants nor feudal lords nor even the most powerful kings willfully and consciously determined the relations of production. Rather, these relations of production came about through material processes and developments which (as Marx defined above) were separate from human consciousness and will. Conversely, human consciousness is heavily conditioned and determined by the material base of society, i.e. the relations and mode of production. Subjective human will does have a role to play in the history-making project, however. For instance, social revolution—brought about through the development of class consciousness—is a prerequisite for the advancement of humanity from one stage of development of the mode of production to the next.

Human philosophy which develops in any given era of class society is heavily conditioned and determined by the material base of that society. This is why Marx and Engels wrote that any investigation into human philosophy must take into consideration the material base (the relations and mode of production) of the society in which they arose (see Annotation 37, p. 60).

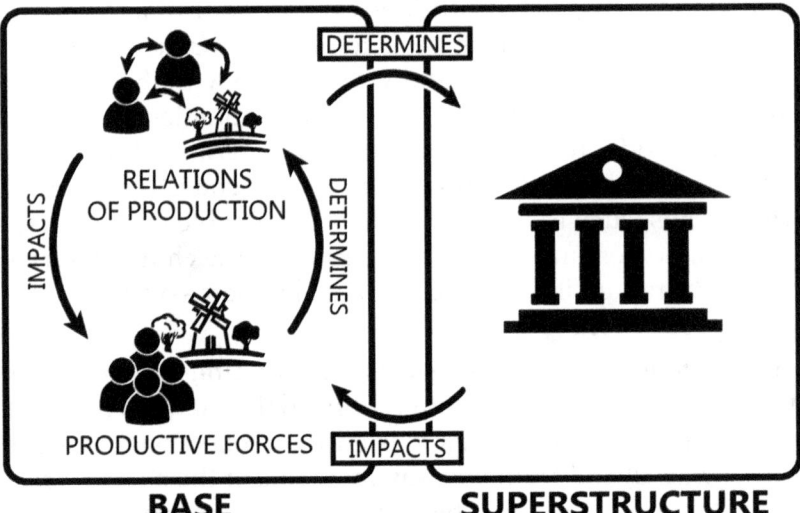

Human society is defined by a relationship between the base and superstructure. The base is largely defined by the material production process, which describes a dialectical relationship between the productive forces and the relations of production.

The Role of Material Production ☭ 59

> **Annotation 37 (continued)**
>
> In *Anti-Düring*, Engels explains the critical importance of the development of productive forces in the historical advancement of human society:
>
>> The materialist conception of history starts from the principle that production [i.e., productive forces], and with it the exchange of the products of production [i.e., relations of production], is the basis of every social order [i.e., superstructural institutions]; that in every society that has appeared in history, the distribution of wealth and with it the division of society into classes or estates is determined by what is produced [material needs], how it is produced [productive forces], and how the products are exchanged [relations of production]. From this point of view, the final causes of all social changes and political revolutions are to be sought, not in the brains of men, not in men's better insight into eternal truth and justice, but in changes in the modes of production and exchange.
>
> Understanding the relationship between the material base and superstructure is key to understanding Social Formation Theory, which is the core of Historical Materialism. According to this theory, productive forces develop until they are no longer suitable with existing relations of production. This eventually leads to a fundamental change in the relations of production and the development of a new social-economic formation with new relations of production and a new mode of production, and this, in turn, leads to changes in the superstructure of society. This pattern of development of human society reflects the Law of Suitability Between the Relations of Production and the Productive Forces (see Annotation 33, p. 48) as well as the Law of the Base Determining the Superstructure of Society (see Annotation 50, p. 90). Social Formation Theory is discussed more in Chapter 4, p. 159.
>
> As an example, productive forces developed under feudalism over the course of many centuries. For most of this time, productive forces were suitable to the prevailing feudal relations of production. Eventually, however, new production technology and many other developments related to the productive forces led to a situation in which productive forces were no longer compatible with the feudal relations of production. This led to a social revolution in which the capitalist class—a newly emerged class which dominated the newly predominant productive forces which had developed under and within feudalism—took primacy and the older ruling classes of feudal lords and monarchs lost their positions as the ruling class, eventually dwindling away into irrelevancy. Meanwhile, the oppressed class of peasants transitioned into a new proletariat or working class, and the wage system of capitalism developed as a new mode of production based on these newly developed productive forces and their corresponding (suitable) relations of production. This change in the material base of society—the transition from a feudal material base to a capitalist material base—led to massive changes to the superstructure of society, so that nearly all superstructure elements of society today are much different from how they manifested under feudalism. The church, political systems, the arts, and prevailing human philosophies have all changed drastically because they are now determined by a capitalist mode of production instead of feudalism. This is how Historical Materialism explains the advance of human society over time. Developments in productive forces lead to shifts in relations of production, and changes in relations of production lead to the development of new forms of class society which lead to changes in the superstructure of human society.

Annotation 37 (continued)

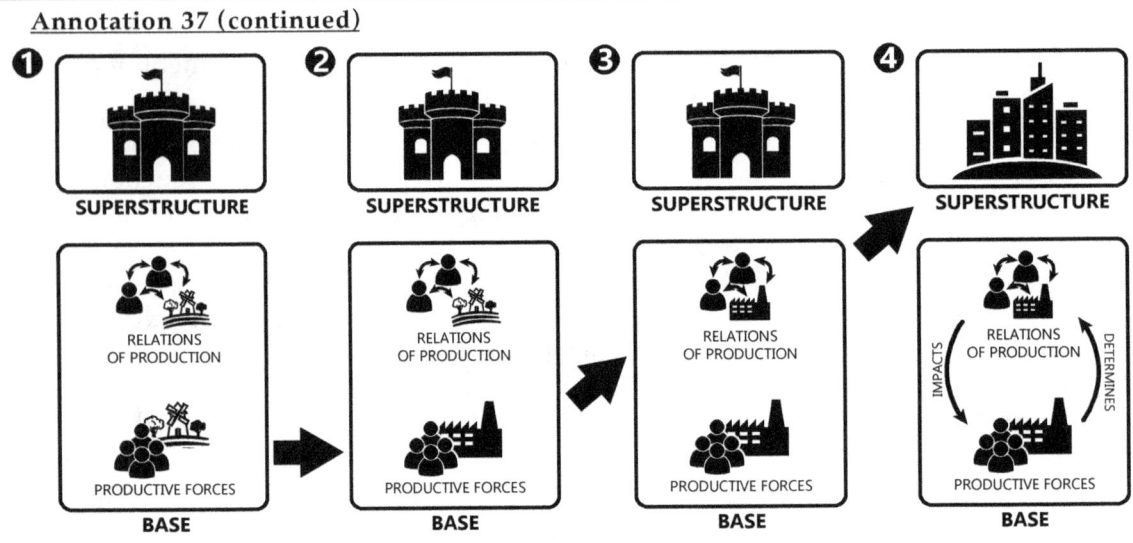

Over time, productive forces develop continuously until they are no longer suitable with relations of production. Eventually, the relations of production must develop into a new form which is suitable with productive forces. These changes in the base of society will, in turn, lead to deep changes to the superstructure of society.

In the preface to *A Contribution to the Critique of Political Economy*, Marx and Engels outline an objective basis for the study of human history:

> In studying such transformations it is always necessary to distinguish between the material transformation of the economic conditions of production, which can be determined with the precision of natural science, and the legal, political, religious, artistic or philosophic – in short, ideological forms in which men become conscious of this conflict and fight it out.

This groundbreaking understanding of human history—which is the material basis of Historical Materialism—transforms the study of history into a scientific field by recognizing the progression of human society through various stages of class society as material processes which have objective and even predictable aspects.

Marx goes on to describe how previous generations of historians failed to put the study of history on a scientific basis due to errors of idealism:

> Just as one does not judge an individual by what he thinks about himself, so one cannot judge such a period of transformation by its consciousness, but, on the contrary, this consciousness must be explained from the contradictions of material life, from the conflict existing between the social forces of production and the relations of production.

Previous generations of historians who believed that history was primarily a study of human consciousness fundamentally understood the nature of the forces which shape and advance human society. By putting emphasis and primacy on the ideas and philosophies of the ruling class, previous historians could have no hope of understanding the history of human development on a scientific basis. Only by studying the underlying material basis of society and its development—through the development of productive forces—can we see history as a phenomenon which has objective and

> **Annotation 37 (continued)**
>
> predictable properties. In other words, the application of the principles and objective laws of Dialectical Materialism—with its understanding of the relationship between the material and consciousness—is what makes Historical Materialism a scientific understanding of history. Historical Materialism helps us to understand that there are underlying material forces (i.e., the development of forces of production and, by extension, relations of production) which lead to superstructural elements of human society. As Marx and Engels go on to explain:
>
>> No social order is ever destroyed before all the productive forces for which it is sufficient have been developed, and new superior relations of production never replace older ones before the material conditions for their existence have matured within the framework of the old society.
>
> In other words, development in human society does not result from development in human consciousness. Superstructural institutions and ideologies such as philosophies, art, and religion do not determine the progress of human society from one mode of production to the next. They *can* impact back on the material base of society. In particular, class consciousness and social revolution are important factors in the advancement of class society.
>
> In the end, the determining factor of human development is the material base. Human society will never advance from one mode of production to the next until the material conditions have been established. These material conditions are always rooted in the development of the productive forces and resulting changes in the relations of production. So long as the productive forces remain suitable and harmonious with the prevailing relations of production, the existing mode of production will continue to dominate human society. However, as soon as productive forces are no longer compatible with the predominant relations of production, new relations will begin to develop which will lead to an advancement to a new mode of production.
>
> No development in human consciousness alone could ever have led to the transition from feudalism to capitalism. No great thinker, philosopher, artist, nor religious figure could have fundamentally shifted the mode of production from feudal relations of production to capitalist relations of production. Only changes to the material base, i.e., developments in productive forces, could lead from one mode of production to the next. Understanding the dynamics between productive forces and the mode of production (as well as the dialectical relationship between the material base of society and the superstructure of society) is what allows Historical Materialism to place the study of human history on an objective, scientific basis. Engels described the objective basis of the development of human society in *Socialism: Utopian and Scientific*:
>
>> ...conflict between productive forces and modes of production is not a conflict engendered in the mind of man, like that between original sin and divine justice. It exists, in fact, objectively, outside us, independently of the will and actions even of the men that have brought it on.

It is thanks to social revolutions that the old relations of production of societies have been replaced by new relations of production which are more suitable to the development needs of the developed productive forces.

Social revolutions thus give way to new forms of relations of production, which in turn allow for the development of productive forces to continue.

> **Annotation 38**
>
> In the framework of Historical Materialism, the term *social revolution* is specifically defined as a social process which culminates in relations of production undergoing an essential change such that a new mode of production develops. Social revolutions are always preceded by the development of productive forces to such a high degree that they are no longer suitable with established relations of production. The newly established relations of production which result from a social revolution must invariably be more suitable to the *development needs* of the newly developed productive forces.
>
> Development needs are the prerequisite conditions which are necessary to stabilize productive forces and establish a new mode of production which can properly accommodate productive forces in the newly developed higher form.
>
> Social revolution is a broad phenomenon in human society which takes place across the span of global human society, though some regions and nations may lag behind and participate more slowly than others in these processes.
>
> For example: feudalism did not transition to capitalism all at once. Instead, the transition was gradual and took place more quickly in some locations than in others. In some nations, like England and the USA, capitalism was established relatively early and the capitalist mode of production set in quickly, whereas in other nations, like Russia and Vietnam, feudal relations of production persisted for much longer. However, once a new mode of production develops, it will eventually transform all of human society. This is partly because the new society's productive forces will exist at such a higher state that the older mode of production cannot hope to compete. Social revolution involves human consciousness and will, as human beings must participate in social activity to bring about revolutionary change in society. However, this conscious activity is determined by the material conditions brought about by the development of productive forces and can never precede those material conditions.
>
>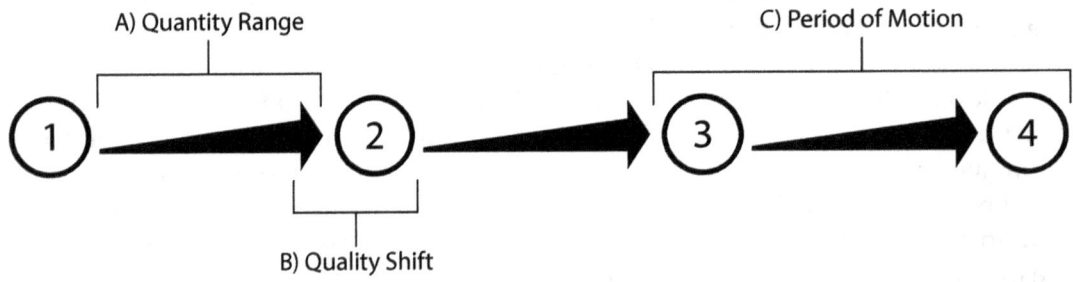
>
> *This diagram shows the anatomy of dialectical development. Over time, changes in quantity lead to shifts in quality. This process is explained in detail in* **Part 1** *starting on p. 163.*
>
> Note that new relations of production initially arise within the older, pre-existing mode of production. Capitalist relations of production first emerged within the feudal mode of production, and for some time capitalist relations of production existed simultaneously with feudal relations of production until a quality shift occurred in the form of social revolution which allowed the capitalist class to take power as the new ruling class, after which the feudal classes gradually transitioned out of power over

> **Annotation 38 (continued)**
>
> human society. This is in accordance with the objective laws and properties of development as described within the framework of Materialist Dialectics: productive forces and new relations of production develop gradually, over time, through a series of quantity shifts, until there is a quality shift (i.e., social revolution) which gives way to the newer, higher mode of production.
>
> The productive forces will continue to develop after a social revolution takes place and a new mode of production is established. Indeed, since the new mode of production will be more suitable with the more developed productive forces, development can occur much more rapidly as soon as the older, obsolete mode of production has given way to the new mode of production.
>
> In *Socialism: Utopian and Scientific*, Engels describes how this process of social revolution took place within the feudal mode of production to give way to the capitalist mode of production. Engels explains that capitalist relations of production initially arose within the feudal mode of production, and development of production forces under these newly developed relations of production soon overpowered feudal relations of production. This led to social revolution which gave the capitalist class primacy over older feudal powers, and once the capitalist class became the ruling class the productive forces could develop more freely and efficiently since they were no longer restrained and hindered by the obsolete feudal mode of production:
>
>> The mode of production peculiar to the bourgeoisie, known, since Marx, as the capitalist mode of production, was incompatible with the feudal system, with the privileges it conferred upon individuals, entire social ranks and local corporations, as well as with the hereditary ties of subordination which constituted the framework of its social organization. The bourgeoisie broke up the feudal system and built upon its ruins the capitalist order of society, the kingdom of free competition, of personal liberty, of the equality, before the law, of all commodity owners, of all the rest of the capitalist blessings. Thenceforward, the capitalist mode of production could develop in freedom.

The relationship between productive forces and relations of production constitute a dialectical contradiction which poses material and technological content against the social-economic form of the production process.

> **Annotation 39**
>
> The universal category pair of content and form is described in Annotation 30 of this book as well as on p. 147 of *Part 1*.
>
> The productive forces are considered to be the content of the material base of human society while the relations of production are the stable social-economic form which the content of productive forces take. Together, this content and form compose the mode of production which exists as the material base of human society in any given period of class society.
>
> This may, at first, seem confusing. However, things become more clear when we remember that within the Dialectical Materialist framework, all things, phenomena,

> **Annotation 39 (continued)**
>
> and ideas are defined by internal and external relationships with one another. These relationships are dialectical in nature, meaning that these relationships lead to change and development within and/or between the related subjects. Thus, we can define all of the concepts mentioned above in terms of Materialist Dialectics:
>
> The social-economic form of humanity simply refers to society; that is to say, all the relationships which human beings have with one another relating to the economic base and social superstructure of society within a given period of history.
>
> A social-economic form can be expressed primarily as a dialectical relationship between the material base and the superstructure. In this relationship, the material base determines the superstructure while the Superstructure can impact back on the material base. This is in line with the Dialectical Materialist understanding of the relationship between the material and human consciousness (see *Part 1*, p. 88).
>
> The material base of human society in a given historical period consists of a dialectical relationship between the productive forces (the content of the material base) and the relations of production (the form of the material base). In this relationship, the content determines the way in which the material base of human society exists, and the form can impact back upon the content.
>
> Now, let's examine the structure of both feudalism and capitalism with these Materialist Dialectical definitions in mind.
>
> **SOCIAL STRUCTURE OF FEUDALISM**   **SOCIAL STRUCTURE OF CAPITALISM**
>
>
>
> **SUPERSTRUCTURE**   **SUPERSTRUCTURE**
>
>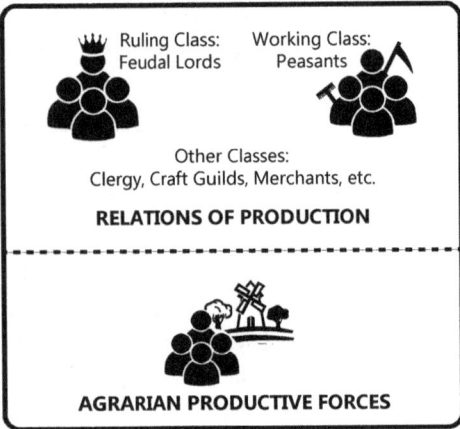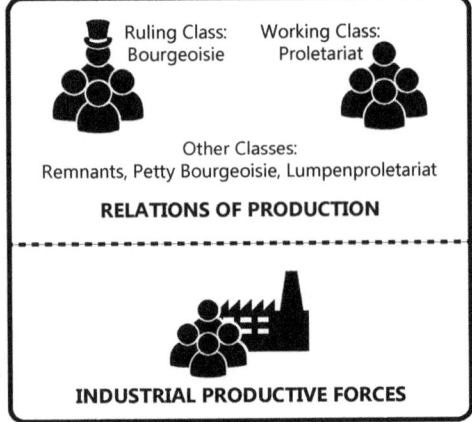
>
> **BASE**   **BASE**
>
> *Feudal society has complex social relations with various classes competing for benefits from the means of production. Capitalism has a simpler class structure with the vast majority of humans relegated to the proletarian working class.*

Annotation 39 (continued)

Content and Form of Feudal Society

Feudalism is a social-economic form of human society which consists of feudal productive forces as content and feudal relations of production as form. Specifically, the feudal productive forces include agricultural resources and technologies including farmland, crops, farm animals, and simple agricultural equipment like plows, hand tools, and so on. Feudal productive forces also include human labor and the labor of beasts of burden. Together, these productive forces are the content of the material base of feudal society.

Feudal relations of production are the social form of the material production process in the material base of feudal society. These relations include several classes, including ruling classes which include nobles, monarchs, and religious clergy, as well as various laboring classes, which predominantly include peasants as well as other laboring classes such as craft guildsmen, merchants, and so on. The relations of production consist of the relationships between all these classes as well as relationships between those classes and other productive forces such as farmland, tools, etc. Feudal relations of production are thus a complex configuration in which nobles own farmlands, peasants work the farmlands, and other classes relate to the productive forces and with each other in various ways.

The relationship between the content (productive forces) and the form (relations of production) of feudal society is dialectical. This means that the productive forces and relations of production lead to changes and development in one another and, by extension, changes and development in the whole of the material base of feudal society. Changes in the material base also lead to changes in the superstructure of society.

Eventually, feudal productive forces developed to such a degree that they were no longer compatible with feudal relations of production. Elements of the merchant and noble classes developed factories and machinery which enabled productive forces to develop to such a high degree that they were no longer compatible with feudal relations of production. This eventually led to social revolution (a quality shift) which gave the newly formed bourgeois class rulership over society. This was the dawn of the capitalist mode of production.

Content and Form of Capitalist Society

Capitalism is a social-economic form of human society which consists of capitalist productive forces as content and capitalist relations of production as form.

Specifically, capitalist productive forces include industrialized resources and technologies including factories and socialized production processes and technologies that include complex machinery, computers and information systems, and various other highly developed production technologies, together with natural resources which are predominantly owned by the capitalist class. Together, these productive forces compose the content of the material base of capitalist society.

Capitalist class structure/relations of production are much more simple than feudal class structure/relations of production. There are two essential classes under capitalism: the ruling capitalist class, which owns nearly all of the means of production such as factories, equipment, and technologies, as well as the proletariat (also known as the working class), which operates the means of production.

> **Annotation 39 (continued)**
>
> The content (productive forces) and form (relations of production) of capitalism have exist in dialectical unity with one another. This relationship defines and develops the material base of society which, in turn, drives the development of the superstructure. This is the basis of Social Formation Theory which is discussed more in Annotation 98, p. 176.
>
> The productive forces of capitalist society have already developed to such a high degree that they are no longer suitable with the capitalist relations of production. This will inevitably lead to social revolution which will allow the proletariat to become the ruling class. Since the proletariat includes the vast majority of human beings on Earth, this will bring about the end of class society and will usher in a new era: a stateless, classless society called communism.

The motion of this contradiction between productive forces and relations of production is a process that passes back and forth between suitability and opposition, in accordance with the Law of Suitability, which is a manifestation of the universal Law of Unification and Contradiction Between Opposites. The contradiction between productive forces and relations of production also follows the Law of Transformation Between Quantity and Quality as well as the Law of Negation of Negation.

> **Annotation 40**
>
> In Materialist Dialectics, motion simply refers to change and development, and all motion/change/development arises from relationships between things, phenomena, and ideas (see *Part 1*, p. 119).
>
> ### The Three Universal Laws of Materialist Dialectics
>
> Materialist Dialectics contains three universal laws which describe the development of all things, phenomena, and ideas. These laws are:
>
> 1. The Law of Transformation Between Quantity and Quality.
> 2. The Law of Unification and Contradiction Between Opposites.
> 3. The Law of Negation of Negation.
>
> These laws are further defined in Appendix C of *Part 1* on p. 248. The Law of Suitability Between the Relations of Production and the Productive Forces is a manifestation of these laws in human society.
>
> ### The Law of Suitability Between Relations of Production and Productive Forces
>
> The Law of Suitability Between Realtions of Production and Productive Forces (also known as the Law of Suitability) states that:
>
> "The development level of productive forces must suit the development level of the relations of production."
>
> Whenever productive forces develop to such a degree that they are no longer suitable with the relations of production, this creates an objective need for the relations of production to change. Until relations of production develop to a more suitable form, the material production processes will be inefficient and many problems will arise.

Annotation 40 (continued)

Engels described how the Law of Suitability led to the rise of capitalist productive forces within feudal society in *Socialism: Utopian and Scientific*:

> Before capitalist production — i.e., in the Middle Ages — the system of petty industry obtained generally, based upon the private property of the laborers in their means of production; in the country, the agriculture of the small peasant, freeman, or serf; in the towns, the handicrafts organized in guilds. The instruments of labor — land, agricultural implements, the workshop, the tool — were the instruments of labor of single individuals, adapted for the use of one worker, and, therefore, of necessity, small, dwarfish, circumscribed. But, for this very reason, they belonged as a rule to the producer himself. To concentrate these scattered, limited means of production, to enlarge them, to turn them into the powerful levers of production of the present day — this was precisely the historic role of capitalist production and of its upholder, the bourgeoisie. In the fourth section of Capital, Marx has explained in detail how since the 15th century this has been historically worked out through the three phases of simple co-operation, manufacture, and modern industry. But the bourgeoisie, as is shown there, could not transform these puny means of production into mighty productive forces without transforming them, at the same time, from means of production of the individual into social means of production only workable by a collectivity of men. The spinning wheel, the handloom, the blacksmith's hammer, were replaced by the spinning-machine, the power-loom, the steam-hammer; the individual workshop, by the factory implying the co-operation of hundreds and thousands of workmen. In like manner, production itself changed from a series of individual into a series of social acts, and the production from individual to social products.

Productive forces were developed to such a high degree that they became hopelessly unsuitable to the feudal relations of production. This led to an objective need for social revolution, so that relations of production could give way to a new capitalist mode of production.

As Engels writes:

> But with the extension of the production of commodities, and especially with the introduction of the capitalist mode of production, the laws of commodity-production, hitherto latent, came into action more openly and with greater force. The old bonds were loosened, the old exclusive limits broken through, the producers were more and more turned into independent, isolated producers of commodities... It was the increasing organization of production, upon a social basis, in every individual productive establishment. By this, the old, peaceful, stable condition of things was ended. Wherever this organization of production was introduced into a branch of industry, it brooked no other method of production by its side. The field of labor became a battle-ground. The great geographical discoveries, and the colonization following them, multiplied markets and quickened the transformation of handicraft into manufacture. The war did not simply break out between the individual producers of particular localities. The local struggles begat, in their turn, national conflicts, the commercial wars of the 17th and 18th centuries.

Annotation 40 (continued)

Once capitalist relations of production and capitalist productive forces overtook the material base of human society, older feudal relations of production simply could not keep up. Thus, the less suitable form of Feudal Society weakened and eventually collapsed, leading to our current era of capitalism.

This historical example illustrates the Law of Suitability in action: once productive forces became so developed that they were no longer suitable with Feudal relations of production, it necessitated the development of relations of production which were suitable with the newly developed productive forces, which were labelled "capitalist." This led to social revolution which established a new Mode of Production in which these capitalist productive forces and capitalist relations of production were suitable with one another in accordance with the Law of Suitability.

The Law of Suitability manifests the Law of Unification and Contradiction Between Opposites of Materialist Dialectics.

According to V. I. Lenin's *Summary of Dialectics*, the Universal Law of Unification and Contradiction Between Opposites states that:

> The fundamental, originating, and universal driving force of all motion and development processes is the inherent and objective contradiction which exists in all things, phenomena, and ideas.

Whenever two subjects exist in a dialectical relationship with one another, they are said to be in unity because they define one another, and they are said to be in contradiction because they develop one another.

The Law of Suitability Between Relations of Production and Productive Forces merely describes how the Law of Unification and Contradiction applies to the content (the productive forces) and social form (relations of production) of the material base of human society.

Specifically, the dialectical relationship between productive forces and relations of production drives the development of the material production process which is defined by this relationship.

The Law of Suitability manifests the Law of Transformation Between Quantity and Quality of Materialist Dialectics.

The Law of Transformation Between Quantity and Quality is defined by Friedrich Engels in *Dialectics of Nature* in the following terms:

> In nature, in a manner exactly fixed for each individual case, qualitative changes can only occur by the quantitative addition or subtraction of matter or motion.

When productive forces and relations of production are suitable with one another, it allows for the efficient development of the relations of production to occur. Eventually, this development rises to such a quantity that productive forces are no longer compatible with existing relations of production. This, in turn, leads to a quality shift as new relations of production arise and replace (or negate) the older, less suitable relations of production.

In this manner, the dialectical relationship between productive forces and relations of production adheres to the Law of Transformation Between Quantity and Quality.

> **The Law of Suitability manifests the Law of Negation of Negation of Materialist Dialectics.**
>
> The Law of Negation of Negation is defined by Engels in *Anti-Dühring* as follows:
>
>> The true, natural, historical, and dialectical negation is (formally) the moving source of all development – the division into opposites, their struggle and resolution, and what is more, on the basis of experience gained, the original point is achieved again (partly in history, fully in thought), but at a higher stage.
>
> Put more simply, this law states that change and development always takes place, eventually, in the form of negation as one contradicting subject overtakes another. The dialectical relationship between productive forces and relations of production clearly adheres to this universal law since the quality shift which occurs when one mode of relation overtakes another is an act of negation. For example, capitalism arose to contradict feudalism and, eventually, negated feudalism to become the predominant mode of production.
>
> Thus, we can see that the Law of Suitability Between Relations of Production and Productive Forces is merely a manifestation of the Three Universal Laws of Materialist Dialectics as they pertain to the development of human society.

By nature, the contradiction between productive forces and relations of production (which defines the material production process) generally drives development in a gradual and sequential manner. It is also possible, however, for sudden rapid developments to occur, or for sequential steps to be bypassed.

> **Annotation 41**
>
> Development of productive forces and relations of production tends to be gradual and sequential in accordance with the universal laws of Materialist Dialectics.
>
> Development is typically gradual in accordance with the Law of Transformation Between Quantity and Quality. In most instances, productive forces are developed relatively slowly in terms of quantity until a quality shift occurs after some threshold has been surpassed. This pattern of development is discussed more in *Part 1*, p. 163.
>
> Development is typically sequential simply because the conditions to bypass a stage of development are rare, and development of human society tends to follow the development of productive forces which themselves rely on gradual and sequential development of science, technology, organizational systems, etc. Marx describes this sequential pattern of development in *A Contribution to the Critique of Political Economy*:
>
>> No social order is ever destroyed before all the productive forces for which it is sufficient have been developed, and new superior relations of production never replace older ones before the material conditions for their existence have matured within the framework of the old society.
>>
>> Mankind thus inevitably sets itself only such tasks as it is able to solve, since closer examination will always show that the problem itself arises only when the material conditions for its solution are already present or at least in the course of formation.
>
> As an example, it would be absurd to imagine that agrarian medieval Europeans under the feudal mode of production might have developed nuclear power plants.

Annotation 41 (continued)

This is because, as Marx described, feudal relations of production and productive forces were not nearly sufficient to produce such technology. Human beings living in the feudal era did not even ponder such matters as nuclear power plants because the problems of nuclear power production had not even presented themselves yet. In that era, the material conditions for the existence of nuclear power plants had not yet developed. A great many intervening steps and developments, including the development of capitalist relations of production and productive forces, had to occur before human beings could begin grappling with the problem of nuclear power generation.

That said, it is possible—and there are historical examples of—bypassing stages of development both in terms of productive forces and relations of production. There were some nations where productive forces rapidly advanced and bypassed stages of development through interaction with foreign cultures. Vietnam, for example, went directly from simple agrarian practices of the feudal era all the way through the era of French colonization and then suddenly and rapidly developed industrialized agricultural processes with the assistance of the Soviet Union starting from the revolutionary era of the 1950s and especially after the end of the revolutionary war in 1975. This allowed Vietnamese farmers to bypass many stages of technological development of productive forces.

In terms of relations of production, Vietnam's society is currently attempting to bypass the capitalist mode of production altogether. That is to say, the Vietnamese people and government are attempting to build towards socialism and eventually communism without ever giving the capitalist class control over the Vietnamese social-economic formation. This attempt at building socialism while bypassing capitalism has gone through several stages already:

- **The Revolutionary Economy (1945-1975):** During which wars were fought against fascist Japan, colonial France, and the imperialist United States to free the Vietnamese people from foreign oppression and the Communist Party of Vietnam was developed into the leading force of social revolution in Vietnam.

- **The Subsidizing Economy (1975-1986):** This was an attempt to move fully and immediately into communist relations of production. These efforts ultimately proved to be too aggressive and unrealistic, as productive forces could not be developed rapidly enough for suitable relations of production to develop.

- **The Socialism-Oriented Market Economy Era (1986-present):** This is the current era of Vietnamese social revolution, during which time market reforms have been implemented in an attempt to develop productive forces without allowing capitalists to take control of the state and economy. The first era of this economy was known as "Đổi Mới," which is Vietnamese for "Renovation." The focus and priority of this era has been the transformation of Vietnam into a medium-income nation with well-developed industrial productive forces. The Đổi Mới era has just successfully come to an end and Vietnam is now entering into the "Rising Nation" era, with the goal of becoming a medium-high-income nation by 2030 and a high-income nation which can implement full socialism by 2045. These efforts and struggles are described in detail by Vietnamese experts using Historical Materialist analysis in Appendix G, p. 254.

> **Annotation 41 (continued)**
>
> In a speech called "Building a People of Socialism," Ho Chi Minh explained that one of the chief goals of Vietnamese social revolution is to build a socialist people with socialist values and manners:
>
>> We won against colonialism and feudalism. Our main mission now is to win against backwardness and poverty, to build socialism, and to make our people live in happiness. That mission is great but also very difficult. But if our Party and our entire people are determined, we will definitely achieve it.
>>
>> In order to build socialism, first and foremost, we need to have socialist people.
>
> In the current era, the people, government, and Communist Party of Vietnam have the ambition to build socialist relations of production over the coming decades while bypassing the domination of Vietnamese society by the capitalist class.
>
> Hastening the development of socialism and the bypassing or termination of capitalist class society is the primary task of Scientific Socialism, which is Part 4 of the volume this text is taken from, and which we hope to translate in the future. The concept of "bypassing" stages of development is discussed more in Annotation 23, p. 34. The role of social consciousness in bringing about social revolution is discussed more in Annotation 67 on p. 115.

The contradiction between the productive forces and the relations of production are the basis for *The Law of Suitability Between the Relations of Production and the Development of the Productive Forces* which states that:

"The development level of productive forces must suit the development level of the relations of production."

This law is the most essential driving force for the movement and development of the mode of production of the material base of human society and, by extension, of the development of human society in its entirety.

> **Annotation 42**
>
> **Summary of Chapter 1**
>
> Dialectical Materialism is a system of philosophy and methodology which asserts that the material determines consciousness while consciousness can impact back upon the material. Materialist Dialectics is a methodology derived from Dialectical Materialism which holds that all things, phenomena, and ideas are constantly changing and developing at all times, and that this change and development is driven by relationships. Materialist Dialectics also holds that all things, phenomena, and ideas are defined by those same relationships.
>
> Human class society in any given stage of development is defined by the dialectical relationship between the material base and the superstructure. This dialectical relationship between the base and superstructure drives the development of human society. Within this development process, the base determines the superstructure while the superstructure is able to impact back on the base. This is in accordance with the Dialectical Materialist understanding of the relationship between the material and conscious activity.
>
> The material base of society is itself defined by the dialectical relationship between

Annotation 42 (continued)

productive forces (the content of the material base) and relationships of production (the social form of the material base). In this relationship, the productive forces determine the relations of production while the relations of production can only impact back on the productive forces. This is in accordance with the properties of the universal category pair of content and form as defined in the framework of Materialist Dialectics (see *Part 1*, p. 147).

The quantity of productive forces develops over time through various innovations in science, technology, organizational systems, etc.

Eventually, productive forces will develop to such an extent that they are no longer suitable with relations of production. At this point, the relations of production will have undergone a quality shift which will eventually lead to relations of production and, by extension, a change in the mode of production and the material base of society. This is in accordance with the Law of Transformation Between Quantity and Quality within the Materialist Dialectical framework (see *Part 1*, p. 163).

The quality shift from one mode of production to the next is carried out through social revolution, which is the process by which one or more ruling classes emerge to dominate the material base. Once the social revolution is complete, human society will enter a new stage of development and the cycle will restart in terms of development of the mode of production which drives the advancement of human society. This process is defined by the Law of Suitability Between Relations of Production and Productive Forces and is also governed by the three universal laws of Materialist Dialectics (see Annotation 40, p. 66).

From all of this we can conclude that the development of all of human society is driven by the development of productive forces. Productive forces determine the relations of production, which determine the mode of production, which determine the material base of human society, which determines the superstructure of human society. Understanding that the productive forces are the driving force of development of human society is what allows us to view history as an objective and somewhat predictable process. This puts the study of human history and society on a scientific basis. This scientific analysis of humanity is the basis of social formation theory, which is the core of Historical Materialism.

In the next section we will examine the material base and superstructure in more detail in order to better understand how the dialectical relationship between the two drives the development of human society.

CHAPTER 2

DIALECTICS OF THE BASE AND SUPERSTRUCTURE

I. DEFINITIONS OF THE BASE AND THE SUPERSTRUCTURE

1. Definition of the base

The concept of the base or material base or economic base refers to the totality of relations of production that constitute the economic structure of the society.

> **Annotation 43**
>
>
>
> *Karl Marx first accurately described the relationship between base and superstructure in* Capital.
>
> As discussed more fully in Annotation 11, p. 16, the word "economy" refers to social activities which aim to solve the following questions:
>
> 1. What to produce?
> 2. How to produce?
> 3. Produce for whom?
>
> The economic base, therefore, encompasses all the aspects of society which relate to humanity's efforts to solve these questions through material production processes. In accordance with the Materialist Dialectical Principle of General Relations (which holds that all things, phenomena, and ideas are defined by internal and external relationships), we can define the material base by the following relationships:
>
> - An internal relationship between productive forces and relations of production.
> - An external relationship with the superstructure of society.
>
> The internal and external relations described above drive change and development of human society in accordance with the universal laws and principles of Materialist Dialectics (see *Part 1*, p. 107). This is the basis of Social Formation Theory (see p. 159).

The base of a society, in all its motion, is made up of:
- The dominant relations of production
- The remnant relations of production
- The new relations of production

<u>Annotation 44</u>

These descriptions of different relations of production which can exist in human society are all relative to the predominant relations of production of the currently existing mode of production.

Dominant relations of production include the relations of production which are currently the most commonly found in the current form of a given society. The class or classes which have control over the dominant relations of production are the ruling class(es).

Remnant relations of production include relations of production which are held over from a previous form of society.

New relations of production include relations of production which are newly emerging and, given enough development, will give way to a new mode of production and a new stage of development for human society.

STRUCTURE OF RELATIONS OF PRODUCTION UNDER FEUDALISM

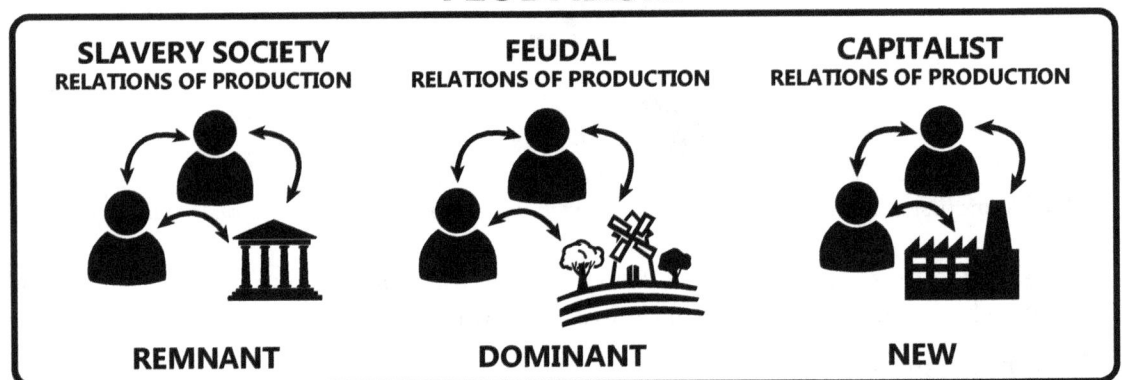

Although the feudal relations of production were dominant throughout the feudal era, remnant productions from the preceding mode of production continued existing in remnant form as capitalist relations of production were also beginning to develop.

As an example: during the feudal era, the dominant relations of production were feudal relations of production, which revolved around ownership of land by noble lords, working of the land by peasants, development of goods by craft guildsmen, trade by merchants, etc. During this era, remnant relations of production from the previous era of ancient slave societies continued to exist, but they were not the predominant relations of production under feudalism. Also, during feudalism, new relations of production—specifically, capitalist relations of production—developed as new classes (the bourgeoisie and the proletariat) began to emerge. An example of this development is how people began producing commodities for exchange at a market, rather than only producing directly for local use, consumption, and subsistence. Another example would be the development of early stock exchanges and joint stock companies, such as the Dutch East India Company[21]. Eventually, the new capitalist relations of production overtook feudal relations of production through social revolution. This led to the current era of capitalism.

---

21 Established in 1602, this was one of the first joint-stock corporations in the world. A monopoly granted by the Dutch government to trade with Asia gave the Company great power and wealth.

> **Annotation 44 (continued)**
>
> Under capitalism, the dominant relations of production are capitalist relations of production, which has the bourgeoisie (or capitalist class) owning the means of production as the ruling class and the proletariat operating the means of production as wage laborers. Even today, there still exist remnant relations of production (for instance, there are still monarchs and nobles in nations like England, Saudi Arabia, and Thailand which continue to possess great wealth and still wield varying degrees of social and political power). There are also new relations of production emerging in socialist nations like Vietnam and Cuba which are attempting to build socialism via a dictatorship of the proletariat with the ambition to eventually do away with capitalism altogether.

Given that development in human society is inevitable [see page 33], each society will eventually manifest some certain new relations of production. These new relations of production form a seed which will eventually overtake the dominant relations of production and give way to a new form of society.

> **Annotation 45**
>
>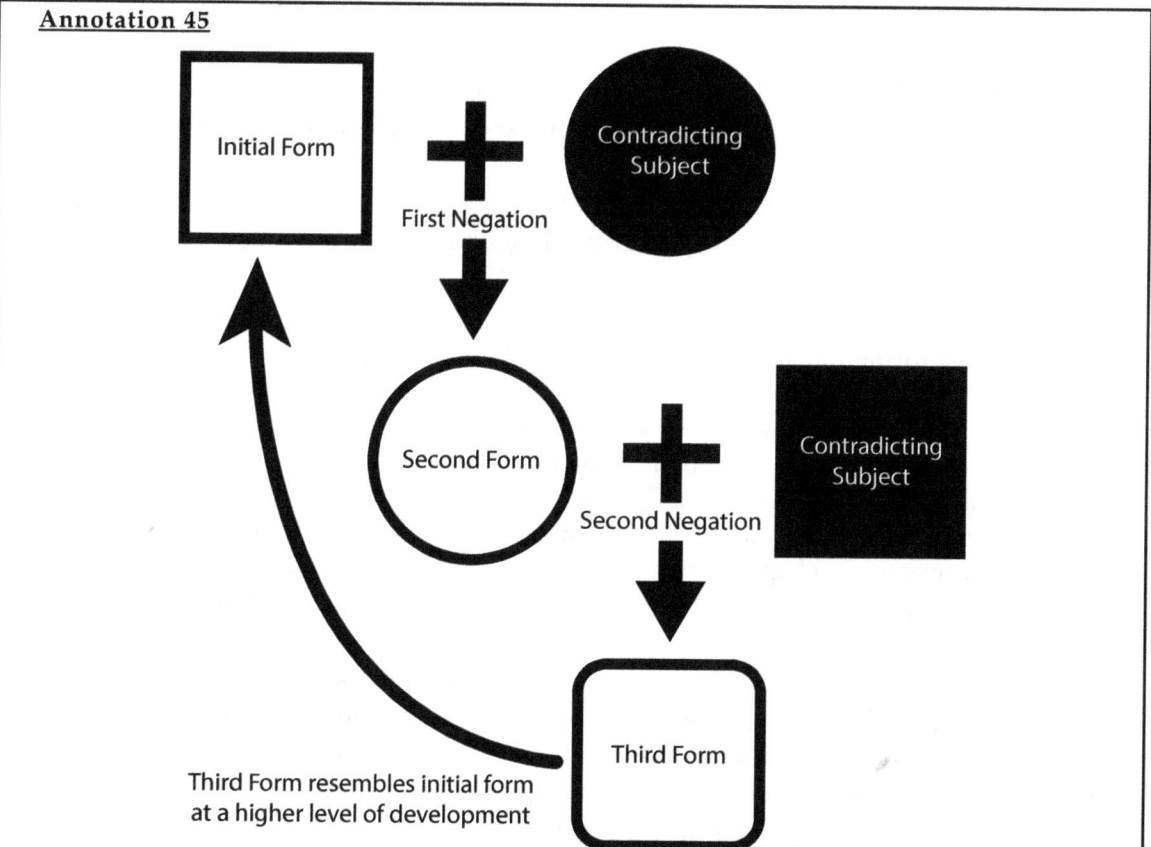
>
> *In dialectical development, characteristics are carried forward from one stage of development to the next from both the initial and contradicting subjects.*
>
> Materialist Dialectics holds that characteristics are carried forward from previous stages of development as a subject transforms through contradiction. These characteristics are carried forward from negating as well as negated subjects which contributed

> **Annotation 45 (continued)**
>
> to the development of the presently existing subject. This is the Materialist Dialectical explanation for why the "seed" of capitalism existed in previous stages of development of human society.
>
> Marx and Engels explained that this seed of capitalism was already present in the feudal system in *Manifesto of the Communist Party*. The embryonic capitalist relations of production soon developed productive forces which were no longer compatible with predominant feudal relations of production. This led to the feudal relations of production being "burst asunder" through social revolution, which resulted in a shift in humanity's mode of production from feudalism to capitalism:
>
>> We see then: the means of production and of exchange, on whose foundation the bourgeoisie built itself up, were generated in feudal society. At a certain stage in the development of these means of production and of exchange, the conditions under which feudal society produced and exchanged, the feudal organisation of agriculture and manufacturing industry, in one word, the feudal relations of property became no longer compatible with the already developed productive forces; they became so many fetters. They had to be burst asunder; they were burst asunder.
>>
>> Into their place stepped free competition, accompanied by a social and political constitution adapted in it, and the economic and political sway of the bourgeois class.
>
> The *Manifesto* also explains that the capitalist mode of production contains the seed of proletarian revolution which will eventually lead to the downfall of capitalism and the end of class society altogether:
>
>> The essential conditions for the existence and for the sway of the bourgeois class is the formation and augmentation of capital; the condition for capital is wage-labour. Wage-labour rests exclusively on competition between the labourers. The advance of industry, whose involuntary promoter is the bourgeoisie, replaces the isolation of the labourers, due to competition, by the revolutionary combination, due to association. The development of Modern Industry, therefore, cuts from under its feet the very foundation on which the bourgeoisie produces and appropriates products. What the bourgeoisie therefore produces, above all, are its own grave-diggers. Its fall and the victory of the proletariat are equally inevitable.
>
> In *Socialism: Utopian and Scientific*, Friedrich Engels explains how the productive forces were already becoming unsuitable to capitalist relations of production even in his day and age, and that this constitutes an objective phenomenon which will eventually lead to social revolution and the end of capitalism:
>
>> The present situation of society — this is now pretty generally conceded — is the creation of the ruling class of today, of the bourgeoisie. The mode of production peculiar to the bourgeoisie, known, since Marx, as the capitalist mode of production, was incompatible with the feudal system, with the privileges it conferred upon individuals, entire social ranks and local corporations, as well as with the hereditary ties of subordination which constituted the framework of its

> **Annotation 45 (continued)**
>
> social organization. The bourgeoisie broke up the feudal system and built upon its ruins the capitalist order of society, the kingdom of free competition, of personal liberty, of the equality, before the law, of all commodity owners, of all the rest of the capitalist blessings. Thenceforward, the capitalist mode of production could develop in freedom. Since steam, machinery, and the making of machines by machinery transformed the older manufacture into modern industry, the productive forces, evolved under the guidance of the bourgeoisie, developed with a rapidity and in a degree unheard of before. But just as the older manufacture, in its time, and handicraft, becoming more developed under its influence, had come into collision with the feudal trammels of the guilds, so now modern industry, in its complete development, comes into collision with the bounds within which the capitalist mode of production holds it confined. The new productive forces have already outgrown the capitalistic mode of using them. And this conflict between productive forces and modes of production is not a conflict engendered in the mind of man, like that between original sin and divine justice. It exists, in fact, objectively, outside us, independently of the will and actions even of the men that have brought it on. Modern Socialism is nothing but the reflex, in thought, of this conflict in fact; its ideal reflection in the minds, first, of the class directly suffering under it, the working class.

In *Anti-Dühring*, Engels explains that the development of capitalist productive forces builds up the proletariat in size and strength, leading to increasing unsuitability between productive forces and capitalist relations of production. This is the seed of communism, already planted within the capitalist mode of production:

> If the introduction and increase of machinery means the displacement of millions of manual by a few machine-workers, improvement in machinery means the displacement of more and more of the machine-workers themselves. It means, in the last instance, the production of a number of available wage-workers in excess of the average needs of capital, the formation of a complete industrial reserve army, as I called it in 1845, available at the times when industry is working at high pressure, to be cast out upon the street when the inevitable crash comes, a constant dead-weight upon the limbs of the working class in its struggle for existence with capital, a regulator for the keeping of wages down to the low level that suits the interests of capital. Thus it comes about, to quote Marx, that machinery becomes the most powerful weapon in the war of capital against the working class; that the instruments of labour constantly tear the means of subsistence out of the hands of the labourer; that the very product of the worker is turned into an instrument for his subjugation. Thus it comes about that the economising of the instruments of labour becomes at the same time, from the outset, the most reckless waste of labour-power, and robbery based upon the normal conditions under which labour functions; that machinery, the most powerful instrument for shortening labour-time, becomes the most unfailing means for placing every moment of the labourer's time and that of his family at the disposal of the capitalist for the purpose of expanding the value of his capital. Thus it comes about that the overwork of some becomes the preliminary condition for the idleness of others, and that modern industry, which hunts

> **Annotation 45 (continued)**
>
> after new consumers over the whole world, forces the consumption of the masses at home down to a starvation minimum, and in doing this destroys its own home market. "The law that always equilibrates the relative surplus-population, or industrial reserve army, to the extent and energy of accumulation, this law rivets the labourer to capital more firmly than the wedges of Vulcan did Prometheus to the rock. It establishes an accumulation of misery corresponding with accumulation of capital. Accumulation of wealth at one pole is, therefore, at the same time accumulation of misery, agony of toil, slavery, ignorance, brutality, mental degradation, at the opposite pole, i.e., on the side of the class that produces its own product in the form of capital... Whilst the capitalist mode of production more and more completely transforms the great majority of the population into proletarians, it creates the power which, under penalty of its own destruction, is forced to accomplish this revolution."
>
> Such inherent and destabilizing contradictions within the capitalist mode of production – i.e., the seed of communism which is contained within capitalism – are the subjects of such great works as *Capital* by Karl Marx and *Imperialism: the Highest Stage of Capitalism* by Lenin and are a key subject of the study of Political Economy.
>
> The end of the capitalist mode of production will end class society entirely, allowing humanity to enter a new era of stateless, classless society, as Marx and Engels explain in the *Manifesto*:
>
>> When, in the course of development, class distinctions have disappeared, and all production has been concentrated in the hands of a vast association of the whole nation, the public power will lose its political character. Political power, properly so called, is merely the organised power of one class for oppressing another. If the proletariat during its contest with the bourgeoisie is compelled, by the force of circumstances, to organise itself as a class, if, by means of a revolution, it makes itself the ruling class, and, as such, sweeps away by force the old conditions of production, then it will, along with these conditions, have swept away the conditions for the existence of class antagonisms and of classes generally, and will thereby have abolished its own supremacy as a class.
>>
>> In place of the old bourgeois society, with its classes and class antagonisms, we shall have an association, in which the free development of each is the condition for the free development of all.

The *dominant* relations of production are those which have risen above all other relations of production. The dominant relations of production set the course of direction for the development of society and define the economic regime of a given society.

The fact that all three types of relations of production exist within the base of any given society reflects the nature of the productive forces as possessing the characteristics of continuous motion and inheritance in development.

> **Annotation 46**
>
> We must avoid thinking of the development of human society in metaphysical terms which misunderstand the ways in which things, phenomena, and ideas change over time. One such metaphysical misconception is that of terminal negation.

Annotation 46 (continued)

Terminal negation is an incorrect view of development which holds that when something is negated it ceases to exist entirely. This misconception is explained more in *Part 1*, p. 185.

Materialist Dialectics holds that negation is a process in which different subjects contradict each other through internal and external relationships, with one subject eventually overtaking the other. When this occurs, the negating subject inherits characteristics from that which it negates. This process of development is continuous, meaning that it is indefinite and is constantly driven by the internal motion of contradiction.

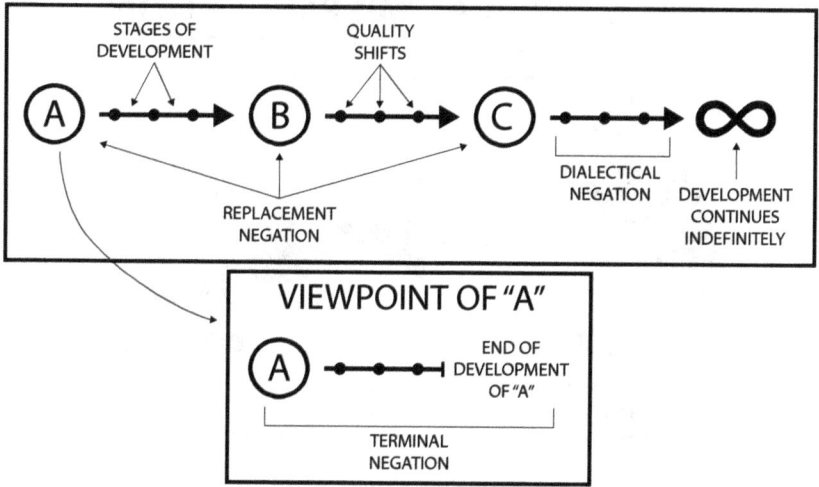

The Materialist Dialectical view of negation holds that negation is not terminal; development continues on after a negation occurs.

Historical Materialism asserts that the development of human society occurs through processes of contradiction and negation which follow the objective laws of Materialist Dialectics. This means that the development of human society must adhere to the principles of continuous motion and inheritance.

Continous Motion in the Development of Human Society

Continuous Motion refers to the fact that all things, phenomena, and ideas are constantly changing and that this change is brought about by internal and external relationships (see *Part 1*, p. 119). Negation processes of human society must adhere to the principle of development, which states that "development is a process that comes from within the thing-in-itself; the process of solving the contradictions within things and phenomena. Therefore, development is inevitable, objective, and occurs without dependence on human will." This means that development and negation of human society stems from internal relations within society which lead to internal contradictions. Development through negation within class society is inevitable and objective and occurs without dependence on human will. In other words, humans do not consciously determine these negations, though the conscious activity of human beings can impact these negation processes in accordance with the Dialectical Materialist conception of the relationship between the material and human consciousness (see *Part 1*, p. 88).

<u>Annotation 46 (continued)</u>

<u>Human society</u> is always continuously changing through developments in <u>quantity</u> which in turn lead to <u>quality shifts</u>. For example, <u>productive forces</u> develop through increases in quantity (quantity of productive output, quantity of efficiency, etc.) and these changes in quantity eventually lead to changes in quality (i.e., negation of one production technology by another, negation of one preferred input material by another, etc.). There are countless examples of such quantity-to-quality negations occurring throughout human history: computers replacing typewriters, cars negating horses, automated factories replacing handcrafts, and so on. Whenever new technologies emerge within the productive forces, they develop gradually, at first only effecting productive forces in terms of quantity until a quality shift occurs.

METAPHYSICAL MISPERCEPTION
OF DEVELOPMENT OF HUMAN SOCIETY

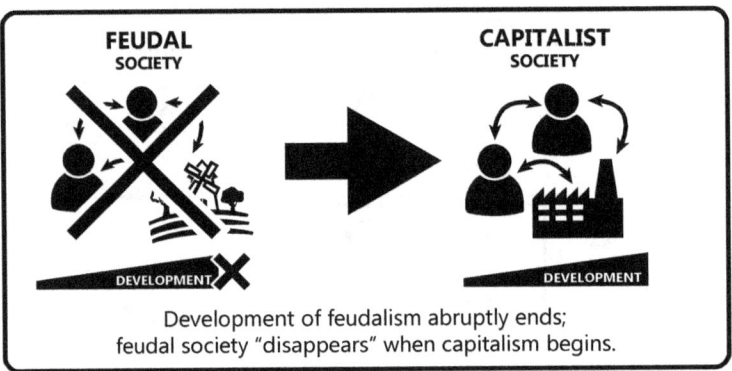

Development of feudalism abruptly ends; feudal society "disappears" when capitalism begins.

HISTORICAL MATERIALIST PERCEPTION
OF DEVELOPMENT OF HUMAN SOCIETY

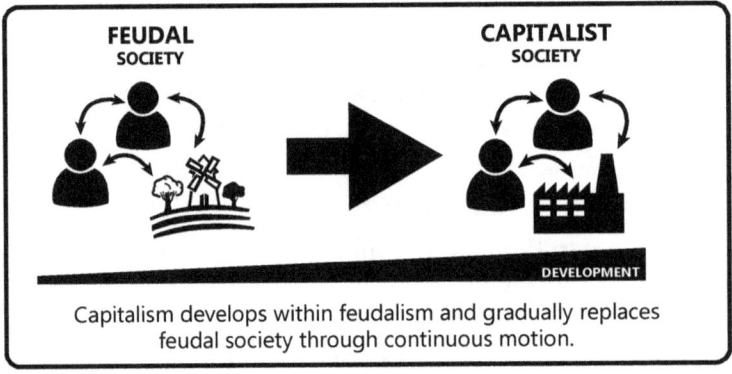

Capitalism develops within feudalism and gradually replaces feudal society through continuous motion.

Historical Materialism holds that society develops in accordance with Materialist Dialectics.

Quality shifts in one aspect of human society will lead to quality shifts in other aspects in accordance with the relationship between matter and consciousness. This means that quality shifts in productive forces lead to quality shifts in relations of production and quality shifts in relations of production lead in turn lead to quality shifts in society's superstructure. This is the basis for the Law of Suitability which is explained in Annotation 33, p. 48.

Annotation 46 (continued)

Inheritance in the Development of Human Society

As stated previously, when one subject negates another, it inherits characteristics and properties from that which it negates.

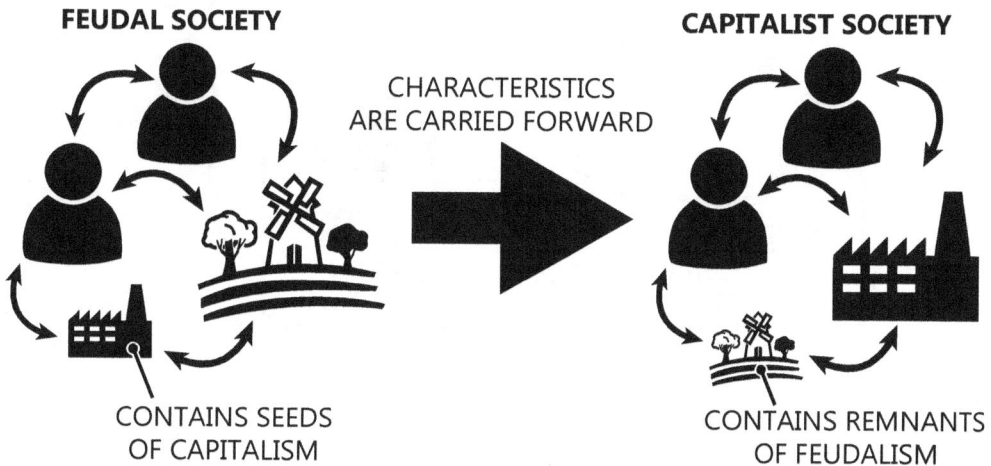

The inheritance principle means that characteristics of one stage of development are carried forward to the next stage. This also means that the present human society contains the "seeds" of the society to come.

Negation processes of human society must adhere to this principle of inheritance, meaning that when a new mode of production negates an older, lower mode of production, it carries characteristics forward from that preceding mode of production. For example, capitalism still possesses characteristics which are inherited from feudalism, such as remnant relations of production (i.e., nobles and monarchs continue to exist even under capitalism) and other characteristics of feudal society which continue to exist both in the base and superstructure of capitalism. Indeed, modern capitalist society even contains inherited characteristics from ancient societies which long predate our current mode of production.

In conclusion, the relations of production constitute a system within society which plays a dual role:

- On one hand, the relations of production serve as the social-economic form of the production process. In this sense, the relations of production govern the maintenance, promotion, and development of the productive forces (which serve as the material content of the production process). This constitutes a dialectical relationship which defines the material production process.
- On the other hand, the relations of production govern the formation of the economic structure of society through mutual development with the socio-political relations of society. This constitutes a dialectical relationship which defines the superstructure of society.

Annotation 47

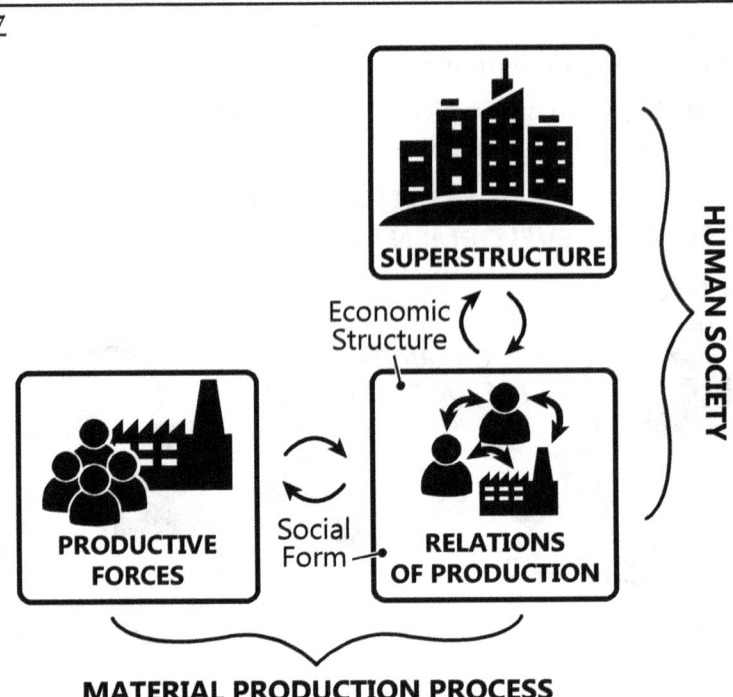

Relations of production define both productive forces (as the social form of the material production process) and superstructure (as the economic structure of human society).

The relations of production are critically important in defining human society. They serve to define both the superstructure and economic base of human society by providing a relatively stable form to both aspects of human society.

Within the economic base, the relations of production serve as the social form of the material production process. In other words, the relations of production constitute a stable set of human relationships which shape and govern a mode of production in a human society.

At the same time, the relations of production provide a stable socio-political form to the superstructure of society. The relations of production define important aspects of human society, such as who has control of the means of production and (in class society) who controls the state. All human institutions and social consciousness forms are determined by economic relations of production.

The role of the state is discussed more in Annotation 100, p. 181. Institutions and social consciousness forms are discussed more in Chapter 2 starting on p. 73.

2. Definition of Superstructure

Marx defined the relations of production as the economic basis of socio-political relations in society, writing:

"The totality of these relations of production constitutes the economic structure of society, the real foundation, on which arises a legal and political superstructure and to which correspond definite forms of social consciousness."[22]

---

[22] *A Contribution to the Critique of Political Economy*, Karl Marx, 1859.

Thus, according to Marx's point of view, the concept of superstructure refers to the entire structural system of social consciousness forms along with corresponding socio-political institutions, which are formed on the economic base.

The superstructure of a given society is a complex structure of relationships that can be analyzed from different perspectives, thereby revealing these relationships as interwoven and constantly developing through mutual impact. From the most general perspective, superstructure can be as consisting of two parts:

1. A system of social consciousness forms including political forms, legal forms, religious forms, etc.
2. A corresponding system of socio-political institutions including states, political parties, religious institutions, etc.

Annotation 48

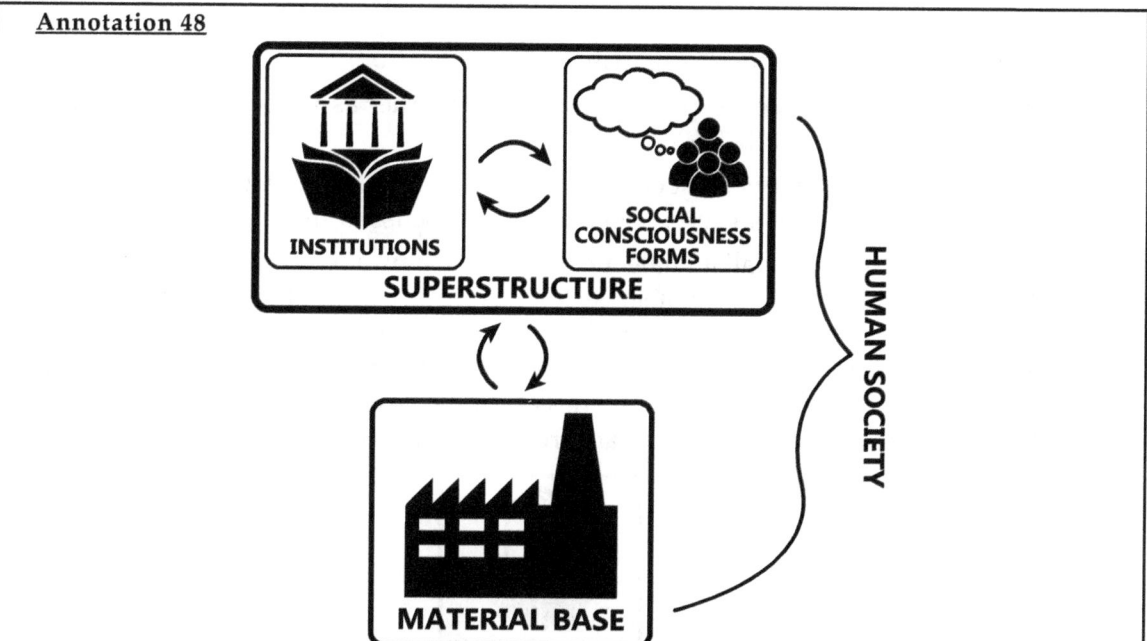

Society's superstructure is defined both by internal relationships between institutions and social consciousness forms and by its external relationship with society's material base.

The superstructure is defined primarily by its external relationship with the material base and by internal relationships between social consciousness forms and corresponding socio-political institutions. The base determines the superstructure, though the superstructure can impact back upon the material base in important ways. This is the Law of the Economic Base Determining the Superstructure of Society, which is explained on p. 90. Within the superstructure, the state is the most significant institution because it has the greatest ability to impact the base (see Annotation 54, p. 100).

Social Consciousness Forms

Social consciousness is human consciousness which is generally shared throughout society. It can be thought of as "collective consciousness," however, it must be understood that there is nothing mystical or supernatural about social consciousness. Social consciousness is simply the body of human consciousness which exists among many human beings in a certain time and place.

Annotation 48 (continued)

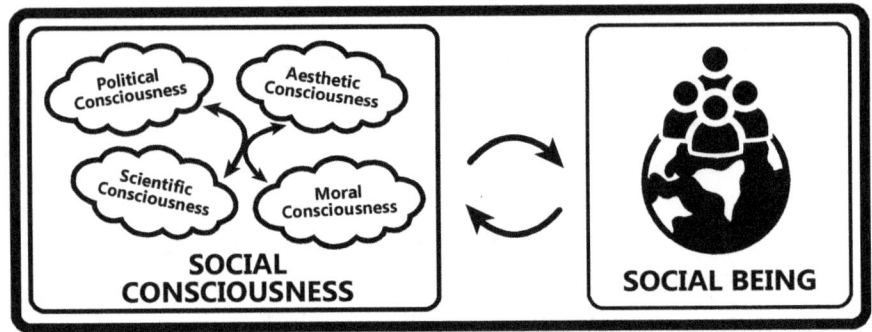

Social consciousness is defined by internal relationships of social consciousness forms and an external relationship with social being.

Social consciousness is defined primarily by these relationships:

Internal relationships between superstructure and all other aspects of social consciousness (see Annotation 61, p. 108-109).

An *external relationship* between social consciousness and social being, which is the material existence of human society. Social being is discussed more starting on p. 106.

Bearing in mind the Materialist Dialectical category pair of content and form, we can understand that a social consciousness form is simply a set of stable relationships which exists within social consciousness. Stability here simply means that a form manifests over time in a manner which is relatively consistent and identifiable. That said, it must also be noted that social consciousness forms—despite this relative stability—never stop changing and developing in accordance with the principle of development.

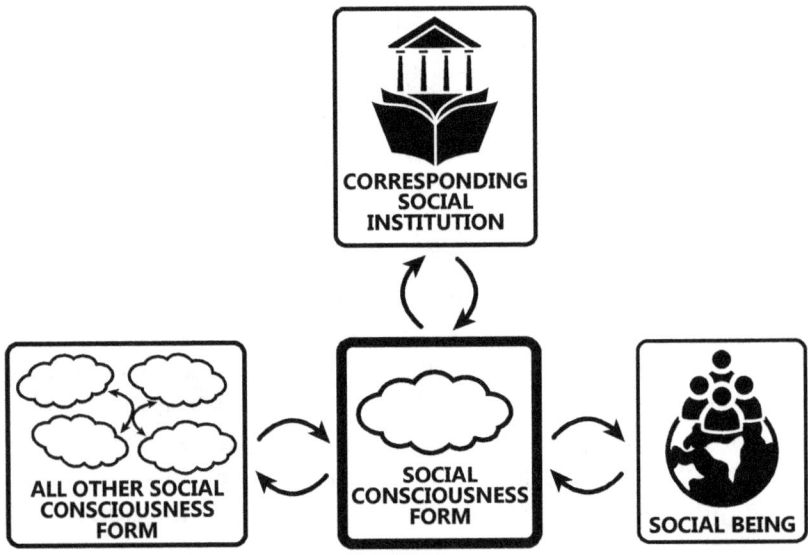

Every form of social consciousness is defined in part by external relationships with corresponding institutions, with social being, and with all other forms of social consciousness.

The content of a *social consciousness form* includes all the various ideas, attitudes, beliefs, and other manifestations of human consciousness which come together as a stable form of social consciousness. Whenever such ideas are packaged together and

> **Annotation 48 (continued)**
>
> held collectively by a group of human beings they become a social consciousness form. Every social consciousness form has a corresponding *socio-political institution.* Such an institution exists to develop and advance its corresponding social consciousness form through dialectical development. Institutions will be discussed more later in this annotation.
>
> A social consciousness form can thus be defined by internal and external relationships:
>
> - *Internal relationships* between the thoughts, ideas, beliefs, and other manifestations of consciousness which compose the social consciousness form.
>
> - *External relationships* with its corresponding institutions, with other social consciousness forms, as well as with social being and the material base of society.
>
> The external relationship which exists between social consciousness forms and socio-political institutions define, in turn, the *superstructure* of society. The dialectical relationship between a social consciousness form and its corresponding institution is, itself, one of content and form.
>
> In this sense, the social consciousness form serves as the content and the institution serves as the social form. Thus, the social consciousness form will determine the existence of its corresponding institution while the institution can impact back on the social consciousness form.
>
> Social consciousness forms manifest in various forms. According to the Vietnamese textbook *Philosophy of Marxism-Leninism*, these forms include:
>
> 1. **Political Consciousness**: A form of consciousness that only exists in class societies which have states. Political consciousness reflects economic and social relationships between classes, peoples, and nations, as well as the attitudes of different classes toward state power.
>
> 2. **Legal consciousness**: The entire system of ideas and opinions which a class holds about the nature and role of law, about the rights and obligations of the state, social organizations and citizens, and about the legality and illegality of human behavior in society, along with human awareness and emotions as they pertain to the enforcement of state laws.
>
> 3. **Moral consciousness**: The totality of concepts, knowledge, and psychological/emotional conditions of human communities pertaining to values of good, evil, conscience, responsibility, happiness, justice, etc., as well as rules for evaluating/regulating behavior between individuals and society, and between individuals within society.
>
> 4. **Aesthetic consciousness**: Consciousness relating to the need to enjoy and create beauty. Among the forms of activities to enjoy and create beauty, art is the highest form of expression of aesthetic consciousness.
>
> 5. **Religious consciousness**: The totality of symbols, emotions, moods, and habits of the masses regarding religious beliefs. Religious ideology is a system of doctrine created and spread in society by clergy and theologians.

Annotation 48 (continued)

In addition to these general forms of social consciousness, there are also two special forms of social consciousness which are particularly relevant to the pursuit of Scientific Socialism:

Scientific knowledge penetrates other forms of social consciousness, serving as the basis for scientific fields which correspond to each form of consciousness. For example: the scientific form of political consciousness is political science, the scientific form of moral consciousness is ethics, the scientific form of artistic consciousness is artistic science, the scientific form of religious consciousness is religious studies, and so on.

Scientific consciousness is an important component of the cognitive theory of Dialectical Materialism. This is discussed more in *Part 1*, p. 214.

"Staying home is loving our country!"
Vietnam's Ministry of Health is a Socio-Political Institution which develops social consciousness related to public health. This poster was created to develop social consciousness among the masses about COVID-19.

Socio-Political Institutions

A socio-political institution is an organization which human beings have created to institute, codify, expand, and develop a corresponding social consciousness form. Whenever human beings develop a social consciousness form and come together to promote, defend, and advance it, it becomes a basis for a socio-political institution.

> **Annotation 48 (continued)**
>
> Such institutions serve social and political functions:
>
> *Social* because they exist, by definition, as organized systems which have been created and developed by a group of human beings to defend, promote, advance, and otherwise develop a corresponding form of social consciousness. Social institutions therefore have an explicitly social function within the superstructure of human society.
>
> *Political* because social consciousness forms and corresponding institutions—as elements of the superstructure—invariably have class character and, therefore, some degree of impact on political struggle to influence the state and benefit from the means of production. Art, for example, invariably reflects some aspect of political consciousness, even if that expression is unintentional.
>
> Examples of socio-political institutions include:
>
> **States**: Socio-political institutions which are the totality of forms of governance over a society by a ruling class. States can take various forms and may be governed in a wide variety of manners. States exist to enforce dictatorship of the ruling class over all other classes.
>
> **Political Parties**: Socio-political institutions which exist to develop, disseminate, and advance political ideologies by codifying political doctrines and programs, disseminating propaganda, recruiting membership from society at large, training and advancing leaders, running political candidates in elections, and so on. In class society, political parties are controlled by a specific class. For example, in capitalist society, most political parties serve the interests of the capitalist class, though opposition parties may exist to represent the interests of remnant or oppressed class interests.
>
> For example, in some nations there are royalist parties which represent the interests of remnant classes such as monarchs and feudal lords. In other nations there are communist parties which represent the working class and seek to put workers in command of society.
>
> **Religious Institutions**: Socio-political institutions which exist for humans to practice and develop religious belief systems. Churches, mosques, and synagogues are all examples of religious institutions.
>
> In addition to the socio-political institution types listed above, there are countless others, including universities, labor unions, industrial associations, and on and on. Institutions and social consciousness forms are determined by the economic base and social being of human society, but they play a very important effect in the development of human society nonetheless and they are capable of impacting back upon the material world. As Engels wrote in a letter to Conrad Schmidt in 1890:
>
>> While the material mode of existence is the primum agens [primary agent, prime cause] this does not preclude the ideological spheres from reacting upon it in their turn, though with a secondary effect.

In a *class society*, and especially in modern societies, the two most important social consciousness forms in the superstructure of society are:

1. Political consciousness forms.
2. Legal consciousness forms.

And the two most important institutions in the superstructure of society are:
1. The political party.
2. The state.

The state is a special apparatus that organizes and exercises power within a class society. On the surface, the state usually presents itself as an organization system that coordinates the shared power of the people in order to manage and control all activities of society and to perform political and social functions along with domestic and foreign affairs functions. In reality, however, every state is a tool to wield power in order to exercise the dictatorship of the ruling class (which is defined as the class that holds the main means of production of society).

> **Annotation 49**
>
> Political and legal consciousness forms are considered the most important social consciousness forms within the superstructure of society because they have the most potential to impact back upon the material base of society. This is because they relate directly to the class structure which exists within a given society's mode of production. The same can be said for political parties and for the state, which are socio-political institutions which reflect and relate the most directly to a society's class structure and material base.
>
>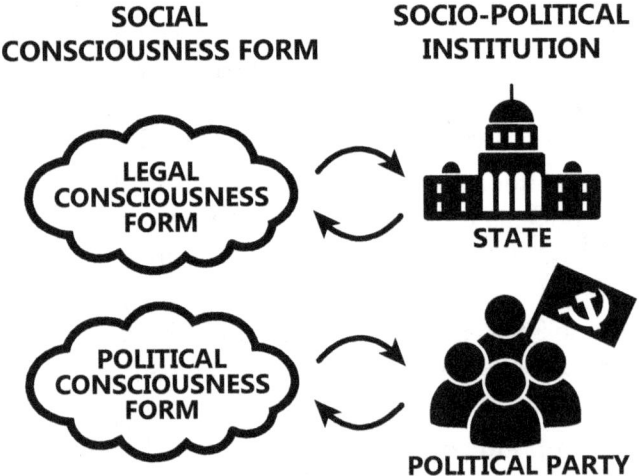
>
> *The most important social consciousness forms and institutions are Legal Consciousness and the corresponding State as well as Political Consciousness and corresponding Political Parties.*
>
> A political party corresponds to a political consciousness form which represents a specific class within society. Political parties are the most effective vehicles for a class to impact back upon the material base by securing benefits from the means of production for that class, building power for that class, and protecting the interests of that class.
>
> A state is a special socio-political institution which a class uses to govern and control a society. Only the ruling class can command a state, and this rulership is known as *class dictatorship*. Under capitalism, the state is controlled by the capitalist class. This means that a powerful but tiny minority of society has dictatorship over the working class which constitutes the great majority of society.

Annotation 49 (continued)

PROCEDURE OF SOCIAL REVOLUTION

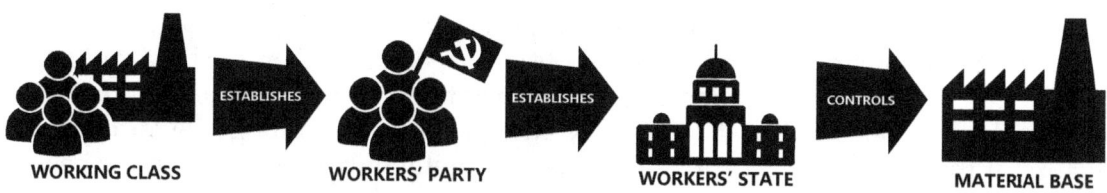

The working class under capitalism has the mission of building a workers' party and establishing a workers' state in order to seize control of the material base of society.

The mission of the working class, according to the principles of Scientific Socialism, is to establish a dictatorship over the capitalist class. This simply means that the vast majority of society—i.e., the workers—control society instead of the tiny minority of capitalists. This can only be achieved by seizing control of the means of production, i.e., the material base of society. This would give the workers the ability to develop state power over society which will, eventually, give the working class the opportunity to finally dismantle class society once and for all.

It is important to note that the state is the most important socio-political institution because it has the most impact on the economic base. This characteristic of the state is discussed more in Annotation 100, p. 181. Class struggle is discussed more in Annotation 55, p. 101.

II. DIALECTICAL RELATIONSHIP BETWEEN THE BASE AND SUPERSTRUCTURE

Base and superstructure are the two basic aspects of society. The base is the economic aspect, and the superstructure is the socio-political aspect. Together, the base and superstructure exist in a dialectical unified relationship with each other, mutually impacting one other. In this dialectical relationship, the base plays a determining role for the superstructure; at the same time, the superstructure constantly impacts back upon the base.

1. The base determines the superstructure

The role which the base plays in determining the superstructure is revealed in many ways:

- Every economic base forms a suitable superstructure to maintain and protect the base.
- Changes in the base create an objective need to have corresponding changes in the superstructure.
- Contradictions in the base are reflected in the contradictions within the superstructure.
- Struggles between different socio-political ideologies as well as conflicts between different socio-political interests all have root causes in class struggle to benefit from the economic base of society.
- The class that owns the means of production of society is also the class that holds state power in the superstructure of society, while other classes are in a subordinate position to that state power.
- State policies and laws, in the end, only reflect the economic domination of the class which owns the means of production of society, and serve the needs of that ruling class.

In short, in any given society, the base determines the superstructure, while the superstructure reflects the base and impacts back upon the base.

Annotation 50

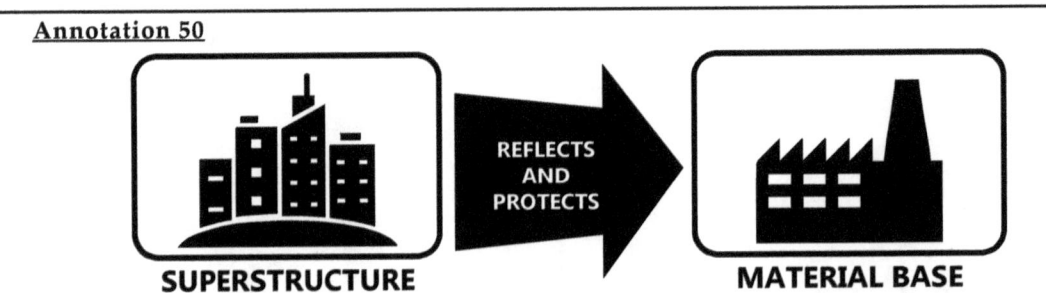

The superstructure reflects and protects the base in accorance with the Law of the Economic Base Determining the Superstructure of Society and the Law of Suitability.

The superstructure has an objective need for suitability with the material base of human society. This need gives rise to Law of the Economic Base Determining the Superstructure. The base and superstructure dialectically define and develop each other: the material base is reflected in the superstructure in countless ways. At the same time, the superstructure develops so as to reflect, protect, and preserve relations of production in order to ensure a stable material production process.

Annotation 50 (continued)

Following are fuller explanations of the various ways in which the determining role of the material base is reflected in the superstructure of society.

1. **Every economic base forms a suitable superstructure to maintain and protect the base.**

Throughout the history of class society, the superstructure of society has served to further the interests of the ruling class through the development of social consciousness forms and socio-political institutions which predominantly reflect the values and interests of the ruling class. As a result, prevailing philosophies and social institutions have always reflected the values and interests of the ruling class in every era of class society. This is explained more in Annotation 13, p. 19.

Examples of Social Consciousness Forms in Class Society:

Most major prevailing **philosophies** have defended and served the interests of the ruling class of the society which produced them. For example, the philosophy of Aristotle defended the institution of slavery in Ancient Greece and extolled the virtue of the land-owning ruling class. Chivalry was a medieval philosophical system which upheld the feudal system which included knighthood and aristocratic notions of "noble birth."

In today's society, most prevailing philosophies in the world uphold and defend the capitalist mode of production.

Legal systems have always historically served the interests of the ruling class. Under feudalism, legal systems upheld the hereditary systems of monarchy and nobility and prevented peasants from participating in governing the state.

Today, under capitalism, the legal systems of most nations heavily favor the capitalist class while suppressing workers in various ways.

Examples of Socio-Political Institutions in Class Society:

During the feudal era, **religious institutions** primarily served the interests of and defended the positions of feudal lords and monarchs. They were also determined by the economic base of feudal society: the church in medieval Europe, for example, controlled feudal landholdings in a similar fashion to noble lords and was financed through tithes and donations secured from the wealthy ruling classes.

Today, most religious institutions defend and reinforce the capitalist mode of production and are determined by the economic base of capitalism; that is to say, they are typically recognized by the capitalist-controlled state and seldom challenge the authority of the ruling capitalist class, but rather normalize capitalist relations of production with practitioners of the religious faith.

States have always predominantly been ruled and governed by the ruling class in every era of history. Under feudalism, the state was controlled directly by monarchs and feudal lords.

Under capitalism, the ruling class controls the states of most nations through financial contributions to political candidates and parties, through lobbying, through bribery and corruption, through corporate influence on governments, and through various other means.

> **Annotation 50 (continued)**
>
> 2. **Changes in the base create an objective need to have corresponding changes in the superstructure.**
>
> Karl Marx explained this concept in the preface of *A Contribution to the Critique of Political Economy*:
>
>> The changes in the economic foundation lead sooner or later to the transformation of the whole immense superstructure.
>
> This was Marx's formulation of the <u>Law of the Economic Base Determining the Superstructure of Society</u>. This law is further defined in the Vietnamese textbook *Philosophy of Marxism-Leninism*:
>
>> The base and the superstructure are two sides of society. They have a dialectical unity with each other in which the base plays a decisive role:
>>
>> Each base will form a corresponding superstructure. The characteristics of the superstructure are defined by the characteristics of its base. In a <u>class society</u>, whichever class rules the economy also has the ruling position of politics and the spiritual/mental life of society. Every contradiction in the economy, in the end, always decides the contradictions in the ideological politics. All the struggles between different ideologies in politics are manifestations of struggles which exist in the economy [relations of production]. All the factors of the superstructure, such as the <u>state</u>, the law, philosophy, religion, and so on, directly and indirectly depend on the base.
>>
>> This process [of changes in the base leading to changes in the superstructure] does not only occur when a social-economic form changes to a new social-economic form [i.e., from feudalism to capitalism], but also occurs within a social-economic form. Even though the changes of the superstructure go hand in hand with the <u>productive forces</u>, the productive forces do not directly change the superstructure. The development of the productive forces change the relations of production which means it directly changes the base, and through that development, the superstructure is changed.
>>
>> The changes in the base leading to changes in the superstructure happen in a very complicated manner. In this process, there are some factors within the superstructure that change very fast in response to changes in the base, such as changes in politics and law. There are also factors that change very slowly, such as religion, art, aesthetics, and so on. There are also factors that are inherited from previous social-economic forms.
>
> 3. **Contradictions in the base are <u>reflected</u> in the contradictions within the superstructure.**
>
> <u>Reflection</u> is the re-creation of the features of one subject in a different subject which occurs when they mutually impact each other through interaction. Reflection occurs in all dialectical relationships between subjects. Reflection is defined in ***Part 1***, p. 64.
>
> Because the base and superstructure have a dialectical relationship with one another, and because the base (as the material component of society) determines the superstructure, reflections of the base in the superstructure are profound and determine the essence

Annotation 50 (continued)

of the superstructure. It should be noted that the superstructure is able to impact back upon the base of society, but it can never determine the base (because of the Dialectical Materialist conception of the relationship between matter and consciousness) and so the reflections of the superstructure found in the base will always be less profound than the reflections of the base found in the superstructure.

In feudal society, for example, such reflections of the contradictions of the base can be found in prevailing and predominant philosophies of that era. Social consciousness forms such as chivalry and fealty in medieval Europe reflected the relations of production of that era and also justified those relations of production, giving the ruling class of monarchs and nobles the most power and prestige in that society.

Similarly, the prevailing philosophies within the capitalist superstructure reflect the capitalist mode of production and material base which determine that superstructure. For example, philosophies of meritocracy, competition, and individualism justify the exploitation of workers by capitalists and otherwise legitimize capitalist relations of production.

Reflections of the superstructure in the base are much more subtle, but they do exist. For example, bourgeois democracy has granted some concessions to workers even in highly developed bourgeois states such as the United States. By developing institutions and social consciousness forms with a working class character, workers have gained workplace safety regulations, child labor laws, etc. Such reforms can improve conditions for workers, but they will never be able to fundamentally alter relations of production.

Similarly, no amount of alteration and change within the bourgeois-controlled state (nor any other socio-political institution) will result in a rearrangement of the relations of production and other essential aspects of the economic base. The only way to fundamentally alter the material base is through social revolution which places the working class in command of the means of production and productive forces of human society. That said, efforts toward changing the superstructure of society can strengthen the position of the revolutionary class and hasten the victory of social revolution over the ruling class. This is important to the mission of Scientific Socialism.

4. **Struggles between different socio-political ideologies as well as conflicts between different socio-political interests all have root causes in class struggle to benefit from the economic base of society.**

Throughout the history of class society, political struggles have stemmed from one prevailing question: who might benefit from the economic base of society?

During the feudal era, there were political struggles between different classes all competing for material benefits from the economic base. Peasants sought to keep more of the crops they grew and to toil under better conditions. Merchants struggled against taxation and hoped to build their wealth. Noble lords struggled against the monarch to hold more power in their own hands, to expand their lands, and to live more comfortable lives. Monarchs fought to maintain rulership over society and to expand the territory of their kingdoms.

Today, under capitalism, class struggle has been reduced primarily to the struggle between the proletariat and the bourgeoisie. Workers struggle for higher wages, lower

Annotation 50 (continued)

taxation of their paychecks, better working conditions, and increased power in society. Capitalists struggle to keep workers suppressed, to drive down wages, and to increase their share of profits while lowering taxes on their capital gains and assets.

The ruling class uses all means available to protect and further their own class interests, including the use of social consciousness forms and socio-political institutions to develop false consciousness within the working class. False consciousness is any human consciousness which does not reflect material reality and objective conditions. In the context of class struggle, the capitalist class seeks to develop false consciousness in workers by limiting and negating class consciousness so that workers will side with the ruling class agenda against their own interests. For this reason, building class consciousness among the working class is an important prerequisite of social revolution.

5. The class that holds the ownership of the means of production of society is also the class that holds state power in the superstructure of society, while other classes are in a subordinate position to that state power.

THE ROLE OF THE STATE UNDER CAPITALISM

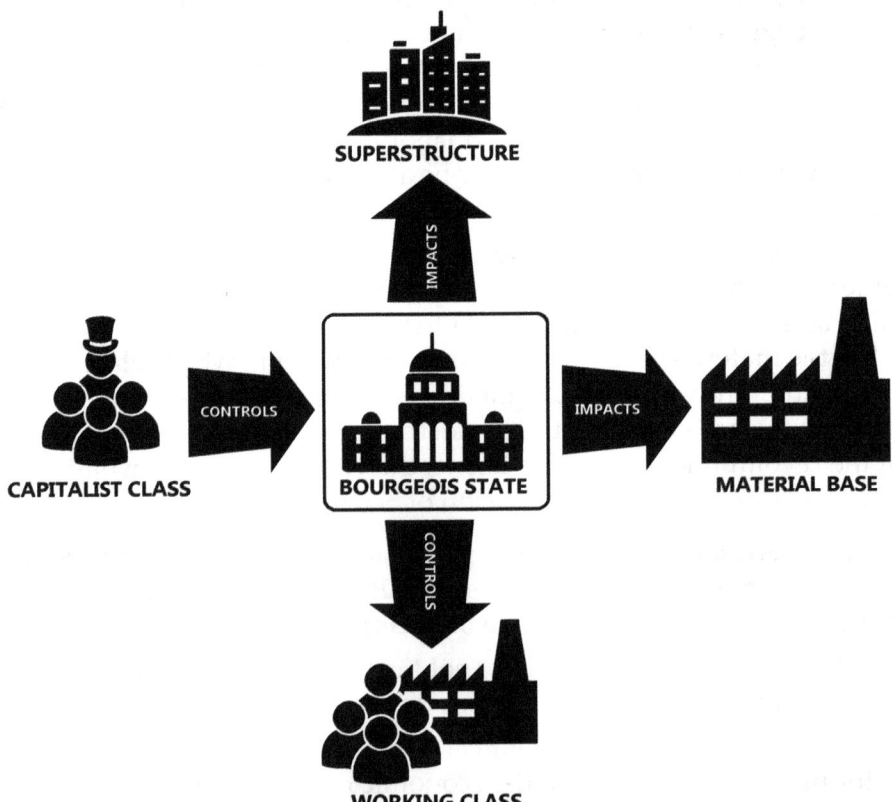

The state is of vital importance in class society because it allows the ruling class to maintain control over the means of production and workers through coercive violence.

In any given class society, the ruling class is the class which owns the means of production. The ruling class of any given class society will always have or gain control of state power. This is a manifestation of the Dialectical Materialist conception of the

Annotation 50 (continued)

relationship between matter and consciousness (see *Part 1*, p. 88): the means of production and economic base, as the material components of society, determine who has control over the state, which—as a socio-political institution—is a manifestation of human social consciousness.

New relations of production always emerge as an objective need once productive forces have developed to such a point that they are no longer compatible with the existing relations of production. In every case throughout history, the new ruling class has gained state power through social revolution. For example, when capitalist relations of production emerged within feudal class society, capitalists seized state power through social revolution as soon as they were able to gain the most power and control over the means of production. The objective need for social revolution caused by unsuitability between productive forces and relations of production is further discussed in Annotation 36 on p. 52.

State policies and laws, in the end, only reflect the economic domination of the class which owns the means of production of society and primarily serve the needs of that ruling class. The ruling class in a class society maintains power over the means of production through state violence. This is the primary function of the state: to enforce stability and established class relations through coercive force. This dynamic is explaned more in Annotation 100, p. 181.

This is vital for understanding the nature of the bourgeois state as well as the functioning of bourgeois-controlled "democracy" in capitalist society.

The character of bourgeois democracy is described well by Lenin in his article "Democracy and Dictatorship," published in *Pravda* in 1918:

> ... Some speak about "pure democracy" and "democracy" in general for the purpose of deceiving the people and concealing from them the bourgeois character of present-day democracy.
>
> Let the bourgeoisie continue to keep the entire apparatus of state power in their hands, let a handful of exploiters continue to use the former, bourgeois, state machine! Elections held in such circumstances are praised by the bourgeoisie – for very good reasons – as being "free", "equal", "democratic" and "universal". These words are designed to conceal the truth, to conceal the fact that the means of production and political power remain in the hands of the exploiters, and that therefore real freedom and real equality for the exploited – that is, for the vast majority of the population – are out of the question.
>
> It is profitable and indispensable for the bourgeoisie to conceal from the people the bourgeois character of modern democracy, to picture it as democracy in general or "pure democracy." And the men who are repeating this, in practice abandon the standpoint of the proletariat and side with the bourgeoisie.
>
> It is sheer mockery of the working and exploited people to speak of pure democracy, of democracy in general, of equality, freedom and universal rights when the workers and all working people are ill-fed, ill-clad, ruined and worn out not only as a result of capitalist wage-slavery. As a consequence of four years of predatory war, the capitalists and profiteers remain in possession of the "property" usurped by them and the "ready-made" apparatus of state power.

> **Annotation 50 (continued)**
>
> This is tantamount to trampling on the basic truths of Marxism which has taught the workers: you must take advantage of bourgeois democracy which, compared with feudalism, represents a great historical advance – but not for one minute must you forget the bourgeois character of this "democracy," its historically conditional and limited character. Never share the "superstitious belief" in the state and never forget that the state, even in the most democratic republic… is simply a machine for the suppression of one class by another.
>
> The dictatorship of the proletariat alone can emancipate humanity from the oppression of capital, from the lies, falsehood and hypocrisy of bourgeois democracy – democracy for the rich – and establish democracy for the poor. [Only it can] make the blessings of democracy really accessible to the workers and poor peasants. [Under bourgeois systems] the blessings of democracy are, in fact, inaccessible to the vast majority of working people.
>
> It is important to understand that when Lenin speaks of a "dictatorship of the proletariat" he is not advocating for tyranny over the masses. It must be kept in mind that the proletariat represents the vast majority of human beings on planet Earth. Building a democracy which exists for, is governed by, and serves the interests of the proletariat, therefore, is far less tyrannical and far more egalitarian than bourgeois democracy which serves and is controlled by the ruling class. As Lenin puts it: "Proletarian democracy is a million times more democratic than any bourgeois democracy."

The dependence of the superstructure on the base is caused by economic necessities which are embedded within all social activities, from legal and political practice to cultural activities of society. Economic necessities are the indispensable need to maintain and develop the productive forces of society.

> **Annotation 51**
>
> "Economic" in the term "economic necessity" refers to relationships having to do with production of the material needs of society as defined in Annotation 81, p. 146. "Necessity" here is synonymous with "obviousness" from the universal category pair of obviousness and randomness as used in Materialist Dialectics. This category pair is discussed in more detail on p. 144 of the *Part 1*, but to briefly summarize:
>
> Obviousness (i.e., necessity) can only apply to material subjects in the material world. Obvious outcomes are outcomes which are certain to happen due to objective laws. Obviousness arises from the internal aspects, features, and relations of physical objects. Example: paper will burn under certain specific conditions because of the internal chemical relations of paper and the objective laws of nature.
>
> Economic necessities are obvious, then, in the sense that they are social activities which *must* be carried out in order for human society to survive. Economic necessities serve, in this manner, as the most fundamental pressure which drives the development of human society and serve as the basis of the Law of Suitability Between Relations of Production and Productive Forces.
>
> Examples: Throughout history, human beings have had an economic need to secure food in order to continue living. In modern times, electricity is an economic necessity because electrical devices are needed to support human life in its current form.

> **Annotation 51 (continued)**
>
> Economic necessities determine aspects of the superstructure of society, and it is in this sense that the superstructure of society is dependent upon the base. Without a functioning economic base and the obligatory processes related to the production of material necessities of human society no other human social activities could occur.
>
> As Engels wrote in a letter to Nikolai Danielson in 1892:
>
>> In essence, the relationship of base and superstructure represents the dependence of social consciousness forms on the material existence [i.e., social being] of society.

2. The superstructure's impact on the base

The superstructure exists as a reflection of the economic base and arises from the need to develop the economic base.

> **Annotation 52**
>
>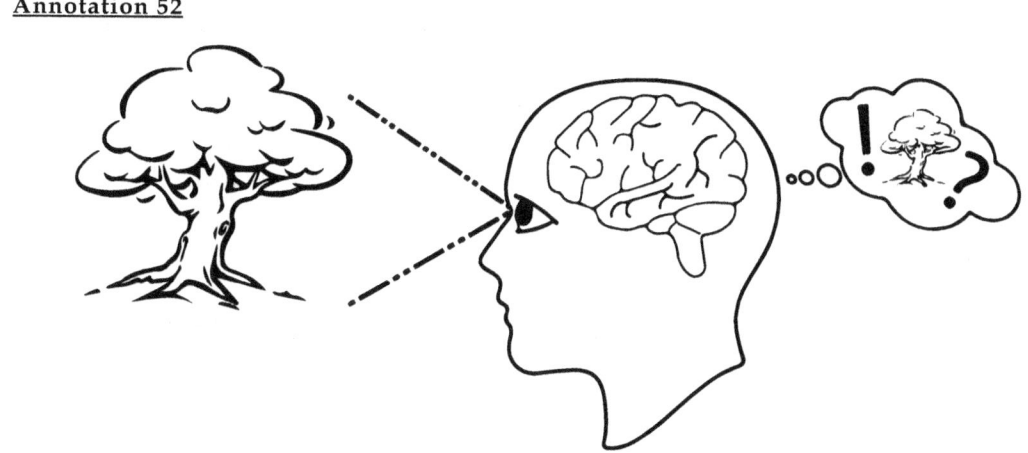
>
> *Consciousness is a reflection of the material world which arises from material processes within the human brain.*
>
> Consciousness itself is a reflection of matter: consciousness reflects the processes of the human brain as well as experiences and data gathered from the material world. This reflection of matter in consciousness is discussed more in **Part 1**, p. 64.
>
> Similarly, the superstructure of society is a reflection of the material/economic base of human society. Superstructural elements such as social consciousness forms and social institutions arise from the conditions of and (are determined by) the material base of society.
>
> As Lenin wrote in "The Three Sources and Three Component Parts of Marxism:"
>
>> Just as man's knowledge reflects nature (i.e., developing matter), which exists independently of him, so man's social knowledge (i.e., his various views and doctrines—philosophical, religious, political and so forth) reflects the economic system of society. Political institutions are a superstructure on the economic foundation. We see, for example, that the various political forms of the modern European states serve to strengthen the domination of the bourgeoisie over the proletariat.

> **Annotation 52 (continued)**
>
> Reflections are always mutual; it is impossible for one subject to change another subject without being changed itself, as explained in *Part 1*, p. 65. However, the material base determines the form of the superstructure of human society, and so human society exists in essence as a reflection of the material base which determines its existence. Engels, in a letter to Joseph Bloch in 1890, wrote:
>
>> We make our history ourselves, but, in the first place, under very definite assumptions and conditions. Among these the economic ones are ultimately decisive. But the political ones, etc., and indeed even the traditions which haunt human minds also play a part, although not the decisive one.

The superstructure is relatively independent and often impacts back on the economic base of society.

> **Annotation 53**
>
> The superstructure of society is "relatively independent" of the material base in a way that is similar to how human consciousness is "relatively independent" of the material world. As Engels wrote in a letter to Conrad Schmidt in 1890:
>
>> The economic movement, upon the whole, asserts itself but it is affected by the reaction of the relatively independent political movement which it itself had set up. This political movement is on the one hand the state power, on the other, the opposition which comes to life at the same time with it. . . so there is reflected in the struggle between government and opposition, the struggle between already existing and contending classes but again in an inverted form, no longer direct but indirect, not as a class struggle but as a struggle for political principles. So inverted is this reflection that it required thousands of years to discover what was behind it.
>
> Engels is saying, here, that the struggles, conflicts, contradictions, and resulting developments which occur within the superstructure of a society occur more or less unconsciously. That is to say, the participants in these struggles do not typically realize that they are engaging in class struggle. Engels further explains this concept using the legal system of the state as an example:
>
>> The reflection of economic relations as principles of law is necessarily also an inverted one. The process takes place without the participants becoming conscious of it. The jurist imagines that he is operating with a priori propositions, while the latter are after all only reflections of the economic process. And so everything remains standing on its head. This inverted reflex so long as it is not recognized for what it is constitutes what we call ideological conceptions. That it is able to exert a reactive influence on the economic basis and within certain limits to modify it, seems to me to be self-evident. The foundations of the law of inheritance, corresponding stages in the development of the family being presupposed, are economic. Nonetheless it would be very hard to prove that, e.g., the absolute freedom of testamentary disposition in England, and the strongly restricted right in France, in all particulars have only economic causes. Yet both methods react in a very significant way upon the economic system in that they influence the distribution of wealth.

> **Annotation 53 (continued)**
>
> In other words, lawyers and judges and other state agents operate on behalf of the bourgeoisie, serving the interests of the bourgeois state, without realizing that they are doing so. This means that political struggle by an oppressed class can lead to impacts in the economic base which might benefit that class. In a letter to J. Bloch, Engels clarified that the relationship between social being and social consciousness is not a *mechanical* relationship, and that economic factors are not the *only* factors which absolutely and unilaterally determine the development of society:
>
>> According to the Materialist Conception of History, the factor which is *in the last instance* decisive in history is the production and reproduction of actual life. More than this neither Marx nor myself ever claimed. If now someone has distorted the meaning in such a way that the economic factor is the only decisive one, this man has changed the above proposition into an abstract, absurd phrase which says nothing. The economic situation is the base, but the different parts of the structure-the political forms of the class struggle and its results, the constitutions established by the victorious class after the battle is won, forms of law and even the reflections of all these real struggles in the brains of the participants, political theories, juridical, philosophical, religious opinions, and their further development into dogmatic systems-all this exercises also its influence on the development of the historical struggles and in cases determines their form. It is under the mutual influence of all these factors that, rejecting the infinitesimal number of accidental occurrences (that is, things and happenings whose intimate sense is so far removed and of so little probability that we can consider them non-existent, and can ignore them), that the economical movement is ultimately carried out. Otherwise the application of the theory to any period of history would be easier than the solution of any simple equation. We ourselves make our history, but, primarily, under pre-suppositions and conditions which are very well determined. But even the political tradition, nay, even the tradition that man creates in his head, plays an important part even if not the decisive one.
>
> This is a refutation of mechanical materialism and an important reminder of the Law of the Relationship Between Social Being and Social Consciousness. Properly understanding and applying this law is especially important in the theory and practice of Scientific Socialism because developing class consciousness, carrying out social revolution, and building a socialist dictatorship of the proletariat are all vital prerequisites to fulfilling the historical mission of the working class. As Engels asked Conrad Schmidt:
>
>> Or else, why are we struggling for the political dictatorship of the proletariat, if political power has no economic effects?

The impact of the superstructure on the base is revealed in many ways.

The superstructure consists of many components which have different positions, roles, and characteristics. These superstructural components determine how the superstructure impacts back on the base.

However, if the superstructure has a state as a component, then all other superstructural components must rely on the state in order to have a strong impact on the base. The state is the superstructural component that has the most direct and the strongest impact on the base of society.

Annotation 54

As discussed in Annotation 16, p. 26, the superstructural components of society include social consciousness forms and their corresponding socio-political institutions. In class society, the state is the social institution which has the most direct impact on the economic base and this plays a tremendous role in securing the position of whichever class controls the state as the ruling class of society. States have not always existed in every human society. It is only with the development of class society that states have developed to stabilize class antagonisms and to serve the agenda of the ruling class, as Engels explains in *The Origin of the Family, Private Property, and the State*:

> The state, then, has not existed from all eternity. There have been societies that did without it, that had no idea of the state and state power. At a certain stage of economic development, which was necessarily bound up with the split of society into classes, the state became a necessity owing to this split.

In the same text, Engels gives a definition of the state and its relation to class conflict:

> The state is... a product of society at a certain stage of development; it is the admission that this society has become entangled in an insoluble contradiction with itself, that it has split into irreconcilable antagonisms which it is powerless to dispel. But in order that these antagonisms, these classes with conflicting economic interests, might not consume themselves and society in fruitless struggle, it became necessary to have a power, seemingly standing above society, that would alleviate the conflict and keep it within the bounds of 'order'; and this power, arisen out of society but placing itself above it, and alienating itself more and more from it, is the state.

Lenin adds to this definition in *The State and Revolution*:

> The state is a product and a manifestation of the irreconcilability of class antagonisms. The state arises where, when and insofar as class antagonism objectively cannot be reconciled. And, conversely, the existence of the state proves that the class antagonisms are irreconcilable.

Engels further explains that the state exists as a coercive force which allows one class to subjugate another through violence which is organized. This organized violence consists "not merely of armed men but also of material adjuncts, prisons, and institutions of coercion of all kinds."

Because states arose from class struggle explicitly to serve the agenda of the ruling class through organized violence, it stands to reason that the end of class society will ultimately result in the end of the state as a component of the superstructure of society. The negation of capitalism will mark the end of class society. Engels explains:

> We are now rapidly approaching a stage in the development of production at which the existence of these classes not only will have ceased to be a necessity, but will become a positive hindrance to production. They will fall as they arose at an earlier stage. Along with them the state will inevitably fall. Society, which will reorganize production on the basis of a free and equal association of the producers, will put the whole machinery of state where it will then belong: into a museum of antiquities, by the side of the spinning-wheel and the bronze axe.

In *Anti-Dühring*, Engels explains how the workers will bring about the end of the state and class society through social revolution:

> **Annotation 54 (continued)**
>
> The proletariat seizes from state power and turns the means of production into state property to begin with. But thereby it abolishes itself as the proletariat, abolishes all class distinctions and class antagonisms, and abolishes also the state as state. Society thus far, operating amid class antagonisms, needed the state, that is, an organization of the particular exploiting class, for the maintenance of its external conditions of production, and, therefore, especially, for the purpose of forcibly keeping the exploited class in the conditions of oppression determined by the given mode of production (slavery, serfdom or bondage, wage-labor). The state was the official representative of society as a whole, its concentration in a visible corporation. But it was this only insofar as it was the state of that class which itself represented, for its own time, society as a whole: in ancient times, the state of slave-owning citizens; in the Middle Ages, of the feudal nobility; in our own time, of the bourgeoisie. When at last it becomes the real representative of the whole of society, it renders itself unnecessary. As soon as there is no longer any social class to be held in subjection, as soon as class rule, and the individual struggle for existence based upon the present anarchy in production, with the collisions and excesses arising from this struggle, are removed, nothing more remains to be held in subjection — nothing necessitating a special coercive force, a state. The first act by which the state really comes forward as the representative of the whole of society — the taking possession of the means of production in the name of society — is also its last independent act as a state. State interference in social relations becomes, in one domain after another, superfluous, and then dies down of itself. The government of persons is replaced by the administration of things, and by the conduct of processes of production. The state is not "abolished." It withers away. This gives the measure of the value of the phrase "a free people's state," both as to its justifiable use for a long time from an agitational point of view, and as to its ultimate scientific insufficiency; and also of the so-called anarchists' demand that the state be abolished overnight.
>
> The role and function of the state under capitalism (as well as the role and function of the state during the socialist transition period between capitalism and communism) is highly relevant to the subjects of both Political Economy and Scientific Socialism.

The impact of superstructural components can affect the base in different ways, and different superstructural components may even contradict one another and impact the base in opposing directions. This reflects the different and opposing interests of different classes within society: some superstructural components will reinforce and maintain the current economic base, while other superstructural components will struggle to abandon the current economic base in favor of establishing a different economic base—in other words, a different social regime.

> **Annotation 55**
>
> Human society is not homogenous and not all human beings want to move society in the same direction, even within the same socio-economic class. As such, within a given human class society, superstructural components will develop to represent the contradicting interests of different groups of people within and between classes.

Annotation 55 (continued)

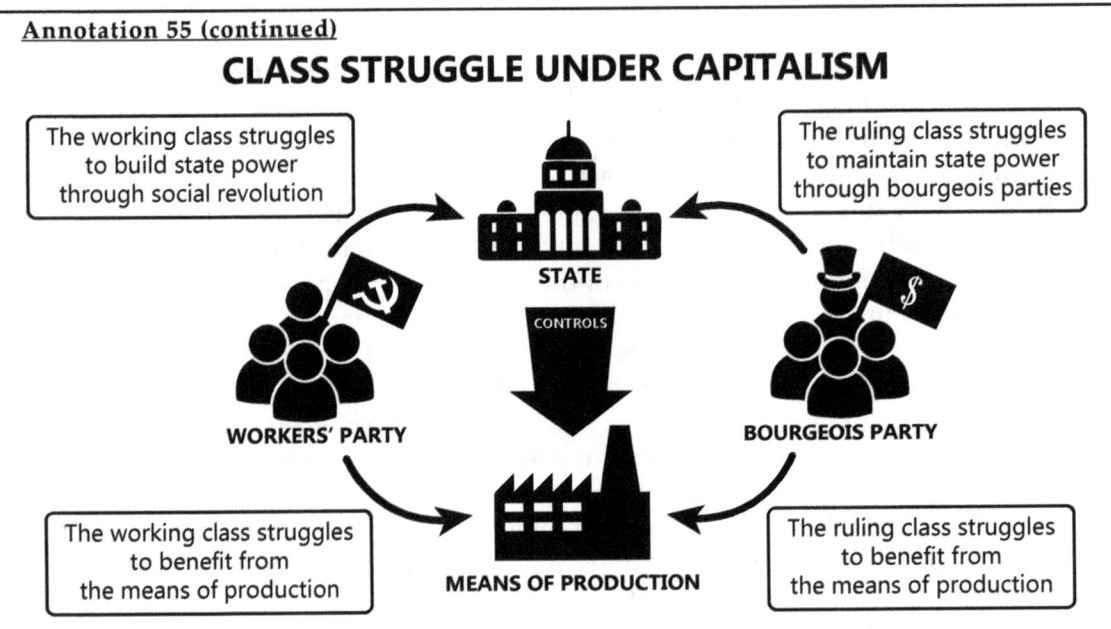

Under capitalism, classes struggle for state power and for benefits from the means of production. The primary institution which humans have developed for class struggle is the political party.

Class struggle is the dialectical contradiction which occurs between various classes as defined by relations of production within class society at a certain stage of development. These objective contradictions which occur in the material base of society also manifest in the superstructure regardless of whether the human beings involved in the class struggle are aware of their class position as it pertains to the material base or not (see Annotation 50, p. 90). Class struggle is the process through which different classes labor and fight to obtain more benefits from the productive forces of society.

Under feudalism, for example, there was a wide variety of superstructural components representing the different classes: churches and monasteries to represent the clergy, craft guilds to represent craftsmen, households consisting of servants and military forces to represent nobles, and so on.

Under capitalism, we can see that capitalist superstructural components exist primarily to advance the interests of the ruling bourgeois class. There also exist petty bourgeois superstructural elements to further the interests of that class, and working class superstructural elements to further the interests of the proletariat.

Many superstructural institutions *claim* to represent the working class yet, in truth, *serve* the interests of the bourgeoisie. There are also some superstructural components that seek to return back to previous relations of production. For example, some modern nations have political parties which seek to restore or strengthen the monarchy and other remnant classes from the feudal era. The most advanced proletariat superstructural elements seek to overthrow capitalist rule and to institute new relations of production. To do this, workers must build worker-controlled political parties which can build power for the proletariat and eventually seize control of the means of production through the construction of a workers' state through social revolution.

The impact of the superstructure on the base can take place in a positive or negative direction, depending on how suitable (or unsuitable) the superstructural components are to the development of the economy. If the superstructural components are suitable to economic development, they will have a positive impact. On the contrary, if they are not suitable, they will have a negative impact by inhibiting and sabotaging economic development.

> **Annotation 56**
>
> As Engels wrote in his letter to Conrad Schmidt of 1890:
>
>> The reaction of the state power upon economic development can take a threefold form. It can run in the same direction, and then the tempo of development becomes accelerated; it can buck up against that development in which case today in every large nation the state power is sure to go to smash for good; or it can block economic development along some directions and lay down its path along others.
>
> Engels' prediction that large nation states which "bucked up against" and resisted economic developments would "go to smash for good" proved prescient. Today there are no large nation states left which have not progressed on from a feudal mode of production; all such remnant states (such as the feudal states of China, the Ottoman Empire, and Russia, all of which managed to last into the 20th century) have, indeed, "gone to smash" and been replaced with higher-stage modes of production.

However, even though the impact of the superstructure on the base takes place in many ways and on many levels, the superstructure cannot play a decisive role in determining the base of society [nor, by extension, of society in general]. The base of society will always determine the ultimate direction of society's development based upon economic necessities.

> **Annotation 57**
>
> Although the superstructure and its components (including political parties, political consciousness, and other forms of organized political activity) cannot determine the material base of society, it is important to understand that they can impact the base significantly and bring about changes which benefit an oppressed class in significant ways. These impacts becomes especially pronounced when productive forces and relations of production are no longer compatible with each other, as is the case presently under capitalism. Because the productive forces are incompatible with capitalist relations of production, it is possible for workers to engage in social revolution to seize the means of production, build a state which they control, impose a dictatorship of the proletariat, and eventually end capitalism and class society altogether. This is the historical mission of the working class and the primary subject in the study of Scientific Socialism. The subjective role of the masses and of individuals in social revolution is discussed in detail in Chapter 6, starting on p. 230.

CHAPTER 3

SOCIAL BEING DETERMINES SOCIAL CONSCIOUSNESS; AND THE RELATIVE INDEPENDENCE OF SOCIAL CONSCIOUSNESS

In the system of Historical Materialism, a fundamental law is that *social being determines social consciousness*. This principle relates to the fundamental opposition between materialist and idealist worldviews of society.[23]

> **Annotation 58**
> Social being and social consciousness are defined in more detail in the next section. In short, social being can be understood as all the material aspects of human society while social consciousness refers to all the ways in which human consciousness manifests in society. The fundamental law of Historical Materialism that "social being determines social consciousness" is rooted in the Dialectical Materialist understanding of the relationship between matter and consciousness (described more in ***Part 1***, p. 88).

Lenin started from the principle that social being determines social consciousness when introducing Marx's system of Historical Materialist views:

> A realization of the inconsistency, incompleteness, and one-sidedness of the old materialism convinced Marx of the necessity of "bringing the science of society... into harmony with the materialist foundation, and of reconstructing it thereupon." Since materialism in general explains consciousness as the outcome of being, and not conversely, then materialism as applied to the social life of humanity has to explain social consciousness as the outcome of social being.[24]

> **Annotation 59**
> Here is an expanded version of the above-quoted passage from *The Materialist Conception of History From Karl Marx* by Lenin:
>
> > A realization of the inconsistency, incompleteness, and one-sidedness of the old materialism convinced Marx of the necessity of "bringing the science of society... into harmony with the materialist foundation, and of reconstructing it thereupon." Since materialism in general explains consciousness as the outcome of being, and not conversely, then materialism as applied to the social life of mankind has to explain social consciousness as the outcome of social being. As Marx writes in *Capital, Vol. I*:
> >
> > > "Technology discloses man's mode of dealing with Nature, the immediate process of production by which he sustains his life, and thereby also lays bare the mode of formation of his social relations, and of the mental conceptions that flow from them." In the preface to his *Contribution to the Critique of Political Economy*, Marx gives an integral formulation of the fundamental principles of materialism as applied to human society and its history, in the following words:

---

23 See ***Part 1***, p. 13.
24 *Karl Marx*, V. I. Lenin, 1914.

> Annotation 59 (continued)
>
> "In the social production of their life, men enter into definite relations that are indispensable and independent of their will, relations of production which correspond to a definite stage of development of their material <u>productive forces</u>.
>
> "The sum total of these relations of production constitutes the economic structure of society, the real foundation, on which rises a legal and political superstructure and to which correspond definite <u>forms of social consciousness</u>. The mode of production of material life conditions the social, political and intellectual life process in general. It is not the consciousness of men that determines their being, but, on the contrary, their social being that determines their consciousness. At a certain stage of their development, the material productive forces of society come in conflict with the existing relations of production, or—what is but a legal expression for the same thing—with the property relations within which they have been at work hitherto. From forms of development of the productive forces these relations turn into their fetters. Then begins an epoch of <u>social revolution</u>. With the change of the economic foundation the entire immense superstructure is more or less rapidly transformed. In considering such transformations a distinction should always be made between the material transformation of the economic conditions of production, which can be determined with the precision of natural science, and the legal, political, religious, aesthetic or philosophic—in short, ideological forms in which men become conscious of this conflict and fight it out.
>
> "Just as our opinion of an individual is not based on what he thinks of himself, so we cannot judge of such a period of transformation by its own consciousness; on the contrary, this consciousness must be explained rather from the contradictions of material life, from the existing conflict between the social productive forces and the relations of production... In broad outlines, Asiatic, ancient, feudal, and modern bourgeois modes of production can be designated as progressive epochs in the economic formation of society."
>
> The discovery of the materialist conception of history, or more correctly, the consistent continuation and extension of materialism into the domain of social phenomena, removed the two chief shortcomings in earlier historical theories. In the first place, the latter at best examined only the ideological motives in the historical activities of human beings, without investigating the origins of those motives, or ascertaining the <u>objective</u> laws governing the development of the system of social relations, or seeing the roots of these relations in the degree of development reached by material production; in the second place, the earlier theories did not embrace the activities of the masses of the population, whereas Historical Materialism made it possible for the first time to study with scientific accuracy the social conditions of the life of the masses, and the changes in those conditions. At best, pre-Marxist "sociology" and historiography brought forth an accumulation of raw facts, collected at random, and a description of individual aspects of the historical process. By examining the totality of opposing tendencies, by reducing them to precisely definable conditions of life and production of the various classes of society, by discarding subjectivism and arbitrariness in the choice of a particular "dominant" idea or in its interpretation, and by revealing

Historical Materialism

> **Annotation 59 (continued)**
>
> that, without exception, all ideas and all the various tendencies stem from the condition of the material forces of production, Marxism indicated the way to an all-embracing and comprehensive study of the process of the rise, development, and decline of socio-economic systems. People make their own history, but what determines the motives of people, of the mass of people, i.e., what is the sum total of all these clashes in the mass of human societies? What are the objective conditions of production of material life that form the basis of all man's historical activity? What is the law of development of these conditions? To all these Marx drew attention and indicated the way to a scientific study of history as a single process which, with all its immense variety and contradictoriness, is governed by definite laws.

I. SOCIAL BEING DETERMINES SOCIAL CONSCIOUSNESS

1. Definitions of social being and social consciousness

The term social being refers to the material life and material conditions of society. The fundamental factors of social being include:

- Mode of material production.
- Factors belonging to natural conditions.
- Geographical circumstances.
- Population.

These factors exist in a dialectical unity, interacting with each other and creating conditions for the survival and development of society in which the mode of material production is the most fundamental factor.

> **Annotation 60**
>
> The term "material base" describes relationships which are involved with material production processes in human society.
>
> **SOCIAL BEING**
>
> | MATERIAL BASE | NATURAL CONDITIONS | POPULATION |
> |---|---|---|
> | • Means of Production
• Human Labor
• Natural Resources
• Relations of Production | GEOGRAPHICAL CIRCUMSTANCES | ALL OTHER MATERIAL ASPECTS OF HUMANITY |
>
> *Social being encompasses the material base and all other material aspects of human society.*
>
> "Social being" is a broader term which encompasses not only the material base but also all other material factors which determine and impact human society. In addition to the material base of society, social being also includes *natural conditions*. Natural conditions include natural phenomena such as weather, climate, ecological factors, etc. Human societies can develop quite differently from one another based on natural con-

Annotation 60 (continued)

ditions. For example, a society which has frequent hurricanes and heavy rainfall might develop much differently from a society which develops in a desert environment.

Similarly, *geographical circumstances* are aspects of social being which can affect the development of human societies in significant ways. For instance, a human society located on an island near the equator will develop quite differently than a human society in a mountainous region with long, harsh winters.

Population is another factor of social being which can affect the development of human society in various ways. A society with a much larger population will be able to perform some industrial processes which a society with a much smaller population might not be able to perform. Population also has a strong correlation with productive forces, since a higher population provides a larger supply of human labor.

There are many other factors of social being, but the factors listed above are the most essential in determining the material conditions of a human society, with the mode of production being the most essential of all. This is because the mode of production can drastically change the ways in which human beings live in terms of material conditions. For example, a nation with a very small population but with a highly developed capitalist and industrialized mode of production would likely have a far more productive material base in terms of economic output than an agrarian feudal society even if the feudal society were to have a much larger population.

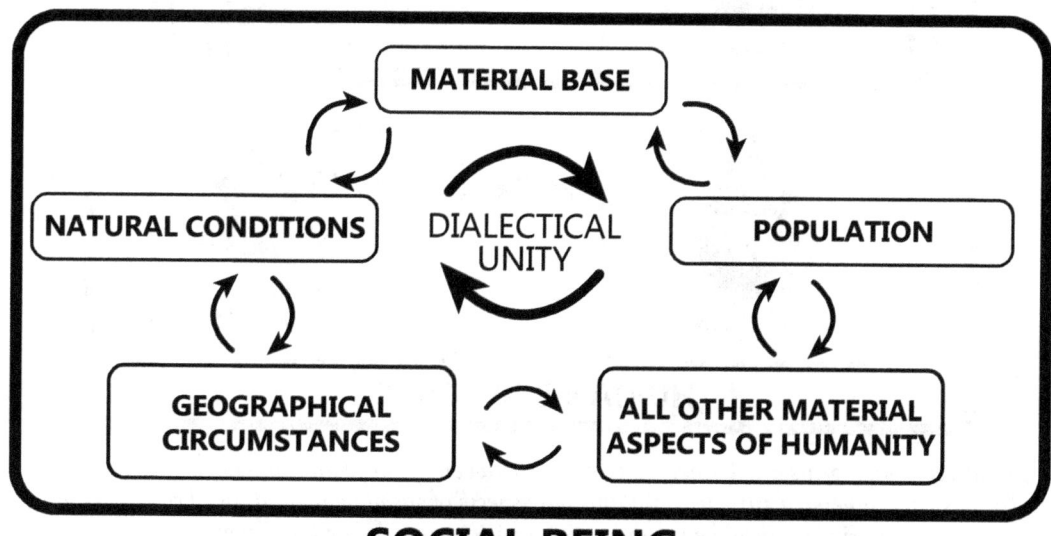

All aspects of social being exist in dialectical unity with one another and mutually develop each other over time.

All aspects of social being (mode of production, natural conditions, geographical circumstances, etc.) exist in dialectical unity with one another. To put it another way, these are all internal relations of social being which define and develop human society at the material level. If, for example, the population of human society grows it will impact natural conditions (i.e., humans will use more natural resources, create pollution, etc.), just as natural conditions impact the material base, and so on.

The term *social consciousness* refers to the mental life of society. Social consciousness arises from social being and reflects the different stages of development of social being.

> **Annotation 61**
>
> Social consciousness refers to ideas and mental life shared within and between groups of human beings. Social consciousness is shared through communication and through social activity. Social consciousness includes various forms of social consciousness as discussed in Annotation 16, p. 26. Social consciousness is defined by a relationship between a social-economic form's superstructure and all other aspects of consciousness within that society.
>
> *Superstructure* is determined by the material base of human society. In class society, a suitable superstructure is created because of objective necessity[25] to defend and stabilize the position of the ruling class.
>
>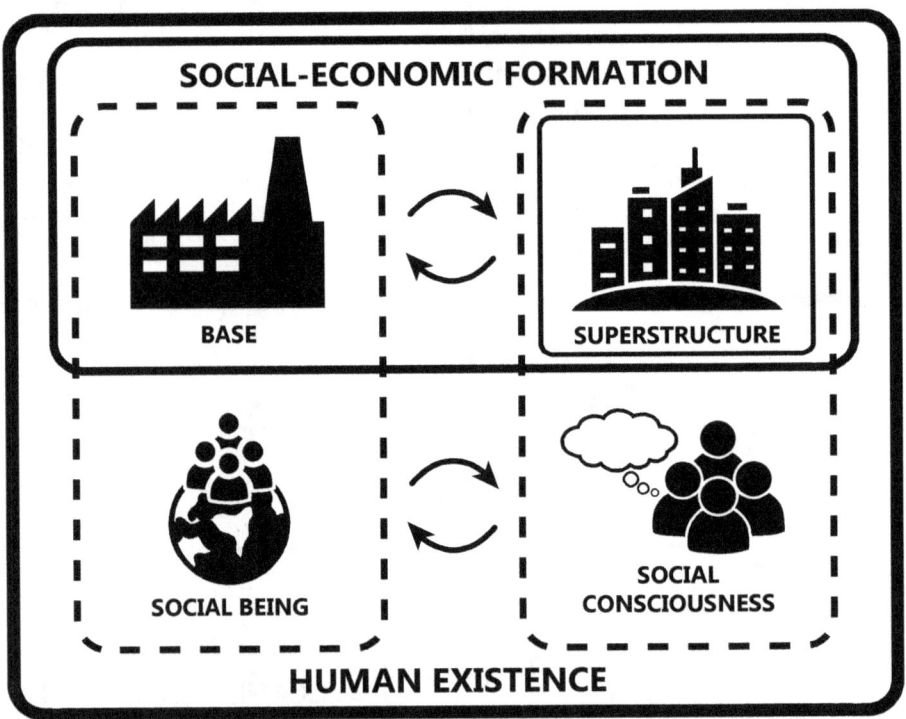
>
> *Social-economic forms are defined by relations between the base and superstructure of society. The base and superstructure are both internal aspects of social being and social consciousness, respectively. Social being and social consciousness define human existence.*
>
> Social consciousness develops from a lower state of direct and immediate observation of the world to higher states of more abstract and general understandings of the world. The lower state of social consciousness is *empirical social consciousness* and the higher state is called *theoretical social consciousness*.
>
> | Concrete | → | Abstract |
> |---|---|---|
> | Empirical Social Consciousness | *develops into* | Theoretical Social Consciousness |

---

25 This objective need is explained in detail in Annotation 50, p. 90.

> **Annotation 61 (continued)**
>
> Social knowledge is knowledge which is held collectively within and between human societies. Social knowledge can exist at a lower level of development as *ordinary social knowledge* or at a higher level of development as *scientific social knowledge*.
>
> | Directly Observed | | Systematically Derived |
> |---|---|---|
> | Ordinary Social Knowledge | → *develops into* | Scientific Social Knowledge |
>
> The textbook *Philosophy of Marxism-Leninism* gives the following definition of ordinary social knowledge:
>
>> Ordinary social knowledge includes all the knowledge, concepts, etc. of people in a certain community which are formed directly from daily practical activities and which have not yet been systematized and generalized into theory. Ordinary social knowledge often vividly and directly reflects many aspects of people's daily lives, and often influences daily life.
>
> Scientific social knowledge is knowledge that has been developed through more systematic and scientific observations and experiments and which is held socially. Based on the content and fields of social life that it reflects, scientific social knowledge can include many different forms: political knowledge, legal knowledge, moral knowledge, religious knowledge, aesthetic knowledge, philosophical knowledge, etc. Scientific knowledge develops from ordinary knowledge as groups of humans work together to seek more formal and systematic understandings of things we experience in daily life.
>
> **Correspondence Between Cognitive Theory of Dialectical Materialism and Historical Materialism**
>
> | | Concrete | Abstract |
> |---|---|---|
> | Dialectical Materialism | Empirical Consciousness | Theoretical Consciousness |
> | Historical Materialism | Empirical Social Consciousness | Theoretical Social Consciousness |
>
> | | Directly Observed | Systematically Derived |
> |---|---|---|
> | Dialectical Materialism | Ordinary Knowledge | Scientific Knowledge |
> | Historical Materialism | Ordinary Social Knowledge | Scientific Social Knowledge |
>
> This conception of social consciousness and social knowledge reflects the more general conception of consciousness and knowledge described by the Cognitive Theory of Dialectical Materialism (see *Part 1*, Annotation 216, p. 210).

There is a dialectical unity between social consciousness and individual consciousness. The relationship between social consciousness and individual consciousness is a relationship of Private and Common.

> **Annotation 62**
>
> The universal category pair of *Private* and *Common* is explained in detail in *Part 1*, p. 128. To briefly review:
>
> *Private* refers to specific things, phenomena, and ideas.
>
> *Common* refers to aspects, factors, and relations shared between private subjects.

Annotation 62 (continued)

Social consciousness represents the *common* aspects of *private* individual consciousness within a society. In other words, social consciousness encompasses all of the ideas, thoughts, attitudes, beliefs, prejudices, and other manifestations of consciousness which are broadly held in common within society.

Note that it is not necessary for all members of human society to *agree* on something for it to be *commonly held* as a social consciousness form within a society. Take, for example, a genre of music. Some people may enjoy listening to the genre, while others might not. What is held in common, regardless, is awareness and impact which the genre has on a society at large (including all the individual humans within society).

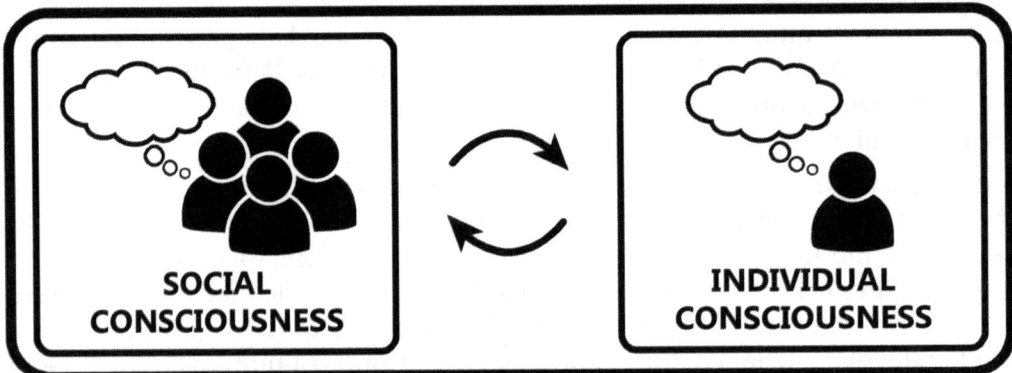

The phenomenon of human consciousness is defined by a relationship between the consciousness of individual human beings and social consciousness.

Individual consciousness and social consciousness have a dialectical relationship with one another, meaning that the consciousness of individuals can impact social consciousness and vice-versa. The work of a single artist, for example, might impact a wider art movement, and wider art movements will also impact the work of individual artists.

Generally speaking, throughout history and even today, human beings have not been fully aware of the true relationship between social being and social consciousness. As Lenin explained in *Materialism and Empirio-Criticism*:

> In all social formations of any complexity—and in the capitalist social formation in particular—people in their intercourse are not conscious of what kind of social relations are being formed, in accordance with what laws they develop, etc. For instance, a peasant when he sells his grain enters into "intercourse" with the world producers of grain in the world market, but he is not conscious of it; nor is he conscious of the kind of social relations that are formed on the basis of exchange. Social consciousness reflects social being—that is Marx's teaching. A reflection may be an approximately true copy of the reflected, but to speak of identity is absurd. Consciousness in general reflects being—that is a general principle of all materialism. It is impossible not to see its direct and inseparable connection with the principle of Historical Materialism: social consciousness reflects social being.

Social consciousness has a very complex structure. The structure of social consciousness can be analyzed from many different perspectives, including [but not limited to]:
- Aspects of Social Consciousness
- Empirical Social Consciousness vs. Theoretical Social Consciousness
- Social Psychology vs. Social Ideology
- Class Analysis of Social Consciousness

Each of these perspectives of analysis is described in more detail below.

> **Annotation 63**
>
> A perspective, or viewpoint, is the starting point of analysis. Various perspectives of social consciousness exist, and these perspectives develop over time. The perspectives of social consciousness which follow are those which are most relevant to Historical Materialist analysis.

Aspects of Social Consciousness

One can analyze different aspects of social consciousness. Each aspect of social consciousness is a reflection of a corresponding aspect of social being. For instance, political being is reflected as political consciousness; legal being is reflected as legal consciousness; moral being is reflected as moral consciousness; religious being is reflected as religious consciousness; aesthetic being is reflected as aesthetic consciousness; scientific being is reflected as scientific consciousness; etc.

> **Annotation 64**
>
> Aspects of social consciousness include such phenomena as art, music, scientific understanding, political ideology, etc. There are countless ways in which human beings have categorized and grouped together aspects of social consciousness, but it must be understood that all of these aspects exist in dialectical unity with each other.
>
> For example, advances in scientific understanding have led to new techniques and ideas about art, art movements can impact political movements, and so on.
>
> In addition, all of these aspects of social consciousness are *determined* by social being.
>
> For example, certain forms of art could not have existed without prerequisite developments in social being (i.e., photography could not have existed before the invention/existence of technologies such as the camera and the photographic process; the modern music industry as it exists today could not have developed before the development of technologies like recorded music as well as the development of the capitalist mode of production).

Empirical Social Consciousness vs. Theoretical Social Consciousness

Over time, aspects of social consciousness will reflect the social base from lower to higher levels—that is to say, with increasing sophistication and accuracy. Social consciousness can be analyzed based on this level of reflection [of the social base], and this analysis requires distinguishing between empirical social consciousness and theoretical social consciousness.

Empirical social consciousness is the sum total of the knowledge and conceptions of people in a certain community. It is formed directly from daily practical activities, which are not yet systematized nor generalized into theory.

Theoretical social consciousness includes ideas and conceptions which have been systematized and generalized into social theories, presented in the form of concepts, categories, and laws. Theoretical social consciousness has the ability to reflect objective reality in a general, profound, and accurate way. It can outline the essential relationships of things and phenomena within a society. Once theoretical social consciousness reaches a high enough level, it becomes possible for systematically formed ideologies to develop.

> **Annotation 65**
>
> As discussed previously in Annotation 61, p. 108, *Empirical Social Consciousness* and *Theoretical Social Consciousness* are concepts which closely relate to the corresponding psychological concepts of *Empirical Consciousnes* and *Theoretical Consciousness* from the cognitive theory of Dialectical Materialism.[26] Social consciousness is a higher form of individual consciousness as it reflects the collective development of the mental life of human beings across society.
>
> **Empirical Social Consciousness**
>
> Empirical consciousness describes consciousness which reflects the process of collecting data about the world through observation, experimentation, and practice.
>
> Empirical social consciousness is empirical consciousness which human beings have developed collectively through social processes into a higher *social form*.
>
> **Theoretical Social Consciousness**
>
> Along the same lines, theoretical consciousness is the indirect, abstract, systematic level of perception in which the nature and laws of things and phenomena are generalized and abstracted.
>
> Theoretical social consciousness is theoretical consciousness which human beings have developed collectively through social processes into a higher social form of consciousness.
>
> **Development of Social Consciousness**
>
> Just as empirical consciousness develops into theoretical consciousness as an individual psychological phenomenon, empirical social consciousness also develops into the higher form of theoretical social consciousness. Theoretical consciousness arises from conscious reflection on accumulated knowledge, as human beings seek to develop general and abstract understanding of the underlying principles of processes we experience in the world. The highest form of theoretical social consciousness is *ideology*. In the article "Social Consciousness in Marxism-Leninism" by Dr. Nguyen Thi Hong Van (professor of science and technology at Posts and Telecommunications Institute of Technology in Hanoi) explains the concept of ideology in more detail:
>
>> Ideology is a high level of social consciousness, formed when people are more aware of their material living conditions. Ideology has the ability to delve deeply into the nature of subjects including social relationships.

---

26 See *Part 1*, p. 210.

> **Annotation 65 (continued)**
>
> Ideology is a theoretical perception of social existence, a system of ideological views (political, philosophical, ethical, artistic, religious, and so on) that is the result of a generalization of social experience. Ideology is formed self-consciously. That is to say, it is formed and propagated in society through social activity which is conscious and intentional.

Ideology, though highly developed consciousness, is not necessarily true and accurate scientific consciousness. It can, indeed, constitute false consciousness, which is consciousness that is misaligned with reality, as Dr. Nguyen explains:

> When studying ideology, it is necessary to distinguish between scientific and non-scientific ideology. Scientific ideology accurately and objectively reflects the material relationships of society. Unscientific ideology also reflects material and social relationships, but in a false, illusory, and objectively distorted form.
>
> As a part of social consciousness, ideology greatly influences the development of science. For instance, throughout history natural science has been highly influenced by ideology. Philosophical consciousness in particular plays an important role in the process of generalizing scientific research.

Social Psychology vs. Social Ideology

Social consciousness can reflect social being with varying degrees of directness or indirectness. Social consciousness which reflects social being directly is social psychology, while social consciousness which reflects social being indirectly is social ideology.

Social psychology is the whole emotional life, mood, aspirations, will, etc. of certain human communities. Social psychology is a direct and spontaneous reflection of living situation of the human beings who compose a society.

Social ideology is the entire system of social conceptions and viewpoints such as politics, philosophy, ethics, art, religion, etc. It is an indirect and self-conscious reflection of social being. Social psychology and social ideology are two levels, two different modes of reflection of social consciousness for the same social being. They have a dialectical relationship with each other but social psychology does not produce social ideology.

> **Annotation 66**
>
> The relationship between Social Psychology and Social Ideology is explained more in *Philosophy of Marxism-Leninism*:
>
> > Social psychology includes all emotions, desires, moods, habits, and so on, which belong to a segment of people or all of society. Social psychology is formed under the direct influence of the daily life of people and it reflects that life. The characteristic of social psychology is that it directly reflects people's daily living conditions. It is a spontaneous reflection, often recording the superficial aspects of social existence. It is incapable of fully, clearly, and deeply outlining the nature of human social relationships.
> >
> > Human concepts of social psychology are still experiential and have not been expressed theoretically. This means that intellectual factors are intertwined with emotional factors. However, the important role of social psychology in the development of social consciousness cannot be denied. Karl Marx, Engels, Lenin,

> **Annotation 66 (continued)**
>
> and Ho Chi Minh attached great importance to studying the people's socio-psychological state in order to understand the people, educate the people, and bring them to actively and voluntarily participate in the struggle for a better society.
>
> Ideology is social consciousness that has attained some level of theoretical awareness of social being. Ideology is a system of viewpoints and ideas (of politics, philosophy, ethics, art, religion, etc.) that are the result of generalization of social experience. Ideology is formed consciously. That is to say, ideology is created by ideologues of certain classes and propagated in society.
>
> It is necessary to distinguish between scientific ideology and non-scientific ideology. Scientific ideology accurately and objectively reflects the material relationships of society. Non-scientific ideology also reflects the material relationships of society, but in a false, illusory or distorted form.
>
> As a component of social consciousness, ideology greatly influences the development of science. The history of natural science has shown the important effect of ideology, especially philosophical ideology, on the process of generalizing scientific research and understanding.
>
> Although social psychology and social ideology exist at two levels and as two different modes of reflection of social consciousness, they have a dialectical relationship with each other. They have the same origin, which is social being. They both reflect social being. Social psychology can contribute to favorable conditions for class members to absorb class ideology.
>
>This can work for or against the development of class consciousness in workers. For example, a ruling class may offer benefits to an oppressed class to reduce or inhibit the development of class consciousness. If conditions deteriorate so that oppressed classes are more dissatisfied with their lives, class consciousness may develop more readily.
>
> It is also possible for agents of a ruling class to use social psychology to influence and sway an oppressed class into opposing their own class interests. For instance, the capitalist class might work to convince workers that their problems stem from other social groups or phenomena to keep them from understanding the nature of class society. False consciousness is often used to divide workers and prevent workers from resisting capitalism.
>
> The textbook *Philosophy of Marxism-Leninism* explains how scientific consciousness which accurately reflets reality can help to develop class consciousness:
>
>> Developing a close relationship between ideology (especially progressive scientific ideology) and social psychology and with a lively and rich social life will help make social ideology and theory less rigid and less faulty. Similarly, social ideology and social theory increase the intellectual aspect of social psychology. Scientific ideology promotes the development of social psychology in a correct and healthy direction which is beneficial to social progress. Anti-scientific and reactionary ideology stimulates the development of more negative elements of social psychology.
>>
>> However, it must be understood that ideology does not stem directly from social psychology, nor is it a direct expression of social psychology.

> **Annotation 66 (continued)**
>
> In other words, it is possible for social psychology and ideology to be at odds with each other. Workers may suffer from capitalist oppression yet still adopt ideology which constitutes false consciousness and this may lead them to support the very system which oppresses them. Similarly, it is also possible for workers who live relatively comfortable lives to have scientific consciousness which allows them to understand the system of capitalism for what it is and to hold progressive views, up to and including class consciousness, as *Philosophy of Marxism-Leninism* explains:
>
>> Any ideology that reflects contemporary relationships also inherits previously existing social theories, ideas and perspectives. For example, medieval religious ideology in Western Europe expressed the interests of the feudal class, but was born directly from idealist philosophical ideas from ancient times and Christian ideology from the early Christian era.
>>
>> The Marxist-Leninist ideology was not directly born from the social psychology of the working class, which was spontaneously fighting against the bourgeoisie at that time, but was a theoretical generalization from the totality of human knowledge, from the experiences of the class struggle of the working class, which at the same time directly inherited the socio-economic and philosophical theories of the late 18th and early 19th centuries.
>>
>> Thus we can see that social ideology is organically related to social psychology and is influenced by social psychology, but it is not simply a "condensation" of social psychology.
>
> Ho Chi Minh explained the importance of deeply understanding the social psychology of the working class in the context of building socialism, writing in *Modify the Working Style*:
>
>> The people are very clever, very enthusiastic, very heroic. Therefore, we [communist cadres] must learn from the people, ask the people, understand the people. Every slogan, every project, every policy must rely on the ideas and experience of the people. We must listen to the people's desires. . . However, this does not mean that we will follow blindly whatever the people say. Cadres must have our own ways of discerning. This means we must discern ideas carefully. We must analyze carefully all classes of the people.

In a class-based society, social consciousness is also class-based, reflecting different and even opposing material living conditions and interests between classes. Each class has its own specific mental life, but the ideology that dominates society is always the ideology of the ruling class.

> **Annotation 67**
>
> In *Critique of Political Economy*, Karl Marx discusses how social consciousness emerges from and is determined by material reality:
>
>> The mode of production of material life conditions the general process of social, political and intellectual life. It is not the consciousness of men that determines their existence, but their social existence that determines their consciousness.

Annotation 67 (continued)

In class society, class consciousness is a form of social consciousness which reflects class struggle. Class consciousness plays an important role in the development of human society from one mode of production to the next. This is because class consciousness is a prerequisite to social revolution.

As productive forces develop, they eventually clash with existing relations of production, leading to new relations of production. This reflects the Law of Suitability (see p. 42). This change in the base drives transformation in the superstructure, per the Law of the Base Determining the Superstructure of Society (see p. 90).

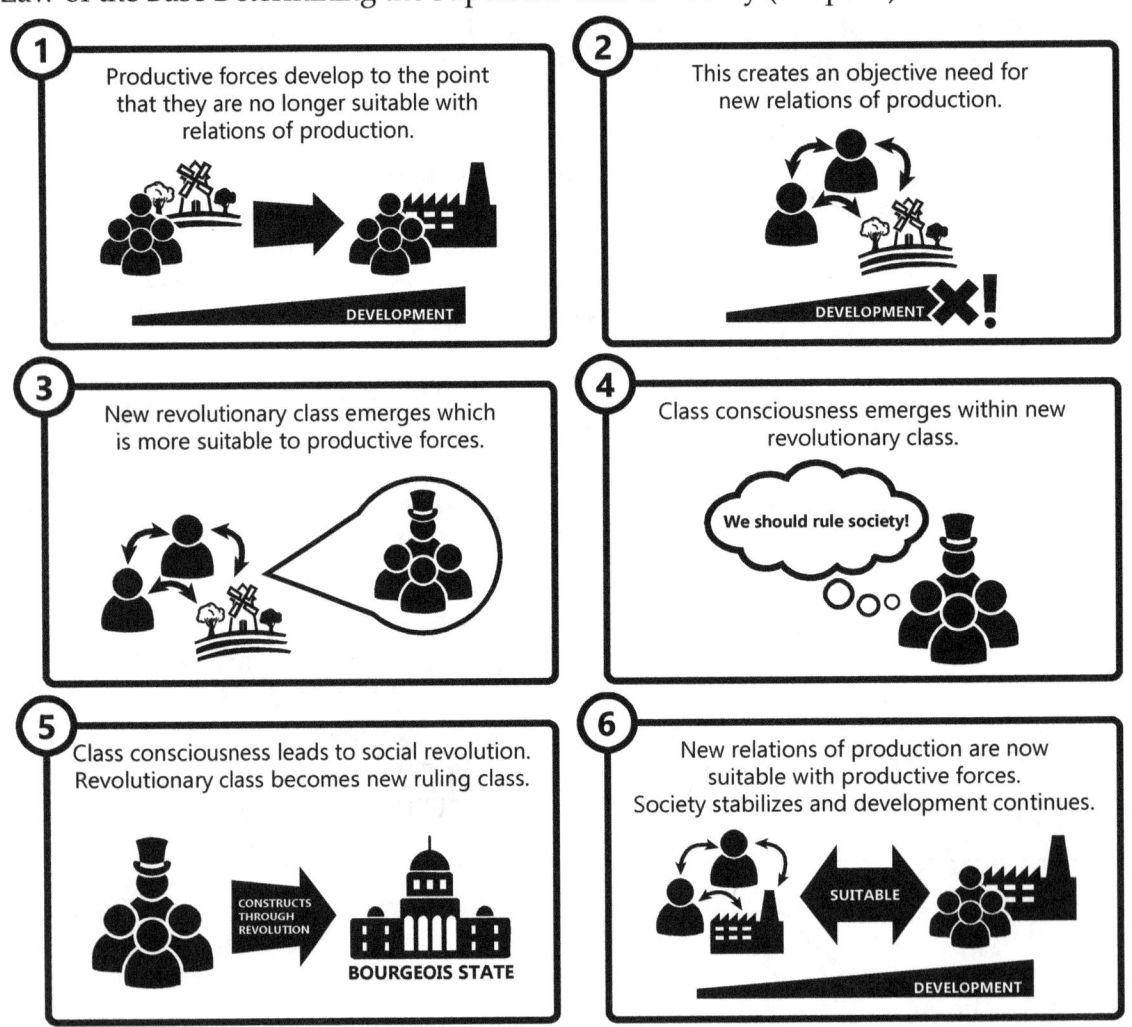

In order for a revolutionary class to take control of society, class consciousness must be developed to a high enough degree that social revolution can be undertaken.

Eventually a new revolutionary class will emerge which is more suitable to newly formed productive forces and relations of production. In time the revolutionary class will develop its own social consciousness and awareness of itself as a class. This is referred to as *class consciousness*.

In class society, social consciousness has a class character, meaning that different classes will think differently about society, the world, and each other. However, it

> **Annotation 67 (continued)**
>
> must be understood that the ruling class of a given society shapes the predominant social consciousness in that society, as Marx explains in *Critique of Political Economy*:
>
>> Just as one does not judge an individual by what he thinks about himself, so one cannot judge such a period of transformation by its consciousness, but, on the contrary, this consciousness must be explained from the contradictions of material life, from the conflict existing between the social forces of production and the relations of production. No social order is ever destroyed before all the productive forces for which it is sufficient have been developed, and new superior relations of production never replace older ones before the material conditions for their existence have matured within the framework of the old society.
>
> This is why all philosophies and ideologies must be studied in the context of the class society and material conditions from which they have emerged and also why the study of philosophy and ideology detached from class analysis is a useless pursuit.[27]
>
> Class consciousness plays a special role in the development of class society because the development of class consciousness by a revolutionary class is a prerequisite to social revolution. Marx cautioned that we must not mistake the necessity for class consciousness to proceed social revolution for an idealist position:
>
>> The weapon of criticism cannot, of course, replace criticism by weapons, material force must be overthrown by material force; but theory also becomes a material force as soon as it has gripped the masses. Theory is capable of gripping the masses as soon as it demonstrates *ad hominem*, and it demonstrates ad hominem as soon as it becomes radical. To be radical is to grasp the root of the matter.
>
> When Marx says that theory must "grip the masses *ad hominem*," he means that the theory must manifest in the actual life conditions and conscious activities of the masses. It is not enough for the masses to simply be *aware* of their own class position and their historical mission to enact social revolution; they must bring these ideas to life by building institutions capable of revolutionary struggle. Of these institutions, the most important is the state, because it allows a class to control the means of production.[28] In order to build a state which represents its own class interests, advanced elements of the revolutionary class must build a revolutionary institution (i.e., a revolutionary party) and a corresponding revolutionary ideology (i.e., revolutionary theory). To make class consciousness a material force, revolutionary theory must serve to develop and instill class consciousness widely within the revolutionary class, and a party is necessary to allow advanced elements of the revolutionary class to struggle and enact social revolution, as Lenin explained in *What is to be Done*:
>
>> Without revolutionary theory there can be no revolutionary movement... the role of the vanguard fighter can be fulfilled only by a party that is guided by the most advanced theory.
>
> If the objective economic conditions of society demand it (i.e., if the economic base is no longer suitable with the superstructure of society), then eventually—through the construction of revolutionary theory which is put into practice by a revolutionary party—the revolutionary class will eventually develop revolutionary theory and a revolu-

---

[27] For further critique of idealist conceptions of history, see Annotation 13, p. 19.
[28] See Annotation 49, p. 88.

> **Annotation 67 (continued)**
>
> tionary party which will guide the masses to a new stage of development; the revolutionary class will become the new ruling class. This process of development reflects the Law of Suitability which is discussed in Annotation 33, p. 48.
>
> In *A Militant Agreement for the Uprising*, Lenin explained that in our present age, a precondition for social revolution by the working class is the development of a Marxist workers' party:
>
>> We see in the independent, uncompromisingly Marxist party of the revolutionary proletariat the sole pledge of socialism's victory and the road to victory that is most free from vacillations.
>
> It must also be understood that social revolution cannot be fully secured until a dictatorship of the proletariat is formed via the construction of a state which is controlled by the working class. This will give the workers' a commanding position over the capitalist class which gives workers control over the means of production. In doing so, political revolution is developed into economic revolution. This allows human society to advance to the next stage of development in accordance with the laws and principles of Historical Materialism and Social Formation Theory.
>
> Bearing all this in mind, the historical mission of the working class can be summarized as follows:
>
> Advanced elements of the working class must build a revolutionary party and develop corresponding revolutionary theory. This superstructural configuration of institution and ideology must be used to develop class consciousness among the working masses and guide them to revolution. This revolution must result in the construction of a workers' state which can bring about the dictatorship of the proletariat. Only through the dictatorship of the proletariat can workers fulfill the historical mission of ending class society once and for all.
>
> Ending capitalism will require a high development of class consciousness among the working class. Until the working class develops class consciousness on a mass level, social revolution and the overthrow of the ruling class of capitalists will remain impossible, despite the fact that the material conditions have already been in place since Marx and Engels were alive. Understanding the role of social consciousness in human society and the role of revolutionary theory and the revolutionary party in the arena of class struggle is therefore of vital importance in the study of both Historical Materialism and Scientific Socialism. Historical Materialist analysis is concerned with processes of development in both social being and social consciousness of human society, while Scientific Socialism is concerned with the practice of developing the working class in order to bring about social revolution and an end to capitalism.

The prevailing social ideology affects the consciousness of all classes in social life. According to Marx and Engels:

> The class which has the means of material production at its disposal, has control at the same time over the means of mental production, so that thereby, generally speaking, the ideas of those who lack the means of mental production are subject to it."[29]

---

29 Karl Marx and Friedrich Engels, *The German Ideology*, 1846.

Annotation 68

In the full passage from which the above quotation is taken, Marx explains in detail the process by which the ideas of the ruling class become predominant in class society:

> The ideas of the ruling class are in every epoch the ruling ideas, i.e. the class which is the ruling material force of society, is at the same time its ruling intellectual force. The class which has the means of material production at its disposal, has control at the same time over the means of mental production, so that thereby, generally speaking, the ideas of those who lack the means of mental production are subject to it. The ruling ideas are nothing more than the ideal expression of the dominant material relationships, the dominant material relationships grasped as ideas; hence of the relationships which make the one class the ruling one, therefore, the ideas of its dominance. The individuals composing the ruling class possess among other things consciousness, and therefore think. Insofar, therefore, as they rule as a class and determine the extent and compass of an epoch, it is self-evident that they do this in its whole range, hence among other things rule also as thinkers, as producers of ideas, and regulate the production and distribution of the ideas of their age: thus their ideas are the ruling ideas of the epoch. For instance, in an age and in a country where royal power, aristocracy, and bourgeoisie are contending for mastery and where, therefore, mastery is shared, the doctrine of the separation of powers proves to be the dominant idea and is expressed as an "eternal law."

In other words, the consciousness of the ruling class is rooted in the material relations of production of society and thus reflects the dominance of the ruling class. Marx goes on to explain how some individuals become dedicated ideologists tasked with systematizing the ideas of the ruling class to higher levels of theoretical consciousness:[30]

> The division of labour, which we already saw above as one of the chief forces of history up till now, manifests itself also in the ruling class as the division of mental and material labour, so that inside this class one part appears as the thinkers of the class (its active, conceptive ideologists, who make the perfecting of the illusion of the class about itself their chief source of livelihood), while the others' attitude to these ideas and illusions is more passive and receptive, because they are in reality the active members of this class and have less time to make up illusions and ideas about themselves.

Marx then introduces the concept of revolutionary class consciousness:

> The existence of revolutionary ideas in a particular period presupposes the existence of a revolutionary class.

Here, Marx is referring to the fact that before revolutionary ideas can be generated, material conditions for those ideas must first be present. These material conditions arise from the development of an economic class which would better suit the newly developed productive forces. This new revolutionary class will eventually develop consciousness of its own existence and its own revolutionary potential, and this class consciousness will eventually lead to social revolution in which the revolutionary class seizes control of the means of production and builds a state to enforce its rule.

---

30 Ideologists are discussed more in Annotation 102, p. 185.

Annotation 68 (continued)

These revolutionary classes emerge from material development which takes place in the social being of human society. Before a revolutionary class can take power and usher in a new stage of development of class society and a new mode of production, they must first stage a social revolution. Before a social revolution can be carried out, the class consciousness of the revolutionary class must be developed to a high level.

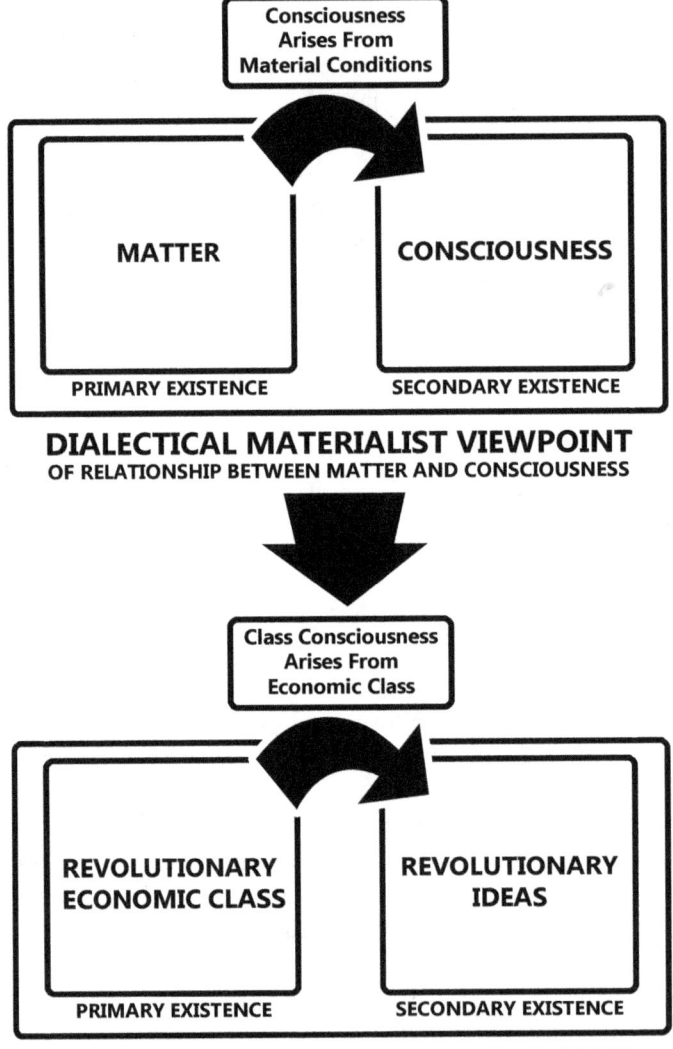

Marx's observation that revolutionary ideas stem from social being has a basis in the Dialectical Materiailst conception of the relationship between matter and consciousness.

Class consciousness, therefore, is the social consciousness of a particular class in society *pertaining to itself and its relations to other classes and the means of production*. As a revolutionary class comes to cement its power over class society, the class consciousness of the new ruling class becomes the predominant consciousness of all of society. This begins to shift, however, as the productive forces develop and eventually reach

Annotation 68 (continued)

a point of development which makes them no longer compatible with the relations of production. At this point, a new revolutionary class emerges and class consciousness begins to develop (based on that material development of the productive forces).

Next, Marx explains how each new stage of development of the mode of production and relations of production leads to dominant social consciousness which must present itself as more "universal" to justify the position of the new ruling class. Marx also critiques historians who do not consider the material conditions which give rise to the philosophies and ideals of any given era of human society:

> If now in considering the course of history we detach the ideas of the ruling class from the ruling class itself and attribute to them an independent existence, if we confine ourselves to saying that these or those ideas were dominant at a given time, without bothering ourselves about the conditions of production and the producers of these ideas, if we thus ignore the individuals and world conditions which are the source of the ideas, we can say, for instance, that during the time that the aristocracy was dominant, the concepts honour, loyalty, etc. were dominant, during the dominance of the bourgeoisie the concepts freedom, equality, etc. The ruling class itself on the whole imagines this to be so. This conception of history, which is common to all historians, particularly since the eighteenth century, will necessarily come up against the phenomenon that increasingly abstract ideas hold sway, i.e. ideas which increasingly take on the form of universality. For each new class which puts itself in the place of one ruling before it, is compelled, merely in order to carry through its aim, to represent its interest as the common interest of all the members of society, that is, expressed in ideal form: it has to give its ideas the form of universality, and represent them as the only rational, universally valid ones. The class making a revolution appears from the very start, if only because it is opposed to a class, not as a class but as the representative of the whole of society; it appears as the whole mass of society confronting the one ruling class.
>
> It can do this because, to start with, its interest really is more connected with the common interest of all other non-ruling classes, because under the pressure of hitherto existing conditions its interest has not yet been able to develop as the particular interest of a particular class. Its victory, therefore, benefits also many individuals of the other classes which are not winning a dominant position, but only insofar as it now puts these individuals in a position to raise themselves into the ruling class. When the French bourgeoisie overthrew the power of the aristocracy, it thereby made it possible for many proletarians to raise themselves above the proletariat, but only insofar as they become bourgeois.

Finally, Marx explains how this process will eventually result in an end to class society. Once the proletarian working class is able to successfully enact social revolution and overtake the capitalist class, there will no longer be any basis for class consciousness, and social consciousness will develop along truly universal lines:

> Every new class, therefore, achieves its hegemony only on a broader basis than that of the class ruling previously, whereas the opposition of the non-ruling class against the new ruling class later develops all the more sharply and profoundly.

> **Annotation 68 (continued)**
>
> Both these things determine the fact that the struggle to be waged against this new ruling class, in its turn, aims at a more decided and radical negation of the previous conditions of society than could all previous classes which sought to rule. This whole semblance, that the rule of a certain class is only the rule of certain ideas, comes to a natural end, of course, as soon as class rule in general ceases to be the form in which society is organised, that is to say, as soon as it is no longer necessary to represent a particular interest as general or the "general interest" as ruling.
>
> Next, Marx discusses the idealist conception of history. Historians in a class society tend to function as ideologists for the ruling class. This leads to three "efforts" which historians undertake to make it seem as though ideas are the driving force of history. In this way, the ruling class is better able to justify its own position by convincing the oppressed classes that the ideas of the ruling class are superior and that those ideas are what drive history (as opposed to material processes and developments in the material base of human society).
>
> According to Marx, in order to promote such an idealist interpretation of history, the ideologists of the ruling class must accomplish the following three tasks:
>
> 1. Separate the ideas of those ruling for empirical reasons, under empirical conditions and as empirical individuals, from these actual rulers, and thus recognize the rule of ideas or illusions in history.
>
> In other words, historians who serve the agenda of the ruling class must draw a distinction between the human beings who rule over society as a ruling class and the ideas which they conceive to justify their own position of power over society. By separating the ideas from the humans themselves, one can ignore the power they have in terms of the material relations of production. This enables ideologists to pretend that the ideas themselves rule over society and advance humanity forward when, in reality, it is the material dominance of the ruling class over the means of production which enable them to push their agenda forward through material processes.
>
> 2. Bring an order into this rule of ideas, prove a mystical connection among the successive ruling ideas, which is managed by understanding them as "acts of self-determination on the part of the concept" (this is possible because by virtue of their empirical basis these ideas are really connected with one another and because, conceived as mere ideas, they become self-distinctions, distinctions made by thought).
>
> In other words, it is necessary to develop a theoretical system of the supposed "rule of ideas" over society. This system of thought must be formulated to convince the oppressed classes that the best ideas are the ones that will rise to the top and advance society forward. Once this idea of the "rule of ideas" is established, then the ideas of the ruling class must be "mystically connected" to the ideas which best serve the agenda of the ruling class. As an example, under capitalism, ideologists often refer to the "free market of ideas" as a theoretical system which advances society forward. These same ideologists then associate ideas which justify capitalism as "winning in the free market of ideas." In this manner, workers can be convinced that capitalists rule over society not because they have the most wealth, power, and control over the means of produc-

Annotation 68 (continued)

tion, but because "their ideas have won in the free market of ideas." This is necessary to keep workers from realizing the true nature of the underlying material base which keeps capitalists in power and to prevent workers from developing revolutionary class consciousness which might threaten the power and position of the ruling class.

3. To remove the mystical appearance of this "self-determining concept" it is changed into a person – "Self-Consciousness" – or, to appear thoroughly materialistic, into a series of persons, who represent the "concept" in history, into the "thinkers," the "philosophers," the ideologists, who again are understood as the manufacturers of history, as the "council of guardians," as the rulers. Thus, the whole body of materialistic elements has been removed from history and now full rein can be given to the speculative steed.

In other words, it is necessary to make the imagined system of the "rule of ideas" seem less mystical and more grounded in reality. In order to make the "rule of ideas" and the dominance of the ideas of the ruling class seem more realistic and acceptable to the oppressed class, historians must fabricate groups of individuals who are "thinkers" in society.

These thinkers are then described as the figures in human society who advance history forward and determine the course of development of human society. In this way, the material processes which actually determine the development of human history can be concealed and the oppressed classes can be made to believe that the ideas of the ruling class are the best ideas formulated by the best thinkers. Next, Marx sarcastically explains that historians who develop such idealist conceptions of history can't seem to accomplish the "trivial insight" of distinguishing between what people think of themselves and who they actually are:

> Whilst in ordinary life every shopkeeper is very well able to distinguish between what somebody professes to be and what he really is, our historians have not yet won even this trivial insight. They take every epoch at its word and believe that everything it says and imagines about itself is true.

Finally, Marx explains that these idealist conceptions of history are only one component of the ideological program of the ruling class:

> This historical method... and especially the reason why [it was formulated], must be understood from its connection with the illusion of ideologists in general, e.g. the illusions of the jurist, politicians (of the practical statesmen among them, too), from the dogmatic dreamings and distortions of these fellows; this is explained perfectly easily from their practical position in life, their job, and the division of labour.

In summary, class society produces historians, politicians, and other such ideologists to develop systems of theoretical consciousness and ideologies which promote, defend, and advance the position and agenda of the ruling class. This is to conceal the fact that the ruling class only has power over society because of the material conditions and processes which give them dominance over the means of production. It is, however, possible for the oppressed class to develop a class consciousness of their own and, once this consciousness has developed to a high enough level, to enact social revolution and take control over the means of production.

> **Annotation 68 (continued)**
>
> In terms of modern capitalism, this is very important to understand for those wishing to liberate the working class. As the working class comes to see the false consciousness which the capitalist class imposes upon society, they will begin to develop a class consciousness of their own. Once a high enough level of class consciousness develops then the resulting social revolution over the capitalist class will eventually lead to the end of class society altogether. This will allow humans to develop social consciousness which universally reflects the will of the people in general without one class dominating and ruling over society.
>
> This makes the historical mission of the working class especially important since only the working class can bring an end to class society.

2. The decisive role of social being in determining social consciousness

One of the great accomplishments of Marx and Engels was the development of materialism to its peak and the construction of a materialist viewpoint of history.[31] This materialist conception of history scientifically solved the problem of the formation and development of social consciousness.

Marx and Engels have thus proven the following statements to be true:

1. The mental life of society [social consciousness] is formed and developed on the basis of material life [social being];
2. The source of social ideology and social psychology cannot be found within social consciousness and social psychology.
3. The source of social consciousness and social psychology is found, not within the human mind, but in physical reality.

> **Annotation 69**
>
> As Marx wrote in his preface to *Critique of Political Economy*:
>
> > Neither legal relations nor political forms could be comprehended whether by themselves or on the basis of a so-called general development of the human mind, but that on the contrary they originate in the material conditions of life
> >
> > ... It is not the consciousness of men that determines their existence, but their social existence that determines their consciousness.
>
> This is the basis for the Law of the Relationship Between the Social Being and Social Consciousness, which states that social being determines social consciousness, while it is also possible for social consciousness to impact back upon material reality and social being. This law of Historical Materialism has an objective basis in the Dialectical Materialist onception of the relationship between matter and consciousness (see *Part 1*, p. 88). The Law of the Relationship Between Social Being and Social Consciousness is further explained in *The German Ideology* by Marx and Engels:
>
> > The production of ideas, of conceptions, of consciousness, is at first directly interwoven with the material activity and the material intercourse of men, the language of real life. Conceiving, thinking, the mental intercourse of men, appear at this stage as the direct efflux [out-flow] of their material behaviour.

---

31 See *Part 1*, p. 37.

Annotation 69 (continued)

In other words, human ideology initially corresponds directly to physical activity which takes place in the real world. As these ideas develop it can appear as though higher forms of consciousness (such as religious or political ideas) are unlinked from the material world. However, consciousness is always rooted in the material world and in the physical activity of human beings, no matter how developed consciousness might become. As Marx and Engels further explain in *The German Ideology*:

> The same applies to mental production as expressed in the language of politics, laws, morality, religion, metaphysics, etc., of a people. Men are the producers of their conceptions, ideas, etc.—real, active men, as they are conditioned by a definite development of their productive forces and of the intercourse corresponding to these, up to its furthest forms. Consciousness can never be anything else than conscious existence, and the existence of men is their actual life-process.

It is crucial to understand the emphasis placed on the fact that ideas originate from "real, active" human beings living out "actual life-processes." This stands in contrast to idealist conceptions of human consciousness which seek to either separate human consciousness from the material world (as with objective idealism), or to deny the existence of the material world altogether (as with subjective idealism). Marx and Engels made it clear that all consciousness is determined by the material world and material labor activities which humans undertake to survive. *The German Ideology* continues:

> If in all ideology men and their circumstances appear upside-down as in a camera obscura, this phenomenon arises just as much from their historical life-process as the inversion of objects on the retina does from their physical life-process.

This statement can seem confusing as it refers to an antiquated optical device: the "camera obscura." A camera obscura projects an image onto a screen, and this projected image appears upside down. Similarly, the lens of the human eye also inverts images when projecting them onto the retina at the back of the human eye.

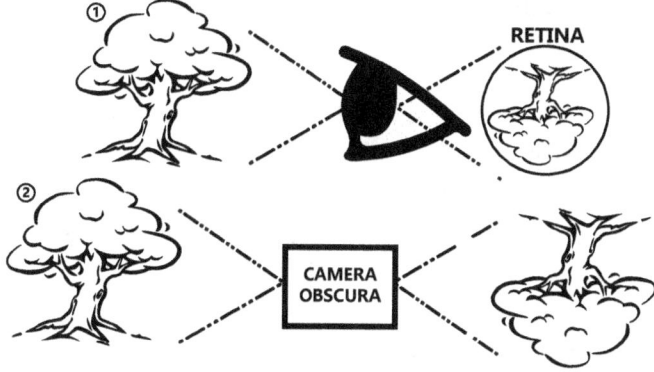

The human eye (1) projects an upside down image on the retina just as a camera obscura (2) projects an upside-down on a screen.

In this passage, Marx and Engels are explaining that false consciousness arises from material conditions and material life processes. In other words, since all consciousness arises from our experiences in the real world, it must also be true that false consciousness arises from our experiences in the real world.

> **Annotation 69 (continued)**
>
> Some idealists (such as empiricists) may assert that inaccurate perceptions of reality are evidence that reality cannot be perceived with any accuracy at all. These idealists argue that human beings can only have subjective perceptions of the world and that consciousness, therefore, is not determined by reality.
>
> Here, Marx explains that misperceptions are, in and of themselves, determined by material phenomena. Just because all consciousness stems from our observations and experiences in the real world, that does not mean that consciousness always reflects reality accurately. Likewise, just because our consciousness does not always reflect reality accurately, that does not mean that consciousness is not determined by reality. It should also be noted here that Lenin's Proof of the Theory of Reflection (see *Part 1*, p. 72) shows that human beings are capable of perceiving the material world with increasing accuracy over time.
>
> To summarize: if a human being believes something that is objectively false, it must be because some objective circumstances of reality are obscuring, skewing, or altering the perceptions of that human being. An example of this would be workers in a capitalist society believing that capitalism is a system which they, as workers, benefit from. This skewed perception of reality is caused by objective material conditions: namely, the capitalist relations of production and the power which capitalists have over such phenomena as education systems, media outlets, and other information sources.
>
> In short, Marx and Engels are simply saying, here, that all human consciousness—whether accurate or inaccurate—is determined by material reality.

The causes of changes within an epoch of society cannot be accurately explained through the analysis of the social consciousness of that society alone. According to Marx:

> One cannot judge such a period of transformation by its consciousness, but, on the contrary, this consciousness must be explained from the contradictions of material life, from the conflict existing between the social forces of production and the relations of production.[32]

> **Annotation 70**
>
> The above quotation is from the preface to *Critique of Political Economy* by Karl Marx. The full passage gives further insight into the development of social consciousness:
>
> > In the social production of their existence, men inevitably enter into definite relations, which are independent of their will, namely relations of production appropriate to a given stage in the development of their material forces of production.
>
> Here, Marx explains that society is formed by humans coming together to produce that which is necessary to sustain human life: food, shelter, etc. This production is independent of human will because humans must carry out this social production or else they will not survive. Therefore, social production processes cannot be considered a choice which humans could willingly decide against undertaking. Material production is an objective need, on a biological level, for the continuation of the species.
>
> Next, Marx explains that:

---

32 Karl Marx, Preface to *A Contribution to the Critique of Political Economy*, 1859.

Annotation 70 (continued)

> The totality of these relations of production constitutes the economic structure of society, the real foundation, on which arises a legal and political superstructure and to which correspond definite <u>forms of social consciousness</u>.

The relationships which human beings have with one another to carry out social material processes are economic relationships. This constitutes the material/economic base of human society. The material base is what primarily drives the development of humanity. A superstructure is also developed based on social consciousness which reflects the material base. Marx continues:

> The mode of production of material life conditions the general process of social, political and intellectual life. It is not the consciousness of men that determines their existence, but their social existence that determines their consciousness.

This is the basis of <u>Social Formation Theory</u>, which is the key to understanding the relationship between the material base and the superstructure of society. Social-economic production (i.e., the material/economic base) determines the superstructure of society. The superstructure can also impact back on the material base. The <u>Law of Suitability Between the Relations of Production and Productive Forces</u> dictates that developments in the <u>productive forces</u> lead to <u>social revolution</u> which in turn allows for society to move on to the next stage of development (see Annotation 33, p. 48).

Social revolution, according to Marx, is a process by which the superstructure undergoes a <u>quality shift</u> and the formerly predominant ruling class is superseded by a new ruling class. This change and development begins with material contradiction (as productive forces grow to such an extent that they are no longer compatible with relations of production) and this determines a contradiction in social consciousness (as new classes emerge which are more compatible with the new, higher level of productive forces). Eventually, the newly developing social consciousness of the new ruling class develops to such a level that they undertake social revolution and overthrow the old ruling class of society. As Marx puts it in *Critique of Political Economy*:

> The changes in the economic foundation lead sooner or later to the transformation of the whole immense superstructure.

This reflects the <u>Law of the Base Determining the Superstructure of Society</u> (see Annotation 50, p. 90).

Thus we see that human society develops in a definite direction, with the development of productive forces driving the development of relations of production, which drives the development of the base, which drives the development of the superstructure and society at large. This reflects the Dialectical Materialist position that matter determines consciousness, as Marx goes on to explain:

> In studying such transformations it is always necessary to distinguish between the material transformation of the economic conditions of production, which can be determined with the precision of natural science, and the legal, political, religious, artistic or philosophic – in short, ideological forms in which men become conscious of this conflict and fight it out. Just as one does not judge an individual by what he thinks about himself, so one cannot judge such a period of transformation by its consciousness, but, on the contrary, this consciousness must

> **Annotation 70 (continued)**
> be explained from the contradictions of material life, from the conflict existing between the social forces of production and the relations of production. No social order is ever destroyed before all the productive forces for which it is sufficient have been developed, and new superior relations of production never replace older ones before the material conditions for their existence have matured within the framework of the old society.
>
> This refutes idealist and metaphysical perspectives of human society and consciousness. Social consciousness does not develop in isolation, in and of itself, metaphysically distinct from the material base of society. Rather, social consciousness develops in dialectical unity with social being, reflecting the Dialectical Materialist conception of the relationship between matter and consciousness [see *Part 1*, p. 88].

The above [materialist] point of view is opposed to the idealist view of society, which:
1. Seeks the origin of consciousness within consciousness itself;
2. Considers consciousness to be the source of all social phenomena which determine social development; and
3. Presents history as a development process of social consciousness without consideration of social being.

The Historical Materialist point of view completely inverts the idealist point of view by affirming that:
1. Social being determines social consciousness;
2. Social consciousness is a reflection of social being; and
3. Social consciousness is dependent on social being.

> **Annotation 71**
> The idealist worldview holds that human consciousness is the primary driving force of change and development in the world. Idealism ignores or downplays the importance of material processes and material conditions in determining human consciousness. Idealist conceptions of history are further discussed in Annotation 13, p. 19.
>
> Historical Materialism is the application of Dialectical Materialist philosophy and methodology to the analysis of human society and human history. This viewpoint of history has revolutionized the way we understand the development of human society and our understanding of social consciousness and its relationship to the material world.
>
> By properly identifying the relationship between social being and social consciousness, Historical Materialism has transformed history into a scientific subject which can be studied on an objective and material basis.
>
> Idealism leads to fundamental misunderstandings about the development of humanity. Idealist ideology holds that philosophy can and should be studied independently of social production processes and the material being of humanity. Disseminating idealist ideology to the oppressed classes also helps to cement the power of the ruling class as explained in Annotation 68, p.119.

Annotation 71 (continued)

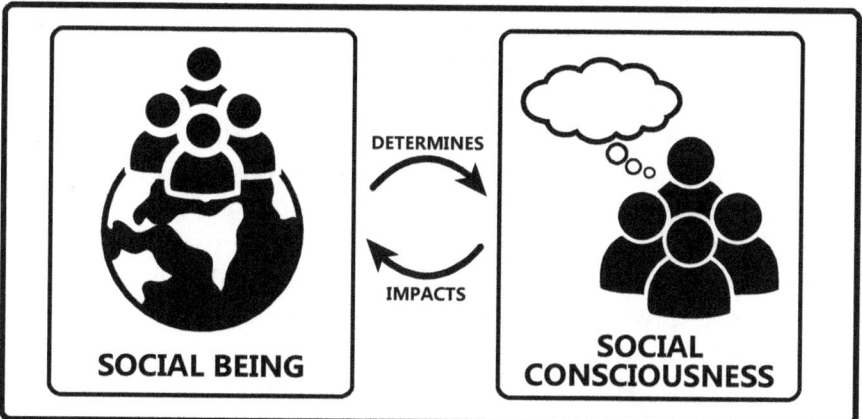

The idealist perspective of human history holds that human ideas shape the development of human society. Historical Materialism perceives human history as a process of dialectical development which is driven by the relationship between social being and social consciousness.

Historical Materialism allows for a much more accurate understanding of the development processes of humanity, including both social being and social consciousness. Historical Materialism also serves the oppressed working class within the context of our present capitalist society because it teaches workers how to understand the relationship between the economic base and the superstructure of society, and it shows that an end to capitalism is inevitable. Armed with this knowledge and a scientific understanding of human society and history, workers can better develop class consciousness, fight false consciousness which is contrived by the ruling class, and build towards social revolution that will put workers in command of human society. This will eventually lead to a stateless, classless society which will allow humans to collectively decide our own destiny as a species once and for all.

Whenever aspects of social being (especially the mode of production) change, aspects of social consciousness (ideas and theories of society, the views on politics, the rule of law, philosophy, ethics, culture, art, etc.) will change accordingly. Therefore, in different historical periods, the theories, opinions, and social ideas which arise are all determined by the conditions of material life [i.e., social being].

The Historical Materialist viewpoint of the origin of social consciousness also asserts that social being determines consciousness not in a simple and direct way, but often through many intermediate stages. Not every thought, concept, or theory of social consciousness clearly and directly reflects the economic relations of the times, and only by seeking a comprehensive perspective can we see clearly the economic relations [i.e., social being] which are reflected in these ideas [i.e., social consciousness].

Annotation 72

Human society is defined by an incredibly complex network of internal and external relationships. Such complexity means that social consciousness could not possibly be entirely determined by the material base. Social consciousness is determined primarily by the material/economic base, but there are countless other factors which affect social consciousness. Such factors include remnants of ideology from previous modes of production as well as emerging social consciousness related to emerging classes which might eventually become the ruling class.

For example: in our current capitalist society there are still many remnants of social consciousness left over from feudal society impacting the social consciousness of today. Medieval literature is still studied, certain remnants of the feudal landlord class still exist in many nations and generate ideas which reflect their remnant class identity, and there are many workers who have already attained class consciousness and are beginning to strive toward social revolution and the overthrow of capitalism. This means that a comprehensive perspective must be sought to understand social consciousness in all its complexity, as well as a historical perspective, to understand how social consciousness is constantly changing and developing.

Recognizing the complexity of social consciousness and its relationship with the material base allows Historical Materialist analysis to yield a much more accurate perception of reality than mechanical materialist conceptions of history.

II. THE RELATIVE INDEPENDENCE OF SOCIAL CONSCIOUSNESS

The Dialectical Materialist viewpoint of society [i.e., Historical Materialism] affirms that social being determines social consciousness, but also clarifies that social consciousness maintains relative independence from social being based on the following evidence:

1. Social consciousness is often out of date compared to social being.
2. Social consciousness can surpass social being.
3. Social consciousness maintains the characteristic of inheritance in its own development.
4. The interplay between forms of social consciousness in their development.
5. Social consciousness can affect social being.

*"Culture is the root of steady development.
Build a healthy cultural environment for the steady development of the nation."*

Annotation 73

All of these points relate to the Dialectical Materialist conception of the relationship between matter and consciousness.

Human society exists as an incredibly complicated dialectical unity between <u>social being</u> and <u>social consciousness</u>. This complexity is made exponentially greater by the fact that all of the countless internal aspects of both social being and social consciousness, in turn, also have dialectical relationships with each other.

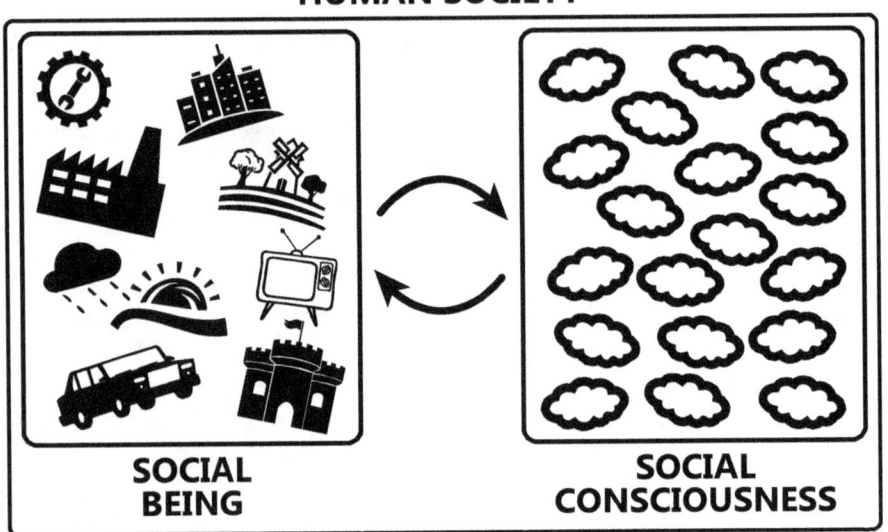

Human society is defined by an incredibly complex system of relationships between aspects of social being and aspects of social consciousness.

This is why a comprehensive perspective is vital for anyone hoping to understand the nature and development of human society. We must always keep in mind when analyzing human society that development between any two things, phenomena, or ideas exists as *mutual* development. Any time one aspect of human society impacts any other aspect of human society, the same is true in the opposite direction. This concept of mutual development is explained in *Part 1*, p. 122.

This applies equally to aspects of social being and aspects of social consciousness, and because the vast system of dialectically interacting relationships between all aspects of human society is so complex, some changes can be very indirect.

As an example, we can look at the development of the smart phone. This invention had far-reaching impacts into countless aspects of both social being and social consciousness in human society. In terms of social being, smart phones have changed material conditions for human beings in many ways. For instance, a great many factories, mines for raw materials, and other infrastructure must be built to sustain the global system of billions of smart phones. Entire industries of smart phone accessories, such as chargers, portable power banks, phone cases, etc., have sprung up. New jobs related to building and developing smart phones and related software have also been developed around the world. These are just some of the ways in which the invention of the smart phone has changed the economic base and social being of human society.

Annotation 73 (continued)

At the same time, the invention of the smart phone has changed social consciousness in countless ways. In many countries, the majority of people spend hours every day using their smart phones. Content designed for smart phones has had far-reaching impact into art categories such as film and video, music, and literature. Apps for smart phones have changed the way many people perform their jobs, hobbies, and social activities. Nearly every aspect of human consciousness has been impacted in some way by smart phones, and all of this activity has also mutually impacted back upon smart phones themselves. As more people use smart phones for photography and video, the hardware and software has developed to include more features and capabilities. As more people use their smart phones to listen to music and videos throughout the day, technologies have developed to make wearing headphones more convenient and comfortable. The social being of smart phone technology has been impacted over time by social consciousness in terms of how humans use smart phones in our daily lives.

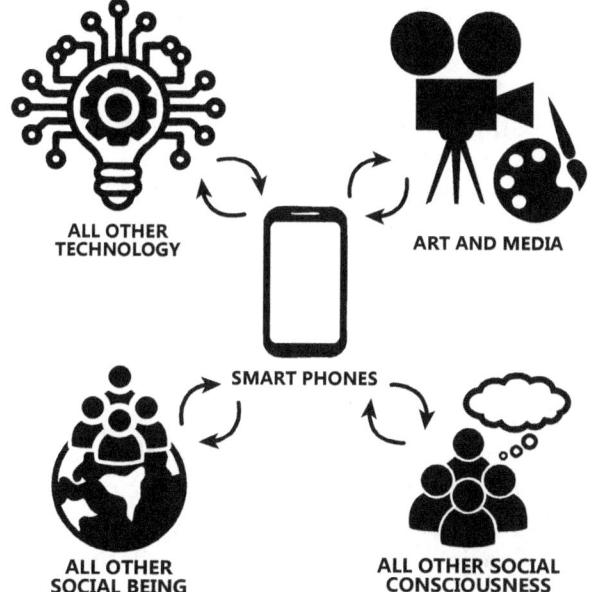

Smart phones exist in dialectical unity with all other aspects of human society.

Smart phone technology in and of itself was developed through the mutual development of various aspects of social being and social consciousness. Advancements in many scientific and technological fields had to be made before smart phones could be invented. Wireless access to high-speed internet connections, for example, were a prerequisite for smart phone technology, in addition to technologies like touch screens and small, high-capacity batteries.

In addition, human social consciousness had to develop before smart phones could have ever been considered a viable technology. The internet had to become a phenomenon that was prominent in human social consciousness in order for the demand for a smart phone with its internet access capabilities to become so ubiquitous. The development of the smart phone was also impacted by such aspects of social consciousness as demand for internet content, the need for new forms of communication such as video calling, and so on.

> **Annotation 73 (continued)**
>
> Social being has determined social consciousness as it relates to the development of smart phone technology. To put it another way: the material reality of smart phone technology determines how humans think about them. This inclues the origin and development of this technology: before the prerequisite technologies such as the internet, touch screens, etc. were developed, it would have been nearly impossible for human beings to imagine the technology of the internet-capable smart phone and impossible to engineer such a device.
>
> This does not mean, of course, that human beings are incapable of speculating about or imagining technologies before they are developed. However, what a human being is capable of imagining is determined by the material conditions that presently exist. In the science fiction of the 1960s and 70s, for example, people could imagine and speculate about handheld communication and computer technology because similar and prerequisite technologies such as telephones and computers already existed at that time. These same ideas could not have developed in more ancient times when such related technologies did not yet exist anywhere in the social being of human society.
>
> The relationship between human beings and smart phones is just one of a virtually infinite number of relationships which define human society. Grasping the complexity and nature of the relationships between and within social being and social consciousness is vital for understanding what is and is not possible in human society. We must understand the essential relationships which define something, including its history of development, before we can consciously change it. This is why Historical Materialism demands that we seek a comprehensive and historical perspective in studying (and attempting to transform) human society.

Social consciousness often lags behind social being

The principle that social being determines social consciousness asserts that changes in social being will inevitably lead to changes in social consciousness as the old social consciousness is negated and gives rise to the new social consciousness. However, in some cases, the transformation of social being does not immediately lead to the transformation of social consciousness. On the contrary, many factors of social consciousness (in both social psychology and social ideology) can persist for a very long time even if its originating social being has been negated. Not all factors of a new social consciousness will arise immediately as soon as a new social being has developed. This is because:

- Social consciousness is only a reflection of social being. In general, social consciousness only changes after social being has changed. Because of the strong, frequent, and direct impact of practical activities, changes to social being take place at such a fast speed that human consciousness cannot keep up with it.
- Habits, traditions, and customs—as well as the backwardness and conservatism of some forms of social consciousness—tend to be very strong.
- Social consciousness is always associated with the interests of certain groups of people and certain classes in history. Therefore, old and outdated ideas are often maintained and propagated by anti-progressive social forces to fight against progressive social forces.

Annotation 74

The theory of consciousness reflection in Materialist Dialectics was conceived of by Marx and Engels and was later expanded and developed by Lenin and other communist theorists. This theory proposes that conscious thought is a reflection of material reality which develops and results from material life-processes. These material life-processes include the motions and activities of human beings in the material world as well as motion and development which occurs within the physical human being.

The theory of reflection thus adheres to the Dialectical Materialist conception of the relationship between matter and consciousness (which holds that consciousness is determined by material life processes and can impact back on the material world through conscious activity), and the theory of reflection also extends to human society and social consciousness. Social being and social consciousness share the same relationship as individual being and consciousness: social consciousness reflects social being and is determined by social being, and can impact back upon social being.

The development of social consciousness reflects our relationships with the material world, and these reflections are incredibly complicated and dynamic. In his "Conspectus of Hegel's *Science of Logic*," Lenin wrote that:

> Cognition is the eternal, endless approximation of thought to the object. The reflection of nature in man's thought must be understood not "lifelessly," not "abstractly," not devoid of movement, not without contradictions, but in the eternal process of movement, the arising of contradictions and their solution.

When contradictions arise in social being, they will eventually manifest in social consciousness, but this is not necessarily an immediate response. For example, when capitalists first began to emerge as a new ruling class, their ideology did not immediately become the predominant ideology all across the world at once in an instant. In many ways, the outmoded feudal ideology remained dominant long after capitalists became the predominant class. In some cases, these outmoded feudal remnants of consciousness persist to this day.

There are even some nations today which are still ruled by feudal-style monarchs despite having a capitalist-dominated economy. In those countries, feudal era ideology still plays a large role in the superstructure of society. There are many other such examples of social consciousness lagging behind social being, such as elements of conservative culture or traditional values which stem from earlier stages of development and modes of production.

Ho Chi Minh explained that one of the missions of communists is to negate reactionary, obsolete, or false consciousness from the working class while developing revolutionary class consciousness. As an example from history: under French colonization and Japanese occupation, Vietnamese culture had been heavily suppressed for several decades. As such, Vietnamese revolutionaries were trying to determine which aspects of traditional Vietnamese culture should be restored and preserved. In a speech in 1958, Ho Chi Minh discussed the manner in which Vietnamese communists should engage with traditional Vietnamese culture:

> When we talk about restoring old things, we mean to restore good aspects and factors of those things while removing bad aspects and bad factors... We should restore, then develop, good aspects and factors and eliminate bad ones.

> **Annotation 74 (continued)**
>
> In an article called "To Become a Good Cadre, One Must Practice Self-Criticism," written in 1945, Ho Chi Minh pointed out the necessity of constantly reviewing ideology to ensure accurate reflection of reality. This is important because reality is constantly changing in accordance with the Principle of Development of Dialectical Materialism. Ho Chi Minh wrote:
>
>> We must know that the objective circumstances change every minute of every day. A policy that might be good today could become obsolete tomorrow. If we fail to willingly criticize our own actions to reject the obsolete and the erroneous, we will never be able to catch up with the circumstances. We will be left behind by agile people with sounder minds.
>
> Social consciousness which lags behind social being is considered a "remnant" of previous forms of human society.

Social consciousness can surpass social being

In affirming the fact that social consciousness is often backwards compared with social being, Historical Materialism at the same time posits that, under certain conditions, human thoughts, especially those of advanced scientific ideas, can precede the development of social being and even predict the future. They can have the effect of organizing and directing human practical activities, and directing that activity to solving problems caused by the mature development of the material life of society. Ultimately, however, the ability to precede social consciousness still depends on social being.

> **Annotation 75**
>
>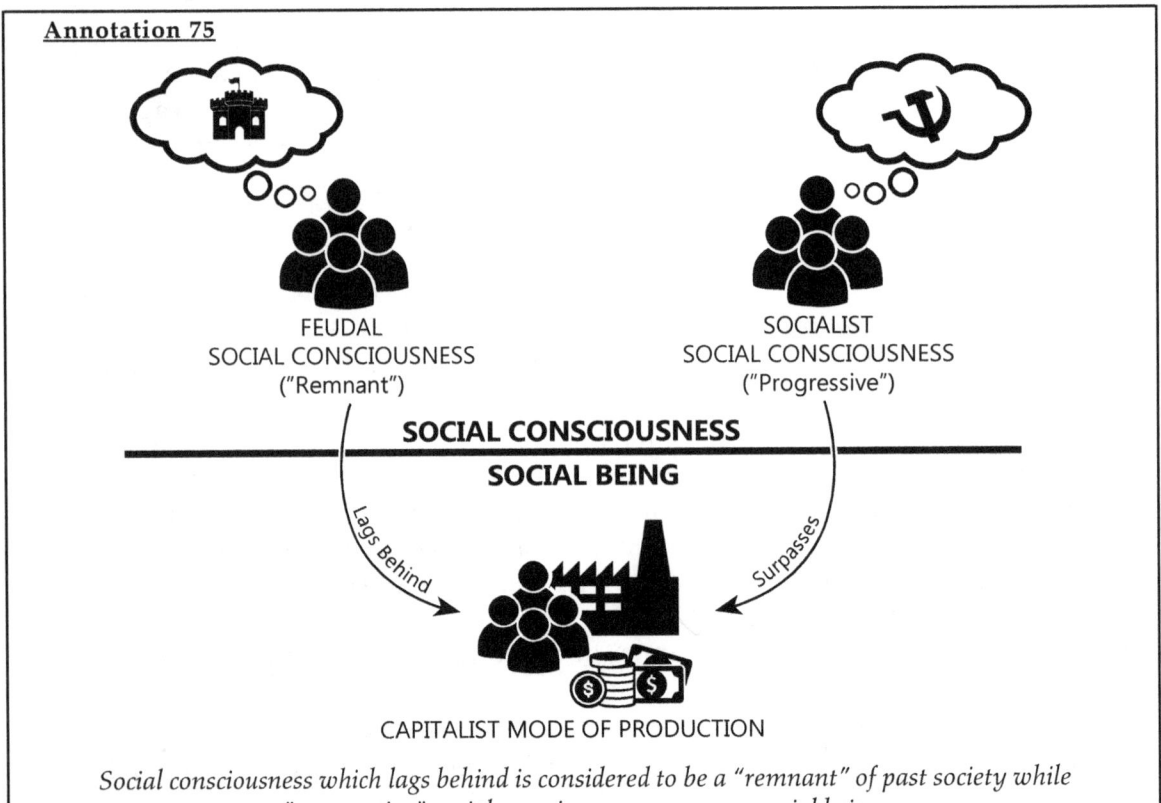
>
> *Social consciousness which lags behind is considered to be a "remnant" of past society while "progressive" social consciousness surpasses social being.*

> **Annotation 75 (continued)**
>
> Scientifically gathered knowledge can often lead to forms of social consciousness which surpass social being. An example of this would be the social consciousness of climate change. Scientists who study the climate, the environment, the weather, and other such fields have been warning human society about climate change for many decades and calling for changes to productive forces which would restrain or reverse climate change. The social being of society at large, however, has lagged behind this social consciousness. The bourgeois states and corporations which have the power to work against climate change have been very slow to affect meaningful change. Some workers recognize the threat of climate change and can essentially predict the future of what will happen to the planet if climate change continues to worsen unchecked but most of society is, conversely, lagging behind and failing to see climate change for the threat that it has been scientifically proven to be.
>
> Another example would be class consciousness under capitalism. Many human beings, including Karl Marx and Friedrich Engels, were able to identify the contradictions of capitalism and the unsustainability of the capitalist mode of production very early on. In this sense they were able to develop social consciousness which surpassed the material base of society, which remains capitalist to this day. Some workers recognize and believe in the eventual downfall of capitalism despite the fact that capitalism is still entrenched as the predominant mode of production on Earth. Such workers surpass the current material base of society and predominant capitalist-imposed social consciousness. Such social consciousness which surpasses social being is considered "progressive" as this social consciousness can lead to advancement to higher stages of development of human society.
>
> Developing the social consciousness of the working class is key to the mission of Scientific Socialism, which seeks to overthrow capitalism through the application of Dialectical Materialist and Historical Materialist theory and practice.

Social consciousness maintains the characteristic of inheritance in its development

The historical development of social consciousness shows that the theoretical views of each era did not appear spontaneously from nothing, but are developed on a foundation of theories inherited from previous ages.

This is simply a manifestation of the inheritance characteristic of development in the development processes of social consciousness. Since social consciousness has inheritance characteristics in its development, it is impossible to fully understand any given idea based only on presently existing economic relations; it is necessary to consider previous stages of development. The development history of consciousness has shown that periods of prosperity or decline in philosophy, literature, art, etc., do not always perfectly line up with periods of economic prosperity or decline.

> **Annotation 76**
>
> Because of the principle of inheritance, social consciousness always contain elements and characteristics which are inherited from previous forms of social consciousness. Such inherited characteristics can take the form of customs, traditions, cultural practices, and so on, and can be reflected in social consciousness in countless ways.

> **Annotation 76 (continued)**
>
> There are, for example, countless ways in which ideas from feudal society have influenced and persisted through to the modern capitalist era, i.e., the establishment of the social institution of the monarchy in a modern capitalist nation like the United Kingdom. Such an institution is clearly a remnant from the feudal era of society. The monarchy does not function in exactly the same way as it did in the feudal era, but it influences social consciousness in countless ways. Even though the bourgeoisie has been the ruling class of the United Kingdom for a very long time, the institution of monarchy and many other remnants of feudal society have been inherited by the modern capitalist society of that nation.

In a class-based society, the inheritance nature of social consciousness is associated with its class character. Different classes inherit different ideas from previous eras. The progressive classes receive the legacy and progressive ideology left behind by the old society.

Lenin emphasized that socialist culture needs to promote the best achievements and traditions of human culture from antiquity to the present on the basis of the Marxist worldview. In "The Task of the Youth Leagues," he wrote:

> Proletarian culture must be the logical development of the store of knowledge mankind has accumulated under the yoke of capitalist, landowner and bureaucratic society.

> **Annotation 77**
>
> The progressive classes are classes which are emerging to become new classes that will be more suitable to emerging productive forces during a transition period where one mode of production is being negated by the next. For example, when capitalism was first beginning to emerge, the progressive classes were the bourgeoisie and the proletariat. The bourgeoisie became the ruling class in the capitalist mode of production while the proletariat became the oppressed working class. Today, the proletariat is the progressive class because it will, in time, become the ruling class as the capitalist mode of production becomes negated within human society.
>
> The following is the full passage from Lenin from which the above quote was taken. In this passage, Lenin emphasizes the importance of understanding and leveraging inheritance in developing the social consciousness of communist revolutionaries:
>
>> We must bear this in mind when, for example, we talk about proletarian culture. We shall be unable to solve this problem unless we clearly realize that only a precise knowledge and transformation of the culture created by the entire development of mankind will enable us to create a proletarian culture. The latter is not clutched out of thin air; it is not an invention of those who call themselves experts in proletarian culture. That is all nonsense. Proletarian culture must be the logical development of the store of knowledge mankind has accumulated under the yoke of capitalist, landowner and bureaucratic society. All these roads have been leading, and will continue to lead up to proletarian culture, in the same way as political economy, as reshaped by Marx, has shown us what human society must arrive at, shown us the passage to the class struggle, to the beginning of the proletarian revolution.

> **Annotation 77 (continued)**
>
> What Lenin means, here, is that "proletarian culture"—i.e., social consciousness of the working class—cannot be developed without a material basis as well as preceding forms of social consciousness. Rather, it must be recognized that the "seeds" of proletarian culture exist in the currently existing social consciousness in accordance with the inheritance principle.
>
> Building class consciousness is a prerequisite to social revolution. This means that workers must build a proletarian culture for ourselves. This culture must recognize the role and mission of the working class in ending capitalism and class society. But this proletarian culture cannot simply be dreamt up in the minds of revolutionaries and then imposed upon workers. Instead, revolutionaries must understand the relationship between social consciousness and social being as well as the processes of development in Dialectical Materialist and Historical Materialist terms. By understanding these relationships and processes of development, it becomes possible for revolutionaries to consciously affect, change, and develop a proletarian culture of class consciousness within the working class over time.
>
> As Lenin further explains, it is the role of revolutionary ideologists to develop positive aspects of social consciousness that are suitable with communism while negating aspects which are reactionary and impede the development of class consciousness:
>
>> When we so often hear representatives of the youth, as well as certain advocates of a new system of education, attacking the old schools... we say to them that we must take what was good in the old schools. We must not borrow the system of encumbering young people's minds with an immense account of knowledge, nine-tenths of which was useless and one-tenth distorted. This, however, does not mean that we can restrict ourselves to communist conclusions and learn only communist slogans. You will not create communism that way. You can become a Communist only when you enrich your mind with a knowledge of all the treasures created by mankind.
>
> This is similar to observations made by Ho Chi Minh about developing the social consciousness of the proletariat (see Annotation 74, page 135).
>
> The Vietnamese textbook *Philosophy of Marxism-Leninism* explains:
>
>> For example, when the bourgeoisie performed its social revolution against feudalism, advanced thinkers of the bourgeoisie restored many materialist and humanist ideas from ancient times. Likewise, the obsolete classes and their thinkers absorbed and restored the anti-progressive social ideas and theories of previous historical periods (i.e., religious and idealist conceptions of the "divine roles" of kings). The feudal class of mediaeval Western European countries during the period of feudal decline tried to exploit Plato's philosophy and idealist elements from the philosophical system of Aristotle of Ancient Greece, using them as the basis of philosophy of Christian teachings.
>>
>> In a similar manner, during the second half of the 19th century and the beginning of the 20th century, reactionary bourgeois forces restored and developed idealist philosophical and religious movements under new names such as neo-Kantianism and neo-Thomism, etc., to fight against the revolutionary movement of the working class and its ideology, Marxism.

Annotation 77 (continued)

The "Divine Role of Kings" was a religious and political ideology that argued that kings had power bestowed upon them directly by God. This was an ancient philosophy which monarchs such as Louis XIV of France restored to justify their rule over society as monarchy and feudalism were challenged in the 18th century. Similarly, the bourgeoisie restored aspects of ancient Greek philosophy to justify their social revolution against feudalism. Examples of this from the French Revolution include Aristotle's conception of "civic fraternity" which was manifested in the French Revolutionary slogan of "Liberty, Equality, Fraternity." As the bourgeoisie cemented itself as the ruling class of society, bourgeois interpretations of "equality" and "fraternity" did not include "equality" as it pertained to relations of production, and workers were deceived into believing that "fraternity" meant that workers should support the power and privilege that capitalists had as it pertained to ownership of the means of production. In this manner, ancient Greek ideas were developed to suit the capitalist mode of production. In other words, the meaning of these concepts shifted to justify and uphold the class position of the newly formed ruling class of capitalists.

A similar shift in the meaning of ideas within social consciousness occurred when capitalism was challenged by Marxism and communist revolutionary movements in the late 19th and early 20th centuries. As the threat of communist revolution increased, bourgeois and religious ideologists began to revive and develop older philosophies originally conceived of by figures from the feudal era such as Immanuel Kant and Thomas Aquinas. These feudal ideas were altered to justify the established social relations of capitalism and to argue against Marxist ideology and communist revolution. This is a manifestation of the inheritance property of Materialist Dialectics within human society: base-level concepts and ideas can be inherited into newer forms of social consciousness.

The interplay between forms of social consciousness in their development

The interplay between forms of social consciousness is a reason why in each form of social consciousness there are aspects and properties that cannot be explained directly by examining social being.

Annotation 78

This relationship is one in which social consciousness is relatively independent of, but also determined by (and can impact back upon), social being. Social consciousness is relatively independent from social being, just as consciousness in general is relatively independent from the material world in general.

Relative independence is not the same as *complete* independence. Complete independence would imply a complete lack of connection between two subjects. Relative independence simply means that one subject has its own development, even if this development is dialectically impacted or determined by another subject. The belief that consciousness can be completely divorced from material reality is a form of idealism.

Consciousness is also not *completely* determined by the material world. Rather, consciousness (though determined by the material world) is capable of impacting back on the material through human conscious activity. The belief that consciousness is completely determined by the material world is a form of mechanical materialism.

Annotation 78 (continued)

It is important to avoid both of these extreme misinterpretations of the relationship between matter and consciousness: idealism and mechanical materialism.

IDEALIST MISCONCEPTION OF THE RELATIONSHIP BETWEEN SOCIAL BEING AND SOCIAL CONSCIOUSNESS

Idealism views consciousness as completely separate from material reality, or upholds the idea that consciousness completely determines the material world. Idealism thus overstates the independence of consciousness from matter.

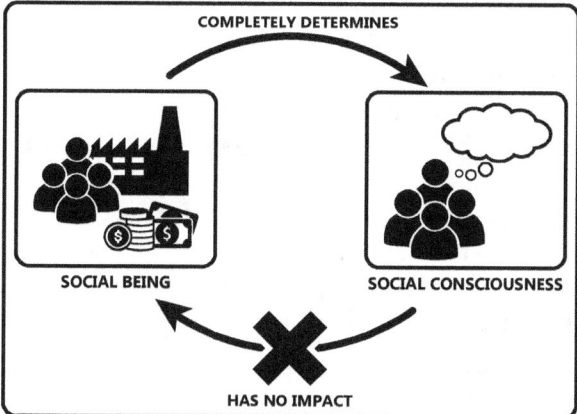

IDEALIST MISCONCEPTION OF THE RELATIONSHIP BETWEEN SOCIAL BEING AND SOCIAL CONSCIOUSNESS

Mechanical Materialism views consciousness as completely determined by the material world and sees consciousness as an illusionary phenomenon that cannot impact back on matter. Mechanical Materialism thus understates the independence of consciousness from matter.

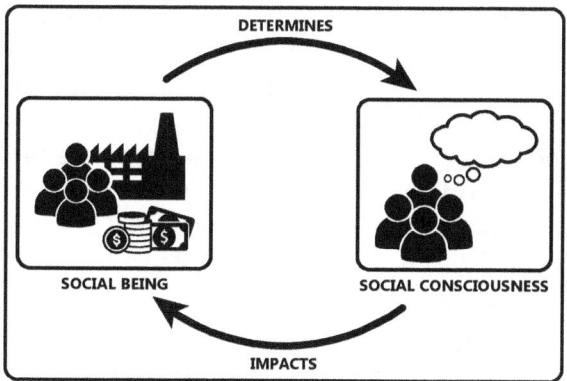

HISTORICAL MATERIALIST CONCEPTION OF RELATIONSHIP BETWEEN SOCIAL BEING AND SOCIAL CONSCIOUSNESS

Dialectical Materialism correctly interprets the relationship between matter and consciousness by viewing consciousness as relatively independent from matter. Matter and consciousness have their own internal development processes, but they also mutually develop one another.

> **Annotation 78 (continued)**
>
> The relative independence of social consciousness from social being reflects the relative independence of consciousness from matter. Social consciousness development is determined by social being, but there are also internal relationships within social consciousness which lead to internal development of social consciousness. Specifically, social consciousness forms can interact with each other to internally develop social consciousness, but ultimately all social conscious forms are derived from and determined by material conditions. It should be noted that this includes false consciousness, which is also determined by material reality (see p. 94).
>
> An example of forms of social consciousness developing each other can be found in the religious traditions of Vietnam. This development reflects the relationship between matter/social being and consciousness/social consciousness. The modern religious practice of Dao Mau involves the worship of Mau, the Mother Goddesses of Vietnam. This religious form of social consciousness originated in and is unique to Vietnam that stretches back over thousands of years. Dao Mau has its roots in ancient Vietnamese society which was matriarchal. Vietnam's earliest religions revolved around the worship of various goddesses of nature such as goddesses of the sun and the moon as well as goddesses of rain, thunder, fire, and so on. During the ancient era in Vietnam this religion was developed to justify and reflect the power of female rulers. Whenever a powerful queen or princess died, Vietnamese religious leaders would build temples to those matriarchal rulers and venerate them as goddesses. Examples of such religious worship of rulers include the two Trung Sisters (empresses of Vietnam who defeated the Chinese Han Dynasty), as well as Duong Van Nga (another queen of Vietnam who helped defeat an invasion led by the Chinese Song Dynasty in the 10th century).
>
> Daoism was another important religious social consciousness form which came to Vietnam in the 2nd century. Daoism also heavily affected ancient Vietnamese religious beliefs. Specifically, Vietnamese people tended to incorporate matriarchal Daoist deities such as the "Mother of Skies," the "Mother of the World of the Dead," etc. Such female deities were synthesized into older matriarchal religious social conscious forms which had already been prevalent in Vietnam.
>
> Vietnamese people began to worship both Dao Mau and Daoist goddesses simultaneously. Over time, Dao Mau began to incorporate more formalized systems of worship which were more similar to Daoist religious practices, such as a clear system of ceremonies, rituals, costumes and so on. This is an example of forms of social consciousness influencing each other in a manner that was relatively independent of material reality. This social consciousness was relatively independent. Examination of Vietnamese social being, in and of itself, throughout these 2000 years of history would not be sufficient to fully understand why Dao Mau exists in its current form today. In order to understand Dao Mau it is necessary to also examine the development of forms of social consciousness in Vietnam.
>
> It is vital to also examine the material conditions and social being of Vietnam to understand Dao Mau in its current form, since Dao Mau reflects and was in many ways determined by historical relations of production such as ancient Vietnamese society which was dominated by matriarchal monarchs, Vietnamese feudalism with its system of royal and noble families, as well as influences from foreign ruling classes such as those in China which determined the development of Daoism.

Annotation 78 (continued)

A painting of the pantheon of goddesses and gods of the Vietnamese Dao Mau religion dating from the late 19th to early 20th century.

Ideology is the most advanced form of social consciousness, as explained in Annotation 65, p. 112. Ideologies have the highest potential to impact the social being and material base of human society through conscious practical activities. The level of impact of ideology on the development of society depends on various factors. This is discussed more in p. 147.

Because ideology's development is so complex, we must differentiate the roles of progressive ideology and anti-progressive ideology as each pertains to social development. As *Philosophy of Marxism-Leninism* explains:

> Historical Materialism holds to the principle that social consciousness is relatively independent and quite complex in its development. Historical Materialism rejects all metaphysical, mechanical, and vulgar viewpoints about the relationship between social being and social consciousness.

The historical development of social consciousness shows that certain forms of consciousness tend to emerge first and have a strong impact on the other forms of consciousness. This pattern of development occurs in almost every historical era and is determined by specific historical circumstances.

In ancient Greece, philosophy and art played a particularly vital role in social consciousness. In medieval Western Europe, religion had a strong influence on all other forms of social consciousness: philosophy, ethics, art, politics, and the rule of law. In Western European countries in the more recent historical period, political consciousness has played a significant role, strongly influencing other forms of social consciousness. In France, from the second half of the 18th century, as in Germany at the end of the 19th century, philosophy and literature were the most important tools for the propagation of political ideas in the arena of the political struggles of the progressive classes.[33] Today, in the interplay between forms of social consciousness, political consciousness still often plays a particularly vital role.

> **Annotation 79**
>
> Different kinds of social consciousness forms will have more prominent and influential roles in the development of different human societies and at different stages of development of those societies.
>
> In Ancient Greece, philosophers such as Plato, Aristotle, and Socrates played an important role in shaping the social consciousness of the Greek people. Ancient Greek artists played a similar role in shaping social consciousness with famous works of art such as statues of Venus de Milo, Zeus at Olympia, Athena etc. Philosophy and art of this era were determined by the material conditions and social being of ancient Greece but were also instrumental in developing the Greek worldview and making Greece one of the most highly developed societies of its era.
>
> Religion played a very important role in the feudal era of medieval Europe. The Catholic Church, as the dominant religion, greatly affected every aspect of Western European society during the feudal era. In most medieval European countries, the Catholic Church and the state had a very close relationship, and the state existed in part to defend the church. The nature of this relationship is defined in a law issued the Catholic church in 1825 known as *Quo Graviora*, which declared:
>
>> Pope Leo the Great defined the role of the state as being a defender of the church's cause and a suppressor of heresies in a letter to the Eastern Roman Emperor Leo I:
>>
>> "You ought unhesitatingly to recognize that the Royal Power has been conferred to you not only for the Rule of the world, but especially for the defense of the Church, so that by suppressing the heinous undertakings you may defend those Statutes which are good and restore True Peace to those things which have been disordered."
>
> In modern capitalist Western Europe, political social consciousness forms have played an important role in the development of social consciousness. As feudalism gave way to capitalism, many new political ideas appeared in Western Europe such as Hegelian Idealism, Kant's humanism, utopianism, and Marxism-Leninism.

---

33 See p. 138.

Annotation 79 (continued)

This emerging political social consciousness also influenced literary and artistic social consciousness in Europe. For instance, European novelists wrote frequently about political aspects of European society. Such works include *Les Miserables* by Victor Hugo, *War and Peace* by Leo Tolstoy, and so on. To this day, political consciousness continues to be the most important form of consciousness in our current world, and it has become the primary battlefield between the capitalist class and the working class. Political social consciousness forms can be found everywhere: in novels, in music, in newspapers, in films, and on social media. The ruling class in the USA has spent billions of dollars producing media, information outlets, and social media platforms which produce propaganda and media which support and defend capitalist relations of production. All of these social institutions exist to defend and advance forms of social consciousness which reflect the agenda of the capitalist ruling class.

An important mission of communists and the working class is to push back against such capitalist social consciousness forms and to build ideologies and social institutions which advance and defend communist social consciousness forms. Developing the social consciousness of the working class is an important prerequisite to social revolution which will lead to a dictatorship of the proletariat and, eventually, an end to capitalism and class society altogether as explained in Annotation 108, p. 203.

The political consciousness of the revolutionary class orients the progressive development of other forms of consciousness.

Annotation 80

Because social revolution must be fulfilled through the construction of a state which enforces the agenda of a ruling class, political struggle is one of the most important battlefields in class struggle. An objective prerequisite for social revolution is that a revolutionary class achieves class consciousness and grasps their own historical mission to build a state and become the ruling class. Therefore, political consciousness—defined as awareness of the importance of controlling the state and, by extension, the means of production—plays a crucial role in the progressive development of all other forms of social consciousness which are dialectically related. For example:

- **Political consciousness must orient morality consciousness:**
  Communists must teach workers about the unethical nature of capitalist exploitation of workers; i.e., that it is unethical for capitalists to steal labor value from workers and that it is unethical for anyone to lack food, healthcare, etc.

- **Political consciousness must orient legal consciousness:**
  Communists must make it clear that the legal system must be on the side of the workers. Communists must struggle to protect workers from unjust laws and to force the government to pass laws that will improve conditions for workers.

- **Political consciousness must orient aesthetic consciousness:**
  Art, entertainment, and other forms of media are vital for influencing the social consciousness of the workers. Communists must, therefore, produce art and media that advances class consciousness while critiquing art and media that serves the agenda of the bourgeoisie.

> **Annotation 80 (continued)**
>
> These are just some of the ways in which communists must use political consciousness to orient all other aspects of social consciousness. It is important to remember the Principle of General Relationships of Dialectical Materialism which states that all things, phenomena, and ideas are dialectically related to each other and mutually develop each other. All social consciousness forms are ultimately related to political consciousness. All of these forms of social consciousness, taken together in unity, impact back on the social being of society.

Social consciousness can affect social being.

Historical Materialism not only criticizes the idealist viewpoint (absolutizing the role of social consciousness), but also rejects the viewpoint of vulgar materialism or "economic materialism" (i.e. negating the positive effect of social consciousness in social life). According to Engels:

> Political, juridical, philosophical, religious, literary, artistic, etc., development is based on economic development. But all these react upon one another and also upon the economic base.[34]

> **Annotation 81**
>
> *Absolutization* refers to holding a belief or supposition as always true in all situations and without exception. This concept is discussed more in *Part 1*, p. 49.
>
> *Idealism* is the position that consciousness determines the material. Idealism is further explained in *Part 1* beginning on p. 48. Idealism absolutizes social consciousness by holding the position that human consciousness determines the material in all situations and without exception.
>
> *Vulgar materialism*, also known as *economic materialism*, is a form of mechanical materialism which holds the opposite position: it absolutizes the supposition that the material fully and completely determines consciousness without exception.
>
> The *Vietnamese Students' Dictionary* defines vulgar materialism as:
>
> > A trend in the mechanical materialist philosophical movement, appearing in Germany in the mid-19th century. Vulgar materialism is a spontaneous reaction of scientific materialism to idealist philosophy (first and foremost, ancient philosophy). It makes the basic principles of materialism poor and crude. . . Not only did they dismiss idealism and religion, but they also dismissed philosophy in general. They wanted to solve all philosophical problems in the concrete study of natural science.
>
> Dialectical Materialism avoids errors of absolutization (which both idealism and vulgar materialism suffer from) by recognizing the true relationship between matter and consciousness: matter determines consciousness while consciousness can impact back upon matter. As Engels goes on to explain in his letter to Borgius:
>
> > It is not that the economic position is the cause and alone active, while everything else only has a passive effect. There is, rather, interaction on the basis of the economic necessity, which ultimately always asserts itself. The state, for in-

---

34 Letter from Engels to Borgius, 1894.

> **Annotation 81 (continued)**
>
> stance, exercises an influence by tariffs, free trade, good or bad fiscal system… So it is not, as people try here and there conveniently to imagine, that the economic position produces an automatic effect. Men make their history themselves, only in given surroundings which condition it and on the basis of actual relations already existing, among which the economic relations, however much they may be influenced by the other political and ideological ones, are still ultimately the decisive ones, forming the red thread which runs through them and alone leads to understanding.
>
> Men make their history themselves, but not as yet with a collective will or according to a collective plan or even in a definitely defined, given society. Their efforts clash, and for that very reason all such societies are governed by necessity, which is supplemented by and appears under the forms of accident. The necessity which here asserts itself amidst all accident is again ultimately economic necessity.
>
> The "economic necessity" which Engels describes here constitutes an objective need which is the primary driver of human history and the development of class society. The primary objective need is the need for suitability between relations of production and productive forces, which is the basis of the Law of Suitability. Objective need which arises in the material base is therefore what drives all class struggle and development of class society, and this same sort of objective need is what will lead to social revolution and the downfall of capitalism and class society. It is therefore highly important that anyone pursuing social revolution should deeply understand the relationship between material and consciousness, between social being and social consciousness, and between the base and superstructure, and how objective/economic needs drive change in human society.

The degree of influence which ideology has on social development depends on many factors, including (but not limited to):

- Specific historical conditions in which the ideology developed.
- The nature of economic relations within the social base at the time of the development of social consciousness which the ideology is derived from.
- The historical role of the class which carries the ideology.
- The accuracy with which the ideology reflects the objective mission of the class which carries the ideology.
- The extent of popular adoption of the ideology among the masses.

> **Annotation 82**
>
> An *ideology* is simply a system of ideas which has been developed and adopted by a group of human beings. The word can also be used to collectively refer to all of the ideologies of human society, i.e., the entire system of human thought as it exists at any given time.
>
> Ideology, as a form of social consciousness, can impact the development of human society but it cannot determine the course of development of human society. This is because only social being and the material base can determine such development.

Annotation 82 (continued)

In order to understand how ideology can impact social development, one must seek a comprehensive and historical perspective. This means understanding how ideology has developed and changed over time as well as the internal and external relationships which led to that development. In particular, this demands the analysis of the ideological factors of these aspects of human society:

Historical Conditions

In seeking to understand how ideology impacts human society, one must examine the historical conditions in which the ideology developed. This is because ideology, like all things, phenomena, and ideas, is constantly changing and developing over time. This change comes about through internal and external relationships which themselves occur and develop over time. Only by understanding the historical development of an ideology can one hope to understand the essence of that ideology and how it might continue to develop into the future. It is also vital to understand the economic relations within the social being at the time of the development of the social consciousness which the ideology is derived from. This is because social being determines social consciousness and thus determines how ideologies can and will manifest in any given stage of development of human society.

For example, one must understand the historical conditions of the 19th century to understand how and why communism developed as it did when Marx and Engels were first formulating its founding principles. One must also understand how those conditions changed and developed in the following decades, into the twentieth century, through the founding of the Soviet Union and various other socialist movements and states, the suppression of communists in capitalist-imperialist nations, and so on, to understand how communism as an ideology has developed and changed as well as how it exists and is developing in our present day.

Economic Relations

The relations of production which exist during the development of an ideology will determine to a great extent how the ideology develops and manifests in human society. Marx and Engels held that studying ideology in and of itself, divorced from the economic conditions in which the ideology arose, was a waste of time which could never lead to complete and accurate understanding. This perspective is discussed more on p. 23.

Take, for example, the development of both communist and capitalist ideology. Neither communist ideology (which holds that workers should seize the means of production from capitalists) nor capitalist ideology (which holds that capitalists should maintain private ownership of the means of production) could have developed in earlier stages of development which preceded private capital.

Both capitalist ideology and communist ideology would have been nonsensical during feudal times when the essential means of production were not privately owned by capitalists and the ruling class consisted of feudal lords. Capitalist relations of production had to first develop as a prerequisite for both communist and capitalist ideologies to develop. In this manner, the relations of production determined the existence of communist and capitalist ideology. Capitalist ideology came into being as a result of an objective need which started within the economic base of society.

> **Annotation 82 (continued)**
>
> **The Historical Role of Class**
>
> Every ideology is developed within the context of class. In order to understand the essence of the ideology, one must first understand the essence of the class which birthed it. This includes not just how the class exists at a given point of time, but also how it developed historically, and how that development led to the development of the ideology itself.
>
> For example, in order to understand communist ideology, one must study the development of the working class. Only by studying the working class: how it originated, how it has struggled against the capitalist class, and how it has changed over time, can one come to understand communist ideology and how it has impacted human society. Similarly, in order to understand bourgeois ideologies one must understand the role and history of the capitalist class, just as one must study the history of monarchs, noble lords, and clergy in order to understand dominant ideologies of feudal society.
>
> It is also important to understand that every class has a "mission." This mission reflects the objective need a class has to pursue its own agenda and to benefit as greatly as possible from the means of production.[35] ***Part 4*** of the volume from which this text is translated, which covers the topic of Scientific Socialism, defines the historical mission of the working class under capitalism:
>
>> The historical mission of the working class is to lead the working people to fight and eliminate capitalism and to erase all exploitative and oppressive regimes to build a new society – namely: socialism, and then communism.
>
> In *Anti-Dühring*, Engels defines the historical missions of the working class as:
>
> 1. Becoming the ruling class by establishing a dictatorship of the proletariat.
>
> 2. Seizing the means of production from the ruling class to end class society.
>
> Engels' outline of this process is discussed more in Annotation 104, p. 193.
>
> **Popularity of Adoption Among the Masses**
>
> Understanding how ideology impacts society requires one to understand the spread of its influence throughout the masses of the human population. The more popularly held an ideology is, the more impact it can have on society at large. This is one reason that capitalists spend huge amounts of resources to spread bourgeois ideologies among the working class throughout history and to our present day.
>
> Understanding how ideas are spread and promoted on the one hand, and how they are suppressed and negated on the other, is critical to understanding how ideology can impact human society. This is critical to the mission of Scientific Socialism, which has a goal of spreading communist ideology to the working masses in order to negate the influence of bourgeois propaganda and indoctrination and to strengthen the resolve of workers to bring about the end of capitalism as quickly as possible. This will also be discussed in ***Part 4***.

It is also necessary to distinguish the role of *progressive* ideology from the role of *reactionary* ideology as it pertains to the development of society.

---

[35] This struggle between economic classes is the basis for political struggle in society. This is explained more in Annotation 107, p. 200.

Annotation 83

A fundamental principle of Dialectical Materialism is the principle of development. This principle holds that change is inevitable. All things, phenomena, and ideas undergo processes of motion and development. Any philosophy, ideology, or strategy which attempts to restrain motion and development is doomed to failure because change can neither be halted nor restrained. Thus, our strategies and actions must align with the material reality that change is inevitable, and we must seek to change the world by impacting processes of development and motion rather than attempting to reverse, restrain, or halt such processes.

Progressive ideology is ideology which accurately reflects reality by correctly interpreting the ways in which human society develops over time. In the context of our current capitalist society, progressive ideology recognizes the role and mission of the working class as the progressive class which will bring about an end to class society. Such ideology is considered progressive because it does not seek to impede or reverse the development of human society, but rather, it seeks to further the progress of humanity in moving towards communism.

Reactionary ideology seeks to impede or reverse the progression and development of human society. In our current capitalist society this most typically means preserving and furthering the power and position of the capitalist class as the ruling class of society. Such ideology is called "reactionary" because it exists as a reaction to the progressive forces of historical development. In the words of *The Communist Manifesto*, reactionaries "try to roll back the wheel of history."

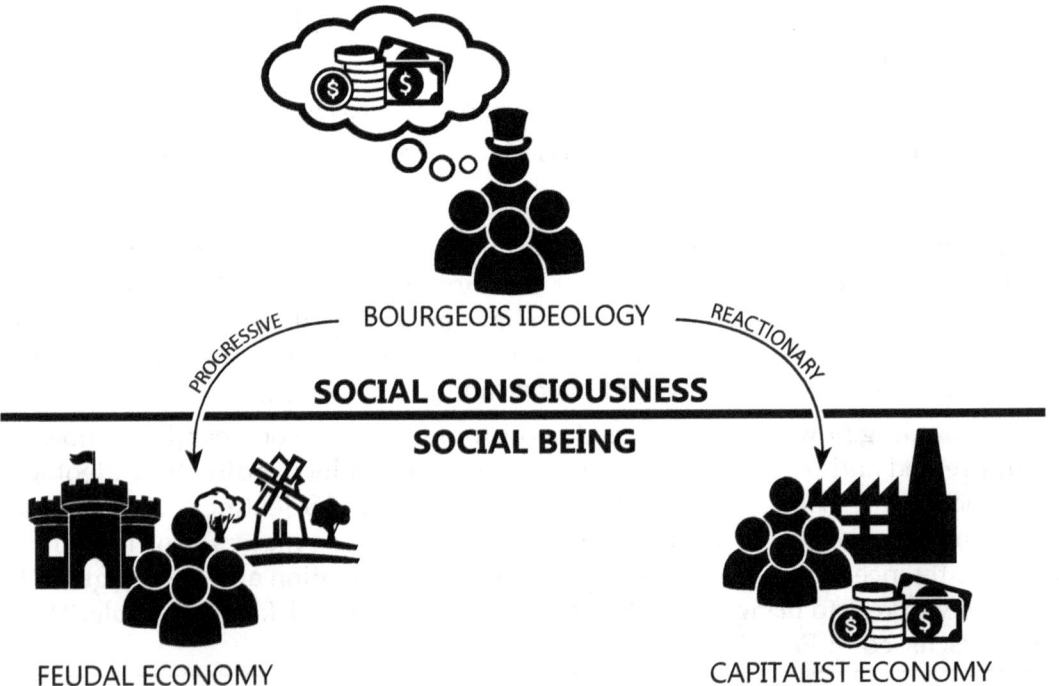

The same ideology may be reactionary or progressive depending on its relationship to present economic conditions and class relations. During the feudal era, bourgeois ideology was progressive. In today's capitalist society, it is reactionary.

> **Annotation 83 (continued)**
>
> There are many variations of ideology which can fall along progressive or reactionary lines. It is necessary to seek a comprehensive and historical perspective to properly identify ideology as progressive or reactionary. Some ideology may have been progressive in past eras but would be considered reactionary today. For instance, during the end of the feudal era, ideology which promoted the power and position of the bourgeoisie was "progressive" in the sense that it sought to move human society's development away from the feudal era. Today, those same ideas would be considered reactionary as they seek to maintain the status quo of class society.
>
> It is also possible for reactionary ideology to falsely pose as progressive ideology. There are many instances, for instance, of reactionary movements claiming to represent the interests of workers or even mixing reactionary ideology in with progressive ideology to corrupt, co-opt, and hamper movements. It is also common for ideology which is idealist, metaphysical, or otherwise flawed to infect progressive ideology. As such, great care must be taken to seek out reactionary elements and characteristics of ideology and to critique and correct them.

Conclusion

Historical Materialism upholds the principle of relative independence of social consciousness. This principle paints a complex portrait of the historical development of social consciousness. It rejects all metaphysical, mechanical materialist, and vulgar materialist conceptions of the relationship between social being and social consciousness.

In summary, according to the Marxist materialist viewpoint, the two fundamental principles of Historical Materialism are:

1. The principle that social being determines social consciousness; and
2. The principle of the relative independence of social consciousness.

These principles serve as fundamental methodological foundations of cognitive and practical activities of Scientific Socialists.[36] Therefore, we must strive to perceive phenomena of social consciousness in the context of the social being which gave rise to it. At the same time, it is also necessary to be able to explain those same phenomena of social consciousness in the context of relative independence from social being.

> **Annotation 84**
>
> These principles are derived from the Dialectical Materialist conception of the relationship between matter and consciousness which is described in *Part 1*, p. 88. Understanding these principles puts Historical Materialism on an objective and scientific basis as explained in Annotation 98, p. 176. In order to affect change in human society it is vital to understand how development processes occur and what drives change and development in human society. Rejection of metaphysical, mechanical, and vulgar materialist conceptions of the relationship of social being and social consciousness is necessary because such conceptions stand as barriers to progress of the mission of Scientific Socialism. The same can be said for idealist conceptions of the relationship between social being and social consciousness.

---

36 Scientific Socialism is a body of theory focused on the practical pursuit of changing the world to bring about socialism and, eventually, communism. This will be the subject of Part 4 of this series.

<u>Annotation 84 (continued)</u>

Metaphysical materialist conceptions of the relationship between social being and social consciousness view social phenomena in a static, abstract manner. Social being and social consciousness, according to this viewpoint, are broken down into fixed categories which do not change over time. For instance, aspects of "human nature" might be seen as unchanging and unalterable characteristics, and metaphysical materialists tend to define humanity by such "innate and unchanging characteristics."

Mechanical materialist conceptions of the relationship between social being and social consciousness view all things, phenomena, and ideas as "machines" which simply carry out predictable and purely physical processes. Such views see as a giant mechanical machine composed of parts which are all essentially isolated from each other and static and unchangeable, simply carrying out material processes which human beings cannot fundamentally alter through conscious activity. Mechanical materialism is therefore a form of vulgar materialism and metaphysical materialism (since it seeks to understand reality by breaking it down into "categories" of "mechanical parts" which are static in nature).

Vulgar materialist conceptions of the relationship between social being and social consciousness essentially deny the role of human consciousness (including social consciousness) and the ability of consciousness to impact on the material world (including social being).

Metaphysical, mechanical, and vulgar materialist viewpoints are all barriers to effective practical activities because they deny the ability for human beings to develop social consciousness and to impact back on social being through conscious activity. Such misconceptions about the nature of reality will invariably hamper and derail efforts to achieve the mission of Scientific Socialism and liberate humanity from the oppression of class society.

Idealist conceptions of the relationship between social being and social consciousness hold that social consciousness determines the development of social being, and that human consciousness is the primary driver and motivating force of human history. Such conceptions deny the objective nature of human history and the principles of development which govern and regulate the development of human society. According to the idealist perspective of human history, development of social consciousness is all that is required to affect change in human society. Ignoring the determining role which social being plays in the development of humanity impedes practical activities by placing too much emphasis on human thought and mental activity while denying the importance of material activity and development.

A common idealist deviation of socialist thought is utopianism, which holds that a perfect society can be conceived of through thought alone, and that socialism can be achieved simply by developing such theoretical models of a utopian society in the mind. Engels rebuked idealist and utopian socialism in *Socialism: Utopian and Scientific*:

> [According to idealist utopians,] socialism is the expression of absolute truth, reason and justice, and has only to be discovered to conquer all the world by virtue of its own power. And as an absolute truth is independent of time, space, and of the historical development of man, it is a mere accident when and where it is discovered. With all this, absolute truth, reason, and justice are different with the

> **Annotation 84 (continued)**
>
> founder of each different school. And as each one's special kind of absolute truth, reason, and justice is again conditioned by his subjective understanding, his conditions of existence, the measure of his knowledge and his intellectual training, there is no other ending possible in this conflict of absolute truths than that they shall be mutually exclusive of one another. Hence, from this nothing could come but a kind of eclectic, average Socialism, which, as a matter of fact, has up to the present time dominated the minds of most of the socialist workers in France and England. Hence, a mish-mash allowing of the most manifold shades of opinion: a mish-mash of such critical statements, economic theories, pictures of future society by the founders of different sects, as excite a minimum of opposition; a mish-mash which is the more easily brewed the more definite sharp edges of the individual constituents are rubbed down in the stream of debate, like rounded pebbles in a brook.
>
> To make a science of Socialism, it had first to be placed upon a real basis.
>
> Historical Materialism avoids the limitations of metaphysical materialism, mechanical materialism, vulgar materialism, and idealism by properly identifying the relationship between social being and social consciousness and by recognizing that human beings can impact social being through socially conscious activity which is the basis for Scientific Socialist theory and practice.
>
> Scientific Socialism is the application of Dialectical Materialist philosophy and Historical Materialist theory in the mission of overthrowing capitalism and building towards the stateless, classless society of communism. Human history is an important subject of study for Scientific Socialists because it is necessary to achieve a historical and comprehensive perspective of humanity and its development in order to affect change in human society.

Therefore, in practice, the revolutionary construction of a new society needs to be carried out along the following lines:

1. Revolution must be carried out simultaneously in the realms of both social being and social consciousness.
2. Changing the old social being is the foundation for changing the old social consciousness.
3. Changes in social being lead to profound changes in social consciousness, and also, conversely, the effects of social consciousness, in certain conditions, can also create drastic and profound changes in social being.

> **Annotation 85**
>
> Revolution can be carried out in the realm of social being by developing a material basis for social revolution. This requires the construction of social institutions such as workers' unions and political parties which can impact back upon the economic base of human society. The most important achievement which workers must strive for is building a state which can function as a dictatorship of the proletariat. This gives workers the greatest ability to impact the material base through conscious activity, and will allow for workers to eventually overcome and negate capitalism once and for all.

Annotation 85 (continued)

Revolution can be carried out in the realm of social consciousness by developing the social consciousness (specifically: the class consciousness) of the working class. This requires developing a Dialectical Materialist worldview in workers, eradicating false consciousness in workers, and fighting against bourgeois and reactionary ideology which is imposed upon workers by the ruling class.

The most effective way to impact and develop social consciousness is to build social institutions which can drive ideological progress through theoretical development and practical activity. This reflects the dialectical unity of theory and practice which is discussed in detail in *Part 1*, Chapter 3, beginning on p. 204.

Revolutionary activities in the realms of social being and social consciousness are dialectically related to one another. For example, improving material conditions for workers will make it easier for workers to develop class consciousness since they might have more free time and resources for education. At the same time, improving class consciousness will lead to workers struggling and fighting for better material conditions, up to and including the development of social revolution and the establishment of working class control of the state.

It is, therefore, vital for workers to understand and leverage a Historical Materialist understanding of human society and the relationship between social consciousness and social being in order to successfully carry out social revolution which will lead to the overthrow of capitalism and class society. As *Philosophy of Marxism-Leninism* explains:

> Social being and social consciousness are two dialectically unified aspects of social life. Therefore, the work of reforming the old society and building a new society must be carried out simultaneously through both social existence and social consciousness. It must be understood that changing social existence is the most basic condition for changing social consciousness. It must be further understood that change must also be sought in the other direction: just as changes in social existence inevitably lead to great changes in the social consciousness of society, social consciousness can also, under certain conditions, create strong and profound changes in social existence.

Engels explained the way in which social consciousness can lead to changes in social being in a letter to Joseph Block in 1890:

> The economic situation is the basis, but the various elements of the superstructure — political forms of the class struggle and its results, to wit: constitutions established by the victorious class after a successful battle, etc., juridical forms, and even the reflexes of all these actual struggles in the brains of the participants, political, juristic, philosophical theories, religious views and their further development into systems of dogmas — also exercise their influence upon the course of the historical struggles and in many cases preponderate in determining their form. There is an interaction of all these elements in which, amid all the endless host of accidents (that is, of things and events whose inner interconnection is so remote or so impossible of proof that we can regard it as non-existent, as negligible), the economic movement finally asserts itself as necessary. Otherwise the application of the theory to any period of history would be easier than the solution of a simple equation of the first degree.

Annotation 85 (continued)

In *What is to be Done*, Lenin explains the role of social consciousness in waging social revolution:

> Without revolutionary theory, there can be no revolutionary movement... The role of vanguard fighter can be fulfilled only by a party that is guided by the most advanced theory.
>
> To thoroughly grasp this methodological principle in the cause of the socialist revolution in our country we must, on the one hand, grasp the importance of the cultural ideological revolution and promote the positive impact of social consciousness on the economic development and industrialization and modernization of the country. On the other hand, we must avoid repeating the mistake of voluntarism in building culture and building a new society.

Voluntarism is a philosophical position and methodological practice of placing subjective will as the primary determinator of decisions and activities. Subjective will includes the goals, desires, and intentions of individual humans and/or groups of human beings. Voluntarism, therefore, is a form of idealism, since it overemphasizes the subjective consciousness of human beings while ignoring the role of matter in determining consciousness.

Lt. Col. Dang Cong Thanh defined the philosophical error of voluntarism in the article "Voluntarism is a Dangerous 'Disease' That Needs to be Avoided," Published in 2020 in Ha Giang Newspaper:

> Willpower is one of the factors that make up a person's character and courage. However, if we only rely on personal willpower without following objective laws, or consider willpower as a "universal key" to solving all problems without starting from a basis of real life, it is voluntarism - one of the manifestations of the disease of "communist arrogance" that can easily cause revolutionaries to fail and deteriorate.
>
> . . .
>
> Voluntarists often have in common the characteristic of examining, perceiving, and evaluating things and phenomena based on subjective feelings. They consider their opinions to be always correct, even "solely correct." Voluntarism used to be one of the mistakes of a segment of communists in the world. These communists considered human will as the primary determinant for reforming and changing the world. This perspective denied the objective laws of nature and society. Voluntarists have hasty thoughts and excessive optimism. They want to quickly achieve results and goals without careful consideration, objective, comprehensive, and thorough evaluation of all issues and aspects. They easily succumb to illusions about subjective strength without anticipating all the difficulties and obstacles caused by both objective and subjective factors.
>
> A number of cadres and party members in the past, when looking ahead, often used "rose-tinted glasses," so they more or less stumbled and made mistakes on the revolutionary path and in practical activities. This was partly due to a lack of scientific information, and partly due to a lack of thorough understanding of the tortuous complexity of the process of building a new social regime.
>
> . . .

Annotation 85 (continued)

Voluntarism manifests itself in many aspects that are difficult to detect at first, but once we become aware of the nature of voluntarism, it becomes much easier to identify. For example: one common cause of voluntarism is the failure by a group of decision-makers to carefully study the actual situation. This leads to inappropriate decisions being made. Another common cause of voluntarism arises from the phenomenon of "new officials, new policies."[37] Many cadres[38] in the early stages of holding leadership positions always appear eager and overly concerned with social approval. Such cadres often wish to quickly create their own mark, so they feel they must put forward programs, plans, proposals, and projects with "positive and brilliant" goals. They set unrealistic targets for beautiful but unfeasible numbers. Ultimately, these ambitious measures cause more harm than good. What is more alarming is that many times voluntarism does not necessarily originate from immature thinking, immature awareness, or hasty thoughts, but rather it originates from very sophisticated group interests. They act in the name of the organization to issue programs and policies that benefit a minority of individuals with power and authority. This leads to many consequences and can even lead to unpredictable socio-economic consequences for the community and the country.

The Need to be Humble and to Learn and Listen to Opposing Opinions:

Speaking about the harmful effects of voluntarism that existed during his lifetime, Vladimir Lenin once said:

"For a proletarian political party, there is no more dangerous mistake than to set its strategy according to subjective will." For cadres and party members, voluntarism and the attitude of imposing personal subjective opinions on the collective are not only prominent manifestations of selfish, narrow-minded, authoritarian, and patriarchal individualism, but also cause suspicion and internal disunity, leading to a loss of fighting power of Party committees and organizations; this hinders the healthy development of agencies, units, localities, and, more broadly, the whole society.

So, how do we prevent, combat, stop, and push back the disease of voluntarism which exists in segments of cadres and Party members, especially those in positions of power today? Finding a satisfactory answer to this problem is not easy if a segment of cadres does not truly have progressive thinking, a spirit of inquiry, a spirit of integrity, and a true sense of service to the country, to the people, and to the common interests of the community and the collective.

Cadres and Party members must have progressive thinking to prevent and eliminate backward remnants in thoughts, in attitudes, and in actions that affect the laws and positive development trends of organizations, agencies, units, and localities. We must have a spirit of learning to humbly receive and accept healthy contributions and criticisms from subordinates, from our fellow cadres, and from others with good professional qualifications. We must have a spirit of integrity to

---

37 This is a Vietnamese expression that describes the tendency for new leaders to enact changes in order to prove themselves.

38 A person or group with a leadership position in a political organization; usually a communist party.

> **Annotation 85 (continued)**
>
> not be influenced by material interests or personal interests in the promulgation of collective policies and decisions.
>
> It is necessary to pay more attention to regularly doing a good job of inspection, supervision, and strengthening control over the personal power of leaders and those with the authority to issue decisions on policies, mechanisms, and policies; promptly detecting and resolutely and strictly handling manifestations of voluntarism and imposition of personal opinions that harm the common interests. This issue has been raised for many years, but in reality, the inspection and supervision work at many Party committees and organizations has not been maintained strictly and effectively; many places have shown signs of laxity and signs of inadequate inspection and supervision. This has led to a situation where a number of leaders, especially top leaders, still do not. . . properly resolve and harmoniously handle the relationship between the collective leadership role and the responsibility of the individual in charge.

Philosophy of Marxism-Leninism describes how voluntarism led to problems in the post-revolutionary historical period of Vietnam which took place just after the end of the war with the USA in 1975. During this period, known as the "Subsidizing Period," Vietnamese communists tried to immediately move Vietnamese society to a stateless, classless society very rapidly.

This was attempted at a time when the productive forces of Vietnam were very undeveloped, especially because of the devastation and destruction caused by the war to the infrastructure and productive capacity of the nation. At the end of the war period, most Vietnamese people were small-scale farmers with very primitive tools and material resources.

> It should be seen that it is only possible to truly create the social consciousness of a socialist society on the basis of thoroughly renovating the traditional small-scale farmer's material way of life and establishing and developing a new method of production on the basis of successfully implementing the cause of industrialization and modernization.

Voluntarism led Vietnamese communists to overemphasize the subjective desire to quickly achieve communism while ignoring the objective material conditions of the era. In objective reality, the productive forces were simply not developed enough to realistically achieve such a rapid transition to a stateless, classless society. These issues of voluntarism as they pertain to the post-war period are discussed more in Annotation 4 of Appendix G, p. 260.

Closely related to the error of voluntarism are the errors of *commandism* and *tailism*. These are mistakes which are made in revolutionary leadership which result whenever revolutionaries do not understand the process and nature of social revolution.

Commandism occurs when revolutionaries do not listen to the people, and instead attempt to unilaterally *command* the people through force of will. This is a form of voluntarism because it reflects a mistaken belief that the subjective will of the revolutionary individual or party can impose its will unilaterally on the masses. It fails to account for the dialectical relationship which exists between more advanced elements of the revolutionary class and the masses at large.

> **Annotation 85 (continued)**
>
> **Tailism** occurs when revolutionaries follow reactionary opinions, attitudes, and false consciousness of the masses blindly. It is, in essence, a failure to utilize proper Dialectical Materialist and Historical Materialist analysis and methodology in theory and practice. As Lenin wrote:
>
>> Surely, it is not [the] function [of the revolutionary party] to drag at the tail of the movement. At best, this would be of no service to the movement; at worst, it would be exceedingly harmful.[39]
>
> The errors of tailism and commandism were further defined by Ho Chi Minh in *Modifying the Working Style*:
>
>> We must always converse with the masses and make sure that we are understood by the masses. This means we must show the masses that we are accountable. If we have bureaucratic manners, if we only command the masses, that means we are not accountable to the masses. In making this mistake, we turn our "commands" into a wall that separates the Party and the government from the masses, and the policies of the Party and the government become detached from the needs of the people... Therefore, we must ask for the masses' opinions in everything. We must always converse with the masses and make sure that we are understood by the masses... But we should also not just blindly do whatever the masses say. (We must) compare different opinions carefully and analyze the class conditions that lead to those opinions. Find the contradictions in those differing opinions to see what is right and what is wrong. Select the right opinions, present them to the people for discussion, and then repeat this process, to gradually raise the people's awareness... We absolutely should not follow the tail of masses. But we must gather the opinions of the masses and utilize them in our leadership. We must take the people's way of comparing, considering, and solving problems, and turn it into a way of leading the people.

---

[39] *What is to be Done?* V. I. Lenin, 1901.

CHAPTER 4

CATEGORY OF SOCIAL-ECONOMIC FORMATION AND THE NATURAL-HISTORICAL PROCESS OF THE DEVELOPMENT OF DIFFERENT SOCIAL-ECONOMIC FORMATIONS

I. CATEGORY OF SOCIAL-ECONOMIC FORMATION

Society is the extraordinarily complex sum total of countless social relationships.

Marx, Engels, and Lenin used Dialectical Materialism to analyze social life in order to formulate scientific theories of human social relations. To be able to develop such scientific theories of human social relations, the relations of production had to be isolated as a subject of study. The examination of these objective economic relations outside of human consciousness allowed the study of human history and society to be placed on an objective basis. Formulating a scientific understanding of human society also required the study of the dialectical relationship between the relations of production and the productive forces.

> **Annotation 86**
>
> At the foundation of Historical Materialism is Social-Economic Formation Theory. This theory holds that every human society exists as a formation which includes an economic base and a social superstructure. The dialectical relationship between the base and superstructure is what defines human society. We can, therefore, use the term "Social-Economic Formation" as a synonym for human society.
>
> Within the relationship between the base and superstructure, the base determines the superstructure while the superstructure can impact back upon the base. This reflects the Dialectical Materialist conception of the relationship between matter and consciousnes: matter determines consciousness, and consciousness can impact back upon the material world. Social-Economic Formation Theory arises from the application of Dialectical Materialist philosophy and Materialist Dialectical analysis in studying human society. The proper understanding of the material basis of the development of human society is the basis for the objective analysis of human history. This is what distinguishes Historical Materialism from all previous methods of analyzing human history and society. As Engels wrote in *Socialism: Utopian and Scientific*:
>
>> The materialist conception of history starts from the proposition that the production of the means to support human life and, next to production, the exchange of things produced, is the basis of all social structure; that in every society that has appeared in history, the manner in which wealth is distributed and society divided into classes or orders is dependent upon what is produced, how it is produced, and how the products are exchanged. From this point of view, the final causes of all social changes and political revolutions are to be sought, not in men's brains, not in men's better insights into eternal truth and justice, but in changes in the modes of production and exchange. They are to be sought, not in the philosophy, but in the economics of each particular epoch.

> **Annotation 86 (continued)**
>
> As Engels goes on to explain, placing our understanding of history on an objective basis is more than a mere philosophical breakthrough. Historical Materialism also has *political* importance, as it creates a basis for the oppressed workers of the world to understand the nature of their own oppression, and such an understanding is a necessary prerequisite for social revolution and liberation from class society:
>
>> The growing perception that existing social institutions are unreasonable and unjust, that reason has become unreason, and right wrong, is only proof that in the modes of production and exchange changes have silently taken place with which the social order, adapted to earlier economic conditions, is no longer in keeping. From this it also follows that the means of getting rid of the incongruities that have been brought to light must also be present, in a more or less developed condition, within the changed modes of production themselves.
>
> Finally Engels explains that the principles of Historical Materialism are not to be "deduced" through reason alone, but must be discovered through material analysis of the economic base (i.e., the "system of production") of human society:
>
>> These means are not to be invented by deduction from fundamental principles, but are to be discovered in the stubborn facts of the existing system of production.
>
> Social-Economic Formation Theory is further explained from p. 159.

They analyzed those economic relations and how they, in turn, related with all other social relations (specifically the relationship with the socio-political superstructure) which led to the clear conclusion that society is a structural system with certain fundamental constituent aspects. These fundamental aspects of society are:

- Productive forces.
- Relations of production (constituting the economic structure of society).
- The superstructure of society.

> **Annotation 87**
>
>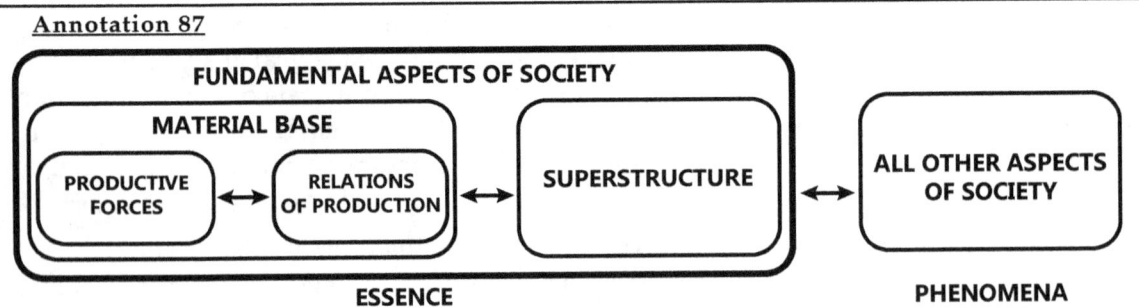
>
> The fundamental aspects of society are those aspects which drive the internal development of society. All other aspects of society are phenomena of those fundamental aspects.
>
> The relationship between productive forces and relations of production constitute the material base of human society, whereas the superstructure of society's internal relationships consists of countless social consciousness forms and their corresponding socio-political institutions. This is the subject of Chapter 1, Section 2, starting on p. 42.

> **Annotation 87 (continued)**
>
> All of these relationships follow the principles and laws of Dialectical Materialism and Materialist Dialectics so that productive forces determine the relations of production whereas relations of production impact back on productive forces, and the material base of society determines the superstructure whereas the superstructure impacts back on the material base [see: Chapter 2, Section 2, starting on p. 90].
>
> The productive forces, relations of production, and superstructure are considered to be the *fundamental* aspects of society because they are the elements which determine the development of human society in essence. This relates to the universal category pair of essence and phenomena. The productive forces, relations of production, and superstructure of society are considered essential because they are the internal relations which determine development and change within human society. Any other aspects of human society that fall outside of the bounds of these fundamental aspects are phenomena; this means that they are externally observable aspects which derive from the fundamental aspects of society.

The relations of production exist both as the economic form which corresponds to the content of the productive forces, and as a constituent aspect of the economic base of society upon which a superstructure (including politics, law, religion, etc.) is built. In the philosophical theory of Historical Materialism, this dialectical system which includes the economic base and superstructure is called the social-economic formation (or "social formation").

> **Annotation 88**
>
> The relationship between content and form is discussed in detail on p. 147 of **Part 1**. The nature of the content/form relationship between productive forces and relations of production are explained in Annotation 39 on p. 63. The relationship between the base and superstructure is explained more in Chapter 1, Section 2, starting on p. 42.

As a basic category of Historical Materialism, the category of social-economic formation has the following definition:

> Society within a certain historical period, composed of a relationship between the predominant relations of production of that society (which suit the development level of the productive forces) and the corresponding superstructure of that society (which is built upon those relations of production).

> **Annotation 89**
>
> Social-economic formation simply refers to a human society as it exists in a certain time and place. The relationship which defines a social-economic formation is the relationship between the base and superstructure.
>
> In Dialectical Materialism, a category is defined as the most general grouping of aspects, attributes, and relations of things, phenomena, and ideas. In Historical Materialism, a social-economic formation can therefore be defined as the most general grouping of aspects, attributes, and relations of human society in a particular stage of development.

> **Annotation 89 (continued)**
>
> The development of human society is driven primarily by the development of productive forces. As the productive forces develop, new relations of production emerge in order to become suitable with the productive forces, and the cycle begins again; eventually, the productive forces will develop once more to such an extent that they become unsuitable to the new relations of production. This leads society to move from one mode of production (defined by the relationship between the productive forces and relations of production) to another. In terms of Materialist Dialectics, each shift from one mode of production to the next can be considered a quality shift which is the result of extended and gradual shifts in quantity of the means of production over time. Quantity and quality are explained more in *Part 1*, p. 163.
>
> The relations of production can only change through social revolution, a process which is described in Chapter 5, Section 2, starting on p. 207.
>
> The superstructure of society is determined by the material base of society as explained in Chapter 2, Section 2, starting on p. 90, and reflects and protects the relations of production as explained in Annotation 50, p. 90.

This scientific conception of society as a "formation" of base and superstructure has provided a scientific methodology for the study of the basic structure of society, allowing us to analyze the extremely complex life of a given society in order to point out the dialectical relationships between its fundamental aspects. This analytical methodology asserts that the motion and development of society is a natural-historical process. This scientific methodology, which allows us to analyze social life and its history of motion and development, is one of the great discoveries of Marxism-Leninism.

> **Annotation 90**
>
> The scientific conception of society as a configuration of a base and superstructure is described in Chapter 2 starting on p. 73. The discovery by Marx and Engels of the objective dialectical development of human society and the formulation of the base/superstructure model of human society is what allows human history to be studied on a scientific basis. Historical Materialism is the term we use to refer to scientific analysis of human history through the framework of Dialectical Materialist analysis. As Lenin wrote in *The Economic Content of Narodism*:
>
>> [Marx's theory of history] applied to social science that objective, general scientific criterion of repetition which the subjectivists declared could not be applied to sociology. They argued, in fact, that owing to the tremendous complexity and variety of social phenomena they could not be studied without separating the important from the unimportant, and that such a separation could be made only from the viewpoint of "critically thinking" and "morally developed" individuals. And they thus happily succeeded in transforming social science into a series of sermons on petty-bourgeois morality... (which) philosophized about the inexpediency of history and about a path directed by "the light of science." It was these arguments that Marx's theory severed at the very root. The distinction between the important and the unimportant was replaced by the distinction between the economic structure of society, as the content, and the political and ideological form.

> **Annotation 90 (continued)**
>
> A "natural-historical process" is a process which arises from nature and is governed by objective laws of nature (natural) and which takes place over time (historical). Humanity has a natural aspect: humanity from nature and is a component of nature and is regulated by objective natural laws. This natural aspect of humanity is explained in more detail in Chapter 6 starting on p. 212.
>
> Furthermore, the development of human society is rooted in objective material processes; namely: the development of the economic base of human society which is composed of productive forces and relations of production. The development of human society occurs independently of human will, although human will and conscious activity (especially political activity) can impact back on the base of society as explained in Annotation 49, p. 88.
>
> Understanding the nature of the relationship between the base and superstructure of society and the ways in which human beings can consciously impact human society is key to the mission of Scientific Socialism.

II. THE NATURAL-HISTORICAL PROCESS OF THE DEVELOPMENT OF SOCIAL-ECONOMIC FORMATIONS

By applying the Theory of Social-Economic Formation to the study of the development of human history, Marx concluded that "the evolution of the economic formation of society is viewed as a process of natural history."

The natural historical nature of the development process of the social-economic formation is proven by the following evidence:

First, the motion and development of society does not follow the subjective will of humans but follows objective laws. These are the laws of the social-economic formation structure itself. These laws include the system of social laws in the fields of economy, politics, culture, science, and so on, but the laws that determine the development of society most fundamentally are:

1. The Law of Suitability Between the Relations of Production and the Productive Forces.
2. The Law of the Base Determining the Superstructure of Society.

> **Annotation 91**
>
> The Law of Suitability Between the Relations of Production and the Productive Forces is defined and explained in Chapter 1, Section 2, starting on p. 42.
>
> The Law of the Base Determining the Superstructure of Society is a closely related law which was first formulated by Marx in *A Contribution to the Critique of Political Economy*:
>
>> At a certain stage of development, the material productive forces of society come into conflict with the existing relations of production or—this merely expresses the same thing in legal terms—with the property relations within the framework of which they have operated hitherto. From forms of development of the productive forces these relations turn into their fetters. Then begins an era of social revolution. With the change of the economic foundation the entire immense superstructure is more or less rapidly transformed.
>
> The objective need for the relations of production to suit the productive forces leads to developments in the base. Eventually these developments in the base of society will lead to developments in the superstructure of society. As Marx explains in *The Poverty of Philosophy*, it is development of the economic base drives constant change in society:
>
>> Social relations are closely bound up with productive forces. In acquiring new productive forces men change their mode of production; and in changing their mode of production, in changing the way of earning their living, they change all their social relations. The hand-mill gives you society with the feudal lord; the steam-mill society with the industrial capitalist.
>>
>> The same men who establish their social relations in conformity with the material productivity, produce also principles, ideas, and categories, in conformity with their social relations.
>>
>> . . .
>>
>> There is a continual movement of growth in productive forces, of destruction in social relations, of formation in ideas.

Social-Economic Formation Theory   165

Annotation 91 (continued)

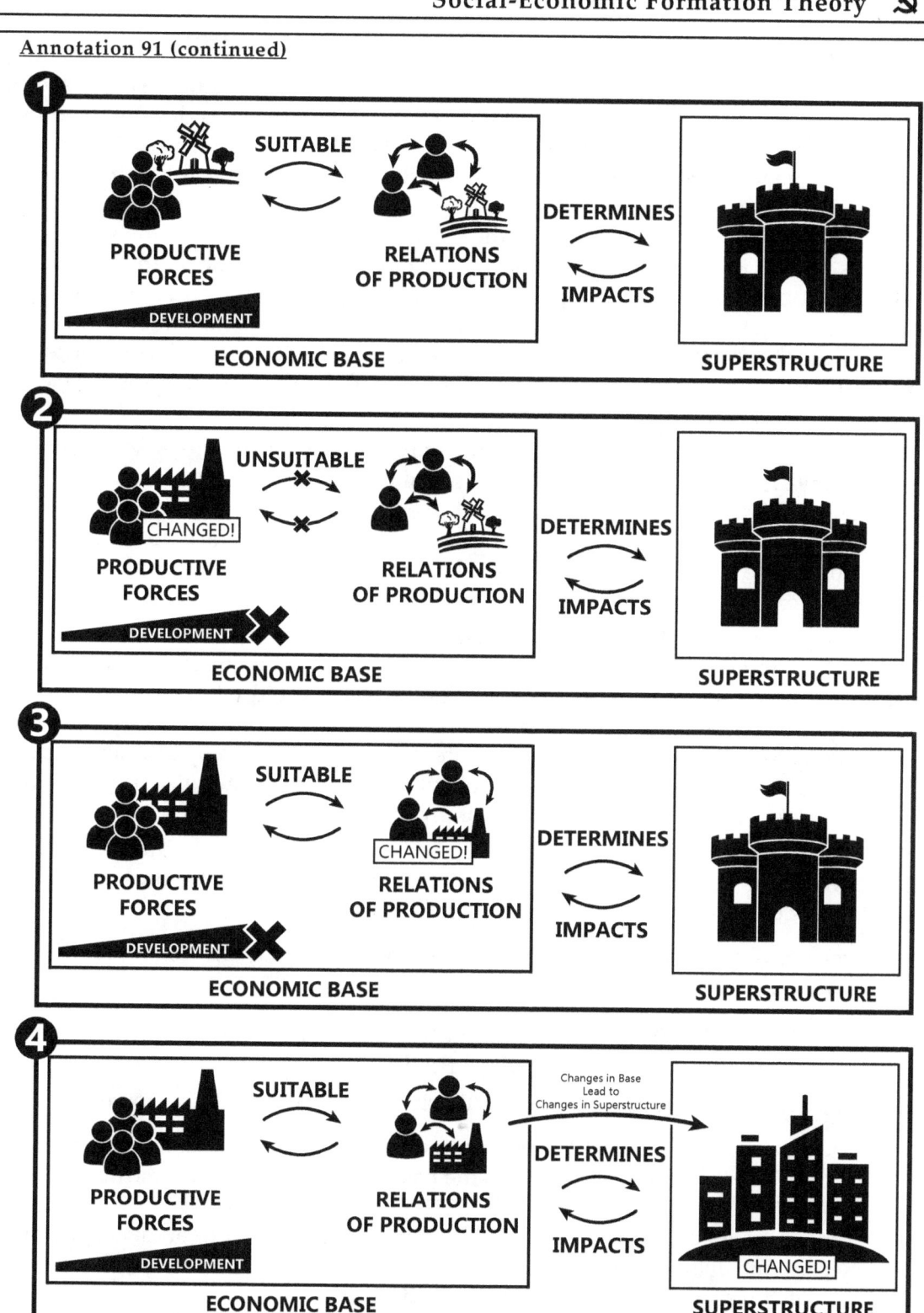

The Law of Suitability Between Relations of Production and Productive Forces is closely linked to the Law of the Base Determining the Superstructure of Society. Together, these laws govern the devleopment pattern of the fundamental aspects of human society.

> **Annotation 91 (continued)**
>
> Whenever productive forces develop to a point that they are no longer suitable with relations of production, human society suffers because progress and development of human society is severely restrained. Human society has an objective need for stability and suitable relations of production which will allow productive forces to resume stable and unrestrained development (see Annotation 36, p. 52). Because the base determines the superstructure, changes in the base will lead to changes in the superstructure. This reflects the Dialectical Materialist conception of the relationship between matter and consciousness which holds that the material determines consciousness while consciousness impacts back upon the material. The base is the material aspect of society while the superstructure is the aspect of social consciousness. Furthermore, the superstructure exists in large part to protect the material base of human society (see: Annotation 50, p. 90).
>
> Within the superstructure of society there are many social institutions which serve this protective role, but the most important social institution of the superstructure in this regard is the state. The state exists to enforce the agenda of the ruling class and to stabilize class relations so that productive forces are allows to develop efficiently continuously. The state serves this function by enforcing the relations of production through coercive violence (see p. 94).
>
> Once social revolution transpires and a new ruling class seizes control of the means of production and develops a state to protect and advance its own class interests, the superstructure of society is (to quote Marx) "more or less rapidly transformed" to reflect and protect the material base and the newly established relations of production. This includes the rapid development of a state which is controlled by and serves the new ruling class and countless other social institutions which otherwise protect and stabilize society's newly formed relations of production.
>
> Understanding both the Law of Suitability Between Relations of Production and Productive Forces and the Law of the Base Determining the Superstructure, we can see the pattern of development of human society:
>
> 1. Productive forces develop to such a point that they are no longer suitable with relations of production.
> 2. This unsuitability restrains the development of the productive forces. This creates an objective need for relations of production to change.
> 3. The relations of production eventually change to suit productive forces.
> 4. Once the material base advances to a new mode of production, the superstructure will rapidly change as well, as the base determines the superstructure.

Second, the origin of all motion and development of society, of human history, and of all social-economic fields are ultimately caused either directly or by the development of the productive forces of society. Lenin once emphasized:

> Only the reduction of social relations to relations of production and of the latter to the level of the productive forces, provided a firm basis for the conception that the development of formations of society is a process of natural history.[40]

---

40 "What the 'Friends of the People' Are and How They Fight the Social-Democrats," V. I. Lenin, 1894.

> **Annotation 92**
>
> The productive forces are the origin of all motion within human society as an internal component of human society and as the material basis of development in human society. This is consistent with fundamental principles of Dialectical Materialist philosophy, including:
>
> - The Dialectical Materialist conception of the relationship between matter and consciousness. This conception holds that the material determines consciousness and consciousness can impact back upon matter. (See: *Part 1*, p. 88)
> - The Principle of Development of Materialist Dialectics. This principle holds that all motion, change, and development originates from internal relations with a thing, phenomenon, or idea. (See: *Part 1*, p. 119)

Third, the development process of social-economic formation, i.e., the replacement of different social-economic formations throughout human history, as well as the development of human social history can be impacted by many subjective factors, but the decisive factor is always the impact of objective laws.

> **Annotation 93**
>
> Subjective factors are factors which can vary across time and place and which can vary from one location to another even within the same social formation of human society. Subjective factors are defined in more detail in Annotation 95, below.
>
> Objective laws are the laws of Materialist Dialectics which apply to all things, phenomena, and ideas in the universe. These laws are listed and detailed in *Part 1*, p. 248 and the application of these laws to human society are detailed in Annotation 37, p. 55 of this book. Objective laws govern, determine, and restrain subjective factors including the ability of human beings to act in the world and to change the world. Subjective factors, therefore, are limited by the objective laws of reality.
>
> Subjectivity and objectivity are explained in detail in Appendix E, p. 244.

Under the influence of objective laws, human history is a process of sequential replacement of social-economic formations: i.e., from original society to slave society to feudalism to capitalism, with the future certainly belong to the communist social-economic formation.

> **Annotation 94**
>
> The principles of development explained in Chapter 2 of *Part 1* apply to human society as they do to all other things, phenomena, and ideas. This means that human society develops through processes of contradiction and negation in accordance with the objective laws of reality. This means that the development of human society can be analyzed and studied like any other natural phenomenon and that certain conclusions and predictions can be drawn from the application and understanding of these laws.
>
> Marx and Engels have proven that communism is inevitably the stage of development that will follow capitalism through careful objective analysis of the political economy of capitalism. Their thorough analysis - in particular the analysis of Marx in *Capital* - show that the productive forces of capitalism are not suitable with the

> **Annotation 94 (continued)**
>
> relations of production and that capitalism contains internal contradictions which are unstable and which will lead to the eventual collapse of the capitalist social formation. Once this occurs, the proletariat (the revolutionary class in our current society) will eventually negate the capitalist class and this will be the end of class society and class struggle.

While affirming the natural-historical characteristic (i.e., the objective-law characteristic) of social change and development, Marxism-Leninism also affirms the role of subjective factors in the development process of human history in general and the history of each specific human community in particular.

Such subjective factors include (but are not limited to):

- Geographical conditions.
- Political power levels of different classes.
- Cultural traditions.
- The international situation.

> **Annotation 95**
>
> Distinguishing the difference between objectivity and subjectivity is crucial for deeper understanding of Dialectical Materialist and Historical Materialist philosophy. The Philosophy of Marxism-Leninism department of Vietnam's Foreign Trade University gives the following explanation of objectivity and subjectivity:
>
> > "Objectivity" refers to everything that exists independently and outside of an active subject and does not depend on the active subject. Objective factors includes objective conditions, possibilities, and laws. In processes of development, objective laws always play the most important role. Objectivity can also be understood as the inherent nature of things, phenomena... In other words, the "objectivity" category is used to refer to all that exists independently of a determined subject, constitutes a practical situation, and regularly affects the determination of the goals, tasks and methods of activity of that subject.
>
> > "Subjectivity" includes everything that constitutes and reflects the level of development of the qualities and capacities of a certain subject. To talk about subjectivity is to talk about the actual internal strength of the subject. "Subjectivity" is also understood as all the qualitative components and capacities of the subject in the activity of perceiving and transforming the object.
>
>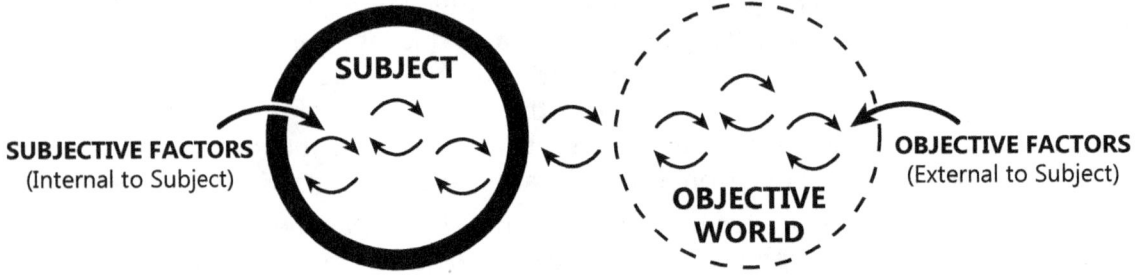
>
> *Subjective factors are internal to the subject being considered and drive its own internal development. Objective factors are external and govern, control, and impact its development.*

Annotation 95 (continued)

A subject is a thing, phenomenon, or idea which exists and develops in the world. This requires the subject to have a certain form. A form is a set of relatively stable relationships which allow the subject to exist and develop over time. According to the Principle of Development, a subject changes and develops over time as a result of internal relationships and contradictions. Subjectivity relates to and describes these internal relationships and contradictions and the internal development of a subject.

Objective factors relate to the external factors, relationships, contradictions, and contradictions in which a subject exists and develops. Of these countless external factors relating to any given subject, the most important are the objective laws which relate to all things, phenomena, and ideas. These include the two basic principles of Dialectical Materialism as well as the three universal laws of Materialist Dialectics.[41]

Both objective and subjective factors play vital roles in development processes, and both must be understood and considered in our analysis of the world.

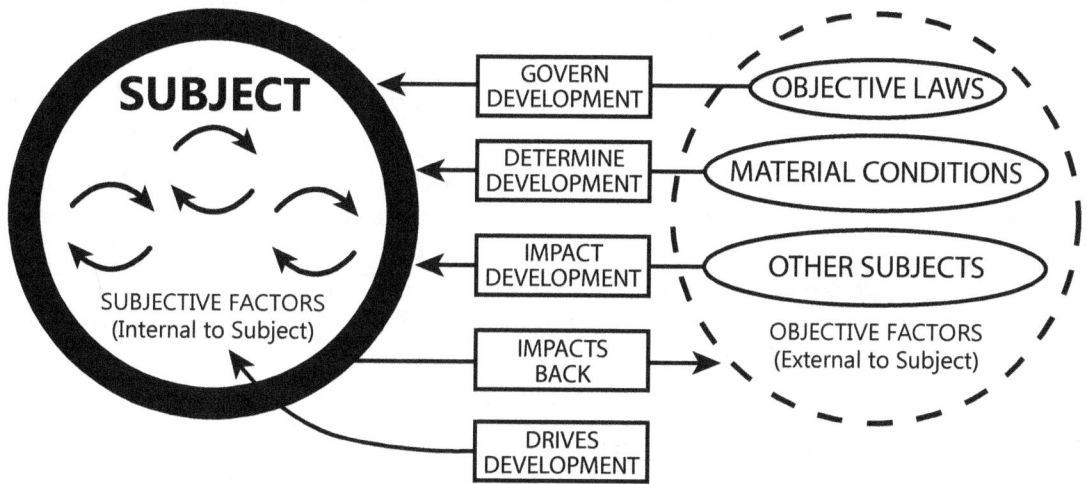

Both subjective and objective factors play important roles in the development of a subject.

Objective factors are important because they can greatly impact and even determine how a subject develops. Objective factors include:

- Objective laws, which govern the development of the subject. All subjects must follow objective laws in the course of their existence and development (i.e., a society must develop in accordance with the objective principles of Social Formation Theory; all things develop in accordance with the universal laws of Materialist Dialectics).

- Material conditions, which determine the development of subjects (i.e., a plant cannot grow without sunlight; a wooden chair can only be made if wood is available; the development of human society is constrained by the capacity of the material production process).

- Other subjects, which can impact back upon the subject in various ways (in accordance with the Principle of General Relationships).

---

41 See *Part 1*: Appendix B, p. 247 and Appendix C, p. 248.

Annotation 95 (continued)

Subjective factors are important because motion and development of a subject is driven by internal relations. This has basis in both the Principle of Development of Dialectical Materialism and the Law of Unification and Contradiction Between Opposites of Materialist Dialectics. As former General Secretary of the Communist Party of Vietnam, Nguyen Phu Trong, wrote:

> Any event or phenomenon has its objective and subjective causes, but in the end, it is the subjective causes that decide it.

This reflects the Law of Unification and Contradiction Between Opposites of Materialist Dialectics, which Lenin summarized as:

> The fundamental, originating, and universal driving force of all motion and development processes is the inherent and objective contradiction which exists in all things, phenomena, and ideas.[42]

In the context of human society and social formation thory, subjective factors are factors which exist as internal relationships and contradictions within a specific social-economic form. The subjective factors of a society in one time and place will be different from the subjective factors of a society in another time and place. These factors also vary from one place to another even within the same social formation.

Objective factors of human society relate to factors which exist externally to the social-economic form as a subject. Objective factors include not just the laws and principles of Dialectical Materialism but also the objective laws and principles of Historical Materialism. Unlike subjective factors, which can vary significantly from one society to another, the objective laws and principles of Historical Materialism apply universally to all human societies in all times and places.

See Appendix E, p. 244 for a full overview of subjectivity and objectivity.

Subjective factors relate to randomness from the Materialist Dialectical category pair of obviousness and randomness. This category pair relates to the predictability of development as determined by whether such development arises from internal relationships or external relationships.

- **Obviousness** refers to factors which have to develop in a certain way based on internal relationships.
- **Randomness** refers to factors which are much less predictable because they are caused by external relationships.

When examining human society and its development, we can identify:

- **Obvious factors** which are relatively predictable and which stem from internal material relationships. Within class society, these obvious factors are primarily related to class struggle: internal struggle related to the material processes which are primarily responsible for the development of class society.
- **Random factors** which are relatively unpredictable and caused by relationships which are external to those obvious material factors. Within class society, these are subjective factors which externally relate to class struggle and impact back on class struggle.

---

42 *Summary of Dialectics*, Vladimir Ilyich Lenin, 1914.

> **Annotation 95 (continued)**
>
> Thus, we can define subjective factors as the relatively random factors which impact a given social group of human beings which exist at a certain stage of development of class society. These factors are considered to be subjective because they relate to internal relationships which impact a specific group of human beings in a specific time in place.
>
> Here are some ways in which subjective factors can manifest and vary within a given social formation:
>
> - **Geographical conditions** can change the ways in which human society manifests and develops in countless ways. For instance, geographical isolation can prevent some groups of human beings from transitioning to the next stage of development of the mode of production along with the rest of the global population. Even today there are some isolated populations which never developed class society at all, though these are extremely rare in our modern day and age. Geographical factors can also impact the rate of development of productive forces and interactions between different groups of human beings in countless ways. For instance, having access to rivers and ports may make transportation of goods, labor, and resource more efficient and this may speed up development of productive forces. The presence or absence of good farmland and other natural resources in a region can also significantly impact the rate of development and other aspects of the development of human society within a region.
>
> - **Political power levels of different classes** can fluctuate over time and vary from one place to another within a social formation. For example, under feudalism there were some nations where peasants had more rights and privileges than other nations. Even within the same nation, one region or town may have different levels of power for different classes. Some cities might generally have stronger labor unions and more benefits for workers, for instance, while others might be more oppressive to workers. This also varies over time as workers strive for more power (and suffer setbacks) through processes of class struggle.
>
> - **Cultural traditions** can significantly impact the ways in which human society develops from one region to the next. Sometimes culture can speed up or slow down the development of productive forces or impede or hasten the development of new relations of production. Cultural traditions can also cause remnant class elements to linger longer in some places than in others. For example, some nations (like the UK and Saudi Arabia) still have cultural practices which include legacy classes from feudal times such as monarchs and nobility, whereas other nations have no such remnant classes present.
>
> - **The international situation** can drastically affect the development and conditions of a social formation. Relationships between nations can vary from peaceful trade and mutual development arrangements which can increase the rate of development of productive forces considerably to more harmful relations such as war, colonization, and competition for markets. Human society can go through periods of general peace and stability or general tension and conflict and these conditions can have significant impact on the development of social formations.

Subjective factors impact each and every human community in countless different ways, allowing for each human community to develop on its own unique path. Thus, subjective factors are the foundation of the richness and diversity of human history. We call this the "richness and diversity characteristic" of social development.

This richness and diversity characteristic allows for certain social-economic formations to "bypass" certain steps in development. Certain objective and subjective conditions must be met in order for such a "bypass" to take place.

> **Annotation 96**
>
> Subjective factors account for the fact that human society does not develop "mechanically" in a perfectly predictable manner. In a letter to Conrad Schmidt, Engels criticizes contemporary thinkers whose analysis of history is purely "mechanical" and fails to account for subjective factors:
>
>> What all these gentlemen lack is dialectics. All they ever see is cause here, effect there. They do not at all see that this is a bare abstraction; that in the real world such metaphysical polar opposites exist only in crises; that the whole great process develops itself in the form of reciprocal action, to be sure of very unequal forces, in which the economic movement is far and away the strongest, most primary and decisive. They do not see that here nothing is absolute and everything relative.
>
> The richness and diversity of humanity stems from all of the countless subjective factors which can impact humans in different times and places. Subjective factors can have such profound impact as to hinder and delay the transition of a society from one stage of development to the next, or to allow it to bypass a stage of development altogether. The passage below comes from an article published by the Cadre Training Political Center of Ben Tre Province in Vietnam and explains how subjective factors can lead to the bypassing of a stage of development of a social formation:
>
>> Because human society is a natural-historical process [see Annotation 90, p. 162], the movement of all social-economic formations happens objectively. However, the development of human society is still attached to the material conditions of the economy and society of each particular nation and each particular people. Because of those subjective factors, each nation will differ in terms of development of their respective social-economic forms. A nation might develop gradually from lower formation to higher formation, or a nation might bypass one or a few formations in the development process. Famous examples include Australia and some Latin American countries which bypassed the social-economic formation of feudalism in the history of their development.
>>
>> Such bypassing does not mainly depend on the subjective will of the people, it is mainly decided by the objective historical conditions. Such differences can manifest even within societies that differ greatly despite existing in the same mode of production. For instance, in Europe during the feudal era, power was held in the hands of many different classes (nobles, peasants, etc.), but in Asia it was more common for nearly all of the power to belong to the king.
>>
>> It is clear that the "bypassing" of stages of development of social-economic formations is not just random, but must obey objective laws.

> **Annotation 96 (continued)**
>
> We have provided more information on Vietnam's ongoing efforts to bypass capitalism in building socialism in the form of several articles and excerpts by Vietnamese communists which can be found in Appendix H, p. 269. We hope that this might give readers more insight into the application of Historical Materialist analysis and methodology in the material world. The objective laws which human society must follow in bypassing, hastening, or delaying development from one stage of development of social formation to the next are the same objective laws which all things, phenomena, and ideas must follow. These are the laws of Dialectical Materialism and Materialist Dialectics which are outlined in *Part 1*, p. 248.

In summary, the history of humanity in general, and of each human community in particular, obey certain objective social laws and are also influenced by numerous other subjective factors. Therefore, the development history of society manifests the characteristic of unity in diversity and diversity in unity.

> **Annotation 97**
>
> Unity in diversity and diversity in unity refers to the Principle of General Relationships of Materialist Dialectics which explains the nature of the internal relationships which define all things, phenomena, and ideas. This principle is explained in detail in Annotation 107 on page 110 of *Part 1*. To briefly summarize: all things, phenomena, and ideas contain countless internal relationships. These relationships are diverse and varied, but they define subjects which exist in unity.
>
>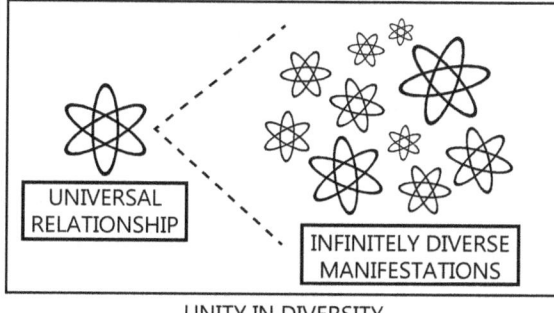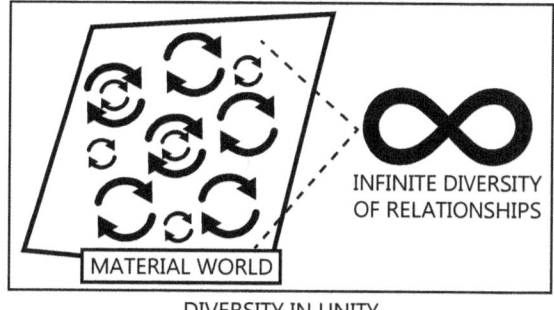
>
> UNITY IN DIVERSITY   DIVERSITY IN UNITY
>
> *"Unity in diversity and diversity in unity" describes an important aspect of the Principle of General Relationships of Materialist Dialectics.*
>
> Like all other things, phenomena, and ideas, humanity adheres to the principle of general relationships and therefore possesses the characteristic of unity in diversity and diversity in unity. Understanding the role of subjective factors in the history, development, and existence of humanity is key to understanding the principle of general development as it pertains to human society.
>
> Humanity as a whole is composed of countless diverse groups, and every group of human beings has subjective factors which distinguishes it from all other groups. All these diverse groups of human beings, considered together, define humanity as a whole. All groups of human beings adhere to the principles and laws of Historical Materialism, which reflects unity in diversity. At the same time, each society develops in a unique manner due to subjective factors, reflecting diversity in unity.

Annotation 97 (continued)

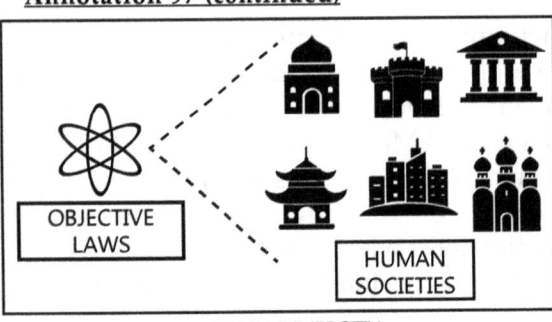
UNITY IN DIVERSITY

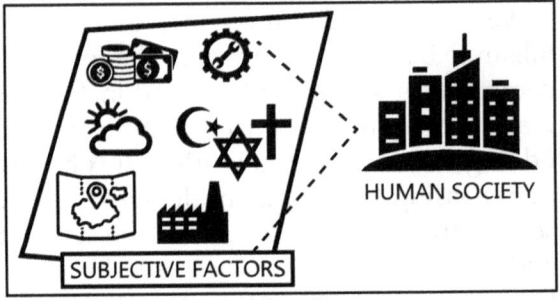
DIVERSITY IN UNITY

"Unity in diversity and diversity in unity" is reflected in human society. All human societies throughout history must obey objective laws, reflecting unity in diversity. Meanwhile, any given human society is impacted by countless subjective factors, reflecting diversity in unity.

As an example, geography is a subjective factor which impacts different societies in different ways. Some groups of human beings have been isolated for longer periods of time than most, which will delay or otherwise change the ways in which they transition from one stage of development to the next. Other societies may have cultural or political aspects which either speed up or slow down development relative to the rest of humanity. However, all human societies must adhere to the objective laws of Dialectical and Historical Materialism, and humanity itself is essentially defined by this diversity in subjective factors and social development.

III. SCIENTIFIC VALUE OF THE THEORY OF SOCIAL-ECONOMIC FORMATION

*"Continuously Struggle,
Rise Up in Strength!"*

Before Marx, *idealism* played a dominant role in social science. The advent of Historical Materialism, the core of which is the Theory of Social-Economic Formation, has provided a truly scientific methodology for the study of human society.

The following three rules must be observed in the Historical Materialist analysis of human society in order to avoid falling into idealism and to ensure that a scientific and material-based methodology is practiced:

First, the Theory of Social-Economic Formation states that:

> Material production is the basis of social life and that the mode of production determines the level of development of society, and thus, material production is also the factor which determines the development level of society and the general course of human history.

Therefore, we must strictly avoid basing our study of the development of human society primarily on the subjective thoughts, ideas, and will of humans. We must, instead, focus on the development level of social production in general and the mode of production in particular with the key is the development level of the productive forces when studying the historical development of any particular human community.

Second, the Theory of Social-Economic Formation also holds that society is not a random, mechanical combination of individuals, but a living organism. Aspects of society exist in a closely unified structural system which interact with each other. Within this system, the relations of production play the fundamental role, determining other social relations. It is an objective criterion which can be used to distinguish different social regimes. Therefore, to accurately explain society, it is necessary to use the scientific abstraction methodology - that is, it is necessary to start from the material relations of production of a society in order to analyze various other aspects of that society (i.e., politics, law, culture, science, etc.) and the mutual relationships between those other aspects.

Third, Social-Economic Formation Theory also holds that the motion and development of society is a natural-historical process. That is to say: social development is a process that takes place according to objective laws, and not according to human subjective will. Therefore, in order to properly understand and effectively solve social problems, it is necessary to study deeply the laws of motion and development of society. Lenin once emphasized that:

> What Marx and Engels called the dialectical method—as against the metaphysical—is nothing else than the scientific method in sociology, which consists in regarding society as a living organism in a state of constant development (and not as something mechanically concatenated and therefore permitting all sorts of arbitrary combinations of separate social elements), an organism the study of which requires an objective analysis of the relations of production that constitute the given social formation and an investigation of its laws of functioning and development.[43]

The three rules above, which are rooted in Social-Economic Formation Theory, together constitute the Historical Materialist methodology, which is the most general methodology in studying society, human history, and human communities.

Annotation 98

The Theory of Social-Economic Formation (also referred to as Social-Economic Formation Theory, or simply Social Formation Theory) is so-named because it is a theory which describe truths about how human societies (and economies) form and develop over time. Social Formation Theory is the core of Historical Materialism as it reflects the foundational role of Dialectical Materialist philosophy in Historical Materialism.

```
┌─────────────────────────────────────────┐
│  ┌───────────────────────────────────┐  │
│  │      SOCIAL FORMATION THEORY      │  │
│  │  Core Theory of Historical Materialism │
│  └───────────────────────────────────┘  │
│        HISTORICAL MATERIALISM           │
│   Dialectical Materialism Applied to the│
│        Analysis of Human Society        │
│                                         │
│        DIALECTICAL MATERIALISM          │
│         Foundational Philosophy         │
└─────────────────────────────────────────┘
```

Social Formation Theory is the core of Historical Materialism which is the application of Dialectical Materialism to the analysis of human society.

Each rule of Historical Materialist methodology is derived from a principle of Social-Economic Formation Theory. Each of these principles, in turn, reflects a foundational aspect of the Dialectical Materialist philosophy. In order to ensure that Historical Materialist analysis is consistent with the underlying philosophical precepts of Dialectical Materialism and the principles of Social Formation Theory, these rules must be closely followed.

---

43 "What the 'Friends of the People' Are and How They Fight the Social-Democrats," V. I. Lenin, 1894.

Annotation 98 (continued)

The table below shows the relationships between Dialectical Materialist philosophy, the principles of Social Formation Theory, and the rules of the methodology of Historical Materialism. Note that each rule of Historical Materialist methodology reflects a principle of Social Formation Theory and that each of these principles, in turn, is grounded in a foundational aspect of Dialectical Materialist philosophy:

Foundation of Dialectical Materialism	Principle of Social Formation Theory	Historical Materialist Methodology Rule
1. Dialectical Materialist conception of relationship between matter and consciousness: Matter determines consciousness.	Material production is the basis of social life, the mode of production determines the level of development of society, and therefore, material production is also the factor which determines the development level of society and the general course of human history	We must strictly avoid basing our study of the development of human society primarily on the subjective thoughts, ideas, and will of humans. We must, instead, focus on the development level of social production in general and the mode of production in particular when studying the historical development of human society.
2. Principle of General Relationships: All things, phenomena, and ideas exist in mutual relationship with each other, regulate each other, and transform each other. Nothing exists in complete isolation.	Society is not a random, mechanical combination of individuals, but a living organism. Aspects of society exist in a closely unified structural system which interact with each other. Within this system, the relations of production play the fundamental role, determining other social relations.	To accurately explain society, it is necessary to use the scientific abstraction methodology - that is, it is necessary to start from the material relations of production of a society in order to analyze various other aspects of that society.
3. Principle of Development: Development is a process that comes from within the thing-in-itself; the process of solving contradictions within things and phenomena. Therefore, development is inevitable, objective, and occurs without dependence on human will.	The development of society is a natural historical process of social development that takes place according to objective laws, and not according to human subjective will.	In order to properly understand and effectively solve social problems, it is necessary to study deeply the laws of motion and development of society.

> **Annotation 98 (continued)**
>
> Following is an explanation of each principle of social formation theory, its basis in Dialectical Materialism, and its corresponding rule of Historical Materialism.
>
> **Principle 1: Matter determines consciousness in human society.**
>
> This principle of Social Formation Theory is rooted in the Dialectical Materialist conception of the relationship between matter and consciousness which holds that matter determines consciousness while consciousness can impact back upon matter. Since matter determines consciousness, it must follow that social being determines social consciousness and that the material base determines the superstructure of society. As Marx wrote in his preface to *A Contribution to the Critique of Political Economy*:
>
>> The mode of production of material life conditions the general process of social, political and intellectual life. It is not the consciousness of men that determines their existence, but their social existence that determines their consciousness.
>
> This is the basis of the first rule of Historical Materialist methodology, which states:
>
>> We must strictly avoid basing our study of the development of human society primarily on the subjective thoughts, ideas and will of humans. We must, instead, focus on the development level of social production in general and the mode of production in particular when studying the historical development of human society.
>
> **Principle 2: Society is an "organism" (a closely unified system of relationships).**
>
> This principle of Social Formation Theory is rooted in the Principle of General Relations of Dialectical Materialism, which holds that all things, phenomena, and ideas exist in mutual relationship with each other, regulate each other, and transform each other, and that nothing exists in complete isolation. Human society can therefore be understood to be defined by internal and external relationships. In *The Economic Content of Narodism*, Lenin explains how human society is thus formed as an "organism" of relations:
>
>> According to Marx's theory, each such system of production relations is a specific social organism, whose inception, functioning, and transition to a higher form, conversion into another social organism, are governed by specific laws.
>
> This is the basis of the second rule of Historical Materialist methodology, which states:
>
>> To accurately explain society, it is necessary to use the scientific abstraction methodology - that is, it is necessary to start from the material relations of production of a society in order to analyze various other aspects of that society.
>
> **Principle 3: Society is a natural historical process of social development governed by objective laws.**
>
> This principle of Social Formation Theory is rooted in the Dialectical Materialist Principle of Development, which states:
>
>> Development is a process that comes from within the thing-in-itself; the process of development is inevitable, objective, and occurs without dependence on human will.
>
> As Engels wrote in *Dialectics of Nature*:

> **Annotation 98 (continued)**
>
> Motion in the most general sense, conceived as the mode of existence, the inherent attribute of matter, comprehends all changes and processes occurring in the universe, from mere change of place right up to thinking... The whole of nature accessible to us forms a system, an interconnected totality of bodies, and by bodies we understand here all material existence extending from stars to atoms, indeed right to ether particles, in so far as one grants the existence of the last named. In the fact that these bodies are interconnected is already included that they react on one another, and it is precisely this mutual reaction that constitutes motion.
>
> It therefore follows that human society, like all other things, phenomena, and ideas, exists in a constant state of development which stems from objective internal and external relationships. This leads to the principle of social formation which states that:
>
> > The motion and development of society is a natural historical process. That is to say: social development is a process that takes place according to objective laws, and not according to human subjective will.
>
> This is the basis of the third rule of Historical Materialist methodology, which states:
>
> > In order to properly understand and effectively solve social problems, it is necessary to study deeply the laws of motion and development of society.
>
> **Application of the Methodology of Historical Materialism**
>
> Following the rules outlined above constitutes the methodology of Historical Materialism. In order to properly practice this methodology in the analysis of human society, it is critical to thoroughly and deeply understand the principles of Social-Economic Formation Theory and their basis in Dialectical Materialist philosophy. When we adhere to the rules of Historical Materialism and the principles of Social Formation Theory, we can be assured that our analysis of human society can be placed upon a scientific basis which aligns with the philosophical worldview and methodology of Dialectical Materialism. A solid understanding of Social-Economic Formation Theory is also an important prerequisite to the studying and pursuing the program of Scientific Socialism, which serves as the basis for an organized political process of bringing about social revolution.

It must be pointed out that the Historical Materialist methodology cannot replace more specific methods used in the study of each specific field of society. Lenin once taught that: "materialism in history has never claimed to explain everything, but merely to indicate the 'only scientific' ... method of explaining history."[44]

> **Annotation 99**
>
> Dialectical Materialism is a universal philosophy. This means that Dialectical Materialism can be used to study and analyze all things, phenomena, and ideas in existence. Historical Materialism is the application of Dialectical Materialist philosophy and methodology specifically to the study and analysis of human society. Other scientific fields (such as the study of physics, medicine, astronomy, and so on) may be analyzed and interpreted through the application of Dialectical Materialist philosophy, but

---

[44] "What the 'Friends of the People' Are and How They Fight the Social-Democrats," V. I. Lenin, 1894.

> **Annotation 99 (continued)**
>
> Historical Materialism is solely focused on the study of the development and existence of humanity.
>
> The three principles of Social Formation Theory and the three rules of Historical Materialist analysis are derived from the universal principles of Dialectical Materialism as applied to the specific study of human society and its development and history. Social Formation Theory is useful for understanding the objective laws which govern the development of humanity and the three rules of Historical Materialist methodology are useful in the application of Historical Materialism to specific inquiries into human society and its historical development.
>
> Together, Social Formation Theory and the methodology of Historical Materialism enable socialists to accurately study and understand all of humanity as well as specific groups of human beings within society, both in our modern contemporary times and throughout history.

CHAPTER 5

THE ROLE OF CLASS STRUGGLE AND SOCIAL REVOLUTION IN THE MOTION AND DEVELOPMENT OF CLASS SOCIETY

I. CLASS AND THE ROLE OF CLASS STRUGGLE IN THE DEVELOPMENT OF CLASS SOCIETY

1. Definition of Class

In *A Great Beginning*, Lenin gave his definition of class:

> Classes are large groups of people differing from each other by the place they occupy in a historically determined system of social production, by their relation (in most cases fixed and formulated in law) to the means of production, by their role in the social organization of labor, and, consequently, by the dimensions of the share of social wealth of which they dispose and the mode of acquiring it.

According to the above definition, division of people in a social community into different and opposing classes is essentially caused by difference in status of different groups within a certain system of social production and opposition between those groups within that system.

These differences in status and oppositions inevitably lead to one class being able to "appropriate the labor of another."[45]

Thus, Lenin asserted:

> Classes are groups of people, one of which can appropriate the labor of another, owing to the different places they occupy in a definite system of social economy.

The essence of class division in a society is the division of people in a social community into the exploiters and the exploited. The reality of human history over the past few millennia has proven that division into opposing classes constitutes exploitation through appropriation of labor throughout history: slave owners exploited slaves in ancient history, landlords exploited serfs in the medieval period, and the bourgeoisie exploits the proletariat during our modern times.

History has also proven that the class which holds the means of production within society occupies the position of mastery of political power and state power. This class [which controls the means of production] will objectively become the dominant class of society, and will appropriate the labor of other classes. Through this domination of political and state power, this ruling class is able to maintain a relatively stable society in the context of class antagonism.

Annotation 100

The state is the social institution which allows a ruling class to exploit and appropriate the labor of oppressed classes through violence and coercion. The state is also the social institution that has the greatest impact on the base. By constructing and controlling the state, the ruling class is able to maintain and stabilize its position of domination over the rest of human society and control of the means of production.

---

45 "A Great Beginning," V. I. Lenin, 1919.

Annotation 100 (continued)

Throughout history, the only way a ruling class has fallen out of power is through the process of social revolution. In the process of social revolution, an emerging progressive class overtakes the previously ruling class (an act of dialectical negation) and ultimately establishes a new state which it controls. Social revolution thus constitutes the development a new social-economic formation which has its own class structure.

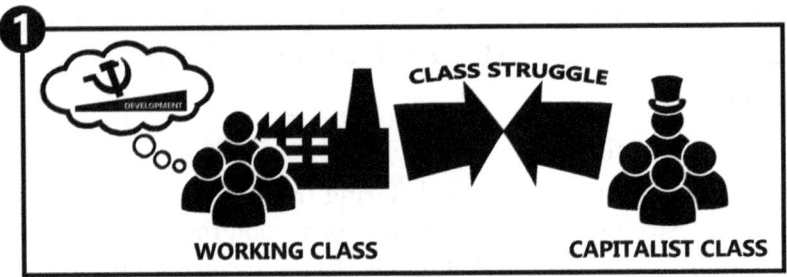
Progressive workers develop class consciousness of the working class.

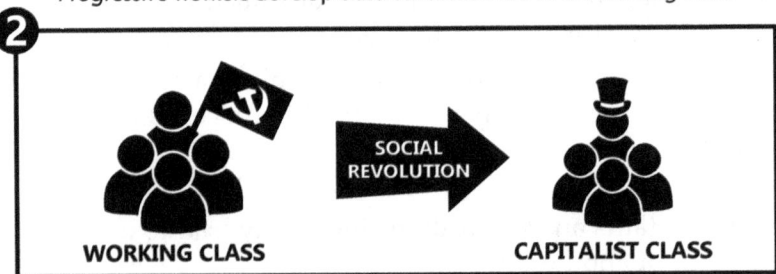
Development of class consciousness eventually leads to social revolution.

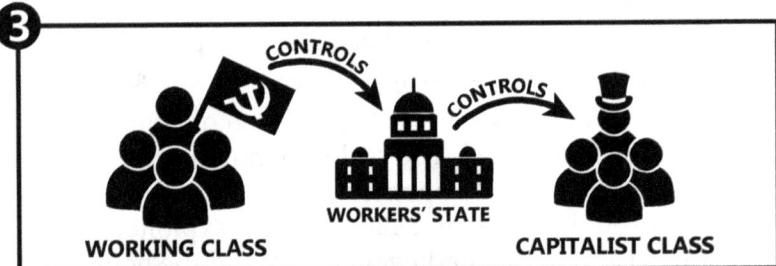
The working class builds a workers' state and a dictatorship of the proletariat.

Once capitalism has been negated completely the state is no longer needed.
A stateless, classless society is established.

The historic mission of the working class is to end class society through social revolution.

In order for workers to end capitalism, a dictatorship of the proletariat must be established through social revolution. This means establishing a worker's state which exists to further the agenda of the working class and to give workers control over the means of production.

> **Annotation 100 (continued)**
>
> Once this process of social revolution is complete and all remnants of the capitalist base and superstructure have been negated there will remain only one class: the united global proletariat. At this point all the humans of the world will collectively control the means of production as a united whole. This will constitute the end of class society altogether and there will no longer be any need for a state to exist. As Lenin wrote in *The State and Revolution*:
>
>> The state is a "special coercive force"... And from it follows that the "special coercive force" for the suppression of the proletariat by the bourgeoisie, of millions of working people by handfuls of the rich, must be replaced by a "special coercive force" for the suppression of the bourgeoisie by the proletariat (the dictatorship of the proletariat). This is precisely what is meant by "abolition of the state as state." This is precisely the "act" of taking possession of the means of production in the name of society.
>
> This is the mission of the working class: to build class consciousness, to enact social revolution, to build a workers' state and dictatorship of the proletariat, and to eventually bring about an end to not just capitalism but class society altogether and the development of a stateless, classless society. The pursuit of this mission is the principle pursuit of Scientific Socialism.

According to this definition, class is not merely a concern of political science alone, but also reflects the objective relationships of the political and economic fields of society, based on the following characteristics:

- Class reflects the objective relationship between the politics and economy of a society.
- Class also reflects the political-economic relationship between groups of human beings in certain historical conditions.
- Class shows not just the differences but also the oppositions of human groups in terms of politics and economics.

Therefore, the analysis of problems of political structure needs to be associated with the analysis of the economic structure of society from a historical point of view.

> **Annotation 101**
>
> In Dialectical Materialism, all things, phenomena, and ideas are defined in terms of internal and external relationships. Class, therefore, is defined by various internal and external relationships. The three primary relationships which define class include:
>
> **The Relationship Between Politics and Economy of a Society**
>
> *Politics* encompass aspects of society's superstructure related to control over and benefit from the state. *Economics* include processes and phenomena which are concerned with securing, providing, and distributing the material needs of life in human society. Class and class society emerge from a dialectical relationship between politics and economy in human society. Historically, whenever one group of human beings came to exploit the labor of others, class society began. The state and political consciousness arose from the objective need to stabilize society and to secure the position of ruling classes over oppressed classes through violence and coercion.

Annotation 101 (continued)

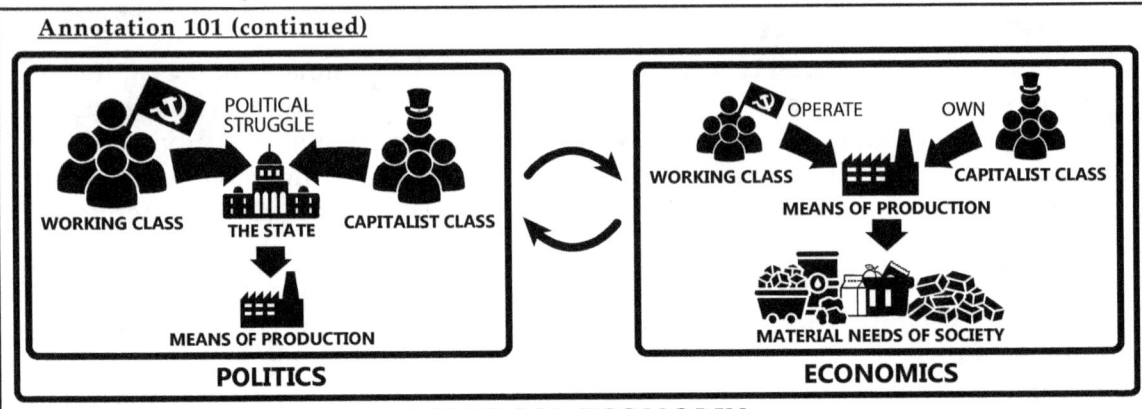

POLITICAL ECONOMY

In class society, politics and economy exist in dialectical unity. Economy encompasses the material production process while politics encompasses class struggle.

Political-Economic Relationships Between Groups of Human Beings

The most important relationships between groups of human beings within class society have to do with the means of production. Such political-economic relationships include:

- The relationship which a group of human beings has with the means of production. Some classes own the means of production while other groups labor and operate the means of production.

- The relationship which one group of human beings has with another group as it pertains to means of production. Within a class society, some groups of human beings appropriate the labor of other groups of human beings and force them to operate the means of production while withholding ownership and control over the means of production.

Under feudalism, some classes (monarchs, feudal lords, religious clergy, etc.) owned land. At this time, land was the most important means of production. These feudal landlords forced peasants to work on the land. This was the primary political-economic relationship of the feudal era. Under capitalism, the primary political-economic relationship is between the capitalist class and the working class. Capitalists own the means of production while workers must operate the means of production in order to survive. Capitalists profit from this relationship and enforce these class relations through the control of the state.

Oppositional Relationships Between Groups of Human Beings

Liberal and metaphysical interpretations of class might define classes based on different characersitics such as levels of income, wealth, and so on. Historical Materialism, as an application of Dialectical Materialism, demands that we define economic classes of human beings by identifying the dialectical contradictions which exist between them. In class society, different classes compete, struggle, and oppose each other to benefit from the means of production. This process of contradiction and development leads, over time, to processes of negation whereby new classes develop and overtake old classes. We call this contradiction and opposition between classes class struggle.

> **Annotation 101 (continued)**
>
> **Historical Perspective of Politics and Economics**
>
> Dialectical Materialism demands that we seek a comprehensive and historical perspective in the analysis of all things, phenomena, and ideas. In the analysis of class society, this means understanding the political oppositions which exist between all classes within a society as well as the development which led to those conditions. For example, in order to understand the political structure of capitalism one must understand feudalism which preceded it. One must understand not just the nature of the capitalist-controlled state of modern society, but also the manner in which the bourgeois state emerged from feudal society. The more deeply we understand the political relationships and the class struggle which underlies political struggle, the more accurate our understanding will be and the more effective our activities which are based upon this understanding.

In order to correctly analyze and solve problems of the political structure of society, it is necessary to not only master the concept of class from the Marxist-Leninist viewpoint, but also to master the concept of social stratification. The concept of social stratification refers to grouping people within the same class according to their specific status and differences in that class such as: blue collar workers, white collar workers, expert workers, etc. On the other hand, this concept is also used to refer to groups of people outside the class structure in a certain society such as: civil servants, intellectuals, small farmers, etc. These social strata all have different relationships with different classes in society.

> **Annotation 102**
>
> Each class within every class society is defined by internal and external relationships. This means that no class is monolithic or homogenous. Rather, every class is defined by internal relationships between internal strata of that class. Here, a stratum simply refers to a defined group within a class which has a certain stable form. Strata are primarily defined by relationships within a class, between classes, and with the means of production. For instance, in feudal society, there were different strata of peasants:
>
> Some peasants owned their own small holdings of land. This was a different stratum from the majority of peasants who worked land which belonged to a feudal lord, but they were all essentially part of the same class. Under capitalism, workers can be further divided into various strata depending on their specific relations to the means of production. For instance, blue collar factory workers who work on a factory assembly line are a different stratum from the white collar engineers who design the factory machines and systems. Both groups are part of the same class—the proletariat—because both sell their labor to capitalists for wages. However, one stratum (the blue collar workers) directly operate the means of production, generally require less education, are typically paid less, etc.
>
> There are other ways to examine and classify strata within a class depending on the point of view of analysis and which relationships are being examined. For example, in some cultures and nations relationships having to do with ethnicity, race, language, caste, or other such factors may play important or defining roles in understanding and distinguishing stratification of classes.

<u>Annotation 102 (continued)</u>

It is common for tension and conflict to exist between different strata of the working class and this must be understood in analyzing class conflict and class society. This can be leveraged in class struggle. For instance, capitalists in our current society commonly set different strata of the working class against each other to weaken and divide the proletariat.

Stratification can also be defined by how members of a class relate specifically to the means of production. One example is the stratification which Karl Marx, Friedrich Engels, and Vladimir Lenin described which exists between intellectual laborers and manual laborers.

Intellectuals are human beings who perform labor in the realm of human and social consciousness. Any human being who works to develop, disseminate, and interpret ideas can, therefore, be considered an intellectual. Intellectuals can serve a wide variety of roles in human society, including: writers, artists, journalists, teachers, medical physicians, lawyers, and so on.

Ideologists are a specific type of intellectual who performs a political role in society. These are intellectuals who specifically work to develop and disseminate the ideology of a particular political party or movement which serves a particular economic class. Ideology is discussed more on p. 112.

Intellectual Laborers are workers who are exploited for profit by capitalists and earn wages by laboring primarily through mental activity. This distinguishes them from most other laborers who work by directly operating the means of production.

Intellectuals and Class Structure

Intellectuals can belong to any economic class. In our current capitalist society there are intellectuals in the working class, the capitalist class, and in the petty bourgeoisie. If a worker receives wages for performing intellectual labor, they are considered to be intellectual laborers. Many intellectuals do not get paid for their intellectual labor. For instance, a factory line worker might run a blog or produce short films as a hobby or side project. In this case, the factory worker would be an intellectual, but not an intellectual laborer.

Intellectuals may also serve the class interests of a different class than the one they occupy. As an example, Friedrich Engels was a member of the bourgeoisie because his family owned many factories and business operations throughout Europe. However, Engels worked as an intellectual for the working class, making him a proletarian ideologist despite being a capitalist. Likewise, there are many workers who perform intellectual labor to serve the agenda for the bourgeoisie.

Some of these bourgeois ideologists perform their labor for wages and are exploited by capitalists. For example, journalists who write articles to further the agenda of the capitalist class in exchange for wages are simultaneously intellectual laborers (because they are exploited as wage laborers) and bourgeois ideologists (because they develop political ideology for the capitalist class). This makes the analysis of intellectuals, ideology, and the human beings who perform intellectual labor quite complex. In the West this complexity has led to much confusion over "intellectuals," "ideologues," "intelligentsia," etc., and their roles in class society. This confusion tends to be related to two factors: semantics and class structure analysis.

Annotation 102 (continued)
Common Misunderstandings about Intellectuals in Class Society

Semantics is a philosophical field of inquiry that pertains to meaning and language. Semantics can lead to confusion and disagreement when different people have strong preferences about different definitions of words. This is especially problematic in metaphysical philosophy, which seeks to categorize all human knowledge into discrete, static, unchanging, specific categories.

Metaphysical semantics generally seek to assign a very specific definition to every individual word. These metaphysical definitions are based on categorization and characteristics. Thus, in a metaphysical philosophical analysis, the word "intellectual" might only have one specific definition which is rooted in a set of criteria and where "intellectuals" would fit into metaphysical categorization. Dialectical Materialist semantics differ from metaphysical semantics in a key way: in Dialectical Materialist analysis, words are discussed and defined based on *internal and external relationships*. This means that Dialectical Materialist analysis demands that language be considered not just in relation to other words, but also in relation to various other factors, such as:

- **The human beings who use the language.** Different people might use the same words differently in different contexts. For example: the way a computer programmer uses the word "virus" in daily speech might be different than how a medical doctor uses the same word.

- **The real-world phenomena that are being described.** As the phenomena change in the real world, the language itself might also change, or the meaning of the same word might change. For example: the word "drive" used in a modern context is usually associated with the operation of automobiles, but this was not the case before the invention and widespread use of automobiles.

In Dialectical Materialist analysis it is important to avoid problems of metaphysical semantics which can lead to unnecessary confusion or even intentional obfuscation and deception when used in bad faith. This has especially been a problem with the use of language surrounding "intellectuals," "intelligentsia," "ideologues," and so on in bourgeois philosophical and political analysis, as well as words such as "class."

For instance, when Lenin refers to an "intellectual class," he is clearly using the word "class" in the sense of "category." The word "class," as used here, does not exclusively refer to "economic class" as it pertains to the class structure of the material base of a political economy. This is evident because economic class is defined by relations between economic classes and relations with the means of production. The fact that intellectual labor can serve both a political function and an economic function makes the analysis of intellectuals and their relationships to class society confusing, especially when muddled by metaphysical analysis. This confusion can be easily cleared up by looking at the underlying relationships which define and develop intellectuals and intellectual labor:

Intellectual labor may (or may not) define someone as a working class member of the proletariat. Whether or not an intellectual would be considered a worker or not depends on their relations to means of production (i.e., whether or not they own their own essential means of production) and whether or not they are wage workers who are exploited by capitalists for profits.

> **Annotation 102 (continued)**
>
> Marx, Engels, and Lenin all wrote of "intellectual labor" and an "intellectual proletariat," which refers to workers who primarily work with their minds and do not directly interface with the essential means of production in their labor. These workers are still part of the working class; they are just a different stratum of the working class and serve a different role in the functioning of capitalism.
>
> Thus, it can be understood that some workers are "intellectual workers," some members of the capitalist class (such as Engels) can be "political intellectuals" who intellectually serve the working class, and so on. This can be easily understood when the underlying relationships which these words represent are properly understood.
>
> Whether a human being should be considered an "intellectual" and how the status of "intellectual" relates to political economy and class structure, must be explored through proper Dialectical Materialist analysis which considers all things, phenomena, and ideas as constantly changing and as defined by the internal and external relationships which lead to those changes.
>
> Metaphysical semantics have been used to distort what Marx, Engels, Lenin, and other Dialectical Materialist philosophers have meant by "intellectual," "intellectual class," etc. These distortions and misunderstandings are easy to clear up with proper Dialectical Materialist analysis and proper application of Materialist Dialectics and Historical Materialist principles.
>
> **Further Clarification of the Role of Intellectuals from Marx, Engels, and Lenin**
>
> In a letter to the International Socialist Students Congress written in 1893, Engles explained the importance of an "intellectual proletariat:"
>
>> May your efforts succeed in developing among students the awareness that it is from their ranks that there must emerge intellectual proletariat which will be called on to play a considerable part in the approaching revolution alongside and among their brothers, the manual workers.
>>
>> The bourgeois revolutions of the past asked nothing of the universities but lawyers, as the best raw material for their politicians; the emancipation of the working class needs, in addition, doctors, engineers, chemists, agronomists and other experts; for we are faced with taking over the running not only of the political machine but of all social production, and in that case what will be needed is not fine words but well-grounded knowledge.
>
> Here, it is clear that Engels interprets the "intellectual proletariat" as workers who perform intellectual labor. In *The German Ideology*, Karl Marx also explicitly defined "mental labor" and "manual labor" as two strata of the working class which are intentionally divided and set against each other by the ruling class:
>
>> The division of labour, which we already saw above as one of the chief forces of history up till now, manifests itself also in the ruling class as the division of mental and material labour, so that inside this class one part appears as the thinkers of the class (its active, conceptive ideologists, who make the perfecting of the illusion of the class about itself their chief source of livelihood), while the others' attitude to these ideas and illusions is more passive and receptive, because they are in reality the active members of this class and have less time to make

<u>**Annotation 102 (continued)**</u>

> up illusions and ideas about themselves. Within this class this cleavage can even develop into a certain opposition and hostility between the two parts, which, however, in the case of a practical collision, in which the class itself is endangered, automatically comes to nothing, in which case there also vanishes the semblance that the ruling ideas were not the ideas of the ruling class and had a power distinct from the power of this class. The existence of revolutionary ideas in a particular period presupposes the existence of a revolutionary class; about the premises for the latter sufficient has already been said above.

In *One Step Forward, Two Steps Back*, Lenin further discussed the divide between intellectuals and manual laborers, using slightly different language:

> The problem that again interests us so keenly today is the antagonism between the intelligentsia and the proletariat. My colleagues (Kautsky is himself an intellectual, a writer and editor) will mostly be indignant that I admit this antagonism. But it actually exists, and, as in other cases, it would be the most inexpedient tactics to try to overcome the fact by denying it. This antagonism is a social one, it relates to classes, not to individuals. The individual intellectual, like the individual capitalist, may identify himself with the proletariat in its class struggle. When he does, he changes his character too. It is not this type of intellectual, who is still an exception among his class, that we shall mainly speak of in what follows. Unless otherwise stated, I shall use the word intellectual to mean only the common run of intellectual who takes the stand of bourgeois society, and who is characteristic of the intelligentsia as a class. This class stands in a certain antagonism to the proletariat.

Reading this paragraph alone, it may be interpreted to mean that Lenin is defining an "intellectual class" in the economic sense, which would make intellectual workers a completely different part of the class structure of capitalism, separate from the working class. However, Lenin immediately specifies that he is talking about political contradiction, not economic contradiction of class structure:

> This antagonism differs, however, from the antagonism between labour and capital. The intellectual is not a capitalist. True, his standard of life is bourgeois, and he must maintain it if he is not to become a pauper; but at the same time he is compelled to sell the product of his labour, and often his labour-power, and is himself often enough exploited and humiliated by the capitalist. Hence the intellectual does not stand in any economic antagonism to the proletariat. But his status of life and his conditions of labour are not proletarian, and this gives rise to a certain antagonism in sentiments and ideas.

In other words, Lenin is pointing out superstructural contradiction and characteristics which cause intellectual laborers to have a general tendency of antagonism with the working class. In other words, Lenin is attempting to explain why intellectuals (of all classes within the capitalist political economy) have a strong tendency to serve the agenda of the ruling class, and how this tendency tends to lead to conflict and antagonism between intellectuals and the majority of the working class.

Lenin did not dismiss Marx and Engles in their conception of intellectual laborers and an intellectual proletariat. On the contrary, he was further developing these ideas

> **Annotation 102 (continued)**
>
> and attempting to further explain the complexity of class relations and divisions which exist between different strata of the working class which Marx had previously identified in *The German Ideology*.
>
> In Lenin's explanation, intellectual laborers are a special stratum of the working class which have unique properties. Namely: intellectual workers do not have a direct relationship with the means of production like manual laborers (such as, for example, factory workers). Instead, they tend to occupy an intermediating role between the ruling class and the vast majority of workers. This means that intellectuals have a tendency to side with whichever class will give them the most benefits, and this leads to an overwhelming tendency to intellectuals supporting the ruling class.
>
> This is not always the case, of course. Lenin himself was an intellectual but he served the proletariat class with his intellectual labor. This means that Lenin's intellectual had, to use his own words, a proletarian characteristic. To put it another way, Lenin was a proletarian ideologist because he developed and furthered the ideology of the proletariat as a revolutionary class. Lenin, Marx, and Engels all identified the tendency for division between intellectual laborers and manual laborers within the working class. There are many causes of this division:
>
> - As stated, intellectuals tend to receive many benefits from serving the interests of the bourgeoisie. On the other hand, openly supporting proletarian revolution can lead to significant economic hardship and many other difficulties for intellectuals.
>
> - In capitalist society, intellectuals tend to receive their education from institutions which are funded, controlled, and owned by the ruling class.
>
> - Likewise, in capitalist society, intellectual institutions such as media outlets, social media platforms, and information sources also tend to be owned and controlled by the ruling class, meaning that most ideas which intellectuals are exposed to on a daily basis will tend to be ideas that serve the interests of the ruling class.
>
> Despite these difficulties, there have been many examples of intellectuals who have risen above this tendency. It is important to properly understand the role and nature of intellectuals. This is because the primary prerequisite for social revolution which will lead to the end of class society is the development of class consciousness, as discussed in Annotation 67, p. 115. This means that proletarian ideologists must develop an effective revolutionary proletarian class ideology and to popularize this proletarian ideology among the working class.
>
> Some of these ideologists might be capitalists, like Friedrich Engels. Others might be intellectual workers, like Vo Nguyen Giap, the great general and political leader of Vietnam who was a school teacher. Many others will be proletarian ideologists who begin as manual laborers, such as Ton Duc Thang, the leader of Vietnam's first union who went on to become an important ideologist and political leader in Vietnam's revolution. Others, like Ho Chi Minh, may develop and change over time. Ho Chi Minh began as a dishwasher and sailor, then became a journalist and writer, and went on to become the ideological leader of Vietnam's entire revolutionary movement.

> **Annotation 102 (continued)**
>
> In the development of social revolution, revolutionary intellectuals must rise above the tendency of antagonism between working class intellectuals and working class material production laborers just as they must undo all other tensions and fractures which divide the working class. Solidification of the proletariat into a class-conscious revolutionary movement can social revolution lead to an end of capitalism and class society.

2. Origin of class

The discovery of class, class antagonism, and class struggle were not a new discovery of Marxism-Leninism. However, one of the new and fundamental findings of Marxism-Leninism was that class, class antagonism, and class struggle are neither the nature of humanity, nor a predestined law, but only a historical phenomenon. Marx asserted that "the existence of classes is only bound up with particular historical phases in the development of production."

The *direct origin* of class division in society is the birth and existence of the private ownership of the means of production, and especially private ownership of the primary means of production in society.

Thus, private ownership of the means of production leads to the possibility that one group may appropriate surplus labor from another.

However, private ownership of the means of production alone is not sufficient to give rise to the separation into classes within society. Another prerequisite is that productive forces be developed to such an extent that labor productivity increases, which gives rise to the development of surplus labor time, which manifests as excess wealth within society.

> **Annotation 103**
>
> There have existed in the past (and even exist today) various human societies which are not class societies. In these societies the means of production are held in common and human beings are not divided up into different classes. This shows that class society is not a fixed characteristic of "human nature."
>
> By studying the development of human society with a comprehensive and historical perspective, Marx and Engels discovered that class society emerged from material and objective processes related to the development of productive forces and corresponding relations of production.
>
> Class society emerged as productive forces reached a level where private ownership of the primary means of production became the most suitable relations of production. The primary means of production are the means of production which are most vital for producing the material necessities of human life. Precisely what constitutes the primary means of production changes as productive forces develop. For example, in feudal times the land was the primary means of production. Today the primary means of production include not just land but factories, machinery, and other components of modern industrial infrastructure.
>
> Class society emerged from the development of surplus labor-time. Marx defines surplus labor-time in *Capital* as the time which a worker spends laboring after pro-

> **Annotation 103 (continued)**
>
> ducing enough labor-value to account for their own reproduction.[46] To put it another way, surplus labor-time is all the time a worker works in excess of the value of that worker's wages.
>
> Surplus labor-time is the source of profit which allows a member of the ruling class to benefit in an exploitative manner from the labor of the oppressed working class. Surplus labor-time generates surplus value, and surplus value generates profits for the ruling class which owns the means of production.
>
> Marx explained in *Capital* that surplus labor is what distinguishes one mode of production from another in the development of human society:
>
>> The essential difference between the various economic forms of society – between, for instance, a society based on slave-labor, and one based on wage-labor, lies only in the mode in which this surplus labor is in each case extracted from the actual producer, the laborer.
>
> This means that over time, as productive forces develop, their suitability with the current relations of production decrease more and more. This means that eventually, once the unsuitability reaches a certain threshold, that mode of production will end and another will take its place.
>
> In the capitalist era, the productive forces continuously become increasingly unsuitable to the relations of production of capitalism. Eventually this will lead to social revolution whereby the working class will take control of society and unseat the capitalist class as the ruling class of society. This will, in effect, end the private ownership of the means of production and class society altogether. The only alternative to this outcome, as stated by Marx and Engels in *The Communist Manifesto*, is "collective ruin:"
>
>> Freeman and slave, patrician and plebeian, lord and serf, guild-master and journeyman, in a word, oppressor and oppressed, stood in constant opposition to one another, carried on an uninterrupted, now hidden, now open fight, a fight that each time ended, either in a revolutionary reconstitution of society at large, or in the common ruin of the contending classes.

Furthermore, private ownership of the means of production is not subject to human subjective will, but rather to an objective law - The Law of Suitability Between Relations of Production and Productive Forces. Therefore, the root origin of class division is an insufficiency of socialization of the productive forces.

When the productive forces reach a high level of socialization, it will become the objective cause of the abolition of private ownership of the means of production and will thus lead to the end of class, class antagonism, and class struggle in society. This constitutes a practical matter of socialism, especially as it pertains to the mission of building the future communist society.

---

46 Marx used the term "reproduction" to refer to processes which allow someone or something to maintain their own existence. In this case, capitalists seek to provide workers with only the bare minimum in wages that would allow the worker to survive and continue working for the capitalist. Workers simultaneously struggle for better benefits from the means of production. This is the basis of political class struggle under capitalism.

Annotation 104

In *Socialism: Utopian and Scientific*, Engels descibes how the operation of the productive forces has become a socialized process under capitalism:

> Before capitalist production — i.e., in the Middle Ages — the system of petty industry obtained generally, based upon the private property of the laborers in their means of production; in the country, the agriculture of the small peasant, freeman, or serf; in the towns, the handicrafts organized in guilds. The instruments of labor — land, agricultural implements, the workshop, the tool — were the instruments of labor of single individuals, adapted for the use of one worker, and, therefore, of necessity, small, dwarfish, circumscribed. But, for this very reason, they belonged as a rule to the producer himself.

In other words, previous modes of production which existed in class societies before capitalism had much lower development of productive forces. The means of production were limited and undeveloped so that the workers who used them tended to own and use them as individuals. This meant that the operation of the productive forces were far more individualized in those preceding societies and the socialization of production was quite limited.

Engels described how the development of capitalism and the development of productive forces led to the socialization of productive forces, meaning that the means of production began to require increasingly concentrated and collectivized operation and use. As industrial processes, factories, complex machinery, and other developments in the productive forces developed, it became impossible for individuals to own and operate individualized means of production.

In order to be competitive in a society which was becoming increasingly dominated by the capitalist mode of production, it became necessary for many human beings to work together to operate the means of production. Simultaneously, these more socialized and collectivized means of production came to be owned privately by a smaller and smaller number of capitalists. As Engels writes:

> To concentrate these scattered, limited means of production, to enlarge them, to turn them into the powerful levers of production of the present day—this was precisely the historic role of capitalist production and of its upholder, the bourgeoisie. In the fourth section of Capital, Marx has explained in detail how since the 15th century this has been historically worked out through the three phases of simple co-operation, manufacture, and modern industry. But the bourgeoisie, as is shown there, could not transform these puny means of production into mighty productive forces without transforming them, at the same time, from means of production of the individual into social means of production only workable by a collectivity of men. The spinning wheel, the handloom, the blacksmith's hammer, were replaced by the spinning-machine, the power-loom, the steam-hammer; the individual workshop, by the factory implying the co-operation of hundreds and thousands of workmen. In like manner, production itself changed from a series of individual into a series of social acts, and the production from individual to social products. The yarn, the cloth, the metal articles that now come out of the factory were the joint product of many workers, through whose hands they had successively to pass before they were ready. No one person could say of them: "I made that; this is my product."

Annotation 104 (continued)

Engels further elaborates that <u>socialized productive forces</u> and the capitalist mode of production gradually and steadily developed well beyond the productive forces of feudal society and individualized productive forces. This meant that the older feudal mode of production could not hope to compete with the newly emerging capitalist mode of production, which produced material necessities and other goods far more efficiently. He states:

> In the midst of the old division of labor, grown up spontaneously and upon no definite plan, which had governed the whole of society, now arose division of labor upon a definite plan, as organized in the factory; side by side with individual production appeared social production. The products of both were sold in the same market, and, therefore, at prices at least approximately equal. But organization upon a definite plan was stronger than spontaneous division of labor. The factories working with the combined social forces of a collectivity of individuals produced their commodities far more cheaply than the individual small producers. Individual producers succumbed in one department after another. Socialized production revolutionized all the old methods of production.

Engels also highlights that, although the means of production came to be used by workers on a <u>socialized</u> basis, the means of production continued to be owned <u>privately</u> by certain individuals: the emerging capitalist class. This was the basis for the development of the two primary classes of capitalism: the bourgeoisie, who own the means of production, and the proletariat, who operate the means of production.

As Engels explains:

> Then came the concentration of the means of production and of the producers in large workshops and manufactories, their transformation into actual socialized means of production and socialized producers. But the socialized producers and means of production and their products were still treated, after this change, just as they had been before — i.e., as the means of production and the products of individuals. Hitherto, the owner of the instruments of labor had himself appropriated the product, because, as a rule, it was his own product and the assistance of others was the exception. Now, the owner of the instruments of labor always appropriated to himself the product, although it was no longer his product but exclusively the product of the labor of others. Thus, the products now produced socially were not appropriated by those who had actually set in motion the means of production and actually produced the commodities, but by the capitalists. The means of production, and production itself, had become in essence socialized. But they were subjected to a form of appropriation which presupposes the private production of individuals, under which, therefore, every one owns his own product and brings it to market. The mode of production is subjected to this form of appropriation, although it abolishes the conditions upon which the latter rests.

Engels identifies a dialectical contradiction between the proletariat and the bourgeoisie, arising from the fact that the operation of the means of production has become socialized while the ownership of the means of production remains individualized. This contradiction means that the productive forces of capitalist society are unsuitable with capitalist relations of production. He writes:

> **Annotation 104 (continued)**
>
>> This contradiction, which gives to the new mode of production its capitalistic character, contains the germ of the whole of the social antagonisms of today. The greater the mastery obtained by the new mode of production over all important fields of production and in all manufacturing countries, the more it reduced individual production to an insignificant residuum, the more clearly was brought out the incompatibility of socialized production with capitalistic appropriation.
>
> The development of the capitalist mode of production eventually overtook and negated the feudal mode of production. However, the contradiction and unsuitability between the socialized productive forces and the individualized ownership of the means of production has led to inherent instability and class struggle within capitalist society.
>
> Engels describes this transformation:
>
>> The first capitalists found, as we have said, alongside of other forms of labor, wage-labor ready-made for them on the market. But it was exceptional, complementary, accessory, transitory wage-labor. The agricultural laborer, though, upon occasion, he hired himself out by the day, had a few acres of his own land on which he could at all events live at a pinch. The guilds were so organized that the journeyman of today became the master of tomorrow. But all this changed, as soon as the means of production became socialized and concentrated in the hands of capitalists. The means of production, as well as the product, of the individual producer became more and more worthless; there was nothing left for him but to turn wage-worker under the capitalist. Wage-labor, aforetime the exception and accessory, now became the rule and basis of all production; aforetime complementary, it now became the sole remaining function of the worker. The wage-worker for a time became a wage-worker for life. The number of these permanent was further enormously increased by the breaking-up of the feudal system that occurred at the same time, by the disbanding of the retainers of the feudal lords, the eviction of the peasants from their homesteads, etc. The separation was made complete between the means of production concentrated in the hands of the capitalists, on the one side, and the producers, possessing nothing but their labor-power, on the other. The contradiction between socialized production and capitalistic appropriation manifested itself as the antagonism of proletariat and bourgeoisie.
>
>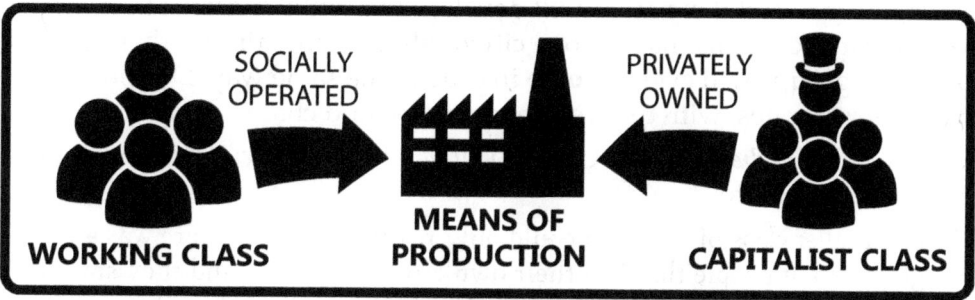
>
> **CAPITALIST RELATIONS OF PRODUCTION**
>
> *Under capitalism, the means of production are socially operated by the working class yet privately owned by the capitalist class. This is a core internal contradiction of capitalism.*

> **Annotation 104 (continued)**
>
> Finally, Engels summarizes the inevitable solution to this contradiction: socialized ownership of the means of production, which can only be accomplished through proletarian social revolution. He describes such a social revolution as the "solution of the contradictions," concluding:
>
>> Proletarian Revolution — Solution of the contradictions. The proletariat seizes the public power, and by means of this transforms the socialized means of production, slipping from the hands of the bourgeoisie, into public property. By this act, the proletariat frees the means of production from the character of capital they have thus far borne, and gives their socialized character complete freedom to work itself out. Socialized production upon a predetermined plan becomes henceforth possible. The development of production makes the existence of different classes of society thenceforth an anachronism. In proportion as anarchy in social production vanishes, the political authority of the State dies out. Man, at last the master of his own form of social organization, becomes at the same time the lord over Nature, his own master — free. To accomplish this act of universal emancipation is the historical mission of the modern proletariat. To thoroughly comprehend the historical conditions and thus the very nature of this act, to impart to the now oppressed proletarian class a full knowledge of the conditions and of the meaning of the momentous act it is called upon to accomplish, this is the task of the theoretical expression of the proletarian movement, Scientific Socialism.

The formation and development of class in history can take place with different forms and different levels in different social communities, and depend on the specific impact of objective and subjective factors on the motion and development process of each human community.

> **Annotation 105**
>
> Every human society has its own unique objective material conditions as well as subjective conditions. Therefore, every society develops in different ways. For this reason, every society will develop differently (even two societies that share the same relations of production).
>
> For example, one capitalist nation will develop differently than another capitalist nation. Even within a capitalist nation, one city might develop differently from another. No two human groups will ever develop in exactly the same way. Development will happen at different rates, with different phenomena and characteristics.
>
> In the book *Study of the Capitalist Class of Vietnam Under French Occupation*, historian Nguyen Cong Binh wrote:
>
>> The capitalist class of Vietnam could only really exist once there was a big enough group of people that had their own economic status, and they started having contradictions with other economic groups that kept them from further developing. Once that contradiction began, capitalists developed class consciousness to defend and fight for the benefit of their own class.

Annotation 105 (continued)

For this reason, the capitalist class of Vietnam had its own process of development. The capitalist class started as a small group of traders and craftsmen in urban areas that produced simple commodities. Once capitalists had developed factories in Vietnam, they began exploiting wage workers. Labor, then, became a commodity. The exploitation of the surplus value of workers became widespread. Commodity and monetary economies overcome the farming economy and with this development the capitalists had become fully developed as a class.

... By the end of 19th century and beginning of the early 20th century, new political and social conditions began to arise. French colonialists invaded and colonized Vietnam. The international capitalist economy – and predominantly the French capitalist economy – arrived in Vietnam and began to dramatically change the economy. The small and simple commodity economy of Vietnam suddenly and drastically developed. Over time, the people who had been exploited by the class of feudal lords came to be exploited, instead, by the French colonial capitalist class. These conditions stimulated the rapid development of capitalism in Vietnam.

In the early days of colonialism until late 19th century, the business of French capitalists in Vietnam was mostly limited to trading and financial lending. The result of this was the emergence of Vietnamese traders, and these traders were the seeds of capitalism in Vietnam. The French government at that time had a policy of monopoly control of foreign trade. Therefore, there existed some Vietnamese small capitalists who traded with French capitalists. This led to the formation of small businesses such as Quang Hung Domestic Trading Company in Hanoi.

... When France joined World War I, a need arose for a huge supply of resources from the colonies to aid the war effort. Vietnam was one of the most heavily affected colonies. This resulted the monopoly policy of French capitalists on foreign trade to be weakened… At that time, French government of Vietnam had reformed the economy to mobilize nearly all the resources of Vietnam to be delivered to France… Vietnam's economy depended tremendously on the French economy, and because of the war, France was unable to invest in Vietnam as much as before… Some Vietnamese capitalists took this as an opportunity to open their own factories in industries such as weaving, oil production, and leather goods… to domestically manufacture products which Vietnam could no longer import. An increasing number of capitalists began using their own money to build factories…

Thus, we can see that colonialism and other factors had a major impact on the development of capitalism in Vietnam. Although the relations of production under capitalism in Vietnam were based on the same contradiction of capitalists exploiting wage workers, the capitalist class rose to prominence through much different circumstances in Vietnam than they did in most European countries. Likewise, the existence of colonial holdings such as Vietnam impacted the way capitalism developed in France. This is the case in every human community: class society develops differently based on material conditions, subjective conditions, and many other factors.

However, it is possible to generalize the process of class formation and development in human communities in history into two basic forms, namely:

- Class formation and development which takes place mainly with the influence of violent factors to separate out commodity producers within the social community.
- Class formation and development which uses economic relations to separate out commodity producers within the social community.

In addition, in historic reality, there are societies impacted simultaneously by both factors.

Annotation 106

The Vietnamese textbook *Philosophy of Marxism-Leninism* explains that:

> Class societies are replaced through processes of contradiction and negation throughout history. Every stage of development of class society has its own class structure. Each class structure includes two primary opposing classes. In the ancient slave society, for example, the two primary classes were those who were enslaved and those who were the owners of slaves. [Under feudalism, the primary classes were peasants and feudal landlords.] Under capitalism, the primary classes are capitalists and workers. The two primary classes of each society are the true products of that society. Simultaneously, they are the classes that determine the existence and the development of the productive forces of that society. The ruling class is the class that represents the essence of that society.

The "primary classes" are defined by their relations to the means of production. Specifically, within class society, the primary classes include the class which owns the means of production and the class which labors to operate the primary means of production. The primary means of production are the means of production which produce the most vital necessities of life.

Economic Classes of Feudalism

Primary Ruling Class	Primary Laboring Class	Other Classes
Feudal Landlords	Peasants	Clergy, Merchants, Craft Guildsmen, etc.

The feudal landlords were considered a primary class under feudalism because they owned the land, which was the primary means of production in the feudal agrarian society. The peasants were considered a primary class under feudalism because they worked the land to produce the vital material needs of society which were needed to sustain human life.

Economic Classes of Capitalism

Primary Ruling Class	Primary Laboring Class	Other Classes
Bourgeoisie	Proletariat	Petty Bourgeois, Lumpenproletariat

Capitalists are considered a primary class under capitalism because they own the means of production of material needs of society (factories, farms, etc.). Workers are considered a primary class because they operate those means of production.

Annotation 106 (continued)

Every class is defined by its relations to other classes and to the means of production. Take, for example, the primary relations of production of feudal society:

Relations between primary classes and primary means of production under feudalism.

- One primary class, the feudal lords, is defined by its relationship with the means of production (the land) and the other primary class (the peasants). The feudal lords own the land and force peasants to labor on the land.

- The other primary class, the peasants, is defined by its relationship with the means of production (the land) and the other primary class (the feudal lords). The peasants labor on the land for the profit and benefit of the feudal lords.

- The means of production – primarily, land – are owned by the feudal lords and labored upon by the feudal lords.

Together, these relationships define the relations of production of feudal society.

Similarly, in capitalist society:

Relations between primary classes and primary means of production under capitalism.

- One primary class, the bourgeoisie, is defined by its relationship with the means of production (factories, machinery, logistics systems, etc.) and the other primary class (the proletariat). The bourgeoisie own the means of production and force the proletariat to labor on the means of production for wages in order to survive.

- The other primary class, the proletariat, is defined by its relationship with the means of production and the other primary class (the bourgeoisie). The proletariat labor with the means of production for the profits of capitalists.

- The means of production are owned by the bourgeoisie and labored upon by the proletariat.

> **Annotation 106 (continued)**
>
> As with feudalism, these relationships between the primary classes and the means of production define the relations of production of capitalist society. The Vietnamese textbook *Philosophy of Marxism-Leninism* further explains such relationships:
>
>> In addition to the two primary classes, each society has other non-primary [or secondary] classes. Among these social groups, some are the remnants of the old mode of production (such as enslaved peoples at the beginning of capitalism). There are also groups who are the seeds for the future mode of production (such as the capitalists and workers of factories at the end of feudal society). Moreover, every class-based society has intermediate classes which are determined by the current mode of production and the ever-present social division of class society. Such classes include the commoners in ancient slave society, the craftsmen and merchants of feudal society, and the petty bourgeoise in capitalist society. In every class-based society there also exist intellectuals who play a very important role in economy, politics, culture, etc.

3. The role of class struggle in the motion and development of class society

According to Lenin, class struggle is "a struggle waged by the masses of those who have no rights, are oppressed and engage in toil, against the privileged, the oppressors and drones; a struggle of the wage-laborers, or proletarians, against the property-owners, or bourgeoisie."[47]

Based on this definition, the *essence of class struggle* is the struggle of those who are politically oppressed and economically exploited (i.e., slaves, serfs, wage-workers) against that oppression and exploitation in order to resolve the conflict of economic and political interests between the oppressor classes and the oppressed classes to different extents and degrees. Depending on different historical conditions, class struggle in different societies can take many different forms, with different scopes and levels, such as: economic struggle, ideological struggle, political struggle, etc.

Throughout history, class struggle has also taken on forms such as: national struggle, religious struggle, cultural, and various other forms.

> **Annotation 107**
>
> Struggle is simply a way of referring to dialectical contradiction between two opposing sides. Class struggle is, therefore, a particular type of contradiction in which two or more classes contradict with one another. The underlying relationships of class society which lead to these contradictions are outlined in Annotation 100 on p. 181.
>
> **Class Struggle** always involves the means of production; namely: who has control over the means of production and who benefits from them. These contradictions of class struggle can take various forms in human society, including (but not limited to):
>
> **Economic Struggle** over the means of production and the material necessities of human life. For example, under feudalism, serfs struggled for a greater share of the crops which they harvested and for access to more common land while feudal lords struggled to take a greater share from the serfs who toiled beneath them and to share less of their wealth with the lords to which they owed fealty. Under capitalism, workers

---

47 *To the Rural Poor*, V. I. Lenin, 1903.

> **Annotation 107 (continued)**
>
> struggle for higher wages and better access to social services such as healthcare and retirement benefits while capitalists struggle to pay less in taxes and to pay their workers less so that they can enjoy more profits.
>
> **Ideological Struggle** over social consciousness forms within the superstructure of society. This is important because false consciousness can hinder and even work against a class if it is widespread, whereas class consciousness and awareness of the true nature of class society can offer great advantages in political and economic struggle. For example, during the feudal era in many nations noble lords and clergy sought to build up within the social consciousness of serfs the idea that the king had the "divine right to rule" from God and that serfs were serving their role in "God's order" by living a life of service to their landlords. Today, under capitalism, the ruling class wages ideological warfare against the working class to convince workers that capitalism is the system which would serve them best and to prevent workers from building class consciousness. This slows the progress of political struggle and even causes a large fraction of workers - even the majority in many countries - to actively serve the interests of the ruling class.
>
> **Political Struggle** over power and control within the state and legal apparatus of a society. Political struggle primarily takes place through political parties. These are social institutions which exist to develop political consciousness forms and ideology, to train leaders, and to build power for the class which controls them. Political struggle is important because the state is the social institution which has the most impact on the material base of society and so building power with (or against) the state is the most effective way for a class to impact the base. Political struggle also leads to social revolution which is the only way a class can change its position to become the ruling class of society.
>
> **National Struggle** has developed along with the social institutions of nations. Nations are social groups of human beings which have developed a common identity over time based on factors such as language, shared history, geographical region, etc. National identities are complex political phenomena which dialectically relate and contradict with other social institutions such as states, political parties and movements, and so on. National struggle can take various forms. In some cases, national struggle can lead to nationalist chauvinism which is a form of false consciousness in which workers are mistakenly led to believe in the false consciousness that their national identity is exceptional or superior to other nationalities, and that national identity and struggle should be prioritized over class struggle. Other forms of national struggle, such as the struggle for colonized nations to develop independence and self-determination and to end colonial and imperial subjugation, can be positive developments so long as they are aligned with class consciousness and the international mission of Scientific Socialism. It is important, therefore, to distinguish positive characteristics (such as national independence movements of colonized peoples) which can be developed to facilitate class struggle from negative characteristics (such as chauvinism and supremacism) which impede class struggle and divide the international working class.
>
> Ho Chi Minh warned communists against nationalist chauvinism in a speech he delivered in 1967:

> **Annotation 107 (continued)**
>
> The Declaration of this Conference reminds us of the need to strengthen education in the spirit of Marxism-Leninism and to fight against opportunist tendencies such as: bourgeois nationalism, chauvinism, dogmatism and revisionism.
>
> It should also be noted that many communists, including Ho Chi Minh, have been described as "nationalists" by bourgeois ideologists in an effort to conflate anti-colonial communist struggle with nationalist-chauvinism. Ho Chi Minh himself distinguished between the struggles of colonized workers and nationalist chauvinists. In an interview with a foreign journalist in December, 1965, Ho Chi Minh said:
>
>> It is probably not true to say that when I was young, I followed "nationalism." Because at that time, I only knew how to love my compatriots, but I did not know any "ism." When I went to Africa, I saw that the colonial people there were also suffering, oppressed, and exploited like the people of Indochina. When I went to European countries, I saw that there were also some very rich people being sinecurists [i.e., benefitting from positions which required very little work], and the working people were very poor. I thought a lot about these things. At that time, the great October Revolution had succeeded in Russia. Lenin had organized the Communist International. Then Lenin developed the "Theses on the Colonial Questions." Those things made me realize that: the working people of Indochina, the people of the colonies, and all the working people who want to liberate themselves must unite and make a revolution. Therefore, I became a Marxist-Leninist.
>
> It is clear from the words and actions of Ho Chi Minh and Vietnamese communists that the "nationalism" they observed was limited to a struggle for national independence from colonial rule. This "nationalism" of colonized communists is not supremacist in nature and exists in the spirit of internationalist collaboration of the working classes around the world and across national boundaries and should not be conflated with national-chauvinism and bourgeois nationalism which seek to advance the interests of one nation over others.
>
> **Religious Struggle** is the struggle for religious institutions and social forms to develop, survive, grow, and overtake other religions in human society. An example of this from Vietnamese history was the religious struggle of Buddhists in the 1960s during the dictatorship of Ngo Dinh Diem and his puppet government. This government promoted a form of Catholic chauvinism which sought to oppress all other religious forms and led to an uprising of Buddhists to help overthrow Ngo Dinh Diem and his regime.
>
> **Cultural Struggle** is the struggle for human culture to develop within human society. See Annotation 74, p. 135 to see comments from Ho Chi Minh on cultural struggle as it pertains to Vietnam.
>
> Note that all these forms of struggle are dialectically related and reinforce one another. For instance, effective ideological struggle can lead to the building and strengthening of political parties which will enhance efforts of political struggle. Political struggle—building power within the state—can lead to the passage of legislation and other legal progress which may benefit a class in economic struggle. Understanding the dynamics and dialectical relationships associated with class struggle is very important to the mission of Scientific Socialism.

To control and suppress the class struggles of laborers and slaves, and in order to maintain and implement their exploitation, the ruling classes throughout history (i.e., slave-owners, feudal lords, and the bourgeoisie) have inevitably resorted to organized violence. This violence has taken the form of the state, which uses armed forces and legal systems to maintain their class dominance.

Therefore, the issue of state authority and state power is the central and fundamental issue of class struggle in society. Any class struggle that does not solve the problem of seizing state power cannot solve the most fundamental problem of the class struggle. However, not every class struggle identifies that state authority and state power as the central issue. Only when the development of class struggle reaches the level of political struggle will that issue become the central and fundamental issue.

The issue of seizing state power is also the fundamental problem of all social revolutions as the peak of the development of class struggle.

The birth and existence of the state is the result of class struggle within a society that has class antagonism. When social contradictions have been pushed to the point of being unresolvable, it is inevitable that the ruling class will need to use force of violence to maintain an orderly society which serves its own will and interests. The state came into being – and exists today - not to resolve contradictions, but to maintain social order in conditions of unresolvable contradictions.

Through over 2,000 years of human history, there have been several distinct types of state, including: the slave-owner state of ancient times, the feudal state of the Middle Ages, and the bourgeois state in capitalist countries in our present time. These states exist as instruments of organized violence, aimed at controlling the class struggle of the working class. Although each type of state can exist in many different forms with many different names (central or decentralized forms of monarchy, constitutional monarchy, aristocratic republics, representative republics, presidential republics, etc.), their class nature remains the same – the state stands as an instrument of class dictatorship which exists to exploit classes of slaves or laborers.

Unlike the above-mentioned types of state, the dictatorship of the proletariat exists as a new type of state: a "half-state," "a state without its literal meaning," existing in the period of transition towards communism. The dictatorship of the proletariat is an instrument of organized violence and a tool of social-economic management controlled by the working class and the working people.

Annotation 108

In *Socialism: Utopian and Scientific,* Engels explained the importance of workers taking control of the state in order to develop a dictatorship of the proletariat and the way in which capitalism itself creates the necessary objective conditions which will allow workers to seize control of the state:

> Whilst the capitalist mode of production more and more completely transforms the great majority of the population into proletarians, it creates the power which, under penalty of its own destruction, is forced to accomplish this revolution. Whilst it forces on more and more of the transformation of the vast means of production, already socialized, into State property, it shows itself the way to accomplishing this revolution. The proletariat seizes political power and turns the means of production into State property.

> **Annotation 108 (continued)**
>
> Engels also explains how the dictatorship of the proletariat will ultimately lead to the end of not only itself, but all states and class society moving forward:
>
>> But [in seizing political power and turning the means of production into state property] it abolishes itself as proletariat, abolishes all class distinction and class antagonisms, abolishes also the State as State.
>
> Engels then explains the essential difference between the dictatorship of the proletariat and all preceding states and forms of class society:
>
>> Society, thus far, based upon class antagonisms, had need of the State. That is, of an organization of the particular class which was, pro tempore, the exploiting class, an organization for the purpose of preventing any interference from without with the existing conditions of production, and, therefore, especially, for the purpose of forcibly keeping the exploited classes in the condition of oppression corresponding with the given mode of production (slavery, serfdom, wage-labor). The State was the official representative of society as a whole; the gathering of it together into a visible embodiment. But, it was this only in so far as it was the State of that class which itself represented, for the time being, society as a whole:
>>
>> in ancient times, the State of slaveowning citizens;
>>
>> in the Middle Ages, the feudal lords;
>>
>> in our own times, the bourgeoisie.
>>
>> When, at last, it becomes the real representative of the whole of society, it renders itself unnecessary.
>
> In other words, once the working class takes control of the state and establishes a dictatorship of the proletariat, the conditions will eventually develop for the end of class society and the necessity and conditions for the existence of a state altogether:
>
>> As soon as there is no longer any social class to be held in subjection; as soon as class rule, and the individual struggle for existence based upon our present anarchy in production, with the collisions and excesses arising from these, are removed, nothing more remains to be repressed, and a special repressive force, a state, is no longer necessary. The first act by virtue of which the state really constitutes itself the representative of the whole of society — the taking possession of the means of production in the name of society — this is, at the same time, its last independent act as a state. State interference in social relations becomes, in one domain after another, superfluous, and then dies out of itself; the government of persons is replaced by the administration of things, and by the conduct of processes of production. The state is not "abolished." It dies out.
>
> The role and nature of the state is discussed more in Annotation 100, p. 181.

Class struggle serves as the basic mode and driving force of social progress and development in the condition of social division that is class antagonism.

According to the Historical Materialist viewpoint, since class division has existed stretching back in history and through to the present day, human history is, in essence, a history of class struggle as it manifests in various forms, and with different degrees, and with different nuances. Class struggle was the struggle of the slaves against the oppression of the slave-owner class; it was the struggle of serfs and peasants against the oppression and exploitation of nobles and kings; it is the struggle of wage workers against the oppression and exploitation of the bourgeoisie. In every form of class society, class struggle has eventually led to social revolution, which gives rise to a new mode of production.

Therefore, class society can only be developed through the resolution of social, political, and economic antagonisms of class – in other words, through class struggle. In this sense, class struggle is not only the driving force of historical development but also the mode of social progress and development.

Taking into consideration the theory of social-economic formation,[48] it follows that the most fundamental mode and driving force of social progress and development is the motion of the mode of production in society.

> **Annotation 109**
>
> A mode is the way or manner in which something exists. According to Historical Materialism, then, it can be understood that the development of class society exists in the mode of class struggle. This simply means that class society develops because of the internal contradiction between different classes which, together, define class society within a given stage of development.
>
> In addition to class struggle, many other contradictions exist within human society. Such contradictions and struggles are detailed and listed in Annotation 107, p. 200 and include religious struggle, national struggle, and so on. None of these other struggles and contradictions, however, define the development of human society from one stage of development (i.e., mode of production) to the next. Only class struggle advances human society forward by fundamentally developing the material base and productive forces of human society.
>
> Class struggle is, in essence, the contradiction which occurs in the social being and material base of human society. All other forms of struggle (national struggle, religious struggle, etc.) are struggles which occur within the superstructure of society. The Dialectical Materialist perspective indicates that the material determines human consciousness whereas consciousness can only impact back on the material. Thus, it follows that class struggle determines all other forms of social consciousness struggle, while social consciousness struggles can impact back upon class struggle.
>
> Ethnic struggle under feudalism was determined by the nature of feudal class society and class struggle. In essence, ethnicities which dominated the primary means of production (i.e., ethnicities which had a high concentration of feudal lords) were socially dominant over ethnicities which were predominantly peasants. For example, English invaders of Ireland developed and maintained dominance over Irish people through the development of feudal land holdings in Ireland.
>
> As feudalism gave way to capitalism, the nature of ethnic domination changed. Instead of dominating Ireland through feudal class relations, Irish workers became proletarianized and dominated through English capitalism. Under both feudalism and capitalism, the ethnic struggle between English peoples and Irish people was determined by the underlying class struggle. However, it is also true that those ethnic

---

48 See p. 159.

> **Annotation 109 (continued)**
>
> struggles impacted back on class struggle. For example, when Ireland secured partial independence from England it weakened English capitalists in most of Ireland and also led to the more prominent development of an Irish bourgeoisie.
>
> Vietnam had a similar pattern of development. The Vietnamese peoples were dominated by French colonialists who coopted the feudal material base of society to implement colonialism. The ethnic struggle between French colonizers and Vietnamese natives was determined by French control of the means of production which was taken by force and through the subjugation of the Vietnamese feudal lords and monarchy. The ethnic struggle between the Vietnamese and French colonizers did impact upon the material base and class struggle, but was essentially determined by class struggle. The class analysis of this history is explained in further detail in Annotation 23, p. 34.

However, in class society, the motion of the mode of production becomes an antagonistic conflict between classes in society. These economic contradictions can only be resolved through political struggle between the opposing classes. Thus, class struggle has become a political mechanism to resolve contradictions in modes of production, and to fulfill the objective need to develop the productive forces, which drives the development of human society.

> **Annotation 110**
>
> The role of the development of the productive forces as the primary driver of the development of human society is discussed more in Annotation 36, p. 52.
>
> Political struggle and social revolution are discussed in more detail in the following section.

II. SOCIAL REVOLUTIONS AND THEIR ROLE IN THE DEVELOPMENT OF CLASS SOCIETY

1. Definition of social revolution and its causes

In a broad sense, social revolution is a qualitative landmark change in all aspects of social life. It is a method of transitioning from an outdated social-economic formation to a new higher level of development. *In a narrow sense*, social revolution is the overthrow of an outdated political system and the establishment of a more progressive political regime run by the revolutionary class.

> **Annotation 111**
>
> It should be noted that not all political actions commonly referred to as "revolutions" in society are true social revolutions in the Historical Materialist sense of the term. For example, in feudal society, there may have been a political revolution in which one monarch deposed another monarch and took power over the feudal state. This would not be considered a social revolution in the Historical Materialist sense of the term because the mode of production and ruling class has not been essentially changed. Similarly, if one bourgeois-dominated party within a capitalist state is overthrown and replaced with by another bourgeois-dominated party then that would not constitute a social revolution.
>
> Instead, within the Historical Materialist framework, such a "revolution" in which power does not shift from one economic class to another would simply be known as a coup d'etat. This phenomenon is described more in Annotation 113, below.

In a society with class antagonism, social revolution is characterized by armed insurrection of the revolutionary class to seize state power. Social revolution also involves the organization, construction, and use of the new state by the revolutionary class to fundamentally and comprehensively renovate all aspects of society. That is to say, the successful social revolution is the beginning of a new social-economic formation.

This means that the problem of state authority is the fundamental problem of all social revolutions. At the same time, every social revolution must go through two stages: the stage of taking power and the stage of organizing and building a new state and a new society.

Social revolution is different from the concept of reform. Reform refers to changes which take place in one or several areas of social life within a social-economic formation in order to improve that social-economic formation. Examples of reform include: economic institutional reform, national administrative reform, education reform, etc.

> **Annotation 112**
>
> Social revolution is the process by which a progressive class overtakes the existing ruling class within society and brings about a new mode of production. Through this process, the revolutionary progressive class constructs a state to preserve and enforce its own agenda and position as the ruling class. The role of the state in human society is described more in Annotation 100, p. 181.
>
> Reform refers to development which takes place within an existing mode of production. In terms of Materialist Dialectics, reform is a process of change and motion to the

> **Annotation 112 (continued)**
>
> material base and/or superstructure of society which does not constitute a quality shift and negation of the mode of production.
>
> **Economic institutional reform** would include change and development in the economic institutions of a society, such as banks and markets. An example of an economic institutional reform in the United States would be moving from the gold standard system of currency to a fiat monetary system in 1971. This led to fundamental changes in the economic institutions of the United States but did not lead to a change in class relations nor a change in the mode of production.
>
> **National administrative reform** refers to change and development in the state itself, such as a change in the leading political party or elected officials or changed to the structure or constitution of the state itself. Such changes may alter the ways in which the ruling class governs the state, but they do not change which class governs the state, so they exist only as measures of reform.
>
> **Education reform** includes change and development within educational institutions of society. Examples would include the development of public schools, changes to university systems, development of vocational training for workers, etc.

The concept of social revolution is also different from the concept of coup d'état. A coup d'état is a struggle for state power status between political factions of the ruling class with no intention of changing class relations. Coup d'états can be peaceful or violent.

The root cause of social revolution is sharp contradiction within the material production of society itself. This contradiction exists between the objective need for development of the productive forces on one side, and the obsolescence of relations of production (which are maintained through force by the ruling class) on the other side. This contradiction cannot be resolved by any economic or political reform, and manifests as class struggle. It is the development of this class struggle that inevitably leads to an outbreak of social revolution.

> **Annotation 113**
>
> Coup d'etat is French for "stroke of state." A more precise translation would be a "sudden decisive exercise of force as applied to the state." A coup d'etat is essentially a faux revolution in the sense that state power does change hands, but remains in control of the same ruling class. To put it another way: it is a changeover in power from one faction of the ruling class to another. In terms of the economic mode of production, the ruling class remains unchanged and the mode of production does not shift from one form to another.
>
> Historical examples of coup d'etats (which did not result in a change in the mode of production) include:
> - The rise of the National Socialist political party under Adolf Hitler in the 1930s which replaced the government of Weimar Germany.
> - The "revolutions" which took place from 1979-1987 in the Republic of Korea which ended the dictatorship of Park Chung-hee and placed different bourgeois-controlled political parties in power.

> **Annotation 113 (continued)**
>
> - The independence granted to Australia from the government of the United Kingdom. Although this transition took place peacefully and without much turmoil, it still constituted a fundamental changeover in control over the state from one faction of the bourgeoisie to another and can therefore be considered a sort of *coup d'etat* in the Historical Materialist sense of the term.
>
> Although each of these political events led to great changes and developments within each respective nation, they did not lead to essential changes in the mode of production and class relations. In each case, the capitalist class remained the dominant class and the proletariat remained oppressed through the capitalist mode of production. Only a revolution which replaces the ruling class with a revolutionary class as the dominant class of society can be considered to be a *social revolution* in the Historical Materialist sense of the term. Such a revolution will lead to a major shift in human society as it negates of the old mode of production and ushers in of a new mode of production.
>
> Social revolution is always preceded by development of the productive forces to such extent that they are no longer compatible with existing relations of production. Thus it must be understood that social revolution is not brought about by individual human beings nor through human will but as a result of objective development of the material base of society. This is explained in more detail in Annotation 36, p. 52. Any "revolution" which does not lead to a new mode of production and new relations of production is essentially an act of reform and/or coup d'etat.

In addition, each social revolution is impacted by subjective factors. The most important subjective factor is the cognitive and organizational development of the revolutionary class (i.e., the class that represents the new mode of production). From this cognitive and organizational development, class struggle advances from spontaneous action to self-conscious action. Once the subjective and objective causes have sufficiently ripened and the revolutionary seizes the revolutionary moment, then it is inevitable that a social revolution will explode and potentially succeed.

> **Annotation 114**
>
> As explained in Annotation 95, p. 168, subjective factors are factors which can vary across time and place and which can vary from one location to another even within the same social formation of human society.
>
> The importance of developing class consciousness as a prerequisite for social revolution is discussed more in Annotation 50, p. 90.

2. The role of social revolution in the development of class society

Social revolution is the mode and driving force of social development. Without social revolutions in history, the process of replacing any given social-economic formation with a new, higher-level social-economic formation would not have taken place. With that in mind, Marx affirmed that: "Revolutions are the locomotives of history,"[49] the mode of developing social-economic formations.

---

49 *The Class Struggles in France* Karl Marx, 1849.

On the other hand, it is thanks to social revolutions that fundamental contradictions of society in the fields of economy, politics, culture, etc. have been resolved, thereby creating a motivation for the progress and development of society. During revolutionary periods, the creative capacity of the masses has been brought into full play, leading to extraordinarily rapid historical developments: "one day is equal to twenty years."[50]

Human history has fully and clearly demonstrated the role of social revolutions that have taken place in the past millennia. Those include:

- The social revolution that made the transition from the original social-economic formation to the slave-owning social-economic formation.
- The revolution that abolished slavery and replaced it with feudalism.
- The bourgeois revolution that toppled the feudal system and established the capitalist regime.
- The proletarian revolution that abolished the bourgeois dictatorship and established a socialist regime – so far, the greatest and most profound revolution in human history, which completely changes the nature of the old socio-political system by thoroughly abolishing the private ownership system that caused class antagonism to begin with, and which has existed for thousands of years in human history.

Annotation 115

In *Socialism: Utopian and Scientific*, Engels summarized the history of social revolution, starting with a description of medieval/feudal society:

> **I. Mediaeval Society** — Individual production on a small scale. Means of production adapted for individual use; hence primitive, ungainly, petty, dwarfed in action. Production for immediate consumption, either of the producer himself or his feudal lord. Only where an excess of production over this consumption occurs is such excess offered for sale, enters into exchange. Production of commodities, therefore, only in its infancy. But already it contains within itself, in embryo, anarchy in the production of society at large.

Next, Engels describes how capitalists performed social revolution to become the new ruling class:

> **II. Capitalist Revolution** — transformation of industry, at first be means of simple cooperation and manufacture. Concentration of the means of production, hitherto scattered, into great workshops. As a consequence, their transformation from individual to social means of production — a transformation which does not, on the whole, affect the form of exchange. The old forms of appropriation remain in force. The capitalist appears. In his capacity as owner of the means of production, he also appropriates the products and turns them into commodities. Production has become a social act. Exchange and appropriation continue to be individual acts, the acts of individuals. The social product is appropriated by the individual capitalist. Fundamental contradiction, whence arise all the contradictions in which our present-day society moves, and which modern industry brings to light.

---

50 From a Statement of the Politburo of Vietnam, 1975.

Annotation 115 (continued)

Engels next describes important factors of capitalist revolution:

> Severance of the producer from the means of production. Condemnation of the worker to wage-labor for life. Antagonism between the proletariat and the bourgeoisie.
>
> Growing predominance and increasing effectiveness of the laws governing the production of commodities. Unbridled competition. Contradiction between socialized organization in the individual factory and social anarchy in the production as a whole.
>
> On the one hand, perfecting of machinery, made by competition compulsory for each individual manufacturer, and complemented by a constantly growing displacement of laborers. Industrial reserve-army. On the other hand, unlimited extension of production, also compulsory under competition, for every manufacturer. On both sides, unheard-of development of productive forces, excess of supply over demand, over-production and products — excess there, of laborers, without employment and without means of existence. But these two levers of production and of social well-being are unable to work together, because the capitalist form of production prevents the productive forces from working and the products from circulating, unless they are first turned into capital — which their very superabundance prevents. The contradiction has grown into an absurdity. The mode of production rises in rebellion against the form of exchange.
>
> Partial recognition of the social character of the productive forces forced upon the capitalists themselves. Taking over of the great institutions for production and communication, first by joint-stock companies, later in by trusts, then by the State. The bourgeoisie demonstrated to be a superfluous class. All its social functions are now performed by salaried employees.

Finally, Engels predicts the outcome of proletarian revolution which will end class society altogether:

> **III. Proletarian Revolution** — Solution of the contradictions. The proletariat seizes the public power, and by means of this transforms the socialized means of production, slipping from the hands of the bourgeoisie, into public property. By this act, the proletariat frees the means of production from the character of capital they have thus far borne, and gives their socialized character complete freedom to work itself out. Socialized production upon a predetermined plan becomes henceforth possible. The development of production makes the existence of different classes of society thenceforth an anachronism. In proportion as anarchy in social production vanishes, the political authority of the State dies out. Man, at last the master of his own form of social organization, becomes at the same time the lord over Nature, his own master — free.

CHAPTER 6

HISTORICAL MATERIALIST VIEWPOINTS ABOUT HUMANS AND THE HISTORY-CREATING ROLE OF THE MASSES

I. HUMANS AND HUMAN NATURE

1. Definition of Humans

Humans are natural beings with social characteristics. There is a dialectical unity between two essential aspects of human beings: the natural aspect and the social aspect.

> **Annotation 116**
>
>
>
> *The natural aspect of humanity is defined by the relationship between humanity and nature; the social aspect is defined by relationships which exist within and between human societies.*
>
> Humans are *natural beings*. This means that humans exist in and as a part of nature. This constitutes a relationship of dialectical unity in which the natural aspect determines the social aspect, but the social aspect can impact back in important ways.
>
> What distinguishes human beings from all other elements of nature is the *social aspect* of humanity. This social aspect describes the ways in which humans can work together to consciously and intentionally develop our material production over time. This social aspect of humanity is further described below beginning on p. 214.

The Natural Aspect of Humanity

The primary material basis which regulates the formation, existence, and development of humanity is the natural world.

> **Annotation 117**
>
> The "natural world" simply refers to the environment which human beings develop within. It is important to note that human beings are not "metaphysically distinct" from nature; rather, humans exist in dialectical unity with nature.

> **Annotation 117 (continued)**
>
> As Engels wrote in *The Part Played by Labor in the Transition from Ape to Man*:
>
>> ...we by no means rule over nature like a conqueror over a foreign people, like someone standing outside nature – but that we, with flesh, blood, and brain, belong to nature, and exist in its midst, and that all our mastery of it consists in the fact that we have the advantage over all other beings of being able to know and correctly apply its laws.

For this reason, a fundamental aspect of human beings is that we have a natural aspect. Therefore, scientific research and discovery of the natural structure and natural origin of humans is an important scientific basis for humans to understand ourselves and to master ourselves in every activity that contributes to the history of humanity.

> **Annotation 118**
>
> The natural aspect of humanity refers to all the characteristics of human beings which arise from dialectical relationship with the natural world. In addition, humans also have a social aspect which is defined by internal relationships which exist between human beings. The natural and social aspects of humanity are explained more in Annotation 119, below.
>
> Because human beings have a natural aspect, it is important to study the natural characteristics, phenomena, and relationships of human beings in order to have a comprehensive understanding of humanity. This means we must study fields like human biology, human evolution, human psychology, and so on if we are to fully understand human society and its development.

The natural aspect of humanity is analyzed from the following two viewpoints:

First, humans are the result of long-term evolution and development in the natural world. The scientific basis of this conclusion has been established by the whole development of materialism and the natural sciences, and, in particular, the Darwinian theory of the evolution of species.

Second, humans are part of the natural world, and at the same time, the natural world serves as an "inorganic body" for humanity.

> **Annotation 119**
>
> In *Economic and Philosophic Manuscript*, written in 1844, Marx wrote that:
>
>> Nature is man's inorganic body—nature, that is, insofar as it is not itself human body. Man lives on nature—means that nature is his body, with which he must remain in continuous interchange if he is not to die. That man's physical and spiritual life is linked to nature means simply that nature is linked to itself, for man is a part of nature."
>
> Marx is describing human beings as having two "bodies" which allow us to exist in the world. Every individual human being has an "organic body" which is simply our physical body in the literal sense. This body allows a human being to live and exist in the world. Similarly, nature serves as an "inorganic body" for all of humanity which we depend upon for life and existence.

Therefore, changes in the natural world as well as the direct or indirect impacts of natural laws determine the existence and development of humans and human society, and human society is the medium of material exchange between humans and the natural world. On the other hand, the changes and activities of humans always impact the natural environment, changing that environment. This is the dialectical relationship between the existence of humanity and other existences of the natural world.

However, humans are not identical with other existences of the natural world. One attribute which particularly defines humanity is its social aspect.

The Social Aspect of Humanity

The social aspect of humanity is expressed by the special relationships which individual humans have with their many social communities, such as: family, class, nation, humankind, and so on. Therefore, in addition to having a natural aspect, humans must also have a social aspect, and, moreover, this aspect is particularly defining of humanity.

> **Annotation 120**
>
> The social aspect of humanity is what distinguishes human beings from all other entities in the natural world. Human beings are different from all other known forms of life because we are able to form societies and to intentionally work and labor together to develop ourselves through conscious labor activity. This social aspect of humanity is further defined in Annotation 122, below.

The social aspect of humanity is analyzed from the following viewpoints:

First, from the viewpoint of origin:

Human beings originated through natural evolution processes and through social origins. The primary factor of social origin is labor. It is through labor processes that we were able to surpass animals to evolve and develop into human beings. This viewpoint of origin is one of the new discoveries of Marxism-Leninism that makes it possible to complete the theory of human origin for the first time in history.

> **Annotation 121**
>
> Labor in the Dialectical Materialist framework refers specifically to conscious human activity. The viewpoint of origin is a starting point of analysis which pertains to the origin of human consciousness and humanity itself. These origins are important because they constitute the starting point for human society.
>
> The relationship between matter and consciousness is consistent and predictable in every aspect of human society and at every stage of development of humanity. Matter always determines consciousness, whereas consciousness can always impact back upon matter.
>
> Human consciousness originated from human labor activities. This origin is described more in *Part 1*, p. 74. This is consistent with the Dialectical Materialist conception of the relationship between matter and consciousness: that matter determines consciousness (while consciousness can impact back upon the material world). Material production processes led to the development of consciousness. The viewpoint of origin is critical for developing a comprehensive and historical perspective of humanity.

> **Annotation 121 (continued)**
>
> Marx explains how conscious labor processes enabled human beings to surpass all other animals in *Economic and Philosophic Manuscripts*:
>
>> Through material production, humans changed nature: "An animal produces only itself, whilst man reproduces the whole of nature."
>
> *Philosophy of Marxism-Leninism* further explains how conscious labor activities led to the development of human beings as distinct from all other animals:
>
>> Social characteristics of humans express themselves in material production. Material production fundamentally demonstrates the social characteristics of humans. Through labor, we create the mental and material means to serve human life. Through labor, humans form conscious thoughts and languages and determine our social relationships. Therefore, labor is the decisive factor in the formation of humanity's social nature as well as the formation of individual personality in a community.

Second, from the viewpoint of existence and development:

Human existence is always governed by social factors and social laws. As society changes, each person also changes accordingly. Likewise, the development of each individual is the premise for the development of human society. Without social relationships, each human being only exists as a pure biological entity that cannot be "human" with the full meaning of that term.

> **Annotation 122**
>
> In the Dialectical Materialist framework, all things, phenomena, and ideas are defined by internal and external relationships. Thus, we must understand that each human being as an individual is defined in large part by relationships with other human beings. These relationships between individual humans, in turn, are the internal relationships which define human society. Relationships are also what drive all change, motion, and development. Hence, we can see that:
>
> 1. Human society is defined by relationships between human beings, and human beings are defined by their relationship with human society.
>
> 2. Change and development of both human society and individual human beings are driven by these dialectical relationships.
>
> These two points, taken together, serve as the basis for the viewpoint of existence and development of human society, which holds that the existence and development of humanity is defined by relationships between individual human beings and human society. This is an important starting point of analysis of both human society and of human beings as individuals and is therefore a critical viewpoint of Historical Materialism. As Marx explained in *Grundrisse*:
>
>> Society does not consist of individuals, but expresses the sum of interrelations, the relations within which these individuals stand. As if someone were to say: Seen from the perspective of society, there are no slaves and no citizens: both are human beings. Rather, they are that outside society. To be a slave, to be a citizen, are social characteristics, relations between human beings A and B. Human being A, as such, is not a slave. He is a slave in and through society.

> **Annotation 122 (continued)**
>
> To put it another way, whether a person is a "slave," a "worker," or a "capitalist" depends entirely on social relations with other human beings. There is no way that a human being could exist in any of these economic classes as an isolated individual. In this manner, society is defined by individuals (who exist in various economic roles) just as individuals are defined by society. This constitutes a dialectical relationship in which society and individuals mutually change and develop one another over time.
>
> The viewpoint of existence and development perceives the social aspect of humanity because it focuses on the fact that human beings are defined by human society.
>
> Taking the natural aspect and social aspect of humanity together, we see that "human nature" is defined by these two essential aspects: human nature is determined by material processes in the natural world and human nature is defined by social inter-relations. In both of these aspects, human nature is constantly changing and developing just like all other things, phenomena, and ideas in existence, in accordance with the Principle of Development of Dialectical Materialism.

Unity of Natural and Social Aspects of Humanity

These two aspects of humankind – the natural aspect and the social aspect - exist in unity, determine each other, impact each other, and transform each other, thereby creating the potential for creative human activity in the world in the process of making human history. Therefore, explaining the creative nature of humans from only the natural aspect or from only the social aspect is one-sided, incomplete, and will inevitably lead to erroneous conclusions in perception and practice.

> **Annotation 123**
>
> The *natural aspect* (i.e., viewpoint of origin) and *social aspect* (origin of existence and development) of humanity exist in unity. This means that they share a dialectical relationship in which they define one another and lead to change and development in one another. Both the natural aspect and the social aspect of humanity contribute dialectically to the *creative nature* of humanity:
>
> The natural aspect determines creativity in human beings because humans must create through labor processes in order to create the necessities for human life. The objective need of human beings to sustain and develop these material needs leads to a creative nature which also results in an objective need to constantly develop the productive forces of human society (see Annotation 6, p. 12).
>
> The social aspect determines creativity in human beings because human beings share and cooperate creative developments through various forms of cultural and material exchange. Creativity is therefore a social process in which individual human beings contribute but also receive and learn from one another in order to develop and improve creative abilities over time.
>
> Because the natural and social aspects of humanity exist in unity they must be examined and understood together. It must be understood that they dialectically impact, determine, and develop one another in order to fully understand the nature of human beings completely. The *natural* labor processes which human beings undertake to provide for our material needs are also *social* processes, since human beings work together

> **Annotation 123 (continued)**
>
> in carrying out and developing these processes. Likewise, the social activity of human beings is determined by labor processes (since, for example, no other social activities can be carried out if human beings do not first have the material necessities for survival) and also impact natural labor processes (for instance, through the social/collective development of productive forces). *Philosophy of Marxism-Leninism* further defines the relationships which define humanity:
>
>> Since humans are a product of nature and society (see Chapter 6, p. 212), the formation and development of humanity are determined by three distinct but unified sets of laws:
>>
>> - The system of natural laws that determines the biological aspects of human beings. These include genetic inheritance and variation, evolution, etc.
>> - The system of psychology and consciousness that exists on the basis of human biology. Factors of consciousness and psychology include emotions, desires, beliefs, willpower, and so on.
>> - The system of social relations that determine the relations between humans within a society.
>>
>> These 3 systems of laws, together, provide a comprehensive and unified perception of human life that includes both biological and social aspects. The relationship between biological and social aspects is the basis for our biological and social needs such as: needs for food, clothes, shelter, reproduction, love, aesthetics, and all other mental values.

2. Human nature

In the history of human philosophy, there have been many different conceptions of "human nature," but those concepts are usually one-sided, abstract, idealist, and/or mystical.

> **Annotation 124**
>
> *Philosophy of Marxism-Leninism* elaborates on various perceptions of "human nature" from various regions and historical periods:
>
> ### Eastern philosophical perception of human nature:
>
>> Throughout more than 2,000 years of history of Chinese philosophy, the issue of "human nature" was always of chief concern. In the search for truth about human nature, two major schools of thought emerged which viewed human nature as a phenomenon of political practice and social virtue. These philosophical systems were *Confucianism*[51] and *Legalism*.[52]

---

51 Confucianism is a religion or a systematic and methodical doctrine that has existed since the 5th century B.C.E. Confucianism is concerned with Humanity. Specifically, Confucianism teaches a way of being a human being in the family and in society.

52 Legalism is a Chinese political philosophy that emerged in the 6th century B.C.E. Legalism advocated strict laws, harsh punishments, and centralized authority to maintain social order and state control. It was rooted in the belief that humans are inherently self-interested and require strong governance to prevent chaos.

> **<u>Annotation 124 (continued)</u>**
>
>> Confucianists believed that humans are essentially good by nature, while Legalists saw human nature as essentially evil.
>>
>> A third philosophical system from China that was deeply concerned with attempting to understand "human nature" was Daoism.[53]
>>
>> Daoist scholars, such as Laozi [one of the greatest thinkers of Daoism] approached this issue from a different angle and concluded that human nature is natural.
>
> It is important to note that Daoist conceptions of "nature" and the "natural world" are quite different from Western conceptions of these concepts. Daoists view "nature" as a mystical system that includes gods, spirits, ghosts, monsters, and other beings which would be considered "supernatural" in most Western philosophical systems.
>
> According to an article on Daoism by Dr. Phan Ngoc from Vietnam's National Center for Social Sciences and Humanities:
>
>> The Chinese Daoists did not imagine a God that created the world. Daoists believed that gods, humans, and the natural universe are unified as one whole. Therefore, they believed that ghosts and gods could control human destiny, and that, likewise, humans could contact ghosts and gods through the intermediaries of witches and mediums. . . [Daoists also believe] that the human body contains thousands of gods and that life is a phenomenon of "Qi" [a supernatural energy]. Daoists believe that humans can achieve immortality through certain spiritual practices: alchemy, qi circulation, and male/female relations.
>
> Thus, the Daoist conception that human beings are "natural" indicates that human beings are part of a mystical universe and can interact with and be influenced by such spiritual entities as gods and ghosts. Indeed, Daoists even believe that human beings contain gods and ghosts and can become immortal gods themselves. This is very different from Western perceptions of "natural human nature" as described below in this annotation. The Vietnamese textbook *Philosophy of Marxism-Leninism* goes on to explain how different philosophical conceptions of human nature influenced philosophical schools in the East:
>
>> These different models and perceptions of human nature became the premises for later schools of philosophy in the search for truth about politics, virtue, and human life.
>>
>> Indian philosophical theorists, especially Buddhists, tended to differ from Chinese philosophies of human nature. Buddhists approached the question of human nature from the angle of deep metaphysical thinking about humans and the human view of life. Buddhists concluded that human beings, on the path towards Enlightenment, are essentially selfless, impermanent, and good. This is one of the unique conclusions of Buddhist philosophy.
>
> Next, it explains different conceptions of human nature in Western idealist philosophical systems:

---

53 Daoism is a Chinese philosophy and spiritual tradition that emerged around the sixth century B.C.E. Daoism centered on living in harmony with the Dao (the "Way"), the natural and universal principle that underlies all existence.

> **Annotation 124 (continued)**
>
> In the West, idealist philosophers focused on rational activity as the basis for human nature. Notable idealist philosophers include Plato of ancient Greece; Descartes of modern French philosophy, and Hegel in the Classic German philosophy. Since they did were not materialists, these philosophers resorted to mysticism in explaining human nature. To Plato, human nature is rooted in the immortal soul which belongs to the "realm of ideas." Descartes argued that human nature is rooted in rationality "a priori." Hegel conceived of human nature in relation to his conceptions of the "absolute ideal."
>
> . . .
>
> In modern Western philosophy, many philosophical trends (such as existentialism) consider the philosophical issues of humans as essential.
>
> Plato's "realm of ideas" is a timeless, unchanging world of perfect, abstract forms or concepts (e.g., beauty, justice, equality) that exist beyond the physical world. According to Plato, the physical world we experience is merely a flawed reflection of these perfect forms. In this conception of reality, humans have an innate ability to recognize such "perfect forms" because our souls once existed in the realm of ideas before being born into the physical world. This explains why we can identify imperfections in the physical world (e.g., recognizing something as "not quite just" or "not truly beautiful")—our souls supposedly remember the perfect forms and strive to reconnect with them through reason and philosophy. This constitutes an idealist and mystical conception of reality that has more in common with spirituality than natural science.
>
> Descartes argued that rationality is an innate, a priori (prior to experience) concept embedded in human nature. Rationality, therefore, is the foundation of knowledge and the basis for understanding truths, such as mathematical and logical principles, which are universally valid and independent of sensory experience. Descartes believed that the capacity for reason is what defines human beings. In his famous statement "cogito, ergo sum" ("I think, therefore I am"), he asserted that the act of thinking proves the existence of the self and highlights the inherent rationality of human nature. This rational capacity allows humans to discern truth, doubt falsehoods, and achieve certainty through clear and distinct ideas. By placing thinking and rationality as the first basis of discovering truth and of existence, Descartes' conceptions of reality and of human nature are distinctly idealist.
>
> Hegel believed in what he called the "absolute ideal:" a unified, dynamic totality of all ideas, history, and consciousness. To Hegel, this absolute ideal represents the complete realization of freedom, reason, and self-awareness in the universe. Hegel believed that human nature is fundamentally tied to the absolute ideal because humans are rational beings who actively participate in its unfolding. In this way, according to Hegel, human nature is not static but is constantly evolving toward greater self-awareness and freedom, ultimately aligning with the absolute ideal. Hegel's conceptions are notable because they accurately perceive human nature as dynamic and constantly changing, which is how Marx and Engels describe human nature in the system of Dialectical Materialist philosophy. The key difference between Hegelian and Marxist conceptions of human nature is that Hegel's system of thought is idealist, placing human consciousness as the first basis of human nature, whereas Marxist philosophy places its understanding of human nature on a material basis.

> **Annotation 124 (continued)**
>
> Existentialism is a Western philosophy that emphasizes individual freedom, choice, and the creation of meaning in a seemingly indifferent or absurd universe. It focuses on subjective experience and the idea that humans define their own essence through their actions and decisions. Existentialism is idealist in the sense that it prioritizes the mind, consciousness, and human agency over material forces of reality. Existentialism asserts that reality is shaped by individual perception, values, and choices rather than by objective, material phenomena, thus putting the conception of human nature on an idealist basis.
>
> Next, *Philosophy of Marxism-Leninism* describes Western conceptions of human nature rooted in various materialist philosophies:
>
>> Many Western materialist philosophers have chosen to view human nature from the perspective of natural science. From ancient times, many Western materialist philosophers have believed that humans have a "natural" nature. These philosophers consider humans to be no different from other creatures, as human beings are also made from matter. Such materialist conceptions of human nature reject mystical interpretations of human nature. One of the most popular such perceptions is Democritus's conclusion that the human body and soul are made from atoms. This is also the premise for the Epicurean philosophical school.
>
> Democritus conceived a materialist view of nature based on a belief that all things, including humans and other animals, are composed of atoms.
>
> Epicurus was a Greek philosopher who developed an empiricist philosophy that was rooted in atomistic materialism. Epicurus had an empiricist view of reality, believing that human sensations are the ultimate basis for discovering truth and understanding human nature.
>
>> These materialist viewpoints were further developed during the Renaissance and in modern times, such as with English and French materialists of the 18th century. This Western materialist conception of human nature was the theoretical premise for the humanist materialist viewpoint of Feuerbach.
>>
>> In essence, Feuerbach's philosophy shifts focus from the divine to the human, asserting that understanding humanity's material and social conditions is key to understanding existence. His ideas heavily influenced Marx and Engels, who built on his materialism while critiquing his lack of emphasis on practical, revolutionary change.
>>
>> Feurbach's conception of humanist materialism also served as a major influence on the theoretical premises of the materialist viewpoint about humans in Marxism.
>
> Feurbach's philosophy of humanist materialism is centered on the idea that religion and metaphysics are projections of human essence. Feuerbach argued that the material world is the only reality, and consciousness arises from material conditions. Marx and Engels were heavily influenced by Feurbach's materialism, but they took issue with his sharp focus on human attributes and activities in isolation from the external material world.
>
> *Philosophy of Marxism-Leninism* concludes by explaining the important role of Marx's conception of human history:

Annotation 124 (continued)

Generally speaking, all philosophical viewpoints before Marx or outside of Marxism [including Feuerbach's conception of humanist materialism] have a fundamental shortcoming: they are one-sided in the approaches and methodologies used to find answers to philosophical questions of human nature. Therefore, in the history of humankind, there were many abstract ideas about human nature and idealist perceptions about human life as well as idealist methods to attempt to liberate humanity. These shortcomings were overcome by the Dialectical Materialist viewpoint of humans and human nature.

Limitations of Viewpoints of Human Nature Prior to Dialectical Materialism

Before the development of Dialectical Materialist and Historical Materialist conceptions of humanity, the idea of "human nature" was quite limited, tending to be:

One-sided, considering the nature of humanity in only one aspect or from a very limited metaphysical perspective (see Metaphysics, *Part 1*, p. 8). Such conceptions of human nature tend to see humanity as static and unchanging or split human beings into metaphysical categories and/or listing characteristics without recognizing the dialectical relationship between humanity and society. According to the textbook *Philosophy of Marxism-Leninism* by Dr. Nguyen Ngoc Long:

> Throughout history, there have been many different perceptions that differentiate humans from animals. For example: humans have been considered as animals that can use tools, animals that have social characteristics, or even animals that can think, etc. All of these perceptions are one-sided because they only emphasize one aspect of the social nature of humans without pointing out the origin of that social nature.

Abstract, considering humanity in terms of "pure philosophy" without taking into consideration the concrete lives of human beings. In *The German Ideology,* Marx demanded that, in examining humanity, we must seek to understand "real, living man."

Idealist, focusing entirely on human conscious activity without recognizing the dialectical relationship between matter and consciousness and the fact that material processes determine human conscious activity.

Mystical, describing human nature as determined by religious or spiritual forces, deities, or other supernatural phenomena. Such conceptions tend to be fideistic in nature, derived from "received wisdom" of religious texts or practices or taken "on faith," rather than being derived from empirical or scientific observations of reality and human activity (see Fideism, *Part 1*, p. 56).

Historically, as Marx and Engels observed, philosophy has tended to exist to justify the ruling class in any given era of class society, and this extended to conceptions of human nature.[54] For example, in the feudal era, "human nature" was conceived of in ways that tended to justify the feudal mode of production and the dominance of the ruling class of feudal lords, who were described as "noble" and inherently superior and separated from peasants and other oppressed classes who were seen as subservient "by nature."

---

54 See Annotation 124, p. 217.

> **Annotation 124 (continued)**
>
> Such limitations are present today in bourgeois philosophy and ideology, which tends to be formulated to defend the capitalist mode of production. For example, a common conception of human nature in bourgeois ideology suggests that human beings are "naturally competitive" or "inherently greedy" and that capitalism thus "harnesses" this "innate capitalist human nature." Capitalism is therefore described in many forms of bourgeois philosophy as a "natural fit" for humanity, even though capitalism has only existed for a very short time in comparison to the thousands of years of human history.
>
> Historical Materialist conceptions of human nature overcome all of these limitations by recognizing the complex nature of humanity, seeking a comprehensive perspective of humanity through the analysis of internal and external relationships, as well as a historical perspective through the analysis of the development of humanity over time. This Historical Materialist conception of humanity is described in more detail in the following section.

In *Theses on Feuerbach*, Karl Marx briefly criticized previous conceptions of human nature and affirmed his new conception: "the human essence is no abstraction inherent in each single individual. In its reality, it is the ensemble of the social relations."

> **Annotation 125**
>
> *Philosophy of Marxism-Leninism* by Dr. Nguyen Ngoc Long further explains the Historical Materialist conception of human nature:
>
>> (Marx's conception of human nature) affirms that: there is no abstract human nature that exists outside of all social and historical conditions and circumstances. Humans are always concrete and specific. This means that humans always live in specific historical conditions at a specific time. In those historical conditions, through our practical activities, humans create material and mental values for the existence and development of our physical and mental health. Humans can only truly express our social nature in that "ensemble of social relations."
>>
>> Such ensembles of social relations include (but are not limited to):
>> - Relations between classes, individuals, and the mode of production
>> - Relations between politics and the economy
>> - Relations between the family, the individual, and society
>>
>> It must be further understood that the above conception of the social nature of humans does not neglect the natural aspect of human life.[55] The natural aspects of humanity exist in unity with social aspects. Even the biological needs of humans also have social characteristics.
>
> For example, human beings need to interact with nature and with other humans to meet even the most basic biological needs. No human being can realistically survive in pure isolation without any other human beings forever.
>
> The Dialectical Materialist philosophical methodology defines humanity and human

---

55 See Annotation 118, p. 213.

> **Annotation 125 (continued)**
> nature in terms of internal and external relationships. This interpretation of human nature correctly asserts that social relations determine human nature through countless processes of development which are driven by these relationships, and that human nature is thus a complex and constantly developing phenomenon in which individual humans interact with and develop human society and vice-versa.

The basic limitation of the intuitive and metaphysical materialist perspective is that it has abstracted and absolutized the natural aspect of humankind and often underestimated the interpretation of humans from its socio-historical perspective. The intuitive and metaphysical materialist perspective essentially recognizes the natural aspect of humanity alone, while ignoring the social aspect.

> **Annotation 126**
> "Intuitive and metaphysical materialism" refers to vulgar forms of materialism which fail to consider the complex social relations which *also* define humanity (along with the material/natural aspect). For instance, such conceptions might suffer from mechanical materialism which hold that human beings are exclusively defined by material processes. This perspective fails to take into account the role of human consciousness which can impact back on material reality through conscious labor activity. Intuitive conceptions of human nature tend to suffer from various deviations from Dialectical Materialism which cause confusion, distortion in perception of reality, and other mistakes and lapses in analysis. Such deviations include:
>
> **Dogmatism** refers to ignoring practical experience and holding pre-established theory and ideas as unalterable truth. Mechanical materialists are often dogmatic in their belief that the material alone accounts for all change and development in the world, ignoring the evidence that conscious activities can impact back on the material world. Dogmatism can also lead to intuitive perceptions of "human nature," wherein people preconceive of their own ideas about "human nature" and ignore all evidence which contradicts those preconceptions.
>
> **Solipsism** is the belief that the *self* is the only basis for truth. Solipsism is the root cause of "intuitive" conceptions of human nature, as it exclusively relies on personal intuition as a basis for "discovering" truth solely in one's own thoughts and ideas.
>
> **Subjectivism** is the centering of one's own self and one's own conscious activities, as well as a failure to test one's own perceptions against material and social reality. Subjectivists, like solipsists, tend to believe that they can reason their way to truth without testing their ideas against objective reality. This tends to lead to intuitive notions of "human nature" that ultimately fail to discover truth.
>
> In ignoring the social aspect of humanity, mechanical materialists neglect to recognize the important ways in which social consciousness can impact back upon social being. This is further explained in Annotation 78, p. 140.

In contrast to the intuitive and metaphysical materialist conception of human nature, the Dialectical Materialist conception of human nature acknowledges the natural aspect, while also analyzing humans from the perspective of socio-historical relations, thereby discovering the social aspect of humanity. Furthermore, the social aspect of humanity is the most essential aspect that makes a person a "person"; that is to say, it is the social aspect of humanity which distinguishes humans from other existences of the natural world. Thus, it is possible to define humans as a natural entity, but as a natural entity with social characteristics. Thus, in reality, human nature is "the ensemble of the social relations" because human society is composed of all relationships between people in all fields, including political, economic, cultural, and so on.

The Dialectical Materialist viewpoint of the social aspect of humanity is the exploration of the formation and development of humanity – and the human ability to create history – through the analysis of the formation and development of social relations in history.

> **Annotation 127**
>
> The Historical Materialist perspective does not consider fields of study such as sociology, anthropology, human biology, psychology, natural history, and human history to be metaphysically distinct from one another. Instead, Historical Materialism examines the dialectical relationship between all of these fields to develop a comprehensive and historical understanding of humanity.
>
> Historical Materialism is fundamentally the study of humanity using the Dialectical Materialist philosophical methodology which seeks understanding through the exploration of internal and external relationships and the development which these relationships cause over time. Thus, it is critical to understand the origin and development of humanity to understand humanity today, to make reasonable predictions about the future, and to affect change in the material world.
>
> Humans are uniquely able to create history because only humans are able to recall, organize, analyze, and interpret historic records through conscious activity. This gives human beings a unique and profound ability to understand how objective reality has developed over time. By analyzing and interpreting history we are able to develop a scientific understanding of how our own society has developed, the objective and material basis for this development, and the objective laws which govern this development.
>
> Historical Materialism is the application of Dialectical Materialist philosophy and Materialist Dialectical methodology to the study and analysis of human history. Historical Materialism exists with the objective of understanding the history and development of capitalism so that it can ultimately be superseded and so that a stateless classless society can be built and human beings can begin collectively writing our own history without the inherent limitations of economic class division.
>
> Marx explained in *Economic and Philosophic Manuscripts* that communism is "the complete return of man to himself as a social being – a return accomplished consciously and embracing the entire wealth of previous development." This means that once human beings have built a communist society it will enable the human species to consciously write our own history in ways that were not previously possible in class society. Rather than being bound to the objective social forces of class struggle, humanity will be free to pursue objectives of our own collective choosing. This will only be possible once human society, the human individual, and the natural world are brought into harmonious unity, and this harmony must be built *consciously*, and *collectively*, by humanity as a whole. This is, in essence, communism as defined by Karl Marx:

> **Annotation 127 (continued)**
>
> This communism, as fully developed naturalism, equals humanism, and as fully developed humanism equals naturalism; it is the genuine resolution of the conflict between man and nature and between man and man – the true resolution of the strife between existence and essence, between objectification and self-confirmation, between freedom and necessity, between the individual and the species. Communism is the riddle of history solved, and it knows itself to be this solution.

From the anthropological viewpoint, i.e., from the viewpoint of the natural aspect of humanity, an enslaved person is simply a person. Only in the economic-political relations of the slave-owning society do they become an enslaved person. Under socialist political-economic relations, the same person would become a free person: a master and creator of history.

Thus, there is no inherent and constant "slave nature" of any person, derived from ethnicity, national origin, etc. The characteristic of being "enslaved" is an objective outcome of socio-political-economic relations under certain historical conditions. When these relationships change, it also creates a change in human nature. Therefore, the liberation of human nature needs to be directed towards the liberation of economic, political, cultural, and social relations, through which the history-creating ability of humans can be promoted.

> **Annotation 128**
>
> Human beings in slave societies are not enslaved because of any characteristic related to biology, national origin, or other subjective characteristics. Rather, human beings become enslaved because of objective material conditions which give rise to the phenomenon of slavery. The Soviet textbook *Fundamentals of Marxism-Leninism* summarizes the material conditions which led to slavery in ancient societies:
>
>> The foundation of the production relations of this system was private ownership not only of the means of production, but also of the workmen themselves as slaves. The slave-owner's property rights over the slaves and over all they produced was determined by the level of development of the productive forces of that epoch. This level was sufficiently high to give rise to the possibility of exploitation of the working people. But at the same time productivity was still so low that exploitation of the workmen and appropriation of a part of what they produced could be accomplished only by reducing the consumption of slaves to a minimum, leaving them just enough to prevent them from dying of hunger.[56]
>
> Throughout history, various societies have attempted to justify exploitative practices such as slavery by developing ideologies which suggest that some groups of human beings are inferior to others. This constitutes false consciousness which has been fabricated by ruling classes to excuse their own abuses against their fellow human beings. In truth, every human being has the capacity to be free and to have a voice and power in society. There is no objective justification for the exploitation or enslavement of any human being.

---

[56] The text from which this passage was taken can be found in full in Appendix K, p. 277.

> **Annotation 128 (continued)**
>
> Class society itself is a manifestation of social relations of human beings and humanity will not be freed from class society through mysticism, technological innovation, nor any other such pursuit outside of the development of class consciousness of the working class. Only working class consciousness can lead to social revolution which will eliminate class society as explained Chapter 5, Section 2, starting on p. 207.
>
> Of all the social relations which exist between human beings, economic relations are most important, as these objective/material relations play a determining role in the existence and development of humanity. This is the basis of Social-Economic Formation Theory which is explained more in Chapter 4 starting on p. 159.

Thus, there are no non-historical humans. We are always attached to certain historical conditions. It is necessary from such a viewpoint to properly explain the ability of humans to create history. The limitations of the history-creating ability of peasants cannot be explained from their nature, but, on the contrary, must be explained from the perspective of the limited level of development of economic, political, and cultural relations of feudal society.

> **Annotation 129**
>
> In order for a "non-historical human" to exist, that human would have to have absolutely no relationship to any other human being, which is inherently impossible. All human beings are products of and participants in social relations, and these social relations lead to the development of human society, and this development is what we call history. *Philosophy of Marxism-Leninism* further explains the historical characteristics of human beings:
>
>> If there were no natural world, no human society, and no history, then there would be no human beings. Therefore, humans are a product of history and of the long-term evolution of the biological world. However, the most important thing to remember is this: humans are always the subject of social history.
>>
>> As social beings, humans engage in practical activities together. We impact nature, change nature, and at the same time in doing so, cause the development of social history. Animals rely on existing conditions of nature. Humans, on the other hand, develop nature with our practical activities, and create a second nature following our purposes.
>
> This "second nature" is the social aspect of humanity.

Thus, humans - from the social nature viewpoint - are a product of history. To the extent that history creates humans, humans also create history to the same extent. This is the dialectical relationship between humans, as the subject of history, and the history that we have created ourselves. Simultaneously, humans are regulated by the history we have created.

> **Annotation 130**
>
> Human society and human history exist in dialectical unity with each other. This is simply a manifestation of the Principle of Development of Dialectical Materialism. This principle states that:

> **Annotation 130 (continued)**
>
> Development is a process that comes from within the thing-in-itself; the process of solving the contradictions within things and phenomena. Therefore, development is inevitable, objective, and occurs without dependence on human will.
>
> Human society is defined by internal and external relationships which cause development and change over time; and human history is simply the sum total of all of those developments over time. Humanity in our present capitalist society and humanity as it existed under feudalism are one in the same. Capitalism and feudalism are simply different stages of development of the same subject: humanity.
>
> *Philosophy of Marxism-Leninism* further explains:
>
>> In the process of changing nature, humans also create our own history. Humans are a product of history and at the same time are the ones that create our own history. Production activities are, on the one hand, the necessary conditions for the existence of humans, and on the other hand, the method that we use to change our life and society. On the basis of fully understanding the social-historical rules, and with both mental and material activities, humans cause the development of society from lower to higher levels, and to make the society more suitable to our needs. There would be no objective laws of development of human society if there were no human activities. And, by extension, there would be no history of the entirety of human society if there were no human activities.

Therefore, it can be seen that the basic limitation of the metaphysical materialist conception of human nature is that it only sees the decisiveness of the historical situations upon humans, but does not see the creative relationship of humans in the process of changing the situation and therefore also changing ourselves.

> **Annotation 131**
>
> This metaphysical/mechanical materialist conception of human nature is rooted in a misunderstanding of the relationship between matter and consciousness.
>
> Such "vulgar materialism" argues that matter and material processes completely dictate human consciousness. Thus, a metaphysical materialist conception of human history would argue that human beings are simply swept up in objective processes of history without any ability to affect the development of human society. Similarly, a metaphysical materialist conception of human nature would argue that human beings lack agency in the world and are unable to affect the world.
>
> The Dialectical Materialist conception argues, in contrast, that matter determines consciousness but that consciousness can impact back on matter through conscious labor activity. Thus, human history is determined by objective material processes but human beings are capable of impacting back on those processes. A Dialectical Materialist conception of human nature must allow for the human ability to impact back on our society and to intervene in historical processes.
>
> Ultimately, the Dialectical Materialist conception of humanity must accurately reflect the conception of the relationship between matter and consciousness without straying into metaphysical materialism, which holds that material processes completely dictate the development of humanity, while simultaneously avoiding idealism, which holds that human consciousness can completely determine material processes.

Marx asserted that:
> The materialist doctrine that men are products of circumstances and upbringing... forgets that it is men who change circumstances, and that the educator must himself be educated."

In the work *Dialectics of Nature*, Engels also argued that:
> Animals also have a history, that of their derivation and gradual evolution to their present position. This history, however, is made for them, and as far as they themselves take part in it, this occurs without their knowledge or desire. On the other hand, the more that human beings become removed from animals in the narrower sense of the word, the more they make their own history consciously...

Therefore, as a social entity, people - through practical activities - affect the natural world and modify the natural world according to their needs for survival and development. At the same time, people also create their own history and carry out the development of that history.

Annotation 132

Humanity is able to consciously develop itself through practical activity, but there are limitations to this conscious development – especially in class society. As Marx wrote in *The Eighteenth Brumaire of Louis Bonaparte*:
> Men make their own history, but they do not make it as they please; they do not make it under self-selected circumstances, but under circumstances existing already, given and transmitted from the past. The tradition of all dead generations weighs like a nightmare on the brains of the living.

Class society is a major impediment to humanity's ability to consciously develop our own history. This is because class society forces humanity to develop in accordance with class struggle - contradiction and opposition which occurs between competing classes of human society. Once class society is abolished entirely humanity will have much more freedom to collectively—and consciously—determine our own social self-development. This is discussed more in Annotation 115, p. 210.

From the Marxist-Leninist scientific conception of humanity, the following important methodological implications can be drawn:

First, it is impossible to scientifically explain human problems only through examining the natural aspect of humanity; it is fundamental to also examine the social aspect of humanity, i.e., the economic and social relations of humans.

Second, the fundamental driving force of the progress and development of society is the capacity of humanity to create history. Therefore, we must promote the creative capacity of each person, because humans are the main driving force of the progress and development of society.

Third, human liberation, in order to promote history-creating ability of humanity, must be directed towards the cause of liberating social-economic relations. In that methodological sense, it can be seen that one of the most fundamental values of the socialist revolution lies in the goal of thoroughly abolishing oppressive and exploitative social-economic relations which suppress the ability of humans to create history. Revolution must also carry out the cause of liberating all of humankind by building socialist and communist social-economic relations in order to establish and develop a society where one person's creation becomes the condition for another's freedom and creativity. That is also the most noble moral philosophy of communism: "One for all and all for one."

> **Annotation 133**
>
> The phrase "one for all and all for one" was made most famous by Alexandre Dumas[57] as the oath of the main characters in his novel *The Three Musketeers*, but its origins go back centuries, originally formulated in Latin as "unus pro omnibus, omnes pro uno."
>
> This slogan became widely adopted by communists around the world during the 20th century. As an example, it was used by Soviet labor brigades of the 1960s and was featured as a principle of the "Moral Code of the Builder of Communism" which was adopted by the Communist Party of the Soviet Union in 1961. In Vietnam, the expression is translated as "một người vì mọi người, mọi người vì một người," and it is commonly used by Vietnamese communists to express the spirit and attitude of communist revolution.
>
> For example, the expression was used in *The Great Unity*, the official newspaper of Vietnam's Fatherland Front during the outbreak of COVID in 2020:
>
>> One for all and all for one refers not only to each person's awareness of the community, but also to the actions and gestures of sacrificing the interests of individuals, organizations, and businesses, joining hands to prevent the epidemic.
>
> Notably, "all for one and one for all" was the favorite motto of Jenny Marx[58], daughter of Karl Marx. The expression was also used by Ho Chi Minh in "What Are Socialist Ideologies and Socialist Manners?" which can be found in Appendix J, p. 276.

---

57 (1802-1870) French novelist and playwright.
58 (1844-1883) *Married name: Jenny Caroline Marx Longuet. Pen name: J. Williams.* One of four daughters of Karl Marx (all named Jenny). Jenny Caroline Marx was, like her father, a socialist writer and activist.

II. DEFINITION OF THE MASSES AND THE HISTORY-CREATING ROLE OF THE MASSES

"50 Year Anniversary of the Liberation of the South of Vietnam — Uphold the Spirit of Unity, Fortitude, and Self-Reliance in Building and Defending the Nation"

1. Definition of the masses

Humans are the creators of history, but not in a way that is individual, discrete, nor isolated. Rather, history is a process of gathering people together into well-organized social communities, led by individuals or organizations, in order to solve historical tasks in the economic, political, and cultural fields of society. We refer to such gathered and organized social community within a society as *the masses*.

The basic forces forming the community of the masses include:

First, workers, who produce material and intellectual wealth. The workers are the basic nucleus of the community of the masses.

Second, people who oppose the oppressive, exploitative ruling class.

Third, social classes and strata that directly or indirectly promote social progress through their activities in all areas of social life.

Humans and the History-Creating Role of the Masses   231

The masses are not an unchanging community, but in fact, are constantly changing in accordance with the changes of historical missions which exist during certain periods and at certain levels of development.

However, the most fundamental force of the masses are the workers who produce material and intellectual wealth for the survival and development of society. In addition, depending on certain historical conditions, the community of the masses may also include different class forces and social classes.

> **Annotation 134**
>
> According to *Philosophy of Marxism-Leninism*:
>
> > The processes of motion and development of history result from the activities of a massive group of people, called "the masses," under the leadership of an individual or an organization to fulfill their purposes and to meet their demands.
> >
> > Based on different social historical conditions and the mission of each era, the masses include different component classes and social strata.
> >
> > In short: the masses consist of groups of people that share a fundamental interest. The masses contain different groups, classes, and social strata who act under the same leadership of a person, organization, or political party to solve the economic-political-social issues of a specific era. . . The masses is a historical category. It changes in accordance with the development of social history.
>
> The transition from feudalism to capitalism can be considered as an example of how "the masses" can change and develop over time.
>
> Under feudalism, the monarch and feudal lords were the ruling class. These rulers of society held power over the working masses, which included peasants, craftsmen, merchants, and other strata of oppressed working people.
>
> Over time, the masses came under the leadership of the emerging revolutionary bourgeois class. The bourgeoisie developed an ideological program of "bourgeois democracy" and organized (through economic employment and political indoctrination) the emerging "working class" into a mass formation of society which it led to social revolution against the old feudal ruling class.
>
> Prior to this development, "the masses" of working people were under the leadership and direction of the feudal class. Monarchs and feudal lords led and directed society to solve the problems of securing food and other necessities so that human life could be sustained.
>
> The bourgeoisie could not have become the ruling class on its own. In order to enact a successful revolution against the feudal class, it became necessary for the bourgeoisie to organize the other oppressed classes into a mass movement which was large and powerful enough to successfully wage social revolution. Only then could society advance to the next stage of development, from feudalism to capitalism. The necessity of social revolution in advancing society is discussed more in Annotation 36, p. 53.
>
> After the bourgeoisie seized leadership of the masses, the character of the masses and all of society fundamentally changed. Now workers are organized under the leadership of bourgeois political parties. Such parties, which are controlled by the capitalist class, are responsible for leading and organizing the masses to provide for the material needs of humanity under capitalism.

> **Annotation 134 (continued)**
>
> Dr. Doan The Anh, professor at the Ho Chi Minh National Academy of Politics, gives the following definition to "social progress:"
>
>> Social progress is the forward path of society. The founders of Scientific Socialism determined that social progress is the process of development of human society from lower levels to higher levels, from one socio-economic form to another, higher socio-economic form, which brings better material and mental/intellectual value, furthering the perfection of human nature. Thus, the connotation of social progress must simultaneously and correspondingly manifest from the development of productive forces to the development of production relations; from the development of the economic base to the development of superstructure; from the development of social being to the development of social consciousness; from improving the standard of living of people and making people free from all oppression, exploitation, injustice, to the comprehensive development and self-mastery of their own lives.
>
> The task of Scientific Socialism – and the historical mission of the working class – is to develop a proletarian leadership for the masses. This can only be achieved through the development of working-class political parties which will eventually enact social revolution and seize control of the state. Once the working masses lead themselves the conditions will finally exist for class society to be dismantled.

2. The history-creating role of the masses and the role of the individuals in history

Before the development of the Marxist-Leninist methodology and the viewpoint of Historical Materialism, historians did not properly perceive the history-creating role of the masses. This was because of the inherent limitations of the theoretical origins of previous studies of human history, including idealist and religious viewpoints as well as metaphysical methods of analyzing problems in society.

According to the Historical Materialist viewpoint, the masses are the true creators of history, and the force that determines the development of history. Therefore, history is, first and foremost, the history of the masses' activities in all fields of society.

Three principles of historical development define and outline the role of the masses in creating history:

First, the masses are the fundamental productive force of every society which directly produce material wealth to meet the needs of existence and development of humans and society. This is the most important need of every society at all times and in all historical periods.

Second, along with the process of creating material wealth, the masses are also the force that directly or indirectly create the intellectual values of society. The masses directly or indirectly "verify" the intellectual values that have been created by generations of humans and individuals throughout history. The activities of the masses are the decisive practical basis and the source of the cultural and mental creations of society. All intellectual values ultimately exist to serve the activities of the masses and only have practical meaning once materialized by the people's practical activities.

Third, the working masses are the fundamental driving force of all revolutions and reforms in history. Human history has proven that no revolution or social reform can succeed if it does not come from the interests and aspirations of the masses. With such meaning, it can be said that the revolution is a "festival of the masses" and that, in that festival, the masses create history rapidly - "one day is equal to twenty years."

Thus, revolutions and social reforms rely upon the masses, and the creativity of the masses also require revolutions and social reforms in order to develop. That is the dialectic of the social development process.

Annotation 135

As Lenin wrote in "Two Tactics of Social-Democracy in the Democratic Revolution:"

> Revolutions are the locomotives of history, said Marx. Revolutions are the festivals of the oppressed and the exploited. At no other time are the masses of the people in a position to come forward so actively as creators of a new social order as at a time of revolution. At such times the people are capable of performing miracles, if judged by the narrow, philistine scale of gradual progress.

Lenin went on to explain the decisive role which class conscious ideologists and leaders must play in guiding the masses to revolution towards social revolution against capitalism:

> But the leaders of the revolutionary parties must also make their aims more comprehensive and bold at such a time, so that their slogans shall always be in advance of the revolutionary initiative of the masses, serve as a beacon, reveal to them our democratic and socialist ideal in all its magnitude and splendour and show them the shortest and most direct route to complete, absolute and decisive victory.

The history-creating role of the masses can never be separated from the specific roles of each individual, especially the roles of individuals in positions of leadership in each community. According to Lenin:

> Not a single class in history has achieved power without producing its political leaders, its prominent representatives able to organize a movement and lead it.

The concept of *individual* refers to every particular human being who lives in a certain social community and is distinguished from other human beings through uniqueness and universality. Accordingly, each individual is a unified whole with both individual and universal characteristics. Individuals are the subjects of labor and of all social relations and consciousness. Through creative labor processes, individuals perform social functions in every period of development in history.

Annotation 136

Social change and revolution results from contradiction between three core subjects:

The masses, which include all working human beings who provide humanity with the essential needs of life.

Individuals, of which the masses are composed.

Ideological revolutionary leaders, who are themselves individual members of the masses, and who help to develop and disseminate the ideological programs which build class consciousness.

> **Annotation 136 (continued)**
>
> Building towards social revolution, therefore, is a dialectical process in which all of these subjects define and develop each other. The masses must develop class consciousness and solidarity to consciously engage in revolution. This means that individuals must be developed over time until enough of the masses are conscious enough to participate in revolution. This means that social revolutionary leaders are needed to inspire, teach, and develop individuals towards social revolution.

As the masses create history, each individual—depending on their position, functions, roles, and specific creative capacity—can participate in the process of creating the history of the masses. In this sense, each individual of every community has "imprinted" its mark on the history-creating process, although the extent and scale of this imprint may vary. However, leaving the deepest imprints in the historical process are often the leaders, and especially great people. Great people are outstanding individuals in the fields of politics, economics, science, art, etc.

In Marxism-Leninism, the concept of *leaders* is often used to refer to outstanding individuals created by the revolutionary movement of the masses who are strongly associated with the masses. In order to become a leader of the masses and be trusted by the masses, a leader must possess the following basic qualities:

First, they must have erudite scientific knowledge and be able to grasp the trends of the motion and development of history.

Second, they must be capable of gathering the masses, unifying the will and actions of the masses in the settlement of historical tasks, and promoting the progress and development of history.

Third, they must be closely attached to the masses, and must sacrifice their own individual interests for the interests of the masses.

In any period and in any social community, if history sets forth tasks that need to be solved, leaders will inevitably emerge from the mass movement who will meet those tasks.

Thus, absolutizing the role of the masses while forgetting the role of the individuals —or absolutizing the role of individuals, leaders, and great people while disregarding the role of the masses—constitutes a failure to properly apply the Historical Materialist methodology in the study of history. Such failure to properly understand the dialectical relationship between individuals and the masses will make it impossible to accurately explain the motion and development processes of human history in general as well as each social community history in particular.

> **Annotation 137**
>
> Before the development of Historical Materialism, a common misconception about society was the "great man" theory of history. This theory held that human history moved forward primarily and essentially because of the actions of individual "great" human beings who moved society forward through their will, intellect, and other personal qualities.
>
> This is an idealist conception of history as it attributes the motion of history to the consciousness of particular individual human beings.

> **Annotation 137 (continued)**
>
> Historical Materialism refutes the "great man" theory of history by recognizing that the primary and essential motion of history is material motion which occurs within the material base and social being of human society. Individuals, including "great" individuals, do play a role in history, but only insomuch as they are able to impact the masses and human society through conscious activity. This is consistent with the Dialectical Materialist conception of human history which states that human consciousness can impact the objective world through conscious labor activities.
>
> Historical Materialism also recognizes that leaders and "great" people emerge from the masses and from the material forces of history. That is to say, every period of class struggle will eventually lead to leaders emerging to impact the rest of society and to develop ideologies which will lead to social revolution. It must be understood that individual leaders, themselves, do not "create" history and do not have any sort of metaphysical/mystical properties such as are ascribed by the "great man" theory of history.
>
> As Engels wrote in a letter to Borgius in 1894:
>
>> Men make their history themselves, but not as yet with a collective will or according to a collective plan. . . Their efforts clash, and for that very reason all such societies are governed by necessity, which is supplemented by and appears under the forms of accident. The necessity which here asserts itself amidst all accident is again ultimately economic necessity. This is where the so-called great men come in for treatment. That such and such a man and precisely that man arises at that particular time in that given country is of course pure accident. But cut him out and there will be a demand for a substitute, and this substitute will be found, good or bad, but in the long run he will be found. That Napoleon, just that particular Corsican, should have been the military dictator whom the French Republic, exhausted by its own war, had rendered necessary, was an accident; but that, if a Napoleon had been lacking, another would have filled the place, is proved by the fact that the man has always been found as soon as he became necessary: Caesar, Augustus, Cromwell, etc.
>
> Scientific Socialism demands that all Scientific Socialists strive to become leaders and to seek greatness by developing class consciousness among the masses, leading the masses, and building and organizing towards social revolution.

The history-creating role of the masses depends on objective and subjective conditions, which include (but are not limited to):
- The development level of the mode of production.
- The awareness level of each individual, each class, or each social force.
- The level of social organization.
- The nature of the social system.

Therefore, the analysis of the historical creative role of the masses needs to be considered from a comprehensive and historical perspective.

The Marxist-Leninist theory of the history-creating role of the masses—as well as the role of individuals—in the historical process has provided an important scientific methodology for cognitive and cultural activities through two significant achievements:

First, the scientific explanation of the decisive role of the masses in making history has erased the error of idealism that has long dominated human consciousness in the analysis of the motivations and forces which create human history, and has provided a scientific methodology for the study and assessment of history through the analysis of the dialectical relations between the masses and individuals.

Second the explanation of the decisive role of the masses has provided a scientific methodology for communist parties to analyze social forces and to organize and build up the people's mass force in the socialist revolution. This allows for the alliance of the working class with the peasantry and the intelligentsia—under the leadership of the communist party—which is the basis through which all possible forces must be gathered to create great impetus in the socialist revolution all the way through to the final victory.

Humans and the History-Creating Role of the Masses

Uphold victory and enthusiastically move forward!

AFTERWORD

This concludes Part 2 of the Vietnamese curriculum of Marxism-Leninism. Parts 1 and 2 of this curriculum, taken together, constitute a full year of study for a typical Vietnamese college student. Taken together, Dialectical and Historical Materialism are the ideological foundation of all Marxist-Leninist theory and practice.

The rest of the curriculum will build upon this foundation by giving students a deeper understanding of class society and the measures that must be taken to bring about its end through social revolution. At the time of publication of this book, we at Banyan House are already in the process of translating and editing the rest of the curriculum, which consists of:

Part 3: Political Economy

This section condenses the three cardinal volumes of Capital by Karl Marx and covers three primary doctrines:

1. The doctrine of value.
2. The doctrine of surplus value.
3. The doctrines of monopolist capitalism and state monopolist capitalism.

Political Economy, in this course, can be considered the application of dialectical materialism and materialist dialectics to the analysis and understanding of the capitalist mode of production from the perspective of the socialist revolutionary movement.

Part 4: Scientific Socialism

This section relies on an established understanding of dialectical materialism, historical materialism, and political economy as a foundation for developing socialist revolution. The three chapters of this section on Scientific Socialism are:

1. The Historical Mission of the Working Class and the Socialist Revolution.
2. The Primary Social-Political Issues of the Process of Building a Socialist Revolution.
3. Realistic Socialism and Potential Socialism.

Moving Forward

We believe that this book, along with Part 1 of the curriculum, provides the reader with enough of a foundation to continue studying Marxist-Leninist works and to begin applying the principles of Historical Materialism in the analysis of human society and its historical development. That said, we highly discourage readers from *self*-study in isolation, just as we discourage individual political action. The best way to study socialism is *alongside other socialists*.

Depending on where you live, you may be able to find political education resources provided by communist parties, socialist book clubs, or other organizations. If such resources aren't available, it should be fairly easy to find study groups, workshops, and affinity groups online where you can study with like-minded comrades.

Afterword 239

"Victory will be ours"

Our most sincere hope is that you will apply what is learned from this curriculum in your daily life and in your political *practice*. As Ho Chi Minh once said:

> To study Marxism-Leninism is to learn the spirit in which one should deal with things, with other people, and with oneself.

In the following pages we provide several appendices which include reference material as well as articles and excerpts from texts which we find to be excellent examples of Historical Materialism applied to the study of humanity by Marxist-Leninist scholars from Vietnam and from the Soviet Union. As with the curriculum itself, we have provided annotations to provide context for the theoretical concepts and terminology being applied. We hope that this material will give you an even deeper insight into how Historical Materialism can be used to analyze the conditions of society and to plan and implement the work of social revolution.

In Closing

We would like to thank, one last time, Gerald Horne and Anthony Ballas for your wonderful introduction to this text as well as David Peat for your invaluable assistance in making this text legible. Finally, we want to acknowledge the monumental work of the Vietnamese scholars who wrote and revised the original text from which this volume is drawn. We also want to recognize once more the donors and supporters who have given us the precious resource of time to translate and annotate this work. If you would like to download the free digital version of this book, support future translation work, or get in touch, you can visit our website:

BanyanHouse.org

We will leave you, once again, with the immortal words of the Manifesto:

WORKERS OF THE WORLD, UNITE!
YOU HAVE NOTHING TO LOSE BUT YOUR CHAINS.

In Solidarity,

- *Luna Nguyen, Translator & Annotations*
- *Emerican Johnson, Editor, Illustrator, & Annotations*

Appendix A

DIALECTICAL MATERIALISM FUNDAMENTALS

This is a summary of the foundational elements of Dialectical Materialism and Materialist Dialectics with corresponding references to *Part 1* of this curriculum:

BASIC PAIRS OF CATEGORIES USED IN MATERIALIST DIALECTICS

Private & Common	Reason & Result	Obviousness & Randomness
See p. 128.	See p. 138.	See p. 144.
Content & Form	Essence & Phenomenon	Possibility & Reality
See p. 147.	See p. 156.	See p. 160.

THE TWO BASIC PRINCIPLES OF DIALECTICAL MATERIALISM

The Principle of General Relationships

"Materialist dialectics upholds the position that all things, phenomena, and ideas exist in mutual relationships with each other, regulate each other, transform into each other, and that nothing exists in complete isolation." From this Principle we derive the *Characteristic of Diversity in Unity* and the *Characteristic of Unity in Diversity*. See *Part 1*, p. 110.

The Principle of Development

"Development is a process that comes from within the thing-in-itself; the process of solving the contradictions within things and phenomena. Therefore, development is inevitable, objective, and occurs without dependence on human will." From this principle we derive the Characteristics of Objectiveness of Development, Generality of Development, and Diversity of Development. — See *Part 1*, p. 124.

THE THREE UNIVERSAL LAWS OF MATERIALIST DIALECTICS

The Law of Transformation Between Quantity and Quality

"In nature, in a manner exactly fixed for each individual case, qualitative changes can only occur by the quantitative addition or subtraction or motion." See *Part 1*, p. 163.

The Law of Unification and Contradiction Between Opposites

"The fundamental, originating, and universal driving force of all motion and development processes is the inherent and objective contradiction which exists in all things, phenomena, and ideas." — See *Part 1*, p. 175.

The Law of Negation of Negation

"The true, natural, historical, and dialectical negation is (formally) the moving source of all development — the division into opposites, their struggle and resolution, and what is more, on the basis of experience gained, the original point is achieved again (partly in history, fully in thought), but at a higher stage." — See *Part 1*, p. 185.

Appendix B

LAWS OF HISTORICAL MATERIALISM

Law of Suitability Between Relations of Production and Productive Forces

"The development level of productive forces must suit the development level of the relations of production."

Whenever productive forces develop to such a degree that they are no longer suitable with the relations of production, this creates an objective need for the relations of production to change. Until the relations of production develop to a more suitable form, human material production processes will be inefficient and many problems will result from this lack of suitability.

See p. 42 for more information.

Law of the Economic Base Determining the Superstructure of Society

"Every economic base forms a suitable superstructure to maintain and protect the base."

Changes in the base create an objective need to have corresponding changes in the superstructure. Contradictions in the base are reflected in the contradictions within the superstructure. Struggles between different socio-political ideologies as well as conflicts between different socio-political interests all have root causes in class struggle to benefit from the economic base of society.

See p. 90 for more information.

Law of the Relationship Between Social Being and Social Consciousness

"Social being determines social consciousness, while social consciousness impacts back upon social being."

This follows the dialectical materialist understanding of the relationship of matter and consciousness. Note that in this relationship, social consciousness maintains *relative independence* (not *complete independence*) from social being.

See p. 124 for more information.

Appendix C

PRINCIPLES OF SOCIAL FORMATION THEORY AND RULES OF HISTORICAL MATERIALIST METHODOLOGY

Foundation of Dialectical Materialism	Principle of Social Formation Theory	Historical Materialist Methodology Rule
1. Dialectical Materialist conception of relationship between matter and consciousness: Matter determines consciousness.	Material production is the basis of social life, the mode of production determines the level of development of society, and therefore, material production is also the factor which determines the development level of society and the general course of human history	We must strictly avoid basing our study of the development of human society primarily on the subjective thoughts, ideas, and will of humans. We must, instead, focus on the development level of social production in general and the mode of production in particular when studying the historical development of human society.
2. Principle of General Relationships: All things, phenomena, and ideas exist in mutual relationship with each other, regulate each other, and transform each other. Nothing exists in complete isolation.	Society is not a random, mechanical combination of individuals, but a living organism. Aspects of society exist in a closely unified structural system which interact with each other. Within this system, the relations of production play the fundamental role, determining other social relations.	To accurately explain society, it is necessary to use the scientific abstraction methodology - that is, it is necessary to start from the material relations of production of a society in order to analyze various other aspects of that society.
3. Principle of Development: Development is a process that comes from within the thing-in-itself; the process of solving contradictions within things and phenomena. Therefore, development is inevitable, objective, and occurs without dependence on human will.	The development of society is a natural historical process of social development that takes place according to objective laws, and not according to human subjective will.	In order to properly understand and effectively solve social problems, it is necessary to study deeply the laws of motion and development of society.

For a full explanation of these principles and rules and how they correspond to foundations of Dialectical Materialism, see Annotation 98, p. 176.

Appendix D

STRUCTURE OF HUMAN SOCIETY

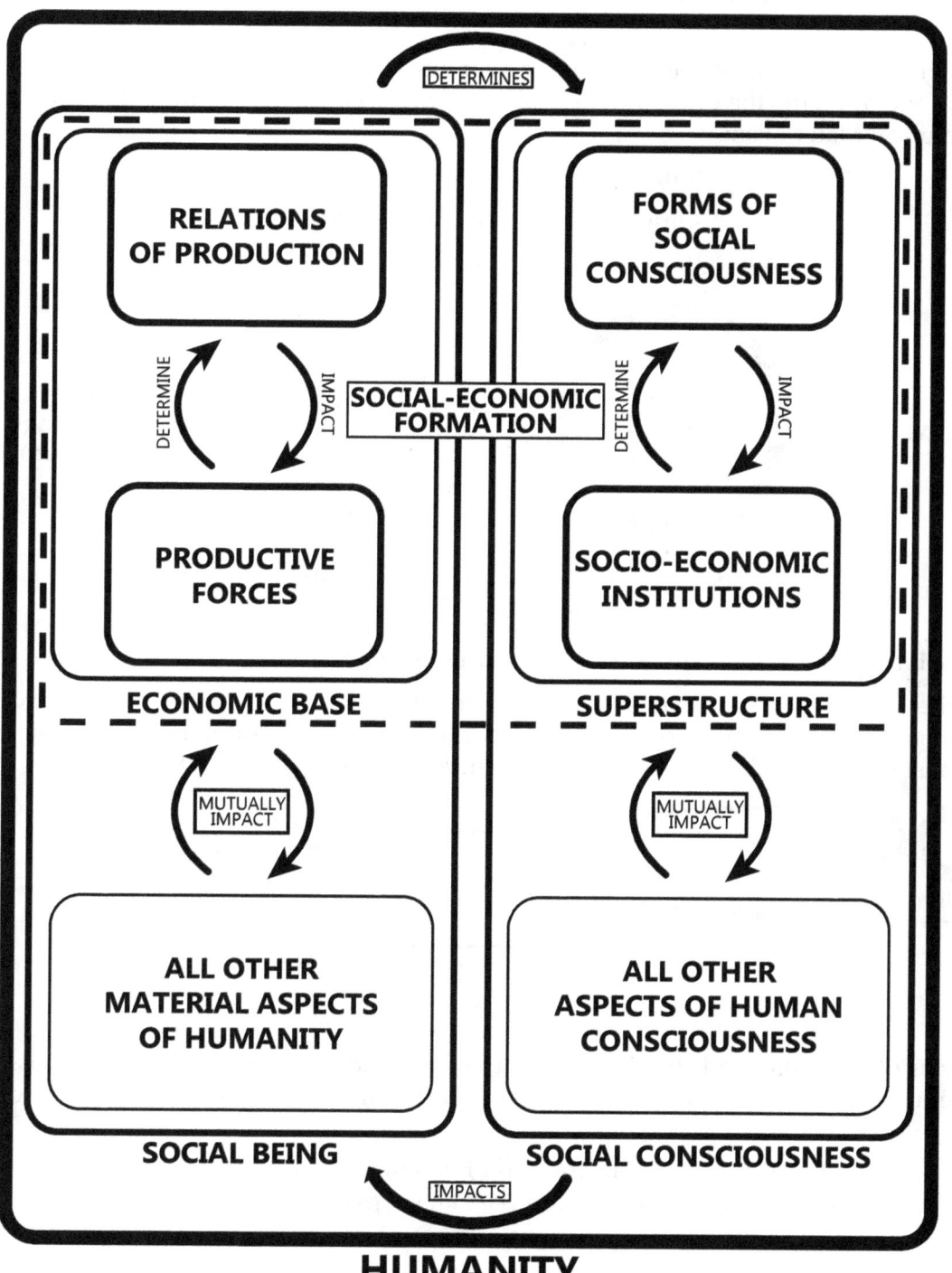

Appendix E

SUBJECTIVITY AND OBJECTIVITY IN DIALECTICAL MATERIALISM AND HISTORICAL MATERIALISM

Distinguishing between subjectivity and objectivity is critically important in understanding and applying the principles of Dialectical Materialism, Materialist Dialectics, and Historical Materialism.

Subjectivity relates to the *internal*.
Objectivity relates to the *external*.
Subjectivity and Objectivity are always *relative*.

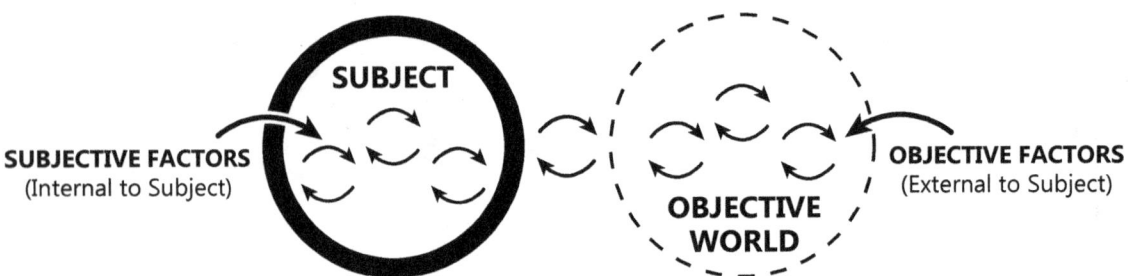

Subjectivity and objectivity are relative concepts which pertain to internal and external relationships.

Objective as the General and Subjective as the Specific

Another way of thinking about subjectivity and objectivity is in terms of the "specific" and the "general." These concepts are related to the private and common category pair of Materialist Dialectics which is discussed more in *Part 1* starting on p. 128.

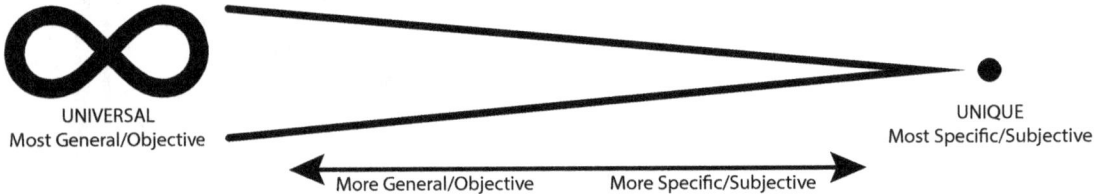

Subjectivity and objectivity also relate to specificity and generality.

In terms of generality and specificity, objective laws and factors generally encompass specific subjects. As objectivity and generality increase, more subjects are encompassed, and vice-versa.

- The most objective laws, factors, and phenomena are factors which are considered *universal* as they encompass all subjects in the universe.
- The most specific factors are considered *unique* as they have only one specific existence in the universe.

All subjects have both universal and unique aspects. This is the principle of *Unity in Diversity and Diversity in Unity* which is further explained in *Part 1* starting on p. 108.

Defining a Subject Through Internal and External Relationships

A subject is a thing, phenomenon, or idea with a stable form which exists and develops over time. Every subject is defined, changed, and developed by internal and external relationships.

- Internal (subjective) relationships drive the internal motion and development of a subject. The combination of all a subject's internal relationships essentially define that subject.
- External (objective) relationships govern the development of a subject via objective laws. External relationships impact and change a subject through processes of dialectical contradiction and negation.

External relationships can further define a subject, especially as part of an encompassing system. For example: a left shoe's external relationship with a right shoe defines it in the context of the encompassing system of "a pair of shoes."

Definition and Characteristics of the Objective

The objective encompasses everything that is external to a subject. What is considered objective depends on the subject at hand.

Examples:

- From the perspective of Bob, Alice is objective.
- Relative to the Earth, the moon is objective. Relative to our Solar System, both the Earth and the moon are subjective.

Definition of Objective Laws

Objective laws are laws which generally and universally govern everything which is relatively subjective to some objective system of relationships.

Objective Laws of Dialectical Materialism and Materialist Dialectics

Dialectical Materialism and Materialist Dialectics constitute a universal philosophy and methodology which encompasses the analysis of all things, phenomena, and ideas. As such, the universal laws of Dialectical Materialism are laws which are theorized to govern and regulate all things, phenomena, and ideas in our universe.

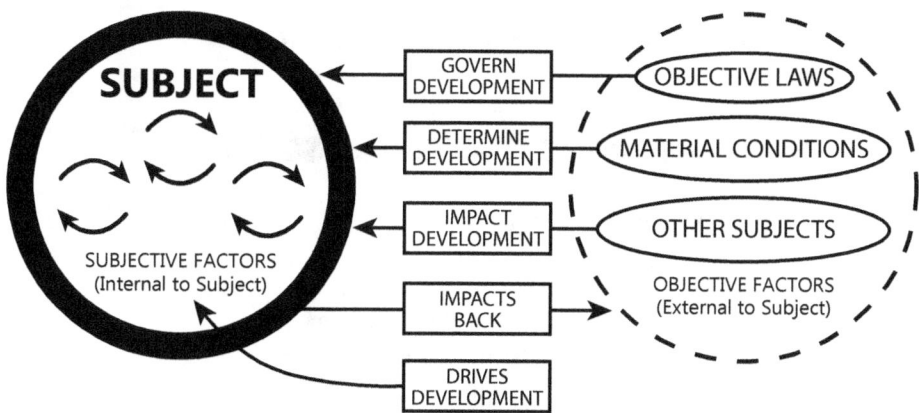

Overview of Subjective and Objective Factors and Properties.

Objective Factors of Humanity

All human beings share certain characteristics, needs, and objective factors/conditions.

Examples:

- All human beings have objective needs which must be met for survival such as food, clothing, shelter, etc.
- All human beings must engage in material production processes to meet objective needs to sustain and reproduce our own lives.
- All human beings evolved in nature; exist in dialectical unity with nature; and are governed by the same laws of nature.

Objective Laws of Historical Materialism

Historical Materialism is the application of Dialectical Materialism and Materialist Dialectics to the analysis of human society. Therefore, the objective laws of Historical Materialism are laws which are theorized to govern and regulate all of human society. In order for a law to be considered objective within the framework of Historical Materialism, it must be objective to *all of humanity*. This means that an objective law of Historical Materialism must apply to all human societies at all times and in all places throughout history.

The laws of Dialectical Materialism and Materialist Dialectics govern humanity just as they govern all other subjects in the universe. The laws and principles of Historical Materialism are derived from—and must not contradict—the laws of Dialectical Materialism and Materialist Dialectics.

Laws of Dialectical Materialism govern all subjects in our universe; Laws of Historical Materialism are rooted in the Laws of Dialectical Materialism and govern all of humanity.

Laws of Historical Materialism Reflect Laws of Dialectical Materialism

Dialectical Materialism asserts a universal conception of the relationship between matter and consciousness: that matter *determines* consciousness while consciousness can *impact* back upon the material world. Historical Materialist theory is *objective* relative to human society, but *subjective* relative to the laws of Dialectical Materialism. The laws of Historical Materialism, therefore, must uphold the universal Dialectical Materialist conception of the relationship between matter and consciousness. Based on these truths, we arrive at this summarization:

> The objective laws of Historical Materialism are laws which govern and regulate all human societies in every time and place in accordance with the universally objective laws of Dialectical Materialism and Materialist Dialectics.

Subjective Factors of Historical Materialism

Within the framework of Historical Materialism, subjective factors are any factors which are not shared universally by all of human society. Subjective factors vary from time and place and contribute to the richness and diversity of human civilization.

Examples:

- Political power levels of different classes can vary over time and lead to drastically different conditions and outcomes for revolutionary activities.
- International relations can impact greatly on human societies. War, colonization, imperialism, and other relations can negatively impact a nation, just as peaceful relations and trade can greatly benefit nations.
- Social consciousness and social psychology can vary significantly and can have great impact in the development of a society; i.e., the development of class consciousness is a prerequisite for social revolution which must be carried out before a society can move from one mode of production to the next.

Subjective Factors are Governed and Regulated by Objective Laws

Subjective factors can significantly impact the development of a specific human society, but they cannot override or contradict the objective laws of Historical Materialism.

- Objective conditions determine the existence of any and every human society. In particular, the economic base of human society plays a determining role in the development of human society because economic processes of material production allow human beings to survive and reproduce in the natural world. As such, the objective laws of Historical Materialism govern and regulate all human societies regardless of subjective factors.
- Subjective factors must also be considered in the analysis of any and every human society because subjective/internal relationships drive the motion and development of every society (just as internal relationships drive the motion and development of all things, phenomena, and ideas).
- Subjective *laws* do exist, but by their nature they are not universal, nor do they pertain to all aspects of human society. Whereas objective laws are inherently eternal, many subjective laws may change and develop over time. Objective laws govern and regulate subjective laws.

Properly Assessing Objectivity and Subjectivity

Our analysis of human society must avoid errors of objectivity and subjectivity:

- We must not absolutize the objective nor should we ignore the subjective. To do so leads to errors of mechanical materialism, empiricism, etc. Such errors falsely assert that only objective factors and laws matter in the development processes of humanity while neglecting to account for subjective factors.
- We must not absolutize the subjective nor should we ignore the objective. To do so leads to errors of idealism and false conceptions of history such as "Great Man Theory." Such errors falsely assert that human consciousness and other subjective factors fully determine the historical development of humanity which contradicts the objective laws of Dialectical Materialism, Materialist Dialectics, and Historical Materialism.

In our analysis of the historical development of humanity, we must properly comprehend the relationship between the objective and the subjective:

- Objective laws govern and regulate human societies, while subjective factors can impact back upon the development path of a specific social-economic formation.
- Objective social existence determines subjective social consciousness but social consciousness can impact back upon social existence.
- The objective economic base objectively determines the development of the subjective superstructure of society, but the superstructure has significant impact on the course of development of a social-economic formation.
- The development of subjective social consciousness is a vital prerequisite to the objective economic transitioning from one stage of development of the mode of production to the next.

The Subjective Role of the Revolutionary Leader

As Marx pronounced in his "Theses on Feurbach:"

> The philosophers have only interpreted the world, in various ways. The point, however, is to change it.

Historical Materialism as an analytical methodology exists to guide the working class to social revolution. This theory empowers the working class by properly teaching us that we have the capability to impact the development of human society through our subjective conscious activities and by helping us understand the objective laws which govern those activities.

The historical mission of the working class is to engage in social revolution which will end capitalism and, eventually, develop humanity into a stateless, classless society. Before such a social revolution can take place, class consciousness must be developed to a high degree. As practitioners of Scientific Socialism, our mission is to understand the subjective role we play as leaders in fulfilling the historical mission of the working class. We must struggle to build class consciousness among the working class with the goal of enacting social revolution, building a dictatorship of the proletariat, and eventually ending class society altogether.

General Vo Nguyen Giap briefing President Ho Chi Minh on the Viet Bac Campaign in 1947. This was the first major victory of the Viet Nam People's Army against the French colonialists under General Giap's command. Photo Source: Archive of Vietnam People's Army

Vo Nguyen Giap (1911-2013), the great general who led Vietnam People's Army to victory against Japan, France, and the USA, had this to say about the importance of distinguishing between objective and subjective factors in his book People's War, People's Army:

> To make everyone thoroughly understand the strategic guiding principle of long-term war was not only a big work of organisation militarily and economically but also a process of ideological education and struggle within the Party and among the people against erroneous tendencies which appeared many a time in the years of the Resistance War. These were pessimistic defeatism which presumed that our country being small, our population thin, our economy backward and our armed forces young and weak, we would be unable to face the enemy, let alone perseveringly to wage a long Resistance War. These were subjectivism, loss of patience, eagerness to win swiftly which came out in the plans of operations of a number of localities at the start of the Resistance War which were unwilling to withdraw their force to preserve our main force, and in their plan of general counter-offensive put forth in 1950 when this was not yet permitted by objective and subjective conditions.

As Vo goes on to explain, a proper understanding of subjective conditions is key to revolutionary victory:

> If guidance in struggle and organisation was not precise, that is to say did not correctly follow the guiding principle of both determination and carefulness, and of knowing how to estimate the subjective conditions and compare the revolutionary forces with the counter-revolutionary forces, we would certainly have met with difficulty and failure.

The subjective factor of revolutionary leadership, therefore, plays a vitally important role in fulfilling the mission of the working class, but we must not over-emphasize or absolutize this role. We as human beings have the ability to impact the world through subjective will, but our actions are governed by objective laws and conditions. For this reason, we must study the objective laws of Dialectical Materialism, Materialist Dialectics, and Historical Materialism. We must understand the laws and characteristics of motion and development and apply them properly in our revolutionary practice. At the same time, we must avoid absolutizing or over-emphasizing objective laws, factors, and conditions in the development of human society.

- Over-emphasizing and absolutizing subjective factors (such as our role as revolutionary leaders) will result in errors of idealism such as commandism.
- Over-emphasizing and absolutizing objective factors or neglecting the vital role we play as revolutionary leaders will result in errors of vulgar materialism such as tailism.

By properly understanding, assessing, and implementing the theoretical concepts of subjectivity and objectivity we can hasten the development of class consciousness and social revolution and the fulfillment of the historical mission of the working class as revolutionary leaders.

Appendices 251

Vo Nguyen Giap, the Great General of Vietnam.

Appendix F

HISTORICAL DEVELOPMENT OF VIETNAM

> **EDITOR'S NOTE:**
> The following passage is from an article called "The Era of the Rising Nation and its Historical Requirements," written by former member of the Communist Party of Vietnam's Central Committe, Dr. Phung Huu Phu, and published in the Vietnamese journal *Communist Review*. It briefly outlines the modern historical development of the Socialist Republic of Vietnam.

Over the past 95 years, under the leadership of the Communist Party of Vietnam which was founded and developed by President Ho Chi Minh, the Vietnamese people have gone through two glorious eras:

The first era is the Era of Independence, Freedom, and Building Socialism (1930 - 1975), which started in 1930 when the Communist Party of Vietnam was born, leading to the great victory of the August Revolution in 1945 and great feats in the resistance wars against invaders (1946 - 1975) and important achievements in the construction of socialism in the North from 1954 - 1975.

The second era is the Era of National Reunification, Renovation, and Development (1975 - 2025), starting with the great victory of the resistance war against the invading American imperialists, which unified the country, bringing the whole nation to socialism in 1975, creating a solid premise for the country under the leadership of the Party to carry out the renovation process starting from the 6th Party Congress in 1986. This era has been a strong and comprehensive development step for the country.

Now, Vietnam is entering the third era, the Era of the Rising Nation [also known as the Era of Rising], which will officially begin with the 14th National Party Congress, marking 40 years of renovation (1986 - 2026).

Each era objectively presents historical requirements which the nation and people must meet in order to successfully implement the identified strategic goals.

In the Era of Independence, Freedom, and Building Socialism (1930 - 1975), Vietnam's vital goals were to abolish the oppressive and exploitative regime of colonialism and feudalism, to become an independent nation, and to move forward to build a new social regime. These strategic goals required the broadest gathering and unification of the masses, leveraging the material conditions of the times, to smash the domination of imperialism and feudalism; to gain and maintain independence and freedom; and to build the initial premises of socialism. Under the correct leadership of the Party, the Vietnamese people highly promoted patriotism and revolutionary heroism, successfully resolved the historical requirements, and excellently fulfilled the strategic goals of the era.

In the Era of National Reunification, Renovation and Development (1975 - 2025), Vietnam's top goals were to overcome poverty and backwardness, to escape from poverty and underdevelopment, to improve the lives of the people, and to establish a worthy international position. Those strategic goals established the historical requirement of comprehensive and synchronous renovation in all areas of social life, the promotion of industrialization and modernization of the country, and the proactive integration of Vietnam into the international community. After nearly fifty years of national reunification and 40 years of renovation, Vietnam has now successfully fulfilled the historical requirements, has successfully renovated, has successfuly escaped from poverty and underdevelopment, has made great achievements of historical significance, and has created a new international position for Vietnam with power, potential, and prestige.

The historical achievements which were made through these two eras of struggle and persistent creative labor have created the premise and solid foundation for Vietnam to enter the third era: the Era of the Rising Nation, starting from the 14th National Congress of the Party. As General Secretary of the Communist Party of Vietnam To Lam wrote:

> This is the era of development, the era of prosperity under the leadership and governance of the Party, successfully building a socialist Vietnam. The destination of the Era of Rising is a rich people, a strong country, a socialist society, standing shoulder to shoulder with the world powers. The top priority in the new era is to successfully implement our strategic goals: by 2030, Vietnam will become a developing country with modern industry and high average income, and by 2045 Vietnam will become a developed socialist country with high income.

The goal of the third era is the synthesis of the goals of the two previous eras, taken to new heights, reflecting the qualitative development of the goal of national independence associated with socialism, and of the dialectical movement of "independence, freedom, and happiness."[1] The new era sets out special historical requirements, requiring the entire Party, the entire people, and the entire military to have deep awareness, determination, and drastic determination to realize our aspiration to develop a prosperous and happy country.

Timeline of the Historical Development of the Socialist Republic of Vietnam

1920 - 1930: Pre-Revolutionary Era
- 1920: Ho Chi Minh discovers Marxism-Leninism.
- 1920 - 1930: Ho Chi Minh and Vietnamese communists lay the groundwork for revolution.

1930 - 1975: Era of Independence, Freedom, and Building Socialism
- 1930 - 1940: Founding of the Communist Party of Vietnam under French colonialism.
- 1940 - 1945: Fascist Japan occupies Vietnam; communist forces resist and repel the invasion.
- 1945 - 1954: War and struggle for independence from France.
- 1954 - 1975: War and struggle to expel imperialist USA.

1975 - 2025: Era of National Reunification, Renovation, and Development
- 1975 - 1986: Subsidizing Period (see Annotation 85, starting on p. 157).
- 1986 - 2025: Doi Moi Period (see Annotation 4 of Appendix G, p. 260).

Present: Era of the Rising Nation
- Goals of becoming a developing country with modern industry and high average income by 2030 and a developed socialist country with high income by 2045.

---

1 This is the motto of the Socialist Republic of Vietnam.

Appendix G

RESOLVING THE PROBLEM OF THE RELATIONSHIP BETWEEN DEVELOPING PRODUCTIVE FORCES AND GRADUALLY BUILDING AND COMPLETING SOCIALIST RELATIONS OF PRODUCTION TO MAKE SURE THEY SUIT VIETNAM'S REALITY

> **EDITOR'S NOTE:**
>
> We have included this article as an example of a practical application of historical materialist and dialectical materialist methodologies as developed by contemporary socialist theorists. Concepts which are mentioned or applied within this text will be annotated with references to related sections of this book. Words that are underlined relate to terms and concepts which can be found in the glossary/index for further study.
>
> This article was originally published in 2014 in *Communist Review*, a political journal of the Communist Party of Vietnam. The author, Dr. Le Huu Nghia, is the Vice-Chairman of the Central Theoretical Council of the Communist Party of Vietnam. This council reviews programs and policies of the Party to ensure a solid grounding in principles of Dialectical and Historical Materialist theory and practice. At the time this was written, over a decade ago, Vietnam was about fourteen years into the era of "Socialism-Oriented Market Economy." This Vietnamese economic model is described in detail in p. 70.
>
> In this article, Dr. Le describes the political-economic development of Vietnam using Historical Materialist analysis. This includes an assessment of challenges and struggles which Vietnam's people have faced, an addressing of previous failures of ideology and practice, and recommendations for policies and programs moving forward. We hope that this document of modern history will give insight into how governing communists use the theoretical methodologies of Dialectical Materialism and Historical Materialism to guide political-economic practice in the real world.

Our Party's platform for national construction during the transition period to socialism (which was supplemented and developed in 2011) has called for special attention to understanding and resolving important relationships in our society, including the relationship "between the development of productive forces and the gradual construction and improvement of socialist relations of production."[2] Recognizing and navigating this relationship and its context within Vietnam's reality will contribute to the achievement of our goals on the path to socialism.

The essence of the law and its expression in practical conditions

The dialectical relationship between the productive forces and the relations of production is defined by a fundamental law of motion and development of human society: the law that relations of production must suit the level of development of productive forces.[3]

---

2   Platform of the Communist Party of Vietnam (2011).
3   This law, also known as the Law of Suitability, is defined and further discussed on p. 47.

Creatively apply Marxism-Leninism and Ho Chi Minh Thought to achieve great victory for the Doi Moi Career!

Good rice, fat pigs, chicken in flocks. Contribute to building a prosperous village

This law was discovered by Karl Marx and is presented in many of his works. This is a fundamental law which pervasively affects the entire course of human history. This law, together with other historical materialist laws, accounts for historical development from lower to higher levels, and from lower social-economic formations to higher social-economic formations.[4] According to this law, the development of social-economic formations is a historical-natural process.

> **Appendix G, Annotation 1**
>
> This process is described as "historical-natural" because it reflects both the social aspect ("historical") and the natural aspect of humanity. The social and natural aspects of human society are described more on p. 212.

The productive forces and the relations of production are the two constituent parts of the mode of production.

The principles of Historical Materialism assert that the relations of production must suit the level of development of the productive forces. To achieve this suitability the relations of production must reflect the level of development of the productive forces while creating conditions and motivations for further development of the productive forces.

It is necessary to understand suitability in a dialectical – as well as in a historical – sense. We must study it as a process in motion: in a dynamic state. Due to its characteristics, the productive forces are a dynamic factor which change quickly, whereas the relations of production are a relatively stable factor which change more slowly. Therefore, the productive forces and the relations of production are two dialectical opposites in the mode of production.

> **Appendix G, Annotation 2**
>
> Dialectical Materialism holds that all motion, change, and development is the result of contradiction. Contradiction arises from a relationship between two subjects. Every relationship leads to change and development in both opposite sides of every contradiction. This is why, in the Dialectical Materialist framework, subjects are defined by internal and external relationships which drive development.
>
> The mode of production is defined by an internal relationship between the relations of production and the productive forces. As "opposites" in this relationship, both the relations of production and the productive forces develop and change over time. This is what drives the development of the mode of production. By extension, the development of the mode of production determines the development of the economic base of society, which in turn drives the development of human society in general.

Marx proved the decisive role of the productive forces in determining the relations of production, while also pointing out the relative independence of the relations of production in relation to the productive forces.[5]

The relations of production have the following characteristics:

---

4   The historical tendency for human society to develop from lower social-economic formations to higher social-economic formations is discussed more on p. 33.
5   See Chapter 3, Section 2, p. 131.

- They impact back on productive forces.
- They regulate the social purpose of production.
- They influence the benefits of producers, thereby forming a system of factors that either promote or inhibit the development of productive forces.

The law that relations of production must suit the level of development of productive forces can be understood as the most fundamental law, the root law, of social development. Social transformation and development ultimately originate from this law.

Unlike natural laws, social laws are laws of human activities.[6] They exist through human activities and regulate human activities and are associated with specific practical conditions and historical circumstances of humanity. Therefore, the understanding and application of social laws, in general, and the law of the suitability of relations of production with the development level of productive forces, in particular, must be suitable to the specific practical conditions of each nation at each stage of national development as well as the motion and development of the international situation.

Consider Russia after the October Revolution of 1917: the country had experienced a moderate period of capitalist development. While fighting the civil war and enemies in foreign nations at the same time, Vladimir Ilyich Lenin and the Bolsheviks thought that it was possible to use wartime communist policy to move rapidly towards communism. However, the social-economic crisis of the Spring of 1921 showed that this was a mistake. Lenin wrote:

> We expected—or perhaps it would be truer to say that we presumed without having given it adequate consideration—to be able to organize the state production and the state distribution of products on communist lines in a small-peasant country directly as ordered by the proletarian state. Experience has proved that we were wrong.[7]

Lenin criticized the delusional disease[8] at that time for not being practical in the application of law. He decided to implement the New Economic Policy (NEP), which consisted of such measures as replacing the food requisition regime with the food tax regime, encouraging the development of commodity-monetary relations and market relations, allowing the development of private business, appeasement policies, allowing the use of bourgeois experts, and so on.

Also, consider China in the period from 1957 to 1960 during the period of the "Three Red Flags," the "People's Commune," and the "Great Leap Forward." This was a period of subjectivist and idealist disease that destroyed the productive forces of a poor and undeveloped country. It is now clear that an improper understanding and application of the dialectical relationship between the productive forces and the relations of production as well as measures which were inconsistent with the practical conditions came at a cost.

---

6 Dialectical Materialist conceptions of humanity hold that humankind are a part of nature, but also distinct from nature. This constitutes a dialectical relationship in which humanity and nature define each other. This is explained more on p. 212.

7 *Fourth Anniversary of the October Revolution*, V. I. Lenin, 1921.

8 In Vietnamese, the term "disease" is often used to refer to deviations from correct dialectical materialist analysis and methodology.

<u>**Appendix G, Annotation 3**</u>

Vietnam's *History Textbook for 9th Grade Students* summarizes this history:

> For a period of twenty years, from 1959 to 1978, China was in turmoil. The starting event was the introduction of the "Three Red Flags" [also known as the Three Red Banners] path with the purpose of quickly succeeding at building socialism.
>
> One of the "Three Red Flags" was the "Great Leap Forward" movement - motivating the masses to produce iron and steel with the goal of quickly achieving 10 million tons of steel and 20 million tons of iron. In only two months (November and December of 1958), the whole nation built over 1 million small scale steel furnaces. After four months, 11 millions tons of steel was produced but much of it was scrap due to low quality.
>
> The economy became chaotic, production decreased, and people's lives were in chaos, with famine breaking out everywhere.

The *International Relations Handbook*, published by Ho Chi Minh City University of Social Sciences and Agriculture, describes this history in more detail:

> The Great Leap Forward was a campaign which was instituted between 1958 and 1961 by Chinese leaders, especially Mao Zedong, to mobilize the masses in order to promote rapid agricultural and industrial development. Unfortunately, this plan failed, leading to one of the worst famines in history. Although the first five-year plan (1953-1957) following the Soviet model achieved some success, the economy still showed many weaknesses, especially in agricultural production. This left China unable to secure export output and to supply food to its growing urban workforce. Feeling dissatisfied with the Soviet-style development model that prioritized heavy industrial development, Mao Zedong believed that mobilizing mass forces could allow China to develop industry and agriculture in parallel with each other.
>
> The Great Leap Forward became national policy in October of 1957. It began with the mobilization of large numbers of farmers to participate in irrigation projects throughout the winter of 1957-1958, and then promoted the transformation of collective organizations into "people's communes" in 1958. In August 1958, under the direction of Mao Zedong, the Central Committee of the Communist Party of China officially announced that such people's communes would be established in all rural areas of China. Mao saw this action as a step forward against the Soviet Union in reforming society, and believed that China would become the most advanced model for world communism. By November of 1958, about 98% of the rural population was organized into about 26,000 communes. Each rural commune had an average of 5,000 households, or 25,000 inhabitants. All property such as land, buildings, and livestock were collectivised and all administrative and productive activities were controlled by the communes. Several urban communes were also established in 1958.
>
> Besides the goal of increasing food production, the National People's Congress (National Assembly) of China in 1958 also identified another goal of the Great Leap Forward program to be a rapid increase in steel production. Mao Zedong hoped that China's Great Leap Forward in Steel Production would surpass Brit-

> **Appendix G, Annotation 3 (continued)**
>
> ain's Steel Production within fifteen years. In August 1958, the Politburo decided to attempt to double steel production within a year. To realize these goals, forces were massed throughout the country, including from officials, professors, students, workers, and farmers. According to estimates, about one million farmers had to leave the fields to participate in the "steel furnace in every garden" project to achieve the set goals. By the fall of 1958 there were about 600,000 such cottage industry steel furnaces throughout China. These furnaces consumed almost all the metal that could be found including kitchen utensils, steel springs, beds, steel fixtures, and so on. A tremendous amount of wood resources such as doors, tables and chairs, furniture, and forest timber was used to fuel the furnaces. The product of this program was low quality steel but it was officially reported to be high quality steel.
>
> Meanwhile, at the central level, ministries and branches lost the ability to monitor agricultural production because the work of collecting statistics and planning was delegated to lower units. At the same time, local administrations falsified agricultural production reports to the central government, claiming bumper harvests despite the fact that crops had failed due to wrong policies, farmers leaving the fields to process steel, and natural disasters.
>
> The subjectivist and idealist errors which led to the problems of this time period were similar to those which Vietnamese communists would make in the 1970s. These errors are futher described below.

In our country [Vietnam], in the period from the IV Congress (1976) through the years just before the VI Congress (1986) of the Party, we suffered from the disease of being subjective, idealist, hasty, and stagnant due to a failure to observe objective laws - especially the Law of Suitability between relations of production with the level of development of the productive forces. We failed to grasp the practical conditions of an economically underdeveloped, poor, and backward country as we dreamed to create advanced relations of production to pave the way for the productive forces to develop. And the results were, of course, the opposite of what we wanted. As the VI Congress of the Communist Party of Vietnam reported:

> Practical experience demonstrated: the productive forces are constrained not only in cases where relations of production are backward, but also when relations of production develop asynchronously, where there are factors that are too advanced compared to the level of development of the productive forces.

At that time, we subjectively wanted to create relations of production that were too advanced in comparison to the level of development of productive forces. This made the contradiction between productive forces and relations of production acute, bringing the country into a social-economic crisis. We had shown signs of impatience when we immediately wanted to abolish non-socialist economic sectors and quickly turn the private capitalist economy fully into a state-owned economy. Moreover, we held on to the bureaucratic, centralized subsidy model for too long, which stifled the development of the country. We were both subjectively impatient and stagnantly conservative, and these two defective characteristics, together, hindered the progress of the revolution.

Appendix G, Annotation 4

The Subsidizing Period was the period of time which began in 1975, immediately following the end of the war between Vietnam and the United States. During the Subsidizing Period, which lasted until 1986, Vietnamese communist leadership attempted to rapidly transform Vietnam into a moneyless, classless society. This period was hampered by *voluntarism,* which is an over-emphasis on subjective will. During the Subsidizing Period, Vietnamese communists attempted to immediately and abruptly abolish all forms of market economy and private ownership at once. Such measures led to a contradiction between relations of production and the level of development of productive forces. In other words, the productive forces of Vietnam were not developed enough to be suitable with the relations of production which Vietnamese communists attempted to implement. The two biggest examples of these policies were:

Money was abolished and replaced by a ration stamp system. With this system, the people would receive all life necessities (such as food, medicine, fertilizer, fabric, etc.) from the government. However, the government did not have enough material resources available to sufficiently supply the people with what was needed, so this led to material privation of the people as well as the establishment of black markets and illegal currencies. This also led to corruption as many bureaucrats who were responsible for dispensing rations took advantage of their positions, accepted bribes, participated in unequal distribution of resources, etc. Coming out of the wartime period, Vietnam simply did not have enough productive output to properly implement such a rationing system. In the end, this ration system led to inequality, hardship, and dissatisfaction for Vietnamese workers.

The abolishment of private ownership of land, which was replaced by communal collectivization of farmland at the village-scale. In the 1950s, Vietnam's Communist government instituted land reform which seized land from feudal lords, colonial occupiers, and capitalists and distributed to peasant families for personal use and cultivation. During this time, each peasant had the right to work on their own plot of land and to keep what they needed to survive, with the surplus given over to the government to support the war effort. In 1975, at the end of the war, the practice of individual land usage was ended. Each village was organized into a commune and all land was to be managed and cultivated by the entire commune collectively. Vietnamese farmers at this time were uneducated in collective management of land and the productive forces of agricultural production were very low. These collective farming operations were poorly organized and individual farmers lacked sufficient incentive, instruction, and material resources to carry out successful collective operations. In addition, a lack of mechanized farm equipment and other modern material resources meant that farm yields were very low. Many farmers saw this system as unfair, since all the products of each farmer's work were collectively taken by the government for redistribution, and this redistribution was also poorly organized and fraught with corruption. This led to dissatisfaction among farm workers and a shortage of food output which severely hindered Vietnam's development. Both of these policies constituted misalignment between the productive forces and relations of production. The war-torn economic base of Vietnam was incapable of producing enough material resources to sustain a massive state superstructure that could oversee a completely planned economy. For these reasons, the attempt to bypass markets entirely and skip directly to a moneyless society failed.

Appendix G, Annotation 4 (continued)

"To build and protect the country, sell more food to the government."
This propaganda poster from the Subsidizing Period reflects the system of collectivized farming which was implemented at the time.

General Secretary of the Communist Party of Vietnam Truong Chinh addressed these mistakes in a speech delivered to the Hanoi Party Congress on October 19, 1986:

> In recent years, we have made the mistake of leftist voluntarism, going against objective laws. That mistake is reflected in the desire to develop heavy industry on a large scale beyond our capacity, maintaining a massive superstructure beyond the capacity of the infrastructure, wanting to quickly eliminate non-socialist economic components... When we made mistakes, we were too conservative, lacking the courage and determination to correct them.

These errors of voluntarism, subjectivism, and idealism all stemmed from good nitentions: the Communist Party of Vietnam wanted to achieve a fully socialist society as quickly as possible and to force socialist relations of production through force-of-will alone without properly accounting for the level of development of productive forces.

Vietnam began attempting to correct these problems with the institution of the Doi Moi ("renovation") reforms in 1986. These reforms focused on opening up Vietnam's economy in an attempt to transition towards a market economy regulated by socialist oversight and controls. This meant restoring a monetary system, allowing Vietnamese people to open their own private businesses, and allowing workers to cultivate their own plots of land. A taxation system was also slowly and carefully implemented

> **Appendix G, Annotation 4 (continued)**
> to fund government operations and social welfare programs. Importantly, capitalist entities were restricted from owning land. Only working farmers were given the right to privately use and cultivate farmland, and every farmer was given a plot of land to cultivate free of charge. This was essential to maintaining socialist characteristics in Vietnam because, even to this day, about 70% of Vietnamese people are farmers.

The misunderstanding of the Law of Suitability which we committed demonstrates the backwardness of theoretical perception and in the application of objective social laws during the Subsidizing Period. We had improper prejudice against the laws of commodity production and disregard for the summation of practical experience. Life taught us a poignant lesson: that we can't be in such a rush that we break the rules.

From the above examples, it is possible to draw some conclusions about common mistakes in perceiving and applying the Law of Suitability Between Relations of Production and Productive Forces, i.e., the dialectical relationship between the productive forces and the relations of production. These common mistakes include:

- Failing to comprehensively and historically understand relations of production.
- Demonizing private ownership and desiring to quickly establish public ownership at any cost.
- Considering private ownership to be outside the essence of socialism and therefore demanding that it be quickly abolished.
- Disregarding organizational-managerial and distributional relations.
- Disregarding the motivation of personal interests of workers.
- Failing to properly understand the dialectical relationship between productive forces and relations of production.
- Separating relations of production from production forces.
- Exaggerating relations of production while underestimating productive forces.
- Disregarding the development and opening up of productive forces.
- Wanting to create advanced relations of production in an attempt to quickly pave the way for the productive forces.
- Wanting to achieve many of the goals of socialism too quickly amidst the conditions of the economic backwardness of a young workers' state which has just gained power.
- Maintaining the bureaucratic subsidizing model for too long
- Ignoring the theories of value, commodity-monetary relations, and market mechanisms, thereby forming a mechanism that restrains the development of productive forces.
- Wanting to create a conformity in all relations of production in different production sectors and different regions/localities (deltas, mountainous areas, remote areas, etc.) with very different levels of development of productive forces, i.e. over-conforming relations of production.

All of the above common mistakes stem from an incorrect perception of the nature of the law that relations of production must suit the level of productive forces as well as a failure to take into account practical conditions when planning and implementing policies, which will inevitably lead to failure.

Doi Moi renovation is the process of properly and gradually understanding and applying the Law of Suitability Between Relations of Production and Productive Forces in the practical conditions of both Vietnam and the wider international situation.

At the VI Congress (1986), which started the Doi Moi renovation, our Party criticized the disease of being subjective and idealist by violating objective social laws, including - first and foremost - the law that relations of production must suit the level of development of the productive forces. Since then, our Congress has learned the important lesson that "the Party must always come from reality, and must respect and act according to objective laws," and must "make relations of production suitable to the level of development of the productive forces, and always contribute to promoting the development of the productive forces." The Doi Moi renovation is essentially a return to adherence to objective social laws, and to the basic principles of Marxism-Leninism which are suitable with the reality of the country and the times.

Over the past 30 years, by implementing the Party's renovation path which is more in line with objective social laws, our people have achieved great and historically significant achievements on the path of building and defending the homeland. In particular, we have made the following great achievements in the perception and application of the Law of Suitability Between Relations of Production and Productive Forces in Vietnam:

- We have become more aware of the dialectical relationship between the productive forces and the relations of production as well as the relevance and contradiction between the two in each stage of development.

- Regarding the economic characteristics of the socialist society that our people have started building, we have moved from the formula "having a highly developed economy based on modern productive forces and public ownership of the main means of production" (1991 Party Program) to the formula "having a highly developed economy based on modern productive forces and suitable progression in relations of production." (Supplementary Party Program of 2011). "Suitability," here, refers to suitability with the level of development of productive forces as well as suitability with Vietnam's objective conditions and socialist orientation.

- We have constantly improved the guideline of developing a socialist-oriented market economy with many forms of ownership, many economic sectors, and many forms of business organization and distribution. All legal economic sectors are important constituent parts of the economy and are equal under the law. They develop together and cooperate in healthy competition. In implementing this guideline through the years of Doi Moi, our Party and State have promulgated many policies and laws to diversify forms of relations of production in order to encourage and promote the development of the productive forces, unleash all potential of production, and create more motivations for workers. These policies and laws relate to innovation and improvement of quality and efficiency of the state economy, especially state-owned enterprises, as well as consolidation and development of the collective economy, the promotion of the private economy, the strong attraction of foreign-investment, improvement of the quality and efficiency of state-owned joint stock enterprises, the development of a mixed economy, and so on.

- The Party and State have also promulgated many policies and laws to improve aspects of the new socialist-oriented relations of production in terms of ownership, organization, management, and distribution. The Party promulgated the Land Law (amended in 2013) which provides for ownership and owner representation as it pertains to land, delineates the rights of land owners and users of means of production, and the State's management rights in the economic field, and determines the role of economic management of the State through orientation, regulation, plans, strategies, and development programs. The Party has diversified forms of distribution according to economic efficiency, and has managed distribution of resources through the social security and welfare system.

- The Party and State have many guidelines and measures to promote industrialization and modernization in order to develop productive forces and create "material cores" for new relations of production. The Party invested to build infrastructure with a number of modern projects, focusing on the transportation system and large urban infrastructure. The Party also implemented economic restructuring towards industrialization and modernization; development of a number of mechanical industries such as shipbuilding, transportation, mining, construction and processing; application of modern scientific and technological achievements, especially information technology; human resource development, especially high-quality human resources; and so on. At the same time, the Party renovated the growth model, restructured the economy; promoted industrialization and modernization in association with the development of the knowledge economy, and improved the competitiveness of the economy, enterprises, and goods and services.

- The Party proactively integrated internationally to bring into full play internal resources, take advantage of external forces, learn and apply achievements in science and technology, knowledge economy, international experience, and so on, in order to develop and modernize our productive forces and consolidate and improve new relations of production. In the years of Doi Moi, our Party and State have adopted many guidelines, policies and measures to strengthen and expand international cooperation, participate in bilateral relations and multilateral organizations such as ASEAN, APEC, ASEM, WTO etc., to strongly attract foreign investment capital (FDI, ODA etc.), to strongly promote trade and investment, to expand import and export markets, and to effectively exploit international cooperation and capital resources. Vietnam has established diplomatic relations with over 170 countries and trade relations with 230 countries and territories, and signed more than 90 bilateral trade agreements and nearly 60 agreements on investment encouragement and protection. Vietnam's international economic integration is deepening.

However, besides the achievements that we had during the recent years of analyzing and resolving the relationship between productive forces and relations of production, there have also been many limitations and weaknesses, new contradictions and new unsuitability between productive forces and relations of production that hinder the development of both productive forces and relations of production.

Although the country has come out of underdevelopment and entered a lower-middle-income country status, it is still a poor country and economically backward. The risk of our economy falling further behind the world and the region is increasing. The goal that by 2020 our country will basically become an industrialized country is difficult to achieve. Currently, the industries of mechanics and manufacturing are underdeveloped, accounting for a very small proportion of GDP. Labor productivity, efficiency, quality, and competitiveness are low, aggregate productivity factor (TFP) is very low. Such a weak productive force will dictate the level and quality of the relations of production and make what we call socialist relations of production impossible to achieve.

Appendix G, Annotation 5

According to an article[9] by Dr. Nguyen Hong Son, Deputy Head of the Central Economic Commission of the Communist Party of Vietnam, this goal of building an industrialized economy in Vietnam was successfully achieved in 2020.

As of the year 2025, the Era of Doi Moi Renovation has come to a successful end and Vietnam is now entering the "Era of the Rising Nation" with the goal of becoming a developing country with modern industry and high average income by 2030 and the goal of becoming a developed socialist country with high income by 2045. The Era of the Rising Nation is defined in more detail in Appendix F, p. 252.

We have not paid comprehensive and synchronous attention in building and improving all aspects of relations of production. There is still a heavy trend of changing ownership regimes rather than improving and renewing management and distribution relationships. It is impossible to call the current relations of production in our country socialist relations of production (in the true sense of the word) because our country is still in the transition period to socialism, is implementing a socialist-oriented market economy, and does not have modern industrial productive forces as the basis for new relations of production. Therefore, it is not advisable to be hasty in building relations of production, but also not to underestimate the gradual construction of relations of production in the socialist orientation, in accordance with the development level of productive forces.

In the program for national construction in the transition period to socialism (supplemented and developed in 2011) and in the 2013 Constitution, the leading role of the state economy is defined. However, in reality, the state economy has not really played a leading role, because in general, productivity, quality, efficiency are low, and have not set an example to lead other economic sectors. Many state-owned enterprises have fallen into the situation of production and business losses, corruption, waste, negativity, loss of state assets, causing a lot of anger in public opinion. State-owned enterprises current-

---

9 "Some Main Contents of the Party's Guidelines and Policies on Industrialization and Modernization Related to Industrial Transformation," published in Communist Review, a political journal of the Communist Party of Vietnam, on November 12, 2024.

ly account for 70% of social investment capital, 50% of state investment capital, 60% of credit of commercial banks and 70% of ODA capital... but the sector contributes only 37% to 38% of GDP.

State-owned enterprises have a much higher ICOR coefficient than the private sector (in the period 2006 - 2010 if calculated from investment capital, the ICOR ratio of the state sector is 9.68 and the non-state sector is 4.01, increasing over the period 2000-2005 by positions of 6.94 (state) and 2.93 (non-state), respectively. The return on capital of state-owned enterprises is lower than that of private enterprises.

> **Appendix G, Annotation 6**
>
> ICOR stands for Incremental Capital-Output Ratio and aims to measure the ratio between investment and growth. In essence, it is measure of inefficiency. A higher ICOR coefficient indicates less efficient productive output compared to initial investment
>
> What Dr. Le is pointing out, here, is that state-owned enterprises in Vietnam have been, on average, less efficient than non-state-owned enterprises in terms of productive output, and that this inefficiency has been increasing over time.

Management of state-owned enterprises is still lax, with unclear delineation of authority and responsibilities of stakeholders and their representatives, especially in terms of capital management. As a result, over time, many enterprises have engaged in rampant spending, often outside of their main industries. They are dominated by selfish interests and violate the laws. Bad debts have increased (by the end of 2012, bad debts of state-owned enterprises accounted for 11.82% of total bad debts in the credit system of organizations and 5.05% of outstanding loans to state-owned enterprises).

The collective economic sector is still small and weak, and many cooperatives in agriculture are just formalizing. They only do input and output services of production. The savings of funds of cooperatives are still very small. The level of science and technology and the scale and management level of cooperatives are very low and cannot compete with individual and household production. The share of the collective economy in GDP is small, falling continuously from 10.1% in 1995 to 5.22% in 2011.

The private sector is identified as an important motivator of the economy, contributing much to GDP growth and creating jobs for workers. However, private enterprises, mainly small and medium-sized enterprises, face many disadvantages in terms of competition, capital sources, and even discrimination in practice due to our mechanisms and policies. In recent years, due to the economic slowdown, tens of thousands of private enterprises and individuals have been dissolved or have ceased operations. The potential of the private sector is huge but we have not yet created conditions for private businesses to thrive and contribute more to society.

The foreign-invested economic sector is an important economic component in contributing to GDP growth and attracting labor resources. The proportion of the FDI sector has increased continuously from 4.2% in 1991 to 18.97% in 2011. However, this sector also has limitations, such as not investing in fields with high technology. Most foreign-invested businesses are at a level of medium technology, or even operate in outdated fields such as processing and assembly. There was little investment in agricultural and rural areas due to less attractive profits. FDI enterprises exploit cheap resources, markets, and human resources in Vietnam to serve their profit goals, leading to the phenomenon of "changing prices," manipulating accounting to falsely report losses, and so on, in order to evade taxes. Another shortcoming of foreign-invested businesses is the transfer of profits abroad.

The above limitations and weaknesses of economic sectors in relations of production have hindered the development of productive forces. The above situation has both objective and subjective causes.

Objectively, the shift from bureaucratic centralization and subsidy mechanisms to a socialist-oriented market mechanism with multiple forms of ownership, management, distribution, and multi-economic sectors is an unprecedented economic model in history, which must be both practiced and learned at the same time. Vietnam is an underdeveloped country striving to move towards the goals of socialism, industrialization, modernization, innovation, and integration into the global economy. In the pursuit of these goals, the activities of theoretical research (and in the practical development of) the market economy there are still a lot of limitations, inadequacies, and problems.

Although these views have been affirmed in the Party's resolution, there are still many differing opinions. For example, some believe that the state economy should play the leading role, some have differing opinions about land ownership and land usage, some have differing opinions about the relationship between the State and the market, about the relationship between the market economy and socialist orientation, and so on. Because there are still many differing opinions as to how to implement our resolutions, the Party's policies are still hesitant, inconsistent and indecisive.

In addition, the Party's social-economic development thought and leadership methods are slow to innovate; awareness of many specific issues is still inconsistent; the implementation by organizations are still indecisive. Many only do what is easy and quit the difficult. State management is still weak; it fails to institutionalize the Party's guidelines into policies and measures in a timely manner. At the same time, there are some policies that are not clear enough or are unsuitable. There a lack of unity and smoothness at all levels and sectors. Some cadres and Party members fell into deterioration in political ideology, morality, and lifestyle, as well as corruption, negativity, and factionalism. Their capacity and qualities did not meet the requirements of the Doi Moi career.

Here are three theoretical and practical measures Vietnam must take to continue to solve the relationship between the development of productive forces and the construction and improvement of relations of production in accordance with Vietnamese reality:

First, continue to promote theoretical research, practical summaries on understanding and applying the law that relations of production must suit the development of productive forces in Vietnam - a backward country with a very low starting point, and is now promoting industrialization, modernization, development of a socialist-oriented market economy, proactively and actively integrating into the world.

Second, continue to improve theoretical thinking on the socialist-oriented market economy, on the ownership and economic sectors, solve problems that are still problematic, unclear, and under different opinions, in order to develop the productive forces. These problems are: the problem of the forms of ownership in our country, the problem of the leading role of the state economy, problems of arrangement, renewal and equitization of state-owned enterprises, problems of the role of collective economy, and cooperative economy, the role as the driving force for development of the private economy in our country, the role of foreign-invested economy, mixed economic issues, and equity economics.

Third, continue to improve the viewpoint on harmonious development between productive forces, relations of production, politics, culture and society. Our Party must:

- Develop new ideas on the socialist-oriented market economy model, on openness and integration, and on economic development methods.
- Clarify the role of the State in the socialist-oriented market economy; relations between the State and the market, between the State and enterprises.
- Promote comprehensive institutional reforms to effectively mobilize and allocate resources; implement the market mechanism and harmoniously settle the relationship between the State and the market in the distribution of production materials; ensuring true equality among all economic sectors.
- Promote the socialization of organizations in the provision of public services (education, healthcare, science and technology).
- Renovate synchronously economy and politics.
- Continue to develop and improve laws and economic policies to create sustainable development.
- Build human resources, appreciate talents, especially in the state management apparatus.
- Renovate the institution to strengthen the effectiveness of law enforcement and policies, promote democracy, and strengthen discipline.
- Build and synchronously improve all types of markets, ensure market principles in the operation of the economy, improve the operation mechanism of all types of markets.

Fourth, the Party must continue to innovate the growth model, and restructure the economy:

- Improve the set of laws on ownership and economic sectors
- Build an independent and self-reliant economy in the process of proactive and active international integration
- Closely link 5 pillars together: economy - politics - culture - society - environment in sustainable development
- Continue innovating distribution mechanisms
- Exercise the people's mastery right and improve the material and spiritual life of the people.

Appendix H

BYPASSING THE CAPITALIST MODE OF PRODUCTION

> **EDITOR'S NOTE:**
> This appendix consists of excerpts and passages from articles and political documents related to the goal of bypassing capitalist relations of production in the development of Vietnam's political-economy. We hope that these writings will give the reader insight into the ways in which Vietnamese communists are attempting to use Historical Materialist analysis in facing the challenge of building a socialist society in the real world.

From the Cadre Training Political Center of Ben Tre Province

The historical characteristic of the movement of social-economic formations points out that the movement of all social-economic formations happens objectively but is still closely attached to the material conditions of the economy and society of each nation and each people. Because of those subjective factors, each nation will have their own movement of their social-economic forms. They might go gradually from lower formation to higher formation, or they might bypass one or a few formations in the development process. The most famous example is Australia and some Latin American countries which bypassed the social-economic formation of feudalism in its own development history.

This "bypassing" does not mainly depend on the subjective will of the people, it is mainly decided by the objective historical conditions. Even when we talk about the same feudalist social-economic formation in Europe, the power was in the hands of many different classes (nobles, peasants, etc.), but in the East it was more common for all the power to belong to the king. It is clear that the "bypassing" of one or a few social-economic formations is not just random, but must obey objective laws.

From "Bypassing Capitalism in the Transitional Period Towards Socialism: Opportunities and Challenges," by Dr. Vu Van Ha, Editor in Chief of *Communist Review*

In the transition to socialism, bypassing capitalism, in the current conditions of Vietnam there are many opportunities and many challenges and difficulties that need to be solved. Opportunities and challenges intertwine and transform into each other. Recognizing opportunities and challenges in the transition to socialism bypassing capitalism in our country today is very important both in theory and in practice.

Our nation transitions to socialism bypassing capitalism not in a direct way, but through intermediate steps. We must build many small bridges to socialism. According to the Decree of the IX Party Congress of 2001, the bypassing of capitalism fundamentally means:

> To forego the establishment of capitalist relations of production and the capitalist superstructure while inheriting the achievements which humanity has secured under the capitalist regime - especially achievements in science and technology - so as to rapidly build the productive forces a modern economy.

The action of bypassing the dominant position of the capitalist relations of production in the economic base of society (which is moving towards socialism) also means that there still exist the capitalist relations of production. Those capitalist relations of production have their own movement and impact on the development of the economy which is moving towards socialism. Therefore, in practice, our policies must make these impacts contribute to our development while simultaneously avoiding their negative impacts.

Relations of production must be suitable with the level of development of the productive forces. When the productive forces in the socialism-oriented market economy are still low, and fractured, we need to build relations of production which suit them. This means that we need to have diverse relations of production to create conditions to leverage our existing resources and open the path for the productive forces to develop.

On the national scale, we bypass the dominant position of the capitalist relations of production, however, at the business-scale (or industrial-zone scale), the capitalist relations of production and the capitalist style of management still exist. They operate according to the economic laws of capitalism. The operation and the dominance of the capitalist relations of production still exist in the production, but they exist in a limited scope of space and time. This scope – in terms of both space and time – is regulated by the laws and regulations of our socialist government.

The bypassing of capitalism and moving towards socialism means that we must not only bypass the dominant position of the capitalist relations of production and the capitalist superstructure, but also, we must bypass the withholding of farmland from farmers, and the withholding of the means of production from workers.

From "Theory of the Transitional Period to Socialism of Marxism-Leninism and its Supplementation and Development of Our Party," Published in the Official Newspaper of the Communist Youth Union of Quang Ninh Province on September 20, 2022

By: Dr. Nguyen Van Quang, Institute of Military Social Sciences and Humanities

In his pursuit of the development of Marxist theory, Vladimir Lenin expanded our theoretical understanding of the complex and prolonged nature of the transition from capitalism to socialism in countries with different levels of development.

In "Greetings to the Hungarian Workers," Lenin wrote:

> For countries that move towards socialism without highly developed capitalism, a fairly long period of transition from capitalism to socialism is required.

The transition from capitalism to socialism is especially complicated in countries with lower levels of development. These countries must not only carry out the task of the transition from capitalism to socialism, but they must also carry out a series of tasks that capitalism should have done before the proletarian revolution broke out. Such tasks include eliminating feudal vestiges, establishing mechanized industry, and so on.

For less developed countries, Lenin states that "the necessity for a prolonged, complex transition through socialist accounting and control from capitalist society (and the less developed it is the longer the transition will take) to one that even approaches communist society."[10]

---

10 "The New Economic Policy And The Tasks Of The Political Education Departments," V. I. Lenin, 1921.

This unique scientific theory is derived from the law: "socialism was born on the basis of the development of capitalism." At the same time, it adheres to objectivity: socialism can be born from a lower starting point than capitalism when there are ripe conditions, premises, and opportunities. These conditions, premises, and opportunities arise from revolutionary practice which make it possible to build a path towards a new society.

> **Appendix H, Annotation 1**
>
> Above, Dr. Nguyen is referencing a law of Scientific Socialism first defined by Karl Marx in *Critique of the Gotha Program*:
>
> > What we have to deal with here is a communist society, not as it has developed on its own foundations, but, on the contrary, just as it emerges from capitalist society; which is thus in every respect, economically, morally, and intellectually, still stamped with the birthmarks of the old society from whose womb it emerges.
>
> In other words, socialism and communism are not built "from scratch" but arise on the foundation of previous stages of development. This is in accordance with:
>
> - The Principle of Development of Dialectical Materialism, which states that all subjects have developed from prior-existing stages of development.
>
> - The inheritance characteristic of development described in Materialist Dialectics, which indicates that characteristics from previous stages of development are carried forward to later stages of development.

Through practical experience gained in the early years of the transition to socialism in Soviet Russia, Lenin arrived at the scientific conclusion that: "all nations will arrive at socialism—this is inevitable, but all will do so in not exactly the same way, each will contribute something of its own to some form of democracy, to some variety of the dictatorship of the proletariat, to the varying rate of socialist transformations in the different aspects of social life."[11]

From there, two basic forms of the transition to socialism were identified:
- **Direct transition** to socialism from developed capitalism.
- **Indirect transition** to socialism while bypassing capitalism.

In the second transitional form – the indirect transition to socialism while bypassing capitalism – Lenin pointed out that the task would be more burdensome, more difficult, and more complicated, because it requires carrying double the load in completing both tasks: that of building socialism in terms of political and social development as well as that of accomplishing the basic achievements of capitalism in terms of scientific development and development of productive forces. Therefore, Lenin emphasized and demanded the necessity of going through many intermediate, transitional steps to successfully build socialism. For example, having to "build small bridges" through the capitalist economy to gradually build socialism. At the same time, he noted that "If we are successfully to solve the problem of our immediate transition to socialism, we must understand what intermediary paths, methods, means and instruments are required for the transition from pre-capitalist relations to socialism."[12]

---

11 "A Caricature of Marxism and Imperialist Economism," V. I. Lenin, 1916.
12 "The Tax in Kind," V. I. Lenin, 1921.

From the Political Program of the Communist Party of Vietnam, 1930

Our country's transitional period towards socialism will take place in international conditions of many profound changes. For now, capitalism still has the potential of economic development because of capitalist achievements in science, technology, management, and so on. Moreover, capitalism is still an unfair and exploitative regime. The most fundamental contradiction of capitalism is between the socialization of the productive forces and the private ownership of the means of production. There is a huge contradiction between different classes in a society, between different groups of capitalists, between different international companies, and between different imperial cores. The contradictions between different capitalist countries are getting deeper and deeper, and the motion of those contradictions themselves, along with the struggles of the working class will decide the fate of capitalism.

. . .

Our nation is in a transitional period towards socialism, bypassing capitalism, from a society that is a colony – partially feudalist, with very low-developed productive forces.

. . .

Entering the transitional period towards socialism in these material conditions, we must be self-reliant and try to develop all of our potential – both materially and ideologically. At the same time, we need to open our relations for cooperation with many countries in the world, to find the right steps, and the right path to successfully build socialism.

From the Political Program of the Communist Party of Vietnam, 1986

The Communist Party of Vietnam reaffirms that the transitional period from capitalism to socialism is a very difficult and long period, and in our country's conditions, where we are moving directly to socialism and bypassing capitalism, that period will be even more arduous and longer.

From the Political Program of the Communist Party of Vietnam, 2021

Our country must continue strongly renovating our ideology, building and completing a stable regime with highly developed economy, politics, culture, environment, and so on. We must solve all difficulties in a timely manner and use all of our resources and potential to create a fast and stable development for the country.

Appendix I

OUR PARTY'S UNDERSTANDING OF THE TRANSITIONAL PERIOD TOWARDS SOCIALISM IN VIETNAM

> **EDITOR'S NOTE:**
> This article was written by By Dr. Le Van Yen of Truth Publishing House, and Dr. Dinh Duc Duy of the Political Cadre Training Center in Binh Duong. It offers an overview of the historic struggles and challenges faced by communists in Vietnam in their attempts to build a socialist society and to liberate Vietnamese workers from colonialist, imperialist, and capitalist oppression. The authors use Historical Materialism as the basis of analysis of Vietnam's modern history.

Vietnam started building socialism in 1954, when the North officially went into the transitional period towards socialism. Ho Chi Minh stated this characteristic of Vietnam during this time: "the most important characteristic of our country in this transitional period is that we are moving from an outdated agrarian country directly towards socialism without going through capitalism."

After the victory of the resistance war against the USA in 1975, the country reunited and the whole entire country finally joined the path of the transitionary period towards socialism. From then until the party started the Doi Moi reforms in 1986 was an entire decade. This was a time when Vietnam tried to build our economy, culture, and society under the terrible conditions resulting from the war, which caused difficulty after difficulty. Moreover, our party did not fully understand that the transitional period towards socialism is a very long period that must go through many steps. Because our party was too idealist and impatient, we wanted to bypass necessary steps. Therefore, at the time of the IV National Assembly in 1976, our party had not identified correctly the targets of the first steps of the transitional period.

From 1976 through 1980, the party wanted to push industrialization forward while we did not have essential and necessary premises. In addition, our economic management style was still very outdated.

At the V Congress of 1982, the party affirmed two primary tasks [to build socialism and to defend the country against all enemies] and concretized several economic policies in the first stage of the transitional period, came up with general targets, and major social-economic policies. However, in implementation of those policies, the party failed to fully understand the situation at hand. The Party was not determined to resolve the problems of impatience and idealism which were mainly expressed in the policy of economic structure, socialist renovation, and management style which led to social-economic crisis.

The VI Congress of 1986 fully understood the material conditions of the country, and with the mindset of looking straight at the truth, speaking out the truth, and determination to renovate, the party affirmed:

> The transitional period of our country towards socialism from a low level
> of production, bypassing capitalism, will obviously be very long and arduous

process. This constitutes a comprehensive, profound, and revolutionary period of renovation. This renovation period is required to build socialism from nothing, and requires us to build up our productive forces, relations of production, and superstructure.

Our party, by this time, understood that this first step is just another small step in a long period of transition. This Congress also pointed out that from that point forward, with a revolutionary and scientific mindset, we must continue developing the established path towards socialism. The Party must develop a more profound political program for the entire revolutionary transition period towards socialism. Based on such a program, the party will build strategies for social-economic development, for technological and scientific development, and for the nation's development.

In 1991, the Soviet Union and the European socialist bloc collapsed, and, unfortunately, even among the ranks of the international communist community, there was a tendency to deny all the achievements of the party, leading to a rejection of the socialist path. In that complicated circumstance, the VII congress, in 1991, established the previously called-for program to build our country in the transitional period towards socialism, stating:

> The transitional period towards socialism in our country is a long period which requires many stages. The target of the first stage is: our society will go through a comprehensive renovation to reach a stable stage and to create the conditions for the development of the next stage.

At the IX Congress of 2001, the Party affirmed: "building socialism without going through capitalism, making the quality changes of society in all fields, is very difficult and complex. Therefore, it must go through a very long period with many stages and many social-economic forms."

Now that the party had a proper understanding of the circumstances of the first stage of the transitionary period, progress could be made in building toward the next stage. The Party realized that the first stage must accomplish the goals of creating a solidly stable society through innovation, which would create conditions for fast development in the next stage. The next stage is to push forward industrialization and modernization and quickly bringing the country out of the low-level of development and building an industrialized nation.

After 25 years of implementing Doi Moi Renovation, from 1986 through 2011, in the XI Congress of 2011, our party announced a political program regarding building the country in the transitional period towards socialism which read:

> Moving towards socialism is the desire of our people. It is the rightful choice of the Communist Party of Vietnam and Chairman Ho Chi Minh, and it is suitable with the development trend of history.[13] The socialist society that our people want to build is a society of: rich people, a strong country, democratic equality, and intellectually developed people, and so on. This is a comprehensive, profound, and revolutionary process. At the same time, it is the complex struggle between the old and the new which creates quality changes in all fields of society. We must go through a long transitional period with many stages and many social-economic forms.

---

13 See Annotation 22, p. 32.

We can say that, before the Doi Moi reforms, the understanding of our Party about the transitional period towards socialism bypassing capitalism was still very simple, but now, in this Renovation time, the Party's understanding about this issue is getting clearer and brighter. The new understanding is that the transitional period towards socialism, bypassing capitalism, in our country, is an objective necessity. It is a long and arduous process with many stages. At the same time, the Party also emphasized that there are still many issues which need to be studied, improved, and developed into our Party's program, alongside the development of the country in the transitional period towards socialism.

Appendix J

WHAT ARE SOCIALIST VALUES AND SOCIALIST MANNERS?

> **EDITOR'S NOTE:**
> The article below was written by Ho Chi Minh to develop the social consciousness of Vietnamese communists. Ho Chi Minh believed that it was necessary to develop these values and manners within Vietnamese workers in order to create the conditions for social revolution against capitalism, imperialism, and colonialism. The role of social consciousness in bringing about revolution is discussed more on p. 94.

* Be aware that you (the working people) are the true owners of the state, and you must have a socialist collective spirit, and you must follow the thought:
  "One for all and all for one."
  Our state now is the state of the working people. Therefore, all workers, farmers, and revolutionary intellectuals must be fully aware that: nowadays, working people are the owners, and not merely wage workers for the exploitative classes, as it was in the old society. We have rights and we have the conditions to build a free and happy life for ourselves. Working people are the collective owners of all means of production and culture. We are all equal in responsibility and benefits. Therefore, everyone must observe the ideology of "one for all and all for one."

* *Individualism*, an attitude of "good for me but not for thee," disorganization, lack of discipline, and other bad behaviors are dangerous enemies of socialism.

* *All for production.*
  Our most important mission now is to develop our production to enhance our people's cultural and material life. If we want socialism, there is no other way than to use all the resources we have to produce. At present, production is the main battlefield of the North of Vietnam.

* *Build socialism with industry and thrift.*
  Our country is still very poor. To have a happy life, we need to have a spirit of self-reliance, and we must be laborious. Labor is our sacred responsibility. It is our source of life and happiness. In our society, there are no low-value jobs. Only lazy people who always rely on others are shameful. The cooks and the cleaners are the same as teachers and engineers. If they do their jobs well, they are all honorable. Anyone who is fearful of difficulties and hardships, or who just want to live on the fat of the land, are the weak ones, and they are not socialist people.

* *To advance to socialism quickly and fiercely but steadily.*
  To produce quickly and greatly with high quality and low prices, we must have revolutionary enthusiasm. But at the same time, we need to thoroughly understand science.

Each working person must have the spirit of daring to think and daring to do, and each must become a progressive worker. Workers, farmers, and intellectuals must strongly believe that we have enough power, courage and knowledge to build a new life.

Appendix K

HISTORY OF CLASS SOCIETY
FROM: *FUNDAMENTALS OF MARXISM-LENINISM*

> **EDITOR'S NOTE:**
> The following is an excerpt from the Soviet textbook Fundamentals of Marxism-Leninism, first published in English in 1963, which details the development of class society from its origins in slave society to the rise of capitalism to the development of the socialist system that will eventually lead to communism and an end to class society. This offers a broad overview of the development of human society from the standpoint of Historical Materialism. As with the main text of this book, words which are underlined can be found in the glossary/index to assist readers in fully understanding the terminology and underlying concepts.

Historical materialism does not impose preconceived patterns on history and does not adapt the events of past and present to fit its own conclusions. On the contrary, it is a scientific generalization of history.

The conclusion that the history of mankind constitutes a succession of socio-economic formations is based on scientifically verified knowledge of the past. Mankind as a whole has passed through four formations—primitive-communal, slave, feudal, and capitalist—and is now living in the epoch of transition to the next formation, the communist formation, the first phase of which is called socialism.

In what follows, we shall try to describe only the most general features of the various socio-economic formations and refrain from entering into the details and secondary features [i.e., subjective factors] in which the history of every country and every epoch abounds.

The Primitive-Communal System

The primitive-communal system was historically the first form of society that arose after man emerged from the animal world, having acquired through a long process of labour the qualities which distinguish him from all other living creatures.

The instruments of labour that mankind possessed in the early primitive-communal system were of the most primitive kind—the club, the stone axe, the flint knife, the stone-tipped spear, the arrow, etc.

. . .

Production relations between people during this era were in accordance with the level of development of the productive forces. With the instruments of labour then available it was impossible by acting in isolation to fight the forces of nature and to secure the means of subsistence.

Only labour performed in common (common hunting, fishing and so on) by all the members of the primitive commune through unity and mutual assistance enabled them to acquire the necessary means of subsistence. Common labour entailed common ownership of the means of production as the basis of the production relations in that epoch. All members of the commune shared the same relationship to the means of production; no one could deprive other members of the commune of the means of production and turn them into their own private property.

Since there was no private property there could be no exploitation. There was simply no surplus that could be taken away from a producer and kept for other members of society. But since there was no exploitation of the labour of others, there was also no need for a special apparatus of coercion. The simple functions of arranging the common affairs were either performed collectively or else entrusted to the most respected and experienced members of the commune.

The special features of this formation are thus determined by the low level of production and the helplessness of man in the face of his formidable natural surroundings.

. . .

In the course of time the primitive-communal system reached a state of decline. The ultimate causes of the destruction of primitive society lay in the development of the productive forces. Men gradually mastered the secret of smelting metals. Stone and wooden implements were replaced by those of metal. Ploughs with metal blades, metal axes, bronze and iron tips for spears, arrows, etc., became widespread. Agriculture underwent further development. Domestication of animals and their use as draught power for tillage greatly increased the productivity of labour. The development of the productive forces (instruments of labour and production skills and the experience of the workmen) led to important social changes.

Social division of labour arose. Agriculture and animal husbandry and then handicrafts emerged as special kinds of labor activity. Exchange of the products of labour began to develop; first between tribes, then within the commune itself. Gradually, the need for common labour practiced by the whole commune disappeared. The tribe and the clan broke up into families, each of which became an independent economic unit. Labour became split up, private property appeared, and with it the possibility of exploitation, for production had now developed to such an extent that human labour power had begun to produce more than was required for the bare subsistence of the workman.

People were prompted to improve their instruments of labour and develop their skills by necessity, and by the desire to make their work easier and to build up stocks of resources to defend against natural disasters. But by changing their instruments of labour they, unwittingly, unconsciously, not even suspecting what social consequences this would have, were paving the way for a profound social revolution—the replacement of the primitive-communal formation by the slave formation. The expanded productive forces of society led to new production relations among people.

The Slave System

The foundation of the production relations of this system was private ownership not only of the means of production, but also of the workmen themselves as slaves. The slave-owner's property rights over the slaves and over all they produced was determined by the level of development of the productive forces of that epoch. This level was sufficiently high to give rise to the possibility of exploitation of the working people. But at the same time productivity was still so low that exploitation of the workmen and appropriation of a part of what they produced could be accomplished only by reducing the consumption of slaves to a minimum, leaving them just enough to prevent them from dying of hunger.

...

This change in production relations also gave rise to a revolution in other spheres of social life.

The relations of cooperation and solidarity that had been characteristic of the primitive commune were superseded by a relationship involving the domination of one section of society over the other, by relations of exploitation, oppression, and implacable enmity. Society was divided into antagonistic classes - the class of slave owners and the class of slaves.

The epoch of slavery placed terrible burdens and hardships on the working people. "The lowest interests - base greed, brutal sensuality, sordid avarice, selfish plunder of common possessions - usher in the new, civilized society, class society; the most outrageous means - theft, rape, deceit, and treachery - undermine and topple the old, classless, gentile society." Thus, Engels describes the period of transition from the primitive-communal system to that of slavery.

The brutal exploitation of the slaves evoked bitter opposition on their part. In order to crush the opposition a special apparatus of coercion - the state - had to be created in place of the former clan and tribal institutions of administration. It was the function of the state to protect the property of the slave owners and to ensure a constant supply of slaves from prisoners of war and also from bankrupt debtors, who were turned into slaves. The birth of the state gave rise to the birth of law, a system of juridical standards and prescriptions expressing the will of the ruling class and protected by the coercive power of the state. New customs and the specific ideology of slave society appeared. Scorn and contempt for physical labour, which now came to be considered an occupation unworthy of a free man, gradually spread among the oppressors; the idea of the inequality of men took firm root.

...

But the time came when the possibilities of progress inherent in the slave mode of production were exhausted, when its production relations turned more and more into fetters hampering the development of the productive forces. Having in their possession cheap slave labour, the slave-owners made no effort to improve the instruments of production. What was more, the slave, who was not interested in the results of his labour, could not be entrusted with complex and costly tools. More and more insistently the needs of the development of the productive forces demanded the abolition of the old production relations.

This could only be accomplished by a social revolution. The classes and groups that suffered most from the slave system and therefore had most to gain from its abolition formed the driving force behind that revolution. For the most part, they were slaves and the poorest section of the freemen. As the contradictions in the old mode of production came to a head, the class conflict grew more and more acute. It took all kinds of forms — from deliberate breaking of the instruments of labour to uprisings involving tens of thousands of people.

In the end, under the combined blows of the uprisings of the working classes and the attacks of neighbouring barbarian tribes, which the slave-owning state, weakened by internal contradictions and conflicts, would no longer resist, the slave system crumbled. It was replaced by a new system of feudalism.

The Feudal System

The foundation of the production relations of this system lies in the feudal lords' ownership of the means of production, primarily of the land (the very concept known as "feudalism" is derived from the Latin word "feodum," the name given to the land distributed by the king to his vassals in return for their military allegiance). The peasants were personally dependent on the feudal rulers, but were no longer completely their property.* The feudal rulers had the right to the labour of the peasants, and latter were obliged to do service for their lords.

Feudal society was marked also by the peasants and craftsmen possessing their personal holdings: the peasant serf had his own plot of land, his personal holding, the products of which remained at his disposal after his obligations to the feudal lord had been met.

* In some countries (for example, Russia) the personal dependence of the peasants on the feudal rulers assumed particularly crude forms, approaching slavery. The landlord could buy and sell peasants, etc.

This special character of the production relations opened up new possibilities for the growth of the productive forces. The direct producer now had a definite material interest in the results of his work. Accordingly, he no longer broke or spoiled his tools, but, on the contrary, looked after them carefully and went out of his way to improve them. Agriculture made further progress; the three-field system of cultivation was evolved and methods of land fertilisation were more and more widely adopted. Even more significant successes were achieved by the craftsmen supplying agricultural instruments, articles of daily life used by feudal rulers and merchants, various kinds of utensils, and also weapons and military equipment. The development of crafts and trade led to the rise of towns. In the course of time the towns became powerful economic, political, and cultural centre s; the cradle of the new capitalist mode of production.

In the epoch of feudalism, many outstanding discoveries that had a great influence on the course of human history were made. Man learned to produce iron out of pig iron, to build sailing ships with keels that were capable of making long voyages, to fashion simple optical instruments (spectacles, telescopes); the compass, gunpowder, paper, book-printing, and mechanical clocks were invented. The muscular power of men and animals was supplemented on an ever wider scale by the force of the wind (windmills and sailing-ships) and of falling water (the water-mill and water-wheel were the simple and widespread engines of the Middle Ages).

The replacement of slave production relations by feudal ones brought about changes in the whole life of society. The principal changes are in class structure. The feudal rulers, with the ownership of the land, became the ruling class. The other basic class of feudal society was the serfs. The relations between these two classes were antagonistic in character and based on an irreconcilable opposition of class interests. The forms of exploitation, although slightly milder than those of slavery, were of a very cruel kind. The exploitation of the peasants was still based on non-economic coercion. The serf experienced the economic stimulus of material incentive only when working on his own personal holding. The greater part of his time was devoted to working for the feudal lord, for which labour he received no reward whatsoever. Here the main incentive to work was fear of punishment, of physical violence, and also of the danger of losing all his personal property, which could be confiscated by the landlord.

Compared with that of slave society, the class struggle in feudal society rises to a higher level. Peasant uprisings sometimes embrace large territories. The strength of the peasants' resistance to the feudals is shown by the peasant wars which shook one country after another: Wat Tyler's Rebellion in England (14th century), the Jacquerie in France (14th-15th centuries), the Hussite wars in Bohemia (15th century), the Peasant War in Germany (16th century), the Taiping Rebellion in China (19th century), the Sikh uprisings in India (17th-48th centuries), the uprisings of Bolotnikov and Razin (17th century) and of Pugachov (18th century) in Russia, etc.

The political and ideological superstructure of feudal society reflects the forms of exploitation and class struggle peculiar to it. To exploit and hold down the serfs, the feudal state had constantly to resort to armed force, which was at the disposal not only of the central authority but also of each feudal lord, who was the absolute master within his own domains and could condemn and punish at will.

The social and economic inequality of feudal society is embodied in legislation. Classes and their various internal strata constitute estates (feudal society being divided into such estates as the nobility, the clergy, the merchants, and the peasantry). The relations between the estates and within each of them are based on a system of strict subordination and personal dependence. The rigidity of social barriers impedes movement from one step of the feudal hierarchy to another. The spiritual life of feudal society is ruled by the Church and religion.

In the course of time, the development of the productive forces comes into contradiction with the production relations prevailing in feudal society and the political and ideological superstructure determined by them. The peasants fight ever more stubbornly against feudal oppression for the right to dispose freely of the products of their economic activity. They endeavour to free themselves from feudal exploitation to obtain the means for improving their husbandry, etc. Large manufacturing establishments based on craft techniques but making extensive use of the division of labour and employing the labour of workmen free from personal dependence spring up alongside the small artisan workshops.

The towns - the bulwark of the young bourgeoisie - vigorously developed. Trade assumed ever wider scope. Merchants with the help of the king's forces seized new markets in overseas countries. The growth of exchange led in its turn to the rapid development of production, which was also facilitated by the scientific and technical discoveries of the sixteenth and seventeenth centuries.

In the midst of the feudal system a new, capitalist mode of production is gradually formed. Its development demands the abolition of the feudal order. The bourgeoisie—the class that now appears as the sponsor of the new mode of production—needs a "free" labor market, i. e., workers who are free both of serf dependence and property, and whose hunger will drive them to the factories. It needs a national market, the removal of tariff and all other barriers created by the feudal rulers. It achieves the abolition of the taxes that pay for the upkeep of the court and the numerous retinues of the nobility, and the destruction of the privileges of the estates. Its aim is to be able to control affairs in all spheres of the life of society.

The bourgeoisie rallies round it all the classes and groups that are dissatisfied with the feudal order, from the peasant serfs and lower strata of the towns, who live in conditions of poverty, humiliation and oppression, to the advanced scientists and writers, who, regardless of their origin, are stifled by the spiritual tyranny of feudalism and the Church.

Thus begins the epoch of bourgeois revolutions.

The Capitalist System

The production relations of capitalism are based on the private ownership by capitalists of the means of production. The capitalist class exploits the class of workers, who are free from personal dependence but are compelled to sell their labor-power because they are deprived of the means of production.

The production relations of capitalism opened up broad opportunities for the development of the productive forces. Large scale machine production, based on the harnessing of powerful forces of nature such as steam, and later electricity, and on the wide application of science to the process of production, comes into being and develops at a rapid pace. Capitalism brings about the division of labour not only within separate countries but between countries themselves, thus creating a world market, and then a world economic system.

And again the changes in the mode of production are followed by changes throughout the life of society.

The capitalist class and the working class become the main classes of society. As before, the relations between them remain antagonistic in character, since they are based on exploitation, on the oppression of the propertyless by the possessors of property. They are the relations of an implacable class struggle. But the methods of exploitation and oppression have radically changed, the prevailing form of compulsion has become economic. The capitalist, as a rule, does not require physical force to make people work for him. Deprived of the means of production, the worker is compelled to do so " voluntarily" - under threat of death by starvation. The relations of exploitation are veiled by the "free" hire of workers by the master, by the buying and selling of labor-power.

The changed methods of exploitation bring about a change in the methods of political rule. The transition takes place from the undisguised despotism of previous epochs to more refined forms of rule, to bourgeois democracy. The unlimited power of the hereditary monarch gives way to a parliamentary republic (or at least a constitutional monarchy), suffrage is introduced, citizens are declared to have certain political freedoms and to be equal before the law. This kind of system is most in accord with the principles of free competition and the free play of economic forces on which capitalism for a long time was based.

All the differences between the political and ideological superstructure of bourgeois society and that of feudalism do not, however, alter the basic fact that it is still a superstructure erected upon relations of private ownership and exploitation. The dominant part of this superstructure is composed of the institutions and ideas of the oppressor class—the bourgeoisie—whose task it is to preserve bourgeois class domination and to ensure the obedience of the exploited masses.

As has been proved today not only in theory but in social practice, the capitalist formation is also temporary, transitory. Increasingly profound antagonisms, above all the contradiction between the social character of production and the private form of appropriation, matured and deepened in the very heart of the system. The only way out of these contradictions is to effect the transition to social ownership of the means of production, i.e., to socialism.

But, as in the past, the transition to a new mode of production is only possible through a social revolution. The force destined to effect this revolution is generated by capitalism itself in the shape of the working class. Rallying to its side all the working people, the working class overthrows the power of capital and creates a new, socialist system free from the exploitation of man by man.

The Socialist System

The socialist mode of production is based on social ownership of the means of production. The production relations of socialist society are therefore relations of cooperation and mutual assistance among workers liberated from exploitation. They correspond to the character of the productive forces, the social character of production being based on social ownership of the means of production.

Unlike the primitive-communal system, the socialisation of the means of production occurs now on the basis of tremendously developed productive forces, culture and man's power over nature. The new system opens up for humanity unlimited opportunities of progress, both in the development of the productive forces and in all other spheres of the life of society.

Such is a very general outline of the basic stages of the development of human society.

Our knowledge of the past provides us with striking confirmation of the scientific validity of the materialist conception of history, the essence of which Marx formulated as follows in the preface to his book *A Contribution to the Critique of Political Economy*:

> In the social production of their life, men enter into definite relations that are indispensable and independent of their will, relations of production which correspond to a definite stage of development of their material productive forces. The sum total of these relations of production constitutes the economic structure of society, the real foundation, on which arises a legal and political superstructure and to which correspond definite forms of social consciousness. The mode of production of material life conditions the social, political and intellectual life process in general. It is not the consciousness of men that determines their being, but, on the contrary, their social being that determines their consciousness. At a certain stage of their development, the material productive forces of society come in conflict with the existing relations of production, or—what is but a legal expression for the same thing—with the property relations within which they have been at work hitherto, From forms of development of the productive forces these relations turn into their fetters. Then begins an epoch of social revolution. With the change of the economic foundation the entire immense superstructure is more or less rapidly transformed.

GLOSSARY & INDEX

Absolutization — Erroneously holding a belief or supposition as always true in all situations and without exception. See *Part 1*, p. 49; *Part 2*: p. 146.

Alexandre Dumas — (1802-1870) French novelist and playwright who wrote *The Three Musketeers*. See *Part 2*: p. 229.

Base — Also known as: Economic Base; Material Base, Objective Base. The material aspect of a social-economic formation; the totality of relations of production that constitute the economic structure of a society which exists in dialectical unity with a superstructure. See also: Economy; Superstructure.
See *Part 1*: p. 23; *Part 2*: p. 73.

Bourgeoisie — See: Capitalist Class.

Bypass — To skip over a stage of development of the mode of production in the historical development of a human society. See *Part 2*: p. 34-37, 69-71, 172-173, 269-272.

Cadre — A person or group of people with a leadership position in a political organization (i.e., within a communist party).

Capitalism — See: Capitalist Mode of Production.

Capitalist Class — The economic class which owns the means of production under the capitalist mode of production.

Capitalist Mode of Production — Also known as Capitalism. The current mode of production of human society in most nations. Typified by mechanized industrial production of goods and private ownership of the means of production by capitalists.

Category — The most general grouping of aspects, attributes, and relations of things, phenomena, and ideas. Different specific fields of inquiry may categorize things, phenomena, and/or ideas differently from one another. See *Part 1*: p. 126

Category Pair — A pair of philosophical categories within materialist dialectics. Materialist Dialectics tend to focus on universal category pairs which can be used to examine the characteristics, relations, and development of all things, phenomena, and ideas. Examples of category pairs include: private and common; content and form; reason and result; essence and phenomena.
See *Part 1*: p. 127.

Change — See: Development.

Class Character — The characteristics and attributes (including aspects of social being as well as aspects of social consciousness) which are typical of an economic class within a social-economic formation. Class character is derived from the relationships which an economic class has with the means of production and with other economic classes in society. See *Part 2*: p. 116, 138.

Class Consciousness — A highly developed form of social consciousness which an economic class develops by becoming aware of its own existence as well as its historical revolutionary mission. See *Part 2*: p. 14, 94, 99, 114-139, 145, 154, 182, 190, 196, 201, 209, 233-235.
See also: Historical Mission.

Class Dictatorship — Rulership of a social-economic formation by a dominant economic class. This rulership is accomplished through the construction and control of a state and maintained through violence. See also: Dictatorship of the Proletariat.

Class Society — A formation of society which separates human beings into groups based on their relation to the means of production and to one another.

Class Struggle — The process through which different classes labor and fight to obtain more benefits from the productive forces of society.

Glossary and Index 285

Commandism	An error in revolutionary leadership which occurs when revolutionaries do not listen to the people and instead attempt to command them through force of will. This is a form of voluntarism because it reflects a mistaken belief that the subjective will of the revolutionary individual or party can impose its will unilaterally on the masses. It fails to account for the dialectical relationship which exists between more advanced elements of the revolutionary class and the masses at large. See *Part 2*: p. 157-158. See also: Voluntarism, Tailism.
Common	See: Private and Common.
Communism	A stateless, classless society. Building a communist society is the goal of Scientific Socialism and is the Historic Mission of the working class.
Comprehensive and Historical Perspective	Also known as Comprehensive and Historical Viewpoint. A perspective which seeks to consider both the historical development subject as well as all internal and external relationships of a subject which determine and impact its development. Dialectical Materialist philosophy demands a comprehensive and historical perspective in order to fully and properly understand reality. See *Part 1*: p. 115, 172, 235. *Part 2*, p. 2, 7, 134, 148, 151, 185, 191, 214, 224, 235. See also: Viewpoint.
Comprehensive Perspective	Also known as Comprehensive Viewpoint. A viewpoint which seeks to consider the internal dialectical relationships between the component parts, factors, and aspects within a thing or phenomenon, and which considers external mutual interactions with with other things, phenomena, and ideas. See also: Comprehensive and Historical Perspective. See *Part 1*: p. 115, 172, 235.
Confucianism	A religion or a systematic and methodical doctrine that has existed since the 5th century B.C.E. Confucianism is concerned with Humanity. Specifically, Confucianism teaches a way of being a human being in the family and in society. See *Part 1*: p. 5; *Part 2*: p. 217.
Content	See: Content and Form.
Content and Form (Category Pair)	*Content* is the philosophical category which refers to the sum of all aspects, attributes, and processes that a thing, phenomenon, or idea is made from. *Form* is the philosophical category which refers to the mode of existence and development of things, phenomena, and ideas. Form thus describes the system of relatively stable relationships which exist internally within things, phenomena, and ideas. Content and form have a dialectical relationship with one another, in which content determines form and form impacts back on content. See *Part 1*: p. 115, 147-155, 166; *Part 2*: p. 45-46, 63, 65, 72, 84-85, 161.
Continuous Motion	Change/development/motion which is constant. Dialectical Materialism's Principle of Development holds that all things, phenomena, and ideas are constantly changing and that this change is brought about by internal and external relationships through processes of contradiction and negation. See also: Development. See *Part 2*: p. 78-80.
Contradiction	A relationship in which two forces oppose one another, leading to mutual development. See *Part 1*: p. 123, 159, 163, 169, 175-191.
Coup d'Etat	A change in governmental rule in which power does not shift from one economic class to another. Not to be confused with social revolution in which a new revolutionary class seizes power over the state and the means of production. See *Part 2*: p. 208-209.
Creativity	The characteristic of human beings which allows human society and production processes to develop over time through conscious activity. See *Part 2*: p. 42-44, 216, 229, 233.

Daoism	A Chinese philosophy and spiritual tradition that emerged around the 6th century B.C.E. Daoism centered on living in harmony with the Dao (the "Way"), a universal principle that underlies all existence. See *Part 2*, p. 218.
Development	The change and motion of things, phenomena, and ideas with a forward tendency: from less advanced to more advanced; and/or from a less complete to a more complete level.
Dialectical Materialism	A universal philosophical and methodological system which forms the theoretical core of a scientific worldview. Dialectical Materialism was first developed by Karl Marx and Friedrich Engels with the express goal of achieving communism. Dialectical Materialism has since been defended and developed by Vladimir Ilyich Lenin as well as many others. Dialectical Materialism is the philosophy upon which Historical Materialism was developed.
Dialectical Negation	See: Negation.
Dialectical Relationship	A relationship in which two things, phenomena, or ideas mutually impact one another, leading to development and negation. See *Part 1*: p. 47, 51, 62.
Dialectical Unity	The universal principle of Materialist Dialectics which states that even though all relationships are diverse and different from one another, they also exist in unity, because all relationships share a foundation in the material world. See *Part 1*: p. 109-110, 125, 130; *Part 2*: p. 38, 173-174. See also: Unity in Diversity.
Dictatorship	See: Class Dictatorship
Dictatorship of the Proletariat	The historical mission of the working class and a prerequisite to communism. A dictatorship of the proletariat is a social-economic formation in which the vast majority of society (i.e., the working class) seizes control of the means of production and constructs a state to enforce its rule over society. Over time, this state will be eliminated, eventually leading to a stateless, classless society. See *Part 1*: p. 26, 33, 35-36; *Part 2*: p. 89, 96, 99, 103, 118, 145, 149, 153, 182-183, 202-204, 208, 210, 271.
Diversity in Unity	The universal principle of Materialist Dialectics which states that even though all relationships are diverse and different from one another, they also exist in unity, because all relationships share a foundation in the material world. See *Part 1*: p. 109-110, 125, 130; *Part 2*: p. 38, 173-174. See also: Unity in Diversity.
Doi Moi Period	The period of Vietnamese history following the Subsidizing Period, which lasted from 1986-2025 which was marked by Doi Moi ("renovation") reforms. These reforms were intended to return Vietnam to adherence to objective laws and to the basic principles of Marxism-Leninism. The Doi Moi Period ended in 2025 after these goals were considered to be successfully accomplished. See *Part 2*: p. 253-268.
Dogmatism	An inflexible adherence to ideals as incontrovertibly true while refusing to take any contradictory evidence into consideration. Dogmatism stands in direct opposition to Materialist Dialectics, which seeks to form opinions and conclusions only after careful consideration of all observable evidence. See *Part 1*: p. 136-137, 174, 217-218, 233; *Part 2*: p. 202, 223.
Economic Aspect (of the Mode of Production)	The economic organization of production processes within a mode of production. See *Part 2*: p. 16-17, 90. See also: Economy.
Economic Base	See: Base.
Economy	The sum total of the dialectical relationships within a human society which are directly related to production, trading, distribution, and consumption of commodities and services in order to meet the demands of that society, given a limitation of available resources.

Empirical Consciousness	The stage of development of consciousness in which perceptions are formed via direct observations of things and phenomena in the natural world, or of society, or through scientific experimentation and systematic observation. See also: Empircal Social Consciousness. See *Part 1*: p. 210-214; *Part 2*: p. 112.
Empirical Social Consciousness	Social consciousness which is formed directly from daily practical activities, not yet systematized nor generalized into theory. See *Part 2*: p. 108, 111-112. See also: Theoretical Social Consciousness.
Empiricism	A broad philosophical position which holds that only experience (including internal experience) can be held as a source of knowledge or truth. Though nominally opposed to idealism, it is considered a faulty (or naive) form of materialism, since it sees the world as only unconnected, static appearances and ignores the reality of dialectical (changing) relationships between objects. See *Part 1*: p. 9-12, 29, 94, 96-97, 100, 218. *Part 2*: p. 22-23, 126, 220.
Engels	See: Friedrich Engels.
Essence	See: Essence and Phenomena.
Essence and Phenomena (Category Pair)	The *essence* category refers to the synthesis of all the internal aspects as well as the obvious and stable relations that define the existence, motion and development of things and ideas. The *phenomena* category refers to the external manifestation of those internal aspects and relations in specific conditions. Essence always determines which phenomena appear, but phenomena do not always accurately reflect essence in human perception; in other words, it is possible to misinterpret phenomena, leading to a misunderstanding of essence, or to mistake phenomena for essence. See *Part 1*: p. 156-160.
Essential	See: Essence and Phenomena.
Essential Class	The economic classes within a social-economic formation which have an essential role in the ownership and/or operation of the means of production. See *Part 2*: p. 65. See also: Essence and Phenomena.
Essential Means of Production	Those means of production which are most essential in the material production process or in a specific labor activity. See *Part 2*: p. 148, 186-187. See also: Essence and Phenomena.
Existentialism	A Western philosophy that emphasizes individual freedom, choice, and the creation of meaning in a seemingly indifferent or absurd universe. It focuses on subjective experience and the idea that humans define their own essence through their actions and decisions. Existentialism is idealist in the sense that it prioritizes the mind, consciousness, and human agency over material forces of reality. Existentialism asserts that reality is shaped by individual perception, values, and choices rather than by objective, material phenomena, thus putting the conception of human nature on an idealist basis. See *Part 2*: p. 219-220.
False Consciousness	Forms of consciousness (ideas, thoughts, concepts, etc.) which are incorrect and misaligned from reality. See *Part 1*: p. 231-233, 237; *Part 2*: p. 12, 14, 31, 94, 113-115, 124-125, 129, 135, 142, 154, 158, 201, 225.
Fideism	The belief that knowledge is received from some higher power. Fideism upholds that all knowledge is pre-existing, and that humanity simply receives it from on high. Dialectical Materialism, on the other hand, argues that knowledge is developed over time through dialectical processes of consciousness and human activity. See *Part 1*: p. 56-57, 209; *Part 2*: p. 221.
Friedrich Engels	(1820-1895) German theorist, politician, philosopher, leader of the international working class, and co-founder of Scientific Socialism with Karl Marx.
Forces of Production	See: Productive Forces.

Form	See: Content and Form
Form of Social Consciousness	A distinct collection of ideas, attitudes, and beliefs which are shared by a group of people in society and which is defended, advanced, and developed by a corresponding social institution. See **Part 2**: p. 19, 26-27, 56, 82, 84-85, 105, 108, 127, 131, 134, 137, 139-140, 142, 144-146, 205, 283.
Forward Tendency of Development	Also known as the Forward Tendency of Motion. The tendency for things, phenomena, and ideas to move from less advanced to more advanced forms through processes of motion and development. See **Part 1**: p. 122-123, 197, 201; **Part 2**: p. 32, 34.
George Wilhelm Friedrich Hegel	(1770 - 1831) German philosophy professor & objective idealist philosopher; developed the system of idealist dialectics which Marx and Engels used as a basis for developing materialist dialectics. See **Part 1**: p. 8-11, 29, 69-71, 97, 98, 100-105, 132, 157, 165, 182, 192, 193-194, 209, 228; **Part 2**: p. 144, 219.
Germ	See: Seed.
Great Man Theory of History	A common misconception about human society which holds that human history moves forward primarily and essentially because of the actions of individual "great" human beings who develop history through their will, intellect, and other personal qualities. This is an idealist conception of history as it attributes the motion of history to the consciousness of particular individual human beings. In contrast, Marxism-Leninism holds that the masses create history (and that leaders are created by the masses) through material processes of history. See **Part 2**: p. 234-235. See also: Leaders.
Hegel	See: George Wilhelm Friedrich Hegel.
Hegelian Idealism	The idealist philosophy upheld by George Wilhelm Friedrich Hegel. See **Part 2**: p. 144.
Historical Materialism	The application of Dialectical Materialist philosophy and Materialist Dialectical methodology to the study and analysis of human history. Historical Materialism exists with the objective of understanding the history and development of capitalism so that it can ultimately be superseded and so that a stateless, classless society can be built and human beings can begin collectively writing our own history without the inherent limitations of economic class division.
Historical Mission	The objective need which an economic class has to pursue its own agenda and to benefit as greatly as possible from the means of production. See: **Part 1**, p. 4, 26, 33; **Part 2**: *Referenced throughout*.
Historical Perspective	Also known as Historical Viewpoint. A viewpoint which demands that subjects be considered in their current stage of motion and development, while also taking into consideration the development and transformation of the subject over time. See **Part 1**: p. 116-118, 125-126, 143, 185, 234; **Part 2**: p. 2, 7, 38, 124, 130, 134, 148, 151, 185, 191, 214, 222-223, 235.
History	Everything that happened in the past. In the context of Historical Materialism, "history" usually refers to *human* history. Human history is the entirety of human activities from its appearance to the present day, including the history of human interaction with nature and the process of human interaction with each other.
Ho Chi Minh	(1890-1969) Communist leader of Vietnam who led revolutionary struggle against colonial France, fascist Japan, and the imperialist USA.
Human History	See: History.

Human Nature	A philosophical concept which refers to the most essential aspects of humanity. Various philosophies have attempted to define human nature. Historical Materialism asserts that human nature has a natural aspect as well as a social aspect, and that these aspects exist in dialectical unity with one another. See *Part 1*: p. 13-14, 78, 85; *Part 2*: p. 14, 152, 191, 212-227, 232. See also: Natural Aspect of Human Nature; Social Aspect of Human Nature.
Human Production	Also known as Human Material Production. Material production processes carried out by human beings.
Human Reproduction	At the individual and family scale: the act of giving birth and raising children to maintain mankind; at the social scale: population growth and human development as socio-bio entities. Not to be confused with "human production" in this text; here, "human production" is used to refer to human material production processes. See *Part 2*: p. 10-13.
Human Society	The collective existence of human beings. Historical Materialism is the study of the development and existence of human society using the framework of Dialectical Materialist philosophy and Materialist Dialectical methodology. See also: Social-Economic Formation.
Human Will	Also known as Human Willpower; Subjective Will; Will; Willpower. The ability for human beings to intentionally impact and change the world through conscious activity practices known as labor. See *Part 1*: p. 12, 113, 124, 161, 175; *Part 2*: p. 25-26, 33, 50, 79, 126, 155, 163, 177-178, 207, 227.
Humanism	A philosophical concept related to the elevation of humanity. The Marxist-Leninist conception of humanism is concerned with the liberation of all human beings through social revolution which will eliminate class society and allow all of humanity to work together without the oppressive structures of class society. See *Part 1*: p. 14, 40; *Part 2*: p. 144, 225.
Idealism	A philosophical position which holds that the only reliable experience of reality occurs within human consciousness. Idealists believe that human reason exclusively or as a first basis is the best way to seek truth.
Ideologist	A specific type of intellectual who performs a political role in society; ideologists specifically work to develop and disseminate the ideology of a particular political party or movement which serves a particular economic class See *Part 2*: p. 186.
Ideology	The highest form of theoretical social consciousness, formed when people are more aware of their material living conditions. Ideology has the ability to delve deeply into the nature of subjects including social relationships. Note: the term "ideology" was also used by Friedrich Engels to refer to the concept of false consciousness. See *Part 1*: p. 231-232.
Inheritance	See: Property of Inheritance.
Inheritance Characteristic	See: Property of Inheritance.
Inheritance Property	See: Property of Inheritance.
Institution	A superstructural entity which has been established by humans within a social-economic formation in order to promote, defend, and develop a corresponding form of social consciousness. See *Part 2*: p. 86.
Intellectual	Human beings who perform labor in the realm of human and social consciousness. Any human being who works to develop, disseminate, and interpret ideas can, therefore, be considered an intellectual. Intellectuals can serve a wide variety of roles in human society, including: writers, artists, journalists, teachers, medical physicians, lawyers, and so on. See *Part 2*, p. 185-191, 200, 276.

Intellectual Laborer	Workers who are exploited for profit by capitalists and earn wages by laboring primarily through mental activity. This distinguishes them from most other laborers who work by directly operating the means of production. See *Part 2*: p. 186.
Internal Development	Also known as Internal Motion; Development Within the Thing-in-Itself. Change/motion/development which occurs within a thing, phenomenon, or idea. Internal Motion is what drives the development of a subject in accordance with the Principle of Development. See *Part 1*: p. 79, 124, 189, 191; *Part 2*: p. 141-142, 160, 168.
Internal Motion	See: Internal Development
Jenny Marx	(1844-1883) *Married name: Jenny Caroline Marx Longuet. Pen name: J. Williams.* One of four daughters of Karl Marx (all named Jenny). Jenny Caroline Marx was, like her father, a socialist writer and activist. See *Part 2*: p. 229.
Karl Marx	(1818-1883) German theorist, politician, philosopher, political economist, founder of Scientific Socialism, and leader of the international working class.
Labor	Any conscious activity performed by humans which changes or develops the world around us. Labor allows humans to engage in material production activity. See *Part 1*: p. 3, 6, 14-17, 23-24, 49, 64, 74-80, 89-90, 93, 95-96, 105, 162, 175, 184, 201, 206, 210, 212, 218; *Part 2*: *Referenced throughout.* See also: Human Will.
Labor Productivity	The amount which a single human being can produce in the workplace. See *Part 2*: p. 32, 34, 191.
Law of Negation of Negation	A universal law of Materialist Dialectics which states that the fundamental and universal tendency of motion and development occurs through a cycle of dialectical negation, wherein each and every negation is, in turn, negated once more. See *Part 1*: p. 163, 185, 195, 198, 200, 201, 202, 227; Part 2: p. 66, 69, 240.
Law of Relationship Between Social Being and Social Consciousness	A law of Historical Materialism which is rooted in the Dialectical Materialist conception of the relationship between matter and consciousness. This law states that social being and social consciousness exist in dialectical unity; and that social being determines social consciousness, while social consciousness can impact back upon social being. See *Part 2*: p. 99, 124, 141.
Law of Suitability	See: Law of Suitability Between the Relations of Production and the Productive Forces.
Law of Suitability Between the Relations of Production and the Productive Forces	A law of Historical Materialism which states that the development level of productive forces must suit the development level of the relations of production. See *Part 2*: p. 18, 42, 48, 59, 66-72, 80, 96, 116, 118, 127, 147, 164-166, 192, 254, 259, 262-263.
Law of the Economic Base Determining the Superstructure of Society	A law of Historical Materialism which states that every economic base forms a superstructure which is suitable to itself in order to maintain and protect the base. This is the basis of Social Formation Theory. See *Part 2*: p. 159.
Law of Transformation Between Quantity and Quality	The universal law of Dialectical Materialism which concerns the universal mode of motion and development processes of nature, society, and human thought, which states that qualitative changes of things, phenomena, and ideas arise from the inevitable basis of the quantitative changes of things, phenomena, and, ideas, and, vice versa, quantitative changes of things, phenomena, and ideas arise from the inevitable basis of qualitative changes of things, phenomena, and ideas. See *Part 1*: p. 163-165, 172-173, 227; *Part 2*: p 66-69, 72.
Law of Unification and Contradiction Between Opposites	The universal law of Dialectical Materialism which states that the fundamental, originating, and universal driving force of all motion and development processes is the inherent and objective contradictions which exists in all things, phenomena, and ideas. See *Part 1*: p. 163, 175, 181; *Part 2*: p. 28-29, 66, 68, 170.

Glossary and Index

Leader	Outstanding individuals created by the revolutionary movement of the masses who are strongly associated with the masses. Note that "leaders" as defined within the framework of Marxism-Leninism are not mystical and do not drive history, themselves, as individuals. Rather, they are put forth from the masses by the material processes of history as explained in *Part 2*, p. 234-236.
	See also: Great Man Theory of History.
Leo Tolstoy	(1828-1910) Russian author who wrote about social problems. See *Part 2*: p. 145.
Legalism	A Chinese political philosophy that emerged in the 6th century B.C.E. Legalism advocated strict laws, harsh punishments, and centralized authority to maintain social order and state control. It was rooted in the belief that humans are inherently self-interested and require strong governance to prevent chaos.
	See *Part 2*: p. 217
Lenin	See: Vladimir Ilyich Lenin.
Lenin's Proof of the Theory of Reflection	Arguments formulated by Vladimir Ilyich Lenin which prove that that the material world must exist outside of and independent from our consciousness; that consciousness can accurately reflect the material world; and that this reflection can become increasingly accurate over time.
	See *Part 1*: p. 72-74; *Part 2*: p. 126.
Marx	See: Karl Marx.
Marxism-Leninism	A system of scientific opinions and theories focused on liberating the working class from capitalism and achieving a stateless, classless, communist society. The core ideas of this system were first developed by Karl Marx and Friedrich Engels, then defended and further developed by Vladimir Ilyich Lenin. Marxism-Leninism has three component parts: the Philosophy of Marxism (i.e., Dialectical Materialism, Materialist Dialectics, and Historical Materialism); the Political Economy of Marxism; and Scientific Socialism. See *Part 1*, p. 1, 22.
Material Base	See: Base.
Material Basis	The underlying material subjects and material conditions which determine forms of consciousness and social consciousness.
Material Conditions	The material external environment in which humans live, including the natural environment, the means of production and the economic base of human society, objective social relations, and other externalities and systems which affect human life and human society. See *Part 1*: p. 6, 22, 40-42, 70-72, 80-81, 87, 92-95, 116-118, 161, 174, 179, 181, 206-207, 210, 229.
Material Production	Practical activity with the aim of transforming objects of the natural world according to the needs of existing humans and the development of society. Material production takes place through human conscious activity which we call labor in conjunction with other factors such as nature, tools, production processes, and so on. See *Part 1*: p. 206-208.
Materialist Dialectics	A scientific system and methodology which is rooted in Dialectical Materialism; Materialist Dialectics are concerned with motion, development, and common relationships, and with the most common rules of motion and development of nature, society, and human thought. See *Part 1*: p. 10, 21, 45-47, 98-202, 227, 237.
Means of Production	Physical inputs and systems used in the production of goods and services, including: machinery, factory buildings, tools, equipment, and anything else used in producing goods and services. See *Part 1*: p. 2-3, 7, 14-16.
Means of Production Factors of the Productive Forces	Factors of productive forces which are related to the means of production; in this dialectical relationship, Means of Production Factors are determined by Worker Factors and impact back upon them. See *Part 2*: p. 44-45.
	See also: Worker Factors of the Productive Forces.
Mechanical Materialism	The erroneous philosophical belief that consciousness is completely determined by the material world and that consciousness cannot impact back upon the material world. See *Part 2*: p. 99, 140-141, 152-153, 223.

Mental Production	The production of ideological programs such as philosophy, religion, art, and so on. See *Part 2*: p. 10-12, 21, 118, 125.
Metaphysical Materialism	An erroneous form of materialism which holds that all change can exist only as an increase or decrease in quantity which is brought about by external causes. See *Part 1*: p. 52; *Part 2*: p. 152-153, 223, 227.
Metaphysics	A branch of philosophy that attempts to explain the fundamental nature of reality. Metaphysical philosophy has taken many forms through the centuries, but one common shortcoming of metaphysical thought is a tendency to view things and ideas in a static, abstract manner. Generally speaking, metaphysics presents nature as a collection of objects and phenomena which are isolated from one another and fundamentally unchanging. See *Part 1*: p. 52; *Part 2*: p. 221-222.
Methodology	A system of reasoning: the ideas and rules that guide humans to research, build, select, and apply the most suitable methods in both perception and practice. Methodologies can range from very specific to broadly general, with philosophical methodology being the most general scope of methodology. See *Part 1*: p. 44.
Mission	See: Historical Mission.
Mode of Production	The manner in which humans carry out the production processes of society within certain historical periods.
Motion	See: Development.
Natural Aspect (of Humanity and of Human Nature)	The aspect of humanity which arises from humanity's dialectical relationship with the natural world. The natural aspect of human nature is the material basis of human development. The natural aspect exists in dialectical unity with the social aspect; this unity is what defined human nature. See *Part 2*: p. 212-216, 222-225, 228, 256. See also: Social Aspect of Human Nature; Human Nature.
Natural-Historical Characteristic of Society	Also known as the Objective-Law Characteristic of Human Society; refers to the properties of human society which universally adhere to objective laws of Dialectical Materialism, Materialist Dialectics, and Historical Materialism. Subjective factors of human society are distinct from objective factors but also important in the development process of human history. See *Part 2*: p. 168.
Natural-Historical Process	A process which arises from nature, is governed by objective laws of nature (natural) and which occurs over time (historical). See *Part 2*: p. 162-164, 172, 176.
Nature	The external world which humans exist in. Nature includes all of the material things and phenomena which surround us and which we interact with and utilize in our daily existence. Humanity and nature exist in dialectical unity and mutually define and develop one another over time.
Negation	The development process through which two contradicting objects mutually develop one another until one is overtaken by the other. In dialectical materialism, negation takes the form of dialectical negation. See *Part 1*: p. 123, 175-176, 183, 185-202.
Negation of Negation	See: Law of Negation of Negation.
Objectivity	See: Objective Factors.
Objective Conditions	See: Objective Factors.
Objective Factors	Factors and conditions which arise from and are governed by objective laws. Objective factors have a dialectical relationship with subjective factors; in this relationship, objective factors play the determining role but subjective factors can also have impact.
Objective-Law Characteristic of Society	See: Natural Historical Characteristic of Society.

Glossary and Index

Objective Laws	The regular, common, obvious, natural, objective relations between internal aspects, factors, and attributes of a thing or phenomenon or between things and phenomena. See *Part 1*: p. 162.
Objective Idealism	A form of idealism which asserts that the ideal and consciousness are the primary existence, while also positing that the ideal and consciousness are objective, and that they exist independently of nature and humans. See *Part 1*: p. 50; *Part 2*: p. 125.
Objective Need	A condition which must inevitably be fulfilled because of objective laws and principles; a situation in which a certain outcome *must* occur because of the essential internal aspects. Such objective needs arise from obviousness.
Obviousness	See: Obviousness and Randomness.
Obviousness and Randomness (Category Pair)	The philosophical category of Obviousness refers to events that occur because of the essential internal aspects of a subject which become reasons for certain results in certain conditions: the obvious has to happen in a certain way, it can't happen any other way. The Randomness category refers to things that happen because of external reasons: things that happen, essentially, by chance, due to impacts from many external relations. A random outcome may occur or it may not occur, and may occur in many different ways. Obviousness and Randomness have a dialectical relationship with one another. See *Part 1*: p. 144-146; *Part 2*: p. 96, 170.
Oppressed Class	An economic class which is forced into labor by a ruling class in the material production process. An oppressed class operates the essential means of production but is restricted from ownership of them.
Ordinary Social Knowledge	All the knowledge, concepts, etc. of people in a certain community which are formed directly from daily practical activities and which have not yet been systematized and generalized into theory. See *Part 2*: p. 108-109. See also: Scientific Social Knowledge.
Perspective	See: Viewpoint.
Phenomena	See: Essence and Phenomena.
Politics	Aspects of human society related to class struggle. In class society, politics exist in dialectical unity with economics and this dialectical configuration is known as a political economy.
Political Economy	The political and economic formation of a class society. Economy encompasses the material production process while politics encompass class struggle. Class society can be defined as these aspects of a society defining one another in dialectical unity.
	Also refers to the Marxist-Leninist field of study related to understanding the political-economic development of class societies and the objective laws which will eventually lead to socialist revolution and the eventual development of communism. This field of study is the subject of *Part 3* of the curriculum from which this text (*Part 2*) is translated. See *Part 2*: p. 183-185
Practice	Also known as Praxis. Conscious activity which improves our understanding, and which has purpose and historical-social characteristics. Used interchangeably with the word "practice" in this text. See *Part 1*: p. 205-206, 235.
Principle of Development	Also known as Principle of General Development. The principle of Dialectical Materialism which states that development is a process that comes from within the thing-in-itself; the process of solving the contradictions within things and phenomena. Therefore, development is inevitable, objective, and occurs without dependence on human will. See *Part 1*: p. 106-108, 118-119, 124-125; *Part 2*: p. 33, 79, 84, 136, 150, 167-170, 177-178, 216, 226.
Principle of General Development	See: Principle of Development.

Principle of General Relationships	A principle of Dialectical Materialism which states that all things, phenomena, and ideas are related to one another, and are defined by these internal and external relationships. See *Part 1*: p. 106-107, 110, 114; *Part 2*: p. 38, 146, 169, 173, 177.
Private	See: Private and Common.
Private and Common (Category Pair)	The Private philosophical category encompasses specific things, phenomena, and ideas; the Common philosophical category defines the common aspects, attributes, factors, and relations that exist in many things and phenomena. Private and Common are relative in nature and have a dialectical relationship with one another. See *Part 1*: p. 128-138; *Part 2*: p. 109-110.
Production	A process in which humans interact with one another, with nature, with tools, and with other factors in order to develop that which is needed to survive. See also: Material Production; Human Reproduction; Mental Production.
Productive Forces	The synthesis of material and mental factors which together form a practical power to transform the natural world according to the needs of human survival and development.
Progressive Class	An economic class which is emerging to be more suitable to emerging productive forces during a transition period where one mode of production is being negated by the next. See *Part 2*: p. 138, 144, 150, 182, 207. See also: Remnant Class; Revolutionary Class.
Proletariat	See: Working Class.
Property of Inheritance (of Dialectical Negation)	Also known as Inheritance Characteristic, Inheritance Property. Inheritance refers to characteristics and attributes being passed along from previous negated forms through processes of contradiction. All things, phenomena, and ideas inherit properties from previous negated forms. See *Part 1*: p. 190-191, 200-203; *Part 2*: p. 40, 78-79, 81, 98, 131, 137-140, 217, 271.
Quality	The unity of component parts, taken together, which defines a subject and distinguishes it from other subjects. See *Part 1*: p. 119-121. See also: Quantity.
Quality Shift	A change in quality which takes place in the motion and development process of things, phenomena, and ideas, occurring when quantity change meets a certain perceived threshold. See *Part 1*: p. 124, 153, 164, 168-174.
Quantity	The total amount of component parts that compose a subject. See *Part 1*: p. 119-121. See also: Quality.
Randomness	See: Obviousness and Randomness.
Reflection	The re-creation of the features of one form of matter in a different form of matter which occurs when they mutually impact each other through interaction.
Reform	Changes which take place in one or several areas of social life within a social-economic formation in order to improve that social-economic formation. See *Part 2*: p. 207-209, 232-233, 250, 254-268, 273-275. See also: Social Revolution.
Relations of Production	The relationships between humans in the process of material production. Relations of production exist in dialectical unity with the productive forces.
Remnant Class	An economic class which is held over from a previous stage of development of human society and is no longer suitable with the mode of production. See *Part 2*: p. 27, 87, 102, 130, 171. See also: Progressive Class; Revolutionary Class.
Replacement	A form of negation in which one subject is replaced with another through dialectical negation. See *Part 1*: p. 186-187; *Part 2*: p. 32-33, 79.

Glossary and Index

Reproduction	See: Human Reproduction.
Revolutionary Class	A class which emerges (initially as a progressive class) to be more suitable to eventually control the means of production in a newly formed mode of production. In time the revolutionary class will develop its own class consciousness and enact social revolution to seize control of the means of production. See *Part 2*: p. 6, 93, 116-121, 123, 135, 145, 157, 168, 189-190, 207, 209. See also: Progressive Class, Remnant Class.
Ruling Class	A class which owns and benefits from the means of production while forcing one or more oppressed classes to operate them.
Scientific Social Knowledge	Knowledge that has been developed through more systematic and scientific observations and experiments and which is held socially. See *Part 2*: p. 108. See also: Ordinary Social Knowledge.
Scientific Socialism	A body of theory and knowledge focused on the practical pursuit of changing the world to bring about socialism through the leadership of the proletariat. Scientific Socialism is the subject of *Part 4* of the curriculum from which this text (*Part 2*) is translated. See *Part 1*: p. 1-2, 21, 37-39.
Scientific Worldview	A worldview that is expressed by a systematic pursuit of knowledge that generally and correctly reflects the relationships of things, phenomena, and processes in the objective material world, including relationships between humans, as well as relationships between humans and the world. See *Part 1*: p. 38-39, 44-45, 48; *Part 2*: p. 1.
Seed	Also known as Germ. Characteristics or properties which will eventually be inherited in future forms through processes of dialectical contradiction and negation. See *Part 2*: p. 3, 75-78, 81, 139, 195, 197, 200.
Sequential	Refers to development processes which tend to occur in a specific sequence, from lower stages of development to higher stages of development, rarely reversing or bypassing any stage. See *Part 2*: p. 34-38, 42-43, 69, 167.
Social Animal	A species in which individuals rely on one another to survive within a collective which is called a society. Specifically, social beings rely on one another to consciously perform material production processes. See *Part 2*: p. 26.
Social Aspect (of Humanity and Human Nature)	The special relationships which individual humans have with their many social communities, such as: family, class, nation, humankind, and so on. The social aspect exists in dialectical unity with the natural aspect of humanity and human nature; both of these aspects mutually define and develop one another. See *Part 2*: p. 214-217, 222-228, 256.
Social Being	The material existence of humanity. Social being exists in dialectical unity with humanity's social consciousness. In this relationship, social being determines social consciousness and is impacted back upon by social consciousness in accordance with the Law of Relationship Between Social Being and Social Consciousness.
Social Consciousness	Human consciousness which is generally shared by society. Social consiousness eists in dialectical unity with humanity's social being. In this relationship, social consciousness is determined by social being and impacts back upon social being in accordance with the Law of Relationship Between Social Being and Social Consciousness.
Social Consciousness Form	See: Form of Social Consciousness.
Social Darwinism	The pseudoscientific belief that animals share a common set of laws, and that human society follows these same laws. According to Social Darwinism, the most fundamental law of animal and human society is competition. See *Part 2*: p. 13.
Social-Economic Form	See: Social-Economic Formation.

Social-Economic Formation	Also known as Socio-Economic Form; Social-Economic Form. A formation of human society which includes an economic base and a social superstructure. The dialectical relationship between the base and superstructure is what defines human society.
Social-Economic Formation Theory	See: Social Formation Theory.
Social Formation Theory	Also known as Social-Economic Formation Theory; Theory of Social Formation. A theory first formulated by Karl Marx and Friedrich Engels which states that social-economic production (i.e., the material/economic base) determines the superstructure of society while the superstructure can also impact back on the material base. This relationship between the base and superstructure drives the formation and development of human society through dialectical processes of contradiction and negation. Social Formation Theory is the core of the Historical Materialist framework of understanding humanity and is itself grounded in the philosophy and methodology of Dialectical Materialism and Materialist Dialectics.
Social Ideology	The entire system of social conceptions and viewpoints such as politics, philosophy, ethics, art, religion, etc. It is an indirect and self-conscious reflection of social being. Social ideology has a dialectical relationship with social psychology but does not produce social psychology. See *Part 2*: p. 8, 111, 113-118, 124, 134.
Social Institution	See: Institution.
Social Production of Life	Social activities which yield all that is necessary to sustain human life (food, shelter, etc.). These social activities lead to social relationships. At any given stage of development of human society, these social activities and relationships constitute an overall mode of production which defines that stage of development for that society. See *Part 2*: p. 19.
Social Psychology	The whole emotional life, mood, aspirations, will, etc. of certain human communities. Social psychology is a direct and spontaneous reflection of living situation of the human beings who compose a society. Social psychology has a dialectical relationship with social ideology but is not produced by social ideology. See *Part 2*: p. 109, 111, 113-115, 124, 134.
Social Revolution	A social process by which relations of production undergo an essential change such that a new mode of production develops. Social revolutions are always predicated by the development of productive forces to such a degree that they are no longer suitable with established relations of production. Therefore, the newly established relations of production which result from a social revolution are more suitable to the development needs of the newly developed productive forces.
Social Stratification	The grouping of people within the same economic class according to their specific status and differences in that class. Such groupings are called strata. See *Part 2*: p. 185.
Socialism	A transitionary political economy in which workers control the means of production through the construction of a workers' state. This constitutes a dictatorship of the proletariat over the capitalist class. The goal of socialism is the development of communism. The systematic pursuit of communism via socialism is known as Scientific Socialism.
Socialization	To own, operate, or otherwise engage in some process collectively with many other human beings.
Socially Necessary Labor-Time	The amount of labor and time needed to produce something within the material conditions of a certain human society. See *Part 2*: p. 52.
Society	See: Human Society; Social-Economic Formation.
Socio-Economic Form	See: Social-Economic Formation.

Socio-Political Institution	See: Institution.
Solipsism	The belief that the self is the only basis for truth. Solipsism is the root cause of "intuitive" conceptions of human nature, since solipsism is simply an improper application of intuition in an effort to "discover" truth solely in one's own thoughts and ideas. See *Part 1*: p. 218; *Part 2*: p. 223.
Stage of Development	The current quantity and quality characteristics which a thing, phenomenon, or object possesses. Every time a quality change occurs, a new stage of development is entered into. Within the framework of Historical Materialism, this term typically refers to stages of development of the mode of production of human society. See *Part 1*: p. 24, 39, 125, 73-174, 179, 190, 196-197, 200, 212, 221.
State	A social institution which exists to wield power in order to exercise the dictatorship of the ruling class.
Strata	A grouping of people within the same class according to their specific status and differences in that class; the result of social stratification. See *Part 2*: p. 6, 185-188, 190, 230-231.
Stratification	See: Social Stratification.
Struggle	Contradiction which takes place between two opposing sides. See also: Class Struggle.
Subjective Conditions	See: Subjective Factors.
Subjective Factors	Factors and conditions which can vary across time and place and which can vary from one location to another even within the same social formation of human society. Subjective factors have a dialectical relationship with objective factors; in this relationship, objective factors play the determining role but subjective factors can also have impact. See *Part 2*: p. 15, 25, 155, 167-174, 196, 209, 244-250, 269, 277.
Subjective Idealism	A philosophical position which asserts that consciousness is the primary existence and that truth can be obtained only or primarily through conscious activity and reasoning. Subjective idealism asserts that all things and phenomena can only be experienced as subjective sensory perceptions, with some forms of subjective idealism even explicitly denying the objective existence of material reality altogether. See *Part 1*: p. 26-27, 50; *Part 2*: p. 125. See also: Objective Idealism.
Subjective Will	See: Human Will.
Subjectivism	A philosophical position in which one centers one's own self and conscious activities in perspective and worldview, failing to test their own perceptions against material and social reality. See *Part 1*: p. 56, 182, 217-218, 233-234; *Part 2*: p. 24, 105, 223, 249, 261.
Subjectivity	See: Subjective Factors.
Subsidizing Period	A period of history in Vietnam which lasted from 1975-1986. During this period, which began immediately after Vietnam's war with the United States, Vietnamese communist leadership attempted to rapidly transform Vietnam into a moneyless, classless society. This period was hampered by voluntarism, which is an over-emphasis on human will. The productive forces of Vietnam were not developed enough to be suitable with the relations of production which Vietnamese communists attempted to implement. The Subsidizing Period was followed by the Doi Moi Period. See *Part 2*: p. 37, 157, 253, 260-262.
Suitability	The applicability of a subject for a specific application or role. See *Part 1*: p. 154.
Superstructure	The totality of social consciousness forms (politics, rule of law, philosophy, ethics, religion, art, etc.), along with corresponding social institutions such as the state, political parties, churches, social organizations, etc., that are formed on a certain economic base. See *Part 1*: p. 23.

Tailism	An error of leadership in which revolutionaries follow reactionary opinions, attitudes, and false consciousness of the masses blindly. See *Part 2*: p. 157-158. See also: Commandism; Voluntarism.
Technical Aspect of the Mode of Production	The aspect of the mode of production which is related to the technology used in production processes to transform objects to suit the needs of humanity. See *Part 2*: p. 16-17.
Terminal Negation	The end of a development process of a thing, phenomenon, or idea. Such negation is only "terminal" relative to the perspective of that which has been negated. See *Part 1*: p. 176, 186-188, 191; *Part 2*: p. 78-79.
Theoretical Consciousness	The indirect, abstract, systematic level of perception in which the nature and laws of things and phenomena are generalized and abstracted. See *Part 1*: p. 210-214, 217-218; *Part 2*: p. 109, 112, 119, 123. See also: Theoretical Social Consciousness.
Theoretical Social Consciousness	Ideas and conceptions which have been generalized within society into social theories, presented in the form of concepts, categories, and laws. Theoretical social consciousness has the ability to reflect objective reality in a general, profound, and accurate way. See *Part 2*: p. 108, 111-112. See also: Empirical Social Consciousness.
Theory of Social-Economic Formation	See: Social Formation Theory.
Thing-in-Itself	The actual material object which exists outside of our consciousness, as it exists outside of our consciousness. See *Part 1*: p. 72-74, 101, 158; *Part 2*: p. 33, 79, 177-178, 227.
Thomas Hobbes	(1588–1679) An English philosopher who was heavily influenced by his experiences in the English Civil War. Having witnessed a great deal of suffering and strife during this period, Hobbes conceptualized human society as a "war of all against all," and believed that human beings were inherently violent and prone to constant conflict with one another. See *Part 1*: p. 53; *Part 2*: p. 13-14.
Thomas Robert Malthus	(1766-1834) An English philosopher who believed that human societies overused resources for population growth and that this invariably led to catastrophe. Malthus had the pessimistic view that over time all societies tend to collapse into disarray as overpopulation led to overconsumption of resources and that this made human society essentially unstable and prone to crisis, war, famine, and so on. See: *Part 2*: p. 13-14.
Transition Period	Periods of development of human society which occur at the threshold between one stage of development of relations of production and the next. Transition periods are times of high instability. See *Part 2*: p. 38, 54, 138, 254, 265, 274.
Unity	A condition in which two subjects mutually define and develop one another through processes of contradiction and negation. Unity is the basis of the Materialist Dialectical principles of Unity in Diversity and Diversity in Unity which are derived from the Principle of General Relationships.
Unity in Diversity	A concept in Materialist Dialectics which holds that within the universal relationships exist within and between all different things, phenomena, and ideas, we will find that each individual manifestation of any universal relationship will have its own different manifestations, aspects, features, etc. Thus even the universal relationships which unite all things, phenomena, and ideas exist in infinite diversity. See *Part 1*: p. 42, 110-111, 114, 125, 130; *Part 2*: p. 38-39, 173-174. See also: Diversity in Unity; Unity.
Universal Category Pair	See: Category Pair

Glossary and Index

Utopianism	The idealist philosophical concept which mistakenly asserts that the ideal can determine the material, and that ideal forms of society can be brought about without regard for material conditions and development processes. See *Part 1*: p. 8, 17-18, 30, 94; *Part 2*: p. 24, 144, 152.
Victor Hugo	(1802-1885) French writer, activist, and politician. Author of *Les Miserables*. See *Part 2*: p. 145.
Viewpoint	Also known as Point of View; Perspective. The starting point of analysis which determines the direction of thinking from which phenomena and problems are considered. See also: Comprehensive and Historical Perspective.
Vladimir Ilyich Lenin	(1870-1924) A Russian theorist, politician, dialectical materialist philosopher, defender and developer of Marxism in the era of imperialism, founder of the Bolsheviks, the Communist Party and the government of the Soviet Union, leader of Russia and the international working class.
Vo Nguyen Giap	(1911-2013) Great General of Vietnam who led Vietnam's People's Army to victory against Japan, France, and the USA. See *Part 2*: p. 249-250.
Voluntarism	An over-emphasis on subjective will. See *Part 2*: p. 155-157, 260-261.
Vulgar Materialism	A form of mechanical materialism which absolutizes the supposition that the material fully and completely determines consciousness without exception. See *Part 2*: p. 146, 152-153, 227.
Will	See: Human Will.
Willpower	See: Human Will.
Worker Factors of the Productive Forces	Factors of the productive forces related to workers who carry out production processes in human society. Worker factors exist in dialectical unity with means of production factors. In this relationship, worker factors play the determining role while means of production factors can impact back upon worker factors. See *Part 2*: p. 44, 46.
Working Class	Also known as the Proletariat. The economic class which operates the means of production under the capitalist mode of production. The working class has the historical mission to engage in social revolution, to build a workers' state, to develop a dictatorship of the proletariat, and to eventually build communism after a transition period of socialism.
Worldview	The whole of an individual's or society's opinions and conceptions about the world, about humans ourselves, and about life and the position of human beings in the world. See *Part 1*: p. 1, 11, 37-39, 44-45, 48, 52, 96, 138, 201, 208-209, 218, 234. See also: Scientific Worldview.

Banyan House
PUBLISHING

For centuries, the banyan tree has been the symbol of communal life in Vietnam.

Traditionally, the entrance to a village is graced by a large and ancient banyan tree. It is in the shade of these trees that villagers gather to socialize, draw water from wells, and make collective decisions together. The drooping accessory trunks represent the longevity of villagers - and of the village itself - while the arching canopy represents the safety and protection of the village. The shape of the banyan tree is seen in the full moon, which casts peaceful light across the Earth to guide travelers in the dark of night.

Vietnam's revolution against Japanese fascism and French colonialism began in 1945 beneath the cover of the Tân Trào Banyan Tree, which still stands in the city of Tuyên Quang.

It is in this deep-rooted, humanistic spirit of collective action that we founded Banyan House Publishing. We hope to deliver volumes which will inspire action and change throughout the village that is our world.

Visit us at:

BanyanHouse.org

www.ingramcontent.com/pod-product-compliance
Lightning Source LLC
Chambersburg PA
CBHW080539030426
42337CB00024B/4801